INTRODUCTION TO SCREEN NARRATIVE

Bringing together the expertise of world-leading screenwriters and scholars, this book offers a comprehensive overview of how screen narratives work. Exploring a variety of mediums including feature films, television, animation, and video games, the volume provides a contextual overview of the form and applies this to the practice of screenwriting.

Featuring 20 contributors, the volume surveys the art of screen narrative and allows students and screenwriters to draw on crucial insights to further improve their screenwriting craft. Editors Paul Taberham and Catalina Iricinschi have curated a volume that spans a range of disciplines including screenwriting, film theory, philosophy and psychology with experience and expertise in storytelling, modern blockbusters, puzzle films, and art cinema. Screenwriters interviewed include Josh Weinstein (The Simpsons, Gravity Falls), David J. Greenberg (Stomping Ground, Used to Love Her), Evan Skolnick (Star Wars: Battlefront, Cuphead: Don't Deal with the Devil!), and Ioana Uricaru (Lemonade, Tales from the Golden Age).

Paul Taberham is an Associate Professor in Film and Animation Studies at the Arts University Bournemouth, UK. He is the author of *Lessons in Perception: The Avant-Garde Filmmaker as Practical Psychologist* (Berghahn, 2018) and the forthcoming *Animated Visions: Theory, History and Aesthetics* (Berghahn, 2024). He is also the co-editor of *Cognitive Media Theory* (Routledge, 2014) with Ted Nannicelli, and *Experimental Animation: From Analogue to Digital* (Routledge, 2019) with Miriam Harris and Lilly Husbands. He is a fellow of the Society of Cognitive Studies of the Moving Image, and on the editorial board for *Animation: An Interdisciplinary Journal*.

Catalina Iricinschi is a Visiting Assistant Professor of Psychology at Franklin & Marshall College. Research interests include event segmentation in film narrative, eye tracking in narrative processing, narrative of belonging and displacement, place and space depiction in film narrative, and Romanian cinema. She has published in journals such as *Cognitive Science, Projections: The Journal for Movie and Mind*, and *i-Perception*, along with the edited anthologies Space in Language and the forthcoming Narrative, Media and Cognition.

INTRODUCTION TO SCREEN NARRATIVE

Perspectives on Story Production and Comprehension

Edited by Paul Taberham and Catalina Iricinschi

Routledge
Taylor & Francis Group

LONDON AND NEW YORK

First published 2024
by Routledge
4 Park Square, Milton Park, Abingdon, Oxon OX14 4RN

and by Routledge
605 Third Avenue, New York, NY 10158

Routledge is an imprint of the Taylor & Francis Group, an informa business

© 2024 selection and editorial matter, Paul Taberham and Catalina Iricinschi; individual chapters, the contributors

British Library Cataloguing-in-Publication Data
A catalogue record for this book is available from the British Library

Library of Congress Cataloging-in-Publication Data
Names: Taberham, Paul, editor. | Iricinschi, Catalina, editor.
Title: Introduction to screen narrative : perspectives on story production and comprehension / edited by Paul Taberham and Catalina Iricinschi.
Description: Abingdon, Oxon ; New York, NY : Routledge, 2024. |
Includes bibliographical references and index.
Identifiers: LCCN 2023011049 (print) | LCCN 2023011050 (ebook) |
ISBN 9781032055213 (hardback) | ISBN 9781032055206 (paperback) |
ISBN 9781003197911 (ebook)
Subjects: LCSH: Motion picture authorship. | Narration (Rhetoric) |
Storytelling in mass media.
Classification: LCC PN1996 .I58 2024 (print) |
LCC PN1996 (ebook) | DDC 791.4302--dc23/eng/20230602
LC record available at https://lccn.loc.gov/2023011049
LC ebook record available at https://lccn.loc.gov/2023011050

ISBN: 978-1-032-05521-3 (hbk)
ISBN: 978-1-032-05520-6 (pbk)
ISBN: 978-1-003-19791-1 (ebk)

DOI: 10.4324/9781003197911

Typeset in Sabon
by KnowledgeWorks Global Ltd.

CONTENTS

Foreword by Patrick Colm Hogan   *viii*
Acknowledgments   *xiii*
List of Contributors   *xiv*

Introduction   1
Catalina Iricinschi and Paul Taberham

1   Dimensions of Narrative   10
   Paul Taberham

PART I
Convention, Deviation, Evolution   **27**

2   Enjoying Classical Hollywood Storytelling   29
   Todd Berliner

3   American Independent Cinema   49
   Geoff King

4   Interview: David J. Greenberg   67

5 Complex Film Narratives: Diegetic Fictionalization
in Christopher Nolan's Fantastical Puzzle Film Cycle   71
Miklós Kiss

PART II
Art Cinema   **93**

6 Realism, Time, and Ambiguity: Narration in Art-Cinema   95
Paul Taberham

7 Interview: Ioana Uricaru   118

8 Pseudo-Narration in Jean-Luc Godard's Late Films   122
András Bálint Kovács

9 Defining a Lynchian Narrative   137
Neil McCartney

PART III
Alternative Media   **149**

10 Television Narrative: Forms, Strategies, and Histories   151
Sean O'Sullivan and Robyn Warhol

11 The Way Toons Tell It: Animation's Narrative Strategies   175
Christopher Holliday

12 Interview: Josh Weinstein   194

13 Video Game Narrative: Concepts and Practices
for Structuring and Infusing Story in Games   197
Dominic Arsenault

14 Interview: Evan Skolnick   218

15 Transmedia Storyworlds and Transmedia Universes   222
Jan-Noël Thon

PART IV
New Perspectives   **237**

16 Two Philosophies of the Screenplay   239
   Enrico Terrone

17 The Absorbed Viewer's Activity   256
   Ed S. Tan and Katalin E. Bálint

18 Narrative Events: Segmenting, Parsing, and Story
   Comprehension   275
   Catalina Iricinschi

Index   296

FOREWORD

Why Study Screenwriting?

Patrick Colm Hogan

There are many reasons to study screenwriting. For example, such study bears on political concerns (e.g., the ways in which social ideologies of class, race, gender, and sexuality develop and are disseminated in mass culture). In keeping with this, the essays that follow speak to many significant issues. I myself happen to be particularly interested in the implications of screenwriting for an account of authorial story-making, how authors create the sequence of events and situations represented in a narrative, an interest shared by a number of the writers in this collection. In connection with this topic, two possible benefits of work on screenwriting will help to illustrate its broad, theoretical import. First, research on screenwriting may challenge some common assumptions about the mental processes engaged by authors. Second, and less obviously, it may challenge some assumptions about human mental processes more generally. Both challenges arise from the fact that there are significant differences between narrative screenplays and prototypical literary narratives, such as novels and short stories—or even stage plays. In the following pages, I will briefly outline some of these differences.

We may divide the most important differences here into three categories: (1) the text, (2) the definitive work of art, and (3) the author. Perhaps the most obvious textual differences between a screenplay and other written narratives result from the difference in the degree to which authors are required to conform to external constraints, thus constraints that do not arise from the nature of the story itself, but from some unrelated matter.[1] Of course, literary works have external constraints. A 30-page "novel" would be too short to publish alone. Today, a 2000-page novel would (usually) be too long to attract a publisher. These are external constraints and authors do need to keep them in mind when writing. But they are very loose and, so to speak, unintrusive constraints, that is, constraints that are relatively unlikely to disrupt other processes of authorial storytelling. Probably the most persistent and intrusive external constraints on literary narratives concern verse forms—for example, for a story in iambic pentameter. This is a "strenuous" constraint in that it requires constant attention from the author. However, it remains a relatively limited constraint in that it affects only one part of the text's verbalization, not its larger story construction, its development of a narrator, or—except for some aspects of word choice—its emplotment (selection, sequencing, emphasis, construal, and so on) of the story.

The situation with screenwriting is very different. There are certainly some external pressures on, say, writers of novels to grab the attention of the reader quickly. Conversely, there are certainly screenplays that ignore or even flout widespread constraints on mainstream cinematic storytelling. However, on the whole, these constraints seem to be enforced with far greater stringency in filmmaking and television production than in most literature. These constraints range from the four-act structure (see Thompson, 1999, pp. 27–36) to the timing of the first song in a Bollywood musical. But to get a clear picture of the strenuous and intrusive character of some constraints on screenwriting, one need only recall the strict timing of episodes in television series. As Parker (1999) explains, "No one minds if a play is five minutes or an hour longer, or shorter, than another play. But someone will chop a sequence or a line of dialogue out of a screenplay if it is a second too long for its slot on television" (p. 3).

The first thing that screenwriting draws our attention to, then, is the importance of monitoring what one produces and how one revises, monitoring guided by self-conscious observation of rules. Again, this is not absent from literary storytelling. But its relatively lesser importance makes it much easier to overlook in the latter case.

The second area of difference is just what constitutes the work of art. A completed novel is the work of art, what we count as the definitive target of study. The same point holds for a stage play. Even if a work is radically cut or systematically adapted in a particular production, we still (usually) consider the play-text to be the (primary) object of our attention. Of course, we are free to discuss a given production and even to consider it a work of art. But (with extremely rare exceptions) production does not displace the play-text, which we identify with play itself. In contrast, in cinema, the film is (almost always) the work of art, what we count as the definitive target of study. The screenplay is (commonly thought of as) merely a means to the film.[2] Just as we may consider a given production as a work of art, we may do this with a screenplay (especially in cases where the screenplay is by an accomplished author, such as William Faulkner). But it is extremely rare for the screenplay to displace the film as what people generally consider to be the work of art.

What, then, happens with the screenplay in cinema and related media? What is its status? In fact, we see an entire range of possibilities. In some cases, the screenplay is more or less binding, with the director, actors, and so forth, trying to remain faithful to the script. In other cases, the screenplay may be considered as more or less plastic, with the director, producer, or others free to cut scenes, re-arrange the order of scenes, change dialogue, and so forth. Indeed, the screenplay may be quite bare, amounting to little more than a set of notes to guide improvisation.

Thus, at the level of the work of art, we see that there are significant differences in the degree to which the screenplay is treated as a significant artifact in the process of storytelling. More precisely, there is a gradient of degrees to which a screenplay may be considered authoritative (and, often related to this, a gradient of degrees to which the screenplay is complete). One theoretical consequence of this observation concerns the degree to which authorial storytelling is or is not a matter of actually generating the story components (events, dialogues, etc.). Filmmaking makes clear that storytelling is often more a matter of selection and arrangement, as when a director in effect takes the screenplay—along with the actors' delivery of lines, the framing and focus of shots determined by the director of photography, and countless other matters—as raw material for creating the film, which again counts as the definitive narrative in this case. It may initially seem that such "receptive" processes are confined to collaborative arts such as film. After all, the novelist does not have different people write, say, dialogue, character descriptions, passages about lighting, and so on, then select from what they have done.[3] However, I have argued in several works (see chapter 1 of Hogan 2013) that this is in effect what an author does with his or her own writing when evaluating whether his or her text is complete, whether what he or she has put together as a text is "right," thus ready to be sent out to the world. (On the relation of these points to auteurism, see chapter 2 of Hogan 2013.)

The final area where screenplays differ rather obviously from literary works is in authorship itself. One striking feature of much screenwriting is that an individual screenplay typically involves many authors. Multiple authorship has two forms. The first is simultaneous; the second is serial. In simultaneous authorship (found primarily in series television), a number of different writers are contributing to the composition of work all at the same time—for example, through a "writers' room" group brainstorming initial ideas or, subsequently, proposing and discussing possible revisions of a draft.[4] In serial multiple authorship, in contrast, one or two writers may be engaged to draft a script, only to be replaced by one or two new writers, who are engaged to revise the script, perhaps in accordance with specific directives from the director or producer. Moreover, this process of replacement may occur a number of times, with earlier writers sometimes returning to take over the revision process at a later stage.

I will conclude with a brief illustration of what implications this may have for an analysis of storytelling. When considering either sort of multiple authorship, theorists trained in cognitive scientific analysis are almost certain to be put in mind of work on "situated cognition." Situated cognition theory stresses several aspects of human mental activity that have often been ignored in classical cognitive science (see Robbins and Aydede, 2009). Two are important here. First, such activity is "embedded," which is to say, that it encompasses a variety of dynamic processes that change continually in response to changing circumstances and to our own actions within those circumstances. Second, such activity is "distributed," which is to say, that no cognition is, so to speak, monadic. Rather, an individual's thoughts and behavior are inevitably reliant on the knowledge, thought, and behavior of others. In relatively straightforward ways, multi-author storytelling involves embedded and distributed cognition. Specifically, each author must respond to the changing content or context of the story, whether the changes are a matter of another author's recent re-drafting of the screenplay or the (as yet unimplemented) recommendations for revision from a writers' group.

I would certainly agree with anyone who asserts that screenwriting highlights the embedded and distributed nature of cognition—though, unlike some of its advocates, I do not see situated cognition as in any way undermining classic cognitive science, with its emphasis on the isolation of enduring cognitive principles. In any event, with regard to authorial storytelling, I see two main consequences. First, distributed cognition recalls the centrality of "theory of mind" processes, the processes whereby we come to (partially) understand—while also (partially) revising—other people's beliefs, feelings, aims, and so forth. For example, when a new writer is engaged to revise a script, he or she must engage with the product of someone else's ideas, etc. On the other hand, the main task of the new author is not one of understanding his or her predecessor. It is, rather, one of understanding the likely response of recipients, thus the film's viewers, whether these are the film's mass audience, influential critics, or the producers of the work. This recipient-oriented understanding is what I have argued to be the main function of the receptive, evaluative response of a single author. In this way, the distributed nature of film once again highlights this receptive aspect of story creation, whether by literary authors or cinematic auteurs.

The second point I would draw out here does not concern differences among individuals, but differences within individuals. For example, faced with an array of ideas for a story, an author is forced to consider what the possible implications of any idea might be, how these might fit with other ideas for the story, and what the likely impact of integrating and developing such ideas might be with respect to a target audience. This is true whether the author is responding to ideas from other people in a brainstorming session or to notes he or she has jotted down to record his or her own ideas over the preceding weeks. Similarly, when faced with a draft of a text, the author needs to determine if that draft needs revision and, if so, how. This is true whether the text is by the author himself or herself or by someone else.

In other words, the prominence of multi-author storytelling in screenwriting may serve to remind us that there is diversity not only across, but also within people. For instance, our ideas for a story are likely to arise in variable contexts from distinct cognitive and affective systems, systems that are sometimes as opaque to one another as are different people.

Again, there are countless ways that the study of screenwriting has consequential implications for understanding such topics as storytelling, mass art, and even human psychology. Indeed, the insights contained in the following essays testify abundantly to the value of such a study. In the preceding pages, I hope merely to have suggested some of the larger, theoretical reasons that we might have expected this happy result (at least given Paul and Catalina's selection of such fine contributors).[5]

Notes

1 By saying that a constraint is "unrelated" to the story, I mean that it does not derive from or even bear on the particular causal or other features of the sequence of events or any other particular aspect of the "storyworld." For example, constraints on just what characters can and do know are constraints that derive from the causal principles of the storyworld (such as whether or not that storyworld includes telepathy). In contrast, the constraint on performance time for a half-hour television episode applies no matter what happens in the story.

2 This is not to say that everyone countenances such a view. For example, Ted Nannicelli has argued that it is misguided (Nannicelli 2013).

3 As my friend, director and producer Ken Kwapis, pointed out to me, something like this does occur with screenplays, where one writer might be brought in to make comedic dialogue funnier, and another to give greater psychological depth to female characters.

4 As with a number of screenwriting practices discussed in this foreword, I am grateful to Ken Kwapis for the preceding information.

5 I am grateful to my friend, screenwriter Brian Hohlfeld, for very helpful comments and suggestions on an earlier draft of this foreword, and for information on which I have drawn repeatedly in the preceding pages.

References

Hogan, Patrick Colm. (2013). *Narrative Discourse: Authors and Narrators in Literature, Film, and Art*. Columbus, OH, Ohio State UP.

Nannicelli, Ted. (2013). *A Philosophy of the Screenplay*. New York, NY, Routledge.

Parker, Philip. (1999). *The Art and Science of Screenwriting*. Exeter, UK, Intellect.

Robbins, Philip and Aydede, Murat. (2009). "A Short Primer on Situated Cognition." In Robbins, Philip and Aydede, Murat (Eds.) *The Cambridge Handbook of Situated Cognition* (pp. 3–10). Cambridge, UK, Cambridge UP.

Thompson, Kristin. (1999). *Storytelling in the New Hollywood*. Cambridge, MA, Harvard UP.

ACKNOWLEDGMENTS

The editors wish to thank Romana Turina, whose passion for storytelling helped inspire this anthology. We also thank Dominic Topp and Emre Çağlayan for their support and friendship, and David Bordwell for his encouragement at the early stages of development, and for his trailblazing work. Thanks also to J. J. Murphy, Wyatt Phillips, and Justin Wyatt for their help in our hour of need.

We also thank our friends at Routledge, Claire Margerison, Sarah Pickles, Andrew Peart, and Rachel Feehan, for their guidance and kindness which made the production of this book straightforward and enjoyable.

Finally, we thank our nearest and dearest: Noelle, Atticus, Ezra and Finlay Taberham, and Eduard Iricinschi for their abiding love and inspiration.

CONTRIBUTORS

Dominic Arsenault is a Full Professor of film and game studies at the Université de Montréal. His main publications revolve around narrative and narration in games, genre, and video game history, notably with his recent *Super Power, Spoony Bards, and Silverware: The Super Nintendo Entertainment System* in the MIT Press's platform studies series. He teaches narratology for film, games and literature, video game screenwriting, and animation film history and theory. He also explores the links between video games and heavy metal music through research and creation with his solo chipmetal project Multi-Memory Controller.

Katalin E. Bálint is an Associate Professor in Media Psychology at the VU Amsterdam in the Netherlands. Her background is in psychology and film studies. Her interdisciplinary research focuses on the media psychology of narratives. She examines narrative experiences, audience members' empathy with story characters, and the role of design components of audio-visual stories in narrative effects. She is a board member of the Society of Cognitive Studies of the Moving Image and the editorial board of the Journal of Media Psychology.

Todd Berliner, Professor of Film Studies at the University of North Carolina Wilmington, teaches film aesthetics, narration, and style and American film history. He is the author of *Hollywood Aesthetic: Pleasure in American Cinema* (Oxford University Press, 2017) and *Hollywood Incoherent: Narration in Seventies Cinema* (University of Texas Press, 2010). He was the founding chair of UNCW's Film Studies Department and the recipient of two Fulbright Scholar awards, including the Laszlo Orszagh Distinguished Chair in American Studies.

David J. Greenberg has written or doctored over 60 screenplays for features, documentaries, and shorts. His feature writing and directing debut *Stomping Ground* premiered at The Philadelphia Independent Film Festival in 2016. He wrote the documentaries *Bonnie & Clyde: Lovers on the Run* (2015) and *Celebrity Skin* (2012) as well as the features *What Matters Most* (2010) and *Used to Love Her* (2013). A 2015 short *Interrogation* won a Special Jury Prize at the L.A. Neo-Noir Film and Literature Festival. His 1995 short film *The True Meaning of Cool* won an award from the American Film Institute. He co-produced the feature *Seclusion* (2023). David graduated from the film program at Temple University and worked in production on both indie films and Hollywood features before shifting focus to screenwriting full-time. David teaches screenwriting and film history and several Philadelphia universities. His book *Screenwriting for Micro-Budget Films* was released by Routledge/Taylor & Francis in 2021.

Patrick Colm Hogan is a Board of Trustees Distinguished Professor in the English Department and the Cognitive Science Program at the University of Connecticut. He is the author of 25 scholarly books, including *Understanding Indian Movies* (2008), *Affective Narratology: The Emotional Structure of Stories* (2011), *Narrative Discourse: Authors and Narrators in Literature, Film, and Art* (2013), and *Style in Narrative* (2021). He has also published a book of poetry, *The Death of the Goddess* (2014), and a novel, *A People Without Shame* (2023).

Christopher Holliday is a Lecturer in Liberal Arts and Visual Cultures Education at King's College London, specializing in Hollywood cinema, animation history, and contemporary digital media. He has published on digital technology and computer animation and is the author of *The Computer-Animated Film: Industry, Style and Genre* (EUP, 2018), and co-editor of the anthologies *Fantasy/Animation: Connections Between Media, Mediums and Genres* (Routledge, 2018) and *Snow White and the Seven Dwarfs: New Perspectives on Production, Reception, Legacy* (Bloomsbury, 2021). Christopher is currently researching the relationship between identity politics and digital technologies in popular cinema and is the curator of the website/blog/podcast www.fantasy-animation.org.

Catalina Iricinschi is a Visiting Assistant Professor of Psychology at Franklin & Marshall College. Her research interests include event segmentation in film narratives, eye tracking in narrative processing, the narrative of belonging and displacement, place and space depiction in film narratives, and Romanian cinema. She has published in journals such as *Cognitive Science*, *Projections: The Journal for Movie and Mind*, *I-Perception*, along with the edited anthologies *Space in Language* and the forthcoming *Narrative, Media, and Cognition*.

Geoff King is a Professor of Film Studies at Brunel University London. He has published numerous books with a particular focus on American independent, art and Hollywood cinema. Books include *American Independent Cinema* (2005), a pioneering work in the study of independent film, and *Indiewood, USA* (2009), the first academic analysis of the "Indiewood" zone in which Hollywood and the independent sector overlap. He has also written books on the indie features *Donnie Darko* (2007) and *Lost in Translation* (2010) and a study of contemporary lower-budget indie cinema, *Indie 2.0: Change and Continuity in American Indie Film* (2014), including analysis of the role of the internet as a new channel of distribution. His more recent work focuses on the way particular forms of cultural value are attributed to different kinds of film, a theme of *Quality Hollywood: Markers of Distinction in Contemporary Studio Film* (2016) and *Positioning Art Cinema: Film Cultural Value* (2019). His latest book is *The Cinema of Discomfort: Disquieting, Awkward and Uncomfortable Experiences in Contemporary Art and Indie Film* (2022).

Miklós Kiss is an Associate Professor of Audiovisual Arts and Cognition at the Department of Arts, Culture, and Media of the University of Groningen, the Netherlands. His research focuses on contemporary audiovisual media through intersecting narrative and cognitive approaches. He is co-author of the books *Film Studies in Motion: From Audiovisual Essay to Academic Research Video* (with Thomas van den Berg, Scalar, 2016) and *Impossible Puzzle Films: A Cognitive Approach to Contemporary Complex Cinema* (with Steven Willemsen, Edinburgh University Press, 2017), and co-editor of the volume *Puzzling Stories: The Aesthetic Appeal of Cognitive Challenge in Film, Television and Literature* (with Steven Willemsen, Berghahn, 2022).

András Bálint Kovács is a Professor at the Film Department of ELTE University, Budapest, Hungary. He teaches the history of modern cinema and the psychology of film perception. He has been visiting professor at École Normale Supérieure, Paris, Université de la Nouvelle Sorbonne, Paris, and at U.C. San Diego. He has been an artistic and script advisor for a number of films including films of Béla Tarr. Currently, he conducts research on the perception of shot scales and causal thinking in film viewing. His major publications include *Screening Modernism* (University of Chicago Press, 2008); *The Cinema of Béla Tarr* (Columbia University Press, 2013); and *Shot Scale Distribution: An Authorial Fingerprint or a Cognitive Pattern?* (Projections: Vol. 8, Issue 2, 2015).

Neil McCartney is currently based in Oxford as an independent researcher and has taught courses at the Department on the Films of Orson Welles and Self-identity in Cinema. He obtained his PhD in Film Studies from the University of Kent under the supervision of Prof. Murray Smith. His doctoral thesis analyzed unconventional character portrayals in film narratives within the wider context of psychological and philosophical theories of self-identity. He is particularly interested in the relationship between real-world selves and fictional film characters, and specifically, the cognitive dissonance generated by films which display a disruption to conventional cinematic norms relating to character portrayal and development. His research is broadly aligned with the cognitivist approach and his other areas of interest include film-as-philosophy, the portrayal of memory and subjectivity in fiction film, and avant-garde deviations from conventional narrative trajectories and continuity of characters.

Sean O'Sullivan is an Associate Professor of English at The Ohio State University. His work connects, in different ways, to the fields of film, television, narrative theory, nineteenth-century British literature and serial storytelling. His publications include a book on the contemporary realist British director Mike Leigh as well as articles and chapters in edited collections on such topics of serial television as *The Sopranos* and episodic storytelling; modernist structure in *Mad Men*; poetic design and the serial season; the afterlives of Krzysztof Kieslowski's *The Decalogue*; *Deadwood* and third seasons; apocalyptic television in Margaret Thatcher's Britain; the limits of satisfaction in Dickens, Eliot, and contemporary serials; and the showrunner Ingmar Bergman's *Scenes from a Marriage* and *Fanny and Alexander*. O'Sullivan has also written recaps of *Mad Men* and *Breaking Bad* for Kritik and Public Books.

Evan Skolnick, with over 30 years of combined story and game development experience at world-class entertainment companies such as Marvel, Activision, and Lucasfilm, brings a unique perspective to narrative experiences across multiple media forms. A BAFTA- and D.I.C.E. Award-nominated video game writer and narrative designer, Skolnick has worked on over 50 games in a narrative capacity, including *Concrete Genie*, indie smash *Cuphead*, *Star Wars 1313*, *Marvel: Ultimate Alliance 2*, *Dying Light*, *The Walking Dead: A New Frontier*, *Star Wars: Battlefront*, and *Mafia III*. Skolnick is an international speaker and the author of the Penguin Random House book *Video Game Storytelling*. Through his tutorials at conferences and game studios, he has imparted core storytelling knowledge to well over a thousand working game development professionals. He currently teaches video game writing at the University of Silicon Valley while continuing to work as a contract game writer, narrative designer and consultant.

Paul Taberham is an Associate Professor in Film and Animation Studies at the Arts University Bournemouth, UK. He is the author of *Lessons in Perception: The Avant-Garde Filmmaker as Practical Psychologist* (Berghahn, 2018) and the forthcoming *Animated Visions: Theory, History and Aesthetics* (Berghahn, 2024). He is also the co-editor of *Cognitive Media Theory* (Routledge, 2014) with Ted Nannicelli, and *Experimental Animation: From*

Analogue to Digital (Routledge, 2019) with Miriam Harris and Lilly Husbands. Paul is a fellow of the Society of Cognitive Studies of the Moving Image, and on the editorial board for *Animation: An Interdisciplinary Journal.*

ED. S. Tan is an Emeritus Professor at the University of Amsterdam. In his work, the psychology of media use and media experience is the central theme. He taught and conducted research on perception, cognition, imagination, and emotions induced by film, television, video games and other media. Tan has (co-)published on film-induced emotion, narrative absorption, and engagement with film and television drama characters.

Enrico Terrone is a Professor of Aesthetics at Università di Genova and Principal Investigator of the European Research Council (ERC) project "The Philosophy of Experiential Artifacts." He was research fellow at the Käte Hamburger Kolleg (Bonn), Gerda Henkel fellow at FMSH (Paris), visiting researcher at Institut Jean Nicod (Paris), and Juan de la Cierva fellow at LOGOS (Barcelona). His areas of inquiry are aesthetics, the philosophy of film and the philosophy of technology. He published papers in international journals such as *The British Journal of Aesthetics*, *The Journal of Aesthetics and Art Criticism*, *Erkenntnis*, *Ergo*, and *American Philosophical Quarterly.* His last book, co-written with Luca Bandirali, was *Concept TV: An Aesthetics of Television Series* (2021, Lexington Books).

Jan-Noël Thon is a Professor and Chair of Media Studies and Media Education at Osnabrück University, Germany. Recent books include *From Comic Strips to Graphic Novels* (co-edited with Daniel Stein, De Gruyter 2013), *Storyworlds across Media* (co-edited with Marie-Laure Ryan, University of Nebraska Press 2014), *Game Studies* (co-edited with Klaus Sachs-Hombach, von Halem 2015), *Transmedial Narratology and Contemporary Media Culture* (University of Nebraska Press 2016), *Subjectivity across Media* (co-edited with Maike Sarah Reinerth, Routledge 2017), *Comicanalyse* (co-authored with Stephan Packard, Andreas Rauscher, Véronique Sina, Lukas R.A. Wilde, and Janina Wildfeuer, Metzler 2019), *Comics and Videogames* (co-edited with Andreas Rauscher and Daniel Stein, Routledge 2021), *Comics and Agency* (co-edited with Vanessa Ossa and Lukas R.A. Wilde, De Gruyter 2022), and *Bildmedien* (co-edited with Frauke Berndt, De Gruyter 2023).

Ioana Uricaru is a Romanian-American filmmaker. She is interested in stories that reconsider the historical past, focuses deeply on the details of lived experience or interrogate the relationship between the United States and the rest of the world. She co-directed the omnibus Tales from the Golden Age (Official Selection, Cannes Film Festival), and co-wrote and directed Lemonade (nominated for the Independent Spirit Someone to Watch Award and winner of several awards in international festivals). Her work has been part of the official selections at the Cannes, Berlin, Sundance, Tribeca, and AFI festivals and was supported by the Cannes Cinefondation Residency and the Sundance Institute Feature Film program. Ioana is a Fellow of the John Simon Guggenheim Memorial Foundation, a Rome Prize recipient, and a Fellow of the American Academy in Berlin.

Robyn Warhol is College of Arts and Sciences Distinguished Professor of English at the Ohio State University. A feminist narratologist and specialist in serialized Victorian novels and television shows, she received the 2022 Wayne C. Booth Lifetime Achievement Award from the International Society for the Study of Narrative for her contributions to narrative theory. The most recent of her ten books include *The Edinburgh Companion to Contemporary Narrative Theories*, co-edited with Zara Dinnen (EUP), *Narrative Theory Unbound: Queer and Feminist Interventions* (Ohio State University Press), co-edited with Susan S. Lanser, and *Love Among the Archives: Writing the Lives of Sir George Scharf, Victorian Bachelor* (Edinburgh UP) which was co-authored with Helena Michie and was the winner of the 2015 NAVSA Best Book of the Year Award. Her current project is a new, improved version of her digital humanities project, "Reading like a Victorian," a website facilitating the synchronic reading of nineteenth-century British serial novels at readinglikeavictorian.osu.edu

Josh Weinstein grew up in Washington, DC, and attended St. Albans School, where he co-founded a humor magazine with his best friend, Bill Oakley. He went to Stanford University, where he was Editor-in-Chief of the school's humor magazine. After university, he was briefly in advertising before becoming a longtime writer for *The Simpsons* and was a showrunner with Oakley for seasons 7 and 8. After the Simpsons, he co-created the cult favorite animated show *Mission Hill and* then wrote for *Futurama*. He also served as a writer for Disney's *Gravity Falls* and co-developed and served as a showrunner for CBBC's critically acclaimed puppet show, *Strange Hill High*. Most recently, he developed the Netflix animated show *Disenchantment* with Matt Groening.

INTRODUCTION

Catalina Iricinschi and Paul Taberham

"What is it about stories, anyway?" This all-too-legitimate question that opens Frank Rose's book on the art of narrative immersion alludes, in its generic format, to a wide array of phenomena regarding the actual writing of stories, the many ways in which stories are presented visually, and the reasons why the recipient/viewer gets caught up in fake and unfamiliar (story) worlds (Rose, 2012, p. 1).

The present anthology was motivated by a quest for a multiple-perspective account of narrative. Specialists from various domains of narrative studies looked at stories and storytelling through the lens of their expertise and outlined their perspectives in the chapters of this collection. Taken together, this multi-disciplinary anthology is designed to bring us closer to answering this deceptively elusive question: "What is it about stories, anyway?" The editors brought together these accounts to highlight (among other goals) the current complexity of film narrative, from its creation to its perception, and to offer views from theoreticians and empirical researchers alongside those of practitioners (screenwriters) and film studies teachers. The present collection builds, inevitably, upon existing work whose contribution to narrative research cannot be overlooked.

There is a wide range of screenwriting manuals, most of which are declaredly geared towards a successful career in Hollywood.[1] These sources are indicative of the screenwriters' expectations regarding the reception of their films. Narratology, however, is a different field: instead of presenting ideals for the screenwriter to aspire to, the narratologist offers top-down analyses of the nature, form and function of narration. Narrative and narration have been explored in an assortment of disciplines and mediums, such

DOI: 10.4324/9781003197911-1

as literature, oral storytelling, graphic novels and music, along with screen media, such as films, television and video games.[2]

Within film studies strictly speaking, the first book-length discussion of film narration was Seymour Chatman's *Story and Discourse Narrative Structure in Fiction and Film* (published in 1980) which introduced the story-discourse dynamic following the syuzhet-fabula distinction from Russian formalism. The process by which the suyzhet (or story) is extracted from the fabula (or discourse) by the mind receiving the visual narrative was largely overlooked in previous research. Story grammarians looked at narrative through a similar focus-on-structure lens. They attributed syntactic structures to narrative discourse, i.e., a syntax very much akin to that regulating the production of correctly formed sentences. Yet again, the focus falls on the production of discourse forms with little consideration for the reception and comprehension of these composites of sound (whether words or other tones) and image (whether still or flickering at our eyes) that have charmed us with their engulfing power for so long.

Film viewers used to be thought of as passive receivers of mere audio-visual entertainment, an otiose process allowing for a brain siesta. As such, the viewers are indeed rather irrelevant. But then why add intricacies to narrative structure, from the simple flashback to the puzzle plot? Why complicate the "syntactic structure" of the narrative if the viewer is in for a "don't make me think" deal? The chronological seamless sequence of events would accomplish just that, wouldn't it? David Bordwell's influential *Narration in the Fiction Film* (published in 1985) promoted an alternative to the prevailing conceptualisations of film narrative of the time: Instead of conceiving of narration as an act of showing (the mimetic conception), or as presupposing a voice which performs an act of telling (diegetic conception), Bordwell foregrounds issues of form and the viewer's mental activity: Observable filmic details interact with the viewer's fluid and dynamic processing. Narration, then, is best understood "as the organization of a set of cues for the construction of a story" (Bordwell, 1985, p. 62).

Edward Branigan's *Narrative Comprehension and Film* followed seven years later, and since then, a wealth of books that explore screen narration (cited throughout this anthology) have been published. Along with this edited collection, Larry A. Brown's *How Films Tell Stories: The Narratology of Cinema* and Warren Buckland's *Narrative and Narration: Analyzing Cinematic Storytelling* are both fine teaching materials for the study of narration. In the realm of cognitive science as reflected in the evolution of film, James Cutting's (2021) *Movies on our Minds* offers a data-driven overview of how the mind interfaces with storytelling conventions. Marina Grishakova and Maria Poulaki's edited collection *Narrative Complexity: Cognition, Embodiment, Evolution* (2019) also offers an overview of the field, along with David Herman's edited collection *Narrative Theory and the Cognitive Sciences*.

Stephen Follows (2019) has illustrated how a film data analyst can offer new insights into screenplay conventions. For example, after analysing 12,309 screenplays, Follows learned that the median length across all scripts was 106 pages, though nearly 70% run between 90 and 120 pages. Horror scripts tended to be the shortest, while animated movies, comedy, drama, sci-fi and historical films were progressively longer. Horror scripts tend to have the fewest speaking characters (an average of 25.8) while historical films have the most (an average of 45.7). Comedies have the fewest scenes (98.5 on average), while action scripts have the most (131.2 on average). The average age of the character who speaks most frequently is 28.3, and they get progressively older with the second, third, fourth and fifth characters – the last of whom is 35.4 on average.

Relevant publications also include Ted Nannicelli's *A Philosophy of the Screenplay* along with George Varotsis' *Screenplay and Narrative Theory: The Screenplectics Model of Complex Narrative Systems*, and Jill Nelmes' edited collection *Analysing the Screenplay*. Focusing more narrowly on the screenplay, the Screenwriting Research Network (SRN) produces the *Journal of Screenwriting* and runs a yearly conference.

The theoretical and empirical approaches to narrative mentioned above have engaged, fairly recently, in cross-domain communication and information exchange with the goal of understanding visual storytelling from all perspectives. The evolution of film form itself is now seen as a "natural selection" process by which successful stories "fit" the engaged and dynamic minds of the viewers. The moving image changed over time, evidently, but not by implementing novelties based solely on disengaged screenwriting in a uni-dimensional feed-forward-like process. Rather, the screen storyteller and the viewer engage in a feedback loop informing and changing each other. This diachronic view of the moving image is void unless seen in tandem with the human mind's increasing film literacy in a fast-paced, and cognitively demanding, technological world.

James Cutting comments, "The idea about evolution of movies [...] is not trivial. It entails continuous variation in, and selection across, attributes of movies over time – where that variation is generated through the art of filmmaking; where selection is governed by fitness; and where fitness is measured against biological, psychological, and cultural constraints of viewers' perceptual and cognitive systems, many of which we've been able to discover only long after filmmakers implemented those changes" (Cutting, 2021, p. 8). Successful stories, consequently, take into account the mind and the eyes of the viewer and make the image move so that the resulting kinesis also makes minds move. The successful story receives its praise and then, we may conjecture, the story creator wonders: What's next? The viewer provides feedback by way of enthusiastic ratings, talk of the town, watching the movie again and again...and then, we may conjecture, wonders: What's next? And so, minds and movies reflect on each other in this feedback loop and emerge with new ways for visual storytelling. With the increasing breadth of media composites, once peripheral narrative formats are now mainstream. Movies evolved, minds evolved, but one factor remains unaltered: *We love stories*.

Stories serve a range of social functions. Fables impart moral lessons to children, myths explain the great mysteries of the world, legends preserve and exaggerate historical events. Carl Plantinga comments that since stories are a fundamental mode of human communication, it should not be surprising that they have extremely varied purposes. Fictional and non-fictional films have been used to "inform, entertain, impress, warn, teach, console, inspire, motivate, consolidate social norms, and make the case for change" (Plantinga, 2018, pp. 22–23). Anton Chekhov famously claimed "The role of the artist is to ask questions, not answer them" (Chekhov quoted in Male, 2019, p. 386). Franz Kafka believed that a story must be "the axe for the frozen sea within us" (Kafka quoted in Sokel, 2001, p. 78) reconnecting us with feelings that might otherwise be unbearable to study, but which need our attention. Stories can reinvigorate our relationship with the outside world when we grow over-familiar with life, dispelling our boredom and ingratitude. Stories have the power to elevate us, make us more cultured, more empathetic and, in George Eliot's words, inspire "nobler emotions" (Eliot, quoted in Neill, 1996, p. 179).

These lofty aspirations for storytelling fit within the category of *magic art*, a term coined by R.G. Collingwood who suggested that magic art of any kind elevates us, it changes the way we see the world and can transform our lives. This is contrasted with *amusement art*, which merely offers entertaining distractions (Collingwood, [1938] 2013). Similarly to this, Iris Murdoch refers to most literature as "self-consoling fantasies" (quoted in Plantinga, 2018, p. 25) which harbours the little potential for self-betterment. This could equally be applied to cinema and screen media more generally. It is simply pleasant, and perhaps serves as an emotional counterbalance to otherwise safe or uneventful lives.

Beyond social and psychological reasons, there may also be biological reasons why we are drawn to stories. At its most basic, the way in which narrative information is organised may be understood as "cognitive play with pattern," like a playground for the mind (Boyd, 2010). We might also be attracted to stories because they feature humanly relevant themes which derive from evolved needs and interests, such as struggles and outcomes, failing and succeeding, escaping harm, loving, being admired and demeaned, being shamed and redeemed, mating, and helping one's offspring thrive (Dissanayake, 2000; Grodal, 2009). Storytelling can also be understood as a simulation of real-life experiences, such as improving social skills by identifying with other people. They can provide a kind of psychological training where we learn about a range of social situations, characters, and plans to confront obstacles and social dilemmas (Oatley, 2011; Gottschall, 2012). Like picturing imaginary scenarios, stories allow us to imagine hypothetical situations without the high-cost experimentation of actual practice. Instead, they provide a low-cost, low-risk surrogate experience which serves as a richly instructional source of information (Dutton, 2009).

Bearing in mind these general considerations on the perennial power of storytelling, the aim of this book is to illustrate the richness of film narrative by bringing together current perspectives on the moving image from different domains of study: philosophy, film studies, and psychology. In addition, screenwriters and teachers of screenwriting contributed brief comments on their practice and expertise that the reader will find interspersed throughout the anthology.

Each chapter in this collection, therefore, outlines a different approach to film narrative discourse thus compiling a mosaic of the multiple research perspectives on the moving image, both traditional and novel. The four parts of the collection delineate the various perspectives on narrative: The dynamic dialogue between convention and deviation in film narrative, a dialogue that alludes to the evolution of film (part I), brings forth art cinema (part II) as defying conventional expression throughout film history. Alternative media formats (part III) highlight television narratives, animated stories, and video games as different degrees of departures from classical film narrative. Transmedial narrative incorporates all these forms in creating story worlds.

Some stories draw us in, some confuse us, some trick us in making wrong predictions, some frighten us...but all stories engage our minds! Directly or indirectly, we interact with the stories we are told even if only by the mere attribution of meaning. The engaged viewer comprehends the narrative through simulation processes of being absorbed in the story world, and through cognitive processes of identifying interrelated narrative units (part IV).

After a short survey of key narrative variables and an account of how screen narration developed from its inception to the present day (Chapter 1), the collection opens with a discussion on how we tell and have been telling stories in cinema: What makes classical Hollywood storytelling enjoyable? Todd Berliner (Chapter 2) challenges the existing narrative unity and clarity explanatory models that, despite their mass accessibility feature, fail "to account for the aesthetic pleasure afforded by disunity in Hollywood storytelling." Disunity in Hollywood exists even in stories characterised by clarity and unity, and even when such disunity violates, at small scales, the logic of the story. If the narrational discourse affords (even a somewhat illusory) story resolution, aspects of disunity may actually increase the aesthetic appreciation of the story. "How does narrative disunity exhilarate our aesthetic response?" Instances of disunity contain elements of surprise that always engage our attention. Efficient humour relies on elements of surprise and incongruity; these very elements make humour enjoyable. Moreover, incongruity resolution is cognitively enjoying and rewarding when performed in a safe environment. Free play affords the same pleasure of solving incongruity in an environment where inconsistencies are not costly. Resolving incongruous information in Hollywood film is, as Berliner argues, an instance of "cognitive play."

Unlike classical Hollywood, independent film (Chapter 3) moves away from the clearly defined plot that "centres" around established goals in a cause–effect dynamic, and de-centres the narrative storyline thus affording film forms that approximate art cinema. Indie film is blind (or blind-folded, at least) to Hollywood's unity criteria and thus allows for fragmented narratives as revolving around a small number of major strands that unfold rather independently of one another, or as varieties of intersecting, multi-strand narrative. Complex characters, forms of ambiguity, narrative structure as a web of narrative strands, indie films replicate the complexity and ambiguity of life.

Puzzle plots display a different kind of complexity (Chapter 4), mostly at the level of deliberate narrative design with the overt intent of inducing perceived cognitive effort on the part of the viewer. Puzzle plots, therefore, are not particularly consistent with the classical Hollywood rules of clarity and unity; puzzle plots are intentionally non-unified, non-linear, and unclear at first sight. Non-linear, inverse, or (multiple) embedded plot trajectories capture the viewer in labyrinthine narrative structures that require a meaningful discovery experience.

Art cinema, yet another instance of film form declaredly departing from mainstream cinema, has enjoyed a well-established status in both the United States and Europe especially with the decline of Hollywood directly following the Second World War. It has received an array of definitions that reveal the degree to which various dimensions of film apply to art film, such as cause–effect logic, realism, and ambiguity. Following an overview of existing approaches to art cinema, Chapter 5 outlines a non-unified model of interconnected modes of art cinema narration in a triangular schema that positions most forms of this film category. The overview of art cinema with its new model for interpretation sets the ground for two "case study" presentations: Jean-Luc Godard's film and its evolution through stylistic periods leading to filmic "short poems expressions" of human life manifestations (Chapter 6); and David Lynch's (Chapter 7) film art featuring recognisable narrative elements alongside surreal elements and plot digressions.

Television narrative, constructing its story world as a familiar environment welcoming the viewer week after week, assumes various thematic formats. Chapter 8 expands on narrative categories and genres that exist in classical film format, but implement episodic or serial structures when designed as television narrative: the western, the police procedural, the anthology series, the sitcom, and the social comedy. In elaborating on each category, actual television series serve as explanative illustrations.

With the development of imagery in virtual information and communication, visual narrative acquired new media formats, such as animation (Chapter 9) and video games (Chapter 10). Animated storytelling, defined in a dynamic dialogue with established narrative and plot constructs, can afford a wide range of novel narration techniques. Given viewers' appreciation of animation (regardless of age), animated narrative gained pedagogical affordances that have made it a multimedia agent of learning. Chapter 10 depicts video games as forms of interactive storytelling (among other platforms) that create the illusion of agency by enabling the player to choose among (limited) alternatives. The author advances the concept "narrative infusion" as video games implement narrative elements while still focusing on player's sense of agency.

Digital media advancements and aspects of film industry akin to corporation-like business approaches allowed for new developments of narrative forms that run across different media resulting in transmedial franchises (Chapter 11). Transmedial franchises introduce a new platform for narrative complexity: the Harry Potter franchise, for instance, comprises all Harry Potter story worlds across all media, along with real-world referents (e.g., Harry Potter Halloween costume), and thus constructs a complex set of Harry Potter "story universes."

Film form in the general sense, including all the variations mentioned above, cannot evolve independent of its creator's and viewer's minds and perception, as the creator and the viewer cannot communicate but through the narrative environment. Novel perspectives from fields of study outside the strictly defined film scholarship invite us to consider screenwriting as the basis for film narrative (Chapter 12) and studies on viewers' cognitive psychology of film (Chapters 13 and 14). Philosophy deals with concepts, it creates concepts, it formulates concepts. The philosophy of screenplay deals with conceptual developments of the act and product of writing for the screen. Chapter 12 elaborates on normative dimensions involved in screenplays defined as "verbal object[s] that should enable one to turn a narrative into a film thereby governing the passage from the design of a film to its production." Screenplays are indeed works of art on a par with the narrative discourse. Presented with a film (or a literary narrative for that matter), the audience experiences a sense of "being there," being present in the world that the story creates, interacting with the fictional characters. The sense of being absorbed in a story world presupposes active cognitive processing from perception to imaginative construction of a world that is sketched only in a fictitious realm. Chapter 13 elaborates upon the cognitive substrates of narrative absorption.

Even fairly simple, linear narrative architectures require cognitive processes for comprehension. Constructing narrative meaning – from the perspective of the audience – has a couple of prerequisites. Forms of narration are rarely chronological orders of events; they can feature flashbacks and flashforwards, for example. The first prerequisite consists of the chronological reorganisation of events. This prerequisite has, in turn, its own prerequisite: identifying the events. Film viewers tend to agree on where the boundaries separating events are. The argument of Chapter 14 focuses on the research methodology used in establishing viewers' event segmentation agreement, and the subsequent stipulations regarding narrative comprehension processes as necessary and sufficient (or insufficient).

The present collection comprises theoretical and empirical approaches to cinematic discourse from Hollywood film to art cinema, and novel implementations of narrative in animation, video games, and franchise platforms. Screenwriters and teachers of film share with the reader insights based on their experiences of working directly with screen narratives. And then there is the human mind all involved in attending and understanding the moving image.

Notes

1 Some of the influential ones include Syd Field's *Screenplay: The Foundations of Screenwriting*, Robert McKee's *Story: Substance, Structure, Style and the Principles of Screenwriting*, David Trottier's *The Screenwriter's Bible: A Complete Guide to Writing, Formatting, and Selling Your Script*, John Truby's *The Anatomy of Story: 22 Steps to Becoming a Master Storyteller* and Blake Snyder's *Save the Cat! The Last Book on Screenwriting You'll Ever Need*.
2 Comprehensive books which cover the area include Mieke Bal's *Narratology: Introduction to the Theory of Narrative*, David Herman, Manfred Jahn and Marie-Laure Ryan's edited collection *Routledge Encyclopaedia of Narrative Theory*, and Peter Huhn et al.'s edited *Handbook of Narratology* (also available online as *The Living Handbook of Narratology*).

References

Bordwell, D. (1985). *Narration in Fiction Film*. Routledge.

Boyd, B. (2010). *On the Origin of Stories: Evolution, Cognition, and Fiction*. Harvard University Press.

Collingwood, R.G. (2013). *The Principles of Art*. Case Press.

Cutting, J. (2021). *Movies on Our Minds: The Evolution of Cinematic Engagement*. OUP USA.

Dissanayake, E. (2000). Art and Intimacy: How the Arts Began. In B. Boyd, J. Carroll, & J. Gottschall (Eds.). *Evolution, Literature, and Film: A Reader*. Columbia University Press.

Dutton, D. (2009). *The Art Instinct: Beauty, Pleasure, and Human Evolution*. OUP Oxford.

Follows, S. (2019). *Defining the average screenplay, via data on 12,000+ scripts*. [online]. stephenfollows.com. Available at: https://stephenfollows.com/what-the-average-screenplay-contains/ [Accessed 8 February 2023].

Gottschall, J. (2012). *The Storytelling Animal: How Stories Make Us Human* (1st ed.). Mariner Books.

Grodal, T. (2009). *Embodied Visions: Evolution, Emotion, Culture, and Film.* Oxford University Press.

Male, A. (2019). *A Companion to Illustration: Art and Theory.* Wiley.

Neill, A. (1996). Empathy and (Film) Fiction. In D. Bordwell and N. Carroll (Eds.). *Post-Theory: Reconstructing Film Studies.* The University of Wisconsin Press.

Oatley, K. (2011). *Such Stuff as Dreams: The Psychology of Fiction* (1st ed.). John Wiley & Sons Inc.

Plantinga, C. (2018). *Screen Stories: Emotion and the Ethics of Engagement.* OUP USA.

Rose, F. (2012). *The Art of Immersion: How the Digital Generation is Remaking Hollywood, Madison Avenue, and the Way We Tell Stories.* W.W. Norton & Co.

Sokel, W. (2001). *The Myth of Power and the Self: Essays on Franz Kafka.* Wayne State University Press.

1

DIMENSIONS OF NARRATIVE

Paul Taberham

A simple-but-comprehensive definition of narrative would be as follows: a chain of events in cause-effect relationship, occurring in coherent time and space. A mere sequence of events does not designate a narrative, as the causal and temporal event relationships are indiscernible. Consider the following: "A radio plays, a house burns down, and a cat gets wet." There are no discernible causal or temporal relations between these events. But if we connect them, a narrative emerges: "A man is at home cooking dinner. He hears on the radio that there is a beer festival taking place near his home. Rushing out, he accidentally leaves the stove on and the kitchen catches fire, triggering his alarm. The fire brigade soon arrives and puts out the flames, accidentally soaking a local cat in the process." Events are causally related now, and they are spatially and temporally oriented.

This is a simple narrative that fits our basic definition, but a vast array of possibilities lie within the way a narrative is *narrated*. That is to say, the causally connected chain of events (narrative) affords a wide range of organisations and recountings (narration). Narratives are constructed along multiple dimensions that sustain and advance the storyline, such as time, space, characters, and events. These dimensions establish relationships that form the internal structure of the narrative. Stories are, therefore, sustained by a scaffolding of connections between events, character relationships, and space-time contextual information. Pre-existing recipes for arrangements of space-time events are mostly framed as screenwriting tenets.

Following Syd Field's influential screenwriting manual, film narratives are generally understood as being structured around three acts: set-up (30 minutes), confrontation (60 minutes), and resolution (30 minutes).[1] *Plot points* occur just before the second and third acts, shifting the story in another

DOI: 10.4324/9781003197911-2

direction (Field, 2005, pp. 51–62). In *Back to the Future* (1985), we shift into act two when Marty (Michael J. Fox) travels back in time and enters Hill Valley in 1955. The third act begins just after his parents are reunited and he needs to rush back to the town's courthouse to catch the lightning strike that will bring him back to the present.

Kristin Thompson, a narratologist who observes screenplays instead of prescribing ideals, has suggested that most films feature four acts of equal length, with Fields' second act breaking in two and a change of direction in the middle: set up (30 minutes), complicating action (30 minutes), development (30 minutes), and climax (30 minutes) (Thompson, 1999, pp. 27–36). In *Back to the Future*, the shift from act two (the complicating action) to act three (the development) occurs at the midpoint where goals are formulated for the two major lines of action: to bring Marty's parents back together, and to return him to 1985 (ibid., p. 90). Midpoints are not always easy to notice, but are clearest in rise-and-fall narratives: in *Scarface* (1983), Tony Montana (Al Pacino) spends the first half of the movie rising from an ex-convict to a wealthy drug lord, and the second half details his downfall; in *Titanic* (1997) the first half is spent following Jack (Leonardo DiCaprio) and Rose's (Kate Winslet) star-crossed lovers romance. At mid-point, the ship collides with an iceberg and the remaining film covers the consequences.

A narrative can also be told in two acts, like *Bambi* (1942) which splits the film into childhood and adulthood, and *Full Metal Jacket* (1987) which spends the first half at boot camp and the second half on the Vietnam War battlefield. There is also block construction, where films are broken into a series of chapters like a book, such as *Barry Lyndon* (1975), *Hannah and Her Sisters* (1985), and *Pulp Fiction* (1994).

Classical Chinese, Korean, and Japanese poems and stories used a four-act structure known as kishōtenketsu, which is still applied today in modern screen narratives. The four stages are introduction (ki), development (shō), twist (ten), and reconciliation (ketsu). Unlike the three-act structure which is considered standard in the West, conflict is not built into kishōtenketsu narratives as prominently, since development is the longest act, and the twist features late in the story. For example, *Kiki's Delivery Service* (1989) begins with Kiki (Minami Takayama), a 13-year-old witch who leaves her home and sets up a delivery service in a new town using her magic broomstick. That's the introduction (ki). Most of the story happens during the development (shō) where she befriends a boy named Tombo (Kappei Yamaguchi) and faces the challenges of growing up and sustaining a work/life balance. Towards the end of the film, the twist (ten) occurs where Tombo is left hanging upside down in an airship accident, and in the reconciliation (ketsu), Kiki rescues him.

Pre-existing templates have also been formulated which are available to the screenwriter. In Hong Kong during the 1970s, movies were planned out by preparing a nine-paragraph plot breakdown, with each paragraph outlining one of the nine 10-minute film reels. The outlines were designed so that the film would have an energetic first reel, a climax in the fourth reel, another climax in the sixth or seventh, and an elaborate dénouement in the last reel or two (Bordwell, 2000, p. 76).

In *The Writer's Journey: Mythic Structure for Writers*, Christopher Vogler (2007) adapts Joseph Campbell's monomyth into a practical guide for screenwriters. It is essentially a coming-of-age narrative with 12 stages (e.g., the call to adventure, refusal of the call, meeting with the mentor) and a cast of character archetypes (e.g., hero, mentor, shapeshifter, trickster, ally, shadow). *Star Wars: Episode IV A New Hope* (1977) and *The Matrix* (1999) are both examples of this. Blake Snyder's *Save the Cat! The Only Book on Screenwriting You'll Ever Need* (2005) offers a 15-point "beat sheet" with various plot points that need to be reached by specific pages of the screenplay (e.g., theme stated on p. 5, catalyst on p. 12, B story on p. 30, dark night of the soul pp. 75–85). *How to Train Your Dragon* (2010) and *Guardians of the Galaxy* (2014) both found success using this template.

A screen narrative can be unified, i.e., self-contained in a single story like *Casablanca* (1942), or episodic – part of a series of stories with their own arcs, which bind together in a larger arc like the *Harry Potter* movie franchise (2001–2011), or a television series such as *The Sopranos* (1999–2007). A story can also be *high-concept* – easy to pitch with a succinct, attention-grabbing premise like *Jurassic Park* (1993) (a dinosaur theme park gone awry).[2] Stories can also be low-concept, which is more focused on character development instead of an attention-grabbing premise, like *Annie Hall* (1977) (a nonlinear chronicle of Alvy Singer and Annie Hall, how they were shaped through life experiences which caused them to fall in love, but ultimately brake up). Or movie narratives can be somewhere on the continuum between these two, with not only a graspable hook but also character development.

A story can also feature a single protagonist (*Dirty Harry*, 1971), or two protagonists (*The Odd Couple*, 1968), or more in a mission team narrative where all protagonists work towards a single goal (*Ocean's Eleven*, 1960/2001). A network narrative (*Nashville*, 1975; *Magnolia* 1999; *Game of Thrones*, 2011–2019) features several characters of equal weighting who are pursuing separate goals, but are connected diffusely "through kinship, friendship, employment, or coincidence in ways that affect their individual fates" (Bordwell, 2016).[3]

In Hollywood films, a protagonist is generally defined by clear-cut traits, motives, and goals. Recognisable archetypes can also be used, such as the renegade cop (Clint Eastwood's Dirty Harry), the child with a big heart (Judy Garland's Dorothy), or the mad scientist (Christopher Lloyd's Doc Bown), to simplify the process of characterisation, making them instantly graspable for general audiences. By contrast, archetypes are typically avoided in art cinema. Like real life, art cinema characters are harder to read or simplify into a narrow selection of core traits, such as Guido Anselmi (Marcello Mastroianni) in *Fellini's 8 ½* (1963). In mainstream screen media, characters can also be one-dimensional (e.g., Voldemort is bad, Superman is good), or they can be multi-dimensional with conflicting traits (e.g., Tony Soprano is both vicious and sensitive, loyal and unfaithful, cautious and impulsive). Central protagonists are usually morally virtuous, but they can also be the villain (*American Psycho*, 2000; *The House that Jack Built*, 2018). The central protagonist will often face two opposing options and will need to choose between them. In *Titanic*, Rose needs to choose between two suitors, one who represents love and another who represents money. In *Goodfellas* (1990), Henry Hill (Ray Liotta) must choose between loyalty to his mobster family, and personal survival by cooperating with the FBI.

Protagonists can undergo an upwards arc, conquering inner-demons like Rick Blaine (Humphrey Bogart) in *Casablanca*, or they can experience a downwards arc – a fall from grace like Michael Corleone (Al Pacino) in *The Godfather* (1972). There is also the flat arc, where the character doesn't require personal change, but rather serves as a catalyst for sparking positive change in the world and characters around them, such as a typical James Bond or Sherlock Holmes story, or Marty McFly (Michael. J Fox) teaching his father to stand up to bullies in *Back to the Future* (Weiland, 2016, pp. 16–17).

Dialogue is not an essential feature of narrative discourse (see: *Les Vacances de M. Hulot*, 1953; *Bellville Rendez-Vous*, 2003) but is usually used in screen narratives to reveal information through exposition, establish character relations, and move the story forward. When used, it usually concise, but can be sprawling, it can also be naturalistic or artificial, direct or laced with subtexts. Local dialect and accents can be used (*Mystic River*, 2003; *The Witch*, 2015), although they are usually avoided. Dialogue can also be used sparingly with the meaning hidden between the words (*No Country for Old Men*, 2007), or it can be snappy, with quick-witted characters sparring with one another through words (*Bringing Up Baby*, 1938; *The Marvelous Mrs. Maisel*, 2017–2023).

Voice-over narration has been used in a variety of ways, from an omniscient narrator who knows all (*The Magnificent Ambersons*, 1942), from a character or multiple characters who are part of the story (*LA Confidential*, 1997; *Spiderman: Into the Spider-Verse*, 2018) or delivered by an onscreen character in a direct address with the audience, personally invested in the events (*Annie Hall*; *Fleabag*, 2016–2019). It can also be a character within the diegetic world who has limited understanding over the onscreen events (*Badlands*, 1973; *Mary and Max*, 2009).

The temporal arrangement of events delineates many narrative constructs; events can unfold in real time (*Rope*, 1948; *Before Sunset*, 2004), but ellipses are normally used where time is skipped forward to the next significant event. Narrative time can be linear, or the chronological order can be scrambled. Flashbacks can be used, offering revelations or reminders to the viewer, and flashforwards can also be used, arousing curiosity as to how the given scenario is going to be set up. A story can begin with the first relevant moment, or it can begin *in media res*, in the middle of the action to quickly grip the viewer.

The flow of information has been handled in a range of different ways in screen narratives. It can progress at variable speeds, moving quickly through dialogue and events, or it can slow to a crawl through contemplative pacing or a set piece such as a fight sequence, a car chase, or a song-and-dance number. Narrative information can be restricted, where we only know as much as the protagonists, or less: in *No Country for Old Men* we spend most of our time with Llewelyn Moss (Josh Brolin), a man who stole a large sum of money he stumbled upon in the desert. Information flow can also be omniscient, where we know more than the onscreen characters: *No Country for Old Men*'s cat-and-mouse narrative occasionally switches between Llewelyn and Anton Chigurh (Javier Bardem), the hitman assigned to retrieve the money. When both points of view are intercut, we know more than the onscreen characters. Stories normally switch from omniscient to restricted and back again – selecting who knows what and when plays a crucial role in the experience of a narrative. Information flow can also be controlled through mise-en-scène, for example, we see a hand pick up the murder weapon in a whodunit, but not who the hand belongs to.

Plot details might only be presented once, but important information is often repeated through *redundancy*, making it abundantly clear to the audience and emphasising their importance. Information can also be foreshadowed, or temporarily withheld through retardation, creating suspense (like a cliffhanger, leaving the protagonist in a precarious situation) or surprise at the moment of revelation (like a twist ending). Using retardation, audiences can be intentionally misled through unreliable narration, such as learning near the end that the story has been the delusions of an asylum inmate (*The Cabinet of Dr. Caligari*, 1920; *Shutter Island*, 2010) or the lead protagonists are the same person with split personality disorder (*Fight Club*, 1999). Plot twists can recontextualise events already seen, such as Malcolm Cole (Bruce Willis) realising at the same time as the audience that he is a ghost late in *The Sixth Sense* (1999), having died near the beginning of the movie.

Screen narratives can be presented without any questions pervading them such as wedding or holiday videos. But narrative fiction is usually *erotetic*, driven by macro questions which dominate the picture from one end to the other (will Dorothy escape Oz and return to Kansas), and micro-questions which sustain our attention and provide the glue that holds the trail of scenes together (why are the munchkins happy to see Dorothy, will she escape the flying monkeys, how will she awaken from the poppy field) (Carroll, 2013, p. 128). Similarly, a dangling cause can be used, "information or action which leads to no effect or resolution until later in the film," providing clarity and forward impetus (Thompson, 1999, p. 12).

Scenes can connect with one another in poetic free association, as in art films like *Gummo* (1997), though they typically operate in unified narratives, where causes and effects follow one another in an unbroken chain across the film. Stories can be embedded within other stories (*Arabian Nights*, 1974; *Inception*, 2010). The denouement usually provides closure, though they can end with a twist or be left open, and a variety of genres with various forms of iconography, subject matter, and emotional effects can be utilised. Genres can also be blended, like *Blade Runner* (1982) (film noir sci-fi) and *Shaun of the Dead* (2004) (comedy-horror). They can also switch mid-stream, such as *From Dusk Till Dawn* (1996) which begins as a fast-talking criminal caper but abruptly turns into a campy horror movie. Tone can vary between films, *Vertigo* (1958) and *North by Northwest* (1959) are both thrillers directed by Alfred Hitchcock, but the first is intense and brooding, while the second is light and comedic.

All of this is to say that there is a lot of possible variation in how a story can be narrated. There are also non-narrative ways of organising information that are easy to understand such as the essay, inventory, instruction manual, index, recipe, prayer, or chronology (Branigan, 1992, p. 1) In these instances, the information is organised for different purposes to narrative, to present an argument, help organise information, or to be instructive.

With a phenomenon as broad and pervasive as storytelling, a variety of disciplines have collectively sought to better understand it. Psychologists, philosophers, narratologists in literature, film, music, and more recently videogames, and of course storytellers and screenwriters themselves reflect on their own craft. All have shed light on the field from different angles, asking an assortment of questions. What is it? Are there guiding principles that make a story compelling? What mechanisms and variables are at play when a narrative is being told? How does it interface with the human mind? How does it vary between mediums?

This book focuses on screen media, serving as the first of its kind to offer a cross-section overview of the breadth of approaches from theory and practice. Much of the anthology will focus on live-action cinema, though television, animation, video games, and transmedia storytelling will also be discussed. In addition, a range of disciplines will feature – film narratology, philosophy, cognitive psychology, and insights from screenwriters.

One of the goals of this collection is to draw together theory and practice – both by gleaning insight from theorists and practitioners, and by offering a collection of chapters that should be of interest to both academics and screenwriters. Traditionally, most branches of film theory have felt very remote from the pragmatics of filmmaking, but screenwriting handbooks and narratological analyses are joined at the hip. If you are a screenwriter (or budding screenwriter) and you want to gain a deeper understanding of the mechanisms, psychological effects, and historical contexts of your creative choices, you can draw from narratological research. In addition, narratologists can also identify storytelling devices that aren't usually discussed in generic screenwriting manuals, which often favour conventional storytelling. This collection straddles both theory and practice with the probing insights of academic analysis, and the practical application and accessibility of screenwriter's manuals.

The (Truncated) Story of Cinematic Narrative

In concise form, we can consider the broad strokes of screen narration from its conception up to the present day. Note that the account is primarily Western-centric, with an initial focus on cinema before other mediums are considered. Materials will be cited where the various movements and eras can be further researched.

In the years closely following the invention of cinema, short films were not detailed narratives. They began as a "cinema of attraction," as Tom Gunning (1986) famously dubbed it, wherein the actuality films and trick films of the time (established by the Lumière Bros and George Méliès, respectively) use the medium not to tell stories, but rather to showcase the technology (Lumière's *Baby's Meal*, 1895) or function more like a stage show (Méliès' *The Magician*, 1898), soliciting spectator attention.

Kristin Thompson (2005, p. 266) comments that extended incidents, "a single drawn-out effect following an initial cause" featured in subsequent films from 1900 to 1906, with comedies being particularly popular. *The European Rest Cure* (1904) features an elderly American man who undergoes a series of misadventures across Europe, falling down walls in Ireland and the Alps, getting drawn into a can-can in Paris, getting robbed in Italy, and being subjected to an excessively vigorous mud bath massage in Germany. On returning home, he is too exhausted to stand. In *Our New Errand Boy* (1905), a rascal is employed by a grocer to deliver his goods. Havoc ensues, and it ends with his victims chasing him, though he escapes unscathed. In both instances, there is a set-up, a series of short gags and a simple resolution.

By the early teens, this "primitive" narrative structure was replaced by "a compressed set of causes and effects" (ibid., p. 266) which were built around a cause, development, crisis, climax, and denouement, with clearly defined protagonists at the helm. Janet Staiger observes that between 1909 and 1917, Hollywood film "developed a specific set of stylistic techniques and a particular arrangement of the systems of narrative logic, time, and space" (2005,

p. 227) which has served as a foundation for the classical mode of film narration ever since, making films unified, easily comprehensible, and entertaining.

The shift from a primitive style of filmmaking into classical narration, then, meant the establishment of several things. Characters moved away from vaudevillian stock figures, becoming instead "psychologically defined, with a range of personality traits from which actions could arise" (Thompson, 2005, p. 269). Audiences were now being asked to consider who the characters are, what their points of view are, what their goals are and how they relate to one another. After 1908, it became uncommon for films to be told in real time. Instead, there were temporal gaps between scenes – hours, days, and even years began to appear, along with non-chronological jumps into flashbacks and flash-forwards (ibid., p. 273). Deadlines also began to feature, limiting, and structuring the temporal span of a movie (ibid., p. 274). Redundancy was also applied, where the storytellers would repeat important information to aid spectator comprehension (ibid., p. 285). Perhaps most significantly, the extended incident (essentially a single drawn-out effect following an initial cause) was replaced with "a unified chain of causes and effects, varied by complicating circumstances (the development), concluding with a definite action which resolves the chain into a final effect (the climax) and which lingers to establish a new situation of stasis at the end" (ibid., p. 266). These basic principles became dominant and have remained the norm in commercial cinema ever since. This is the essence of classical narration.

Actively resisting the norms set by Hollywood, from 1925 to 1933, Soviet filmmakers developed what David Bordwell later termed *historical-materialist* narration. These types of narratives can be characterised by their strong didactic principles which sought to offer a lesson about the world (a *roman à thèse*) rather than mere entertainment (Bordwell, 1985, p. 235). Characters become prototypes (representatives of a broader social class) instead of individual protagonists furnished with complex psychology, which was considered bourgeois (ibid., p. 236). Sergei Eisenstein's early films *Strike* (1925), *Battleship Potemkin* (1925) and *October: Ten Days That Shook the World* (1928) went further in capturing the communal spirit of revolutionaries by using collective protagonists instead of nameable individuals. Overt narration was commonplace in this tradition, defamiliarising classical norms of space and time (ibid., p. 237), and montage editing was used liberally. Due to the fact these early films have not been heavily emulated and normalised since, they still look radical today.

Returning to Hollywood, the 1930s brought about the popularisation of dialogue and sync sound. But the next period of screen storytelling to have been discussed in detail – again by Bordwell, is in his book *Reinventing Hollywood: How 1940s Filmmakers Changed Movie Storytelling*. While narrative experiments within Hollywood featured in piecemeal form in the 1920s and 1930s, in a climate of healthy experimentation, mainstream storytelling became more complex and adventurous in the 1940s: anti-heroes also now featured, flashbacks were used in new and novel ways, an increased level of character subjectivity featured along with hallucinations and dreams, voice-over commentary was used, and characters would turn to address the viewer mid-scene. Scenes would also be replayed from multiple viewpoints with some of them turning out to be false. These new adventurous narratives found a home in movies such as *Our Town* (1940), *Lydia* (1941), *The Locket* (1947), and *Sorry, Wrong Number* (1948).

In Europe during the 1940s, art cinema began to develop as a practice which operated in distinct ways to mainstream cinema both institutionally and in its use of narration. Once again, Bordwell wrote on this type on narration in his seminal essay *The Art Cinema as a Mode of Film Practice* ([1979], reprinted 2007). Beginning with the Italian Neorealists before spreading across the rest of Europe, these films would feature looser cause-effect linkages than classical narration, realist themes, authorial expressivity, and sometimes an absence of goals on the part of the main protagonist. Films such as *Bicycle Thieves* (1948), *La Strada* (1954), *The 400 Blows* (1959), *Cries and Whispers* (1972), *L'Enfant* (2005), and *Amour* (2012) all follow this tradition. The critical success of Akira Kurosawa's *Rashomon* (1950) also opened the door to Western audiences recognising a similar film culture in Japan at the time. Compared to more commercial cinema, this type of art cinema does not necessarily put high demands on viewer comprehension, but they are generally more intellectually and emotionally demanding. Ambiguity also began to feature prominently in some art cinema narratives, such as *Last Year at Marienbad* and *That Obscure Object of Desire* (1977), walking a fine line between waking and dream logic. In addition, movies like *Pickpocket* (1954) and *Red Desert* (1964) paved the way for what is known today as slow cinema, offering a more reflective and unhurried experience than what movie-goers normally experience.

Focusing on American cinema again, the New Hollywood movement[4] took shape in the late 1960s, with *Bonnie and Clyde* (1967) noted as a particular watershed moment (Elsaesser, 2004, p. 37). Prototypical films of the movement include *Easy Rider* (1969), *Harold and Maude* (1971), *A Woman Under the Influence* (1974), *Dog Day Afternoon* (1975), *One Flew Over the Cuckoo's Nest* (1975), and *Taxi Driver* (1976). This period has been the subject of an array of books,[5] with Todd Berliner's *Hollywood Incoherent: Narration in Seventies Cinema* paying particular attention to the ways in which the films from this movement were narrated. He comments:

Influenced, in part, by Asian and European art cinema of the 1950s and 1960s – with its looser narrative structure, elliptical flashbacks, radical changes in mood, and emphasis on character ambiguity – seventies film-makers, working within the classical Hollywood model, tested that model's flexibility by adapting the radical techniques of more truly subversive filmmakers to Hollywood's classical form.

(Berliner, 2010, p. 5)

American filmmakers who had grown up in the 1950s and 1960s aspired to foster an indigenous film culture that was capable of the same lofty modes of storytelling and subject matter they had seen coming from Europe and Asia. *Five Easy Pieces* (1970) resembled the psychological dramas of Ingmar Bergman, *Two-Lane Blacktop* (1971) featured a pacing and austere performance style reminiscent of Michelangelo Antonioni or Robert Bresson's films. *Eraserhead* (1977) appeared to continue the legacy of surrealist filmmakers Jean Cocteau and Luis Buñuel. The art cinema sensibility was also blended with Hollywood genre movies, such as *The Godfather* as a gangster movie, and *Chinatown* (1974) as a film noir. However, marked by the commercial success of *Jaws* (1975) and *Star Wars: Episode IV A New Hope*, along with the commercial failures of *Heaven's Gate* (1980) and *One From the Heart* (1981), the New Hollywood movement with its more radical approach to narration had drawn to a close by the early 1980s.

The 1980s marked two new beginnings in American cinema. The first was a period of high concept studio-driven pictures, the modern Hollywood blockbuster with films like the original *Indiana Jones* trilogy (1981, 1984, 1989), *Top Gun* (1986), and *Dirty Dancing* (1987).[6] This change could be accredited, in part, to the influence of Syd Field's book *Screenplay: The Foundations of Screenwriting* which was first published in 1979. The increase in pacing, more liberal use of special effects and emphasis on franchising caused Wheeler Winston Dixon to declare the "collapse of narrative" in American cinema (Dixon, quoted in Bordwell, 2006, p. 5). Bordwell challenges this in *The Way Hollywood Tells It: Story and Style in Modern Movies*, asserting that time-honoured principles of plot construction and narration have been maintained in a variety of ways in modern Hollywood, sometimes revitalising classical principles imaginatively (Bordwell, 2006, p. 16). Likewise, Kristin Thompson refers to mainstream movies of the 1980s and 1990s such as *Back to the Future*, *The Hunt for Red October* (1990), *The Silence of the Lambs* (1991), and *Groundhog Day* (1993) as fitting a narrative tradition she calls "modern classicism." That is to say, fundamental techniques of narrative progression, clarity, and structure remain unchanged, albeit intensified (Thompson, 1999, pp. 10–27).

Rising from the ashes of New Hollywood, the second new beginning in American cinema during the 1980s was the development of modern independent film. With early tentative steps including Jim Jarmusch's *Stranger Than Paradise* (1984) and Steven Soderbergh's *Sex, Lies and Videotape* (1989), the movement gained momentum in the 1990s with a new spring of directors such as Miranda July, Todd Solondz, Wes Anderson, Charlie Kaufman,

Sofia Coppola, Alexander Payne, Richard Linklater, P.T. Anderson, and Spike Jonze. Continuing into the 2000s and 2010s, the indie movement splintered into sub-movements such as American Eccentric Cinema, metamodern, New Sincerity, and mumblecore. Collectively, independent film has been credited as having "revitalised American cinema" (Murphy, 2007, p. 2), reintroducing an art-cinema sensibility into the American cinematic bloodstream. But the term as it is commonly understood may be taken as operating on a continuum with Daniel Kwan and Daniel Scheinert's *Everything Everywhere All at Once* (2022) on the more commercial end (sometimes known as "indiewood"), and Gus Van Sant's *Elephant* (2003) closer to the art cinema tradition.[7]

J.J. Murphy describes independent cinema as a hybrid form, "borrow[ing] freely from classical Hollywood and art cinema" in turn making it a "laboratory for more innovative storytelling" (ibid., p. 24). For instance, protagonist arcs and inner transformations don't always take place, antagonists might be absent, and the formation of the heterosexual couple is less common. *Gummo* and *Slacker* (1990) defy three-act structure and leave out clear causal connections between scenes. Lead protagonists shift midstream in *Fargo* (ibid., pp. 18–22). Dialogue can meander and characters can chit-chat without advancing the plot, as they do in *Reservoir Dogs* (1992). Gus Van Sant's later work and Jim Jarmusch notably draw from the conventions of slow cinema.

The next noteworthy concept connected to screen narration is not a specific movement, but a term that has been applied to movies made in Hollywood, Europe, and Asia: post-classical narration. This term has been the subject of controversy, with some suggesting that film narration has remained decidedly classical (see: Thompson, 1999, pp. 336–352; Bordwell, 2006, p. 180). The most detailed defence of the notion of post-classical narration comes from Eleftheria Thanouli, in her book *Post-Classical Cinema: An International Poetics of Film Narration*. She suggests that while there hasn't been a fundamental shift in the way stories are told, movies like *Natural Born Killers* (1994), *Fight Club, Magnolia, Moulin Rouge!* (2001), *Amélie* (2001), and *City of God* (2002) suggest a new tendency in film narration for a particular strand of movies.

To briefly summarise some of the main traits of post-classical narration as Thanouli casts it, there is an archaeological attitude to classical genre, complex chronology, and self-conscious narration. Instead of using the screen as a window to an imaginary world, the screen is used as a "windowed world," a graphic space with abundant special effects and a faster editing pace than studio-era movies (2009, pp. 177–181). Like the New Hollywood of the late 1960s and 1970s, post-classical cinema is best understood as a movement rather than the new norm. Overall, Hollywood remains decidedly classical with films such as *Jurassic World: Fallen Kingdom* (2018) and *Bad Boys for Life* (2020) serving as the highest grossing movies in their respective years.

The final term to be introduced here with a distinctive narrational strategy is the puzzle film, which has been gaining currency since the late 2000s. The puzzle film draws together international art cinema with American independent film and found its way into Hollywood. Echoing some of the key traits of post-classical narration, Warren Buckland defines the puzzle film as featuring elements such as "a fragmented spatiotemporal reality; time loops; a blurring of the boundaries of different levels of reality; unstable characters with split identities or memory loss; multiple, labyrinthine plots; unreliable narrators; and over coincidences" (Buckland, 2014, p. 5).

The European film *Run Lola Run* (1998) with its forking path narrative pointed the way for this new approach, along with the Asian movies *Infernal Affairs* (2002), *In the Mood for Love* (2002) and *Oldboy* (2003). The puzzle film also blossomed in American cinema around the same time, notably through Christopher Nolan's *Memento* (2000) and *Inception*, and in work by other directors such as *Donnie Darko* (2001), *Synecdoche, New York* (2008), and *Source Code* (2011).[8] It has also expanded into television with the German time-travel series *Dark* (2017–2020) and often fits the narratives in the animated show *Rick and Morty* (2013–). *Black Mirror: Bandersnatch* (2018) has also explored the form as an interactive film.

Beyond Cinematic Narration

Cinema has been the primary focus so far, but television, videogames, animation, and transmedia narratives all bring additional considerations. This collection features individual chapters dedicated to all these mediums, but some key narrational distinctions will be outlined here. Animation, for example, bears a lot of crossovers with live action, but there is the notable exception that during the golden age of 7-minute shorts from the mid-1940s to the early 1960s with Warner Bros. and MGM shorts, gag-based story structures similar to the live action shorts of the 1900s, i.e., set up, string of gags, closure.

In transmedia narratives, stories are dispersed across different mediums. Franchises *Star Wars* and *The Matrix*, for example, are best known for their movies but there are also canonical and non-canonical comic books, novels, animations, and video games which expand on the lore and fill in gaps which weren't essential to the main plot of the movies. The novel *Bloodline* (2016), for example, explains what Princess Leia (Carrie Fisher) was doing during the intervening years between *Episode VI Return of the Jedi* (1983) and *Episode VII The Force Awakens* (2015). The videogame *Enter the Matrix* (2003) provides additional contextual information which serves as a backdrop to the events of the second two films in the original Matrix trilogy.

Narration in videogames features its own set of particularities, notably driven by the fact that they are interactive. A game like *Pong* (1972) doesn't feature a strictly defined narrative, though the game's player-computer interface does approximate, in its incipient form, an interactive "story" medium: the stick on the left bounced the ball, so the stick on the right bounced it back. Some games are linear, such as *Outrun* (1986) where you simply drive a car to the finish line as fast as possible while avoiding obstacles. In linear stories, the progress of the story happens at "story nodes" (Ince, 2006, p. 49), i.e., at certain checkpoints, or at the beginning of each level like *Sonic the Hedgehog* (1991). When a game is nonlinear, there are two principal types of narrative: branching and foldback (Adams, 2013, pp. 227–228). A branching game begins with all characters at the same place, and then progresses down increasingly divergent paths as a result of the choices made during a moment of narrative division. *Heavy Rain* (2010), for example, has 20 different endings. By contrast, *The Witcher 3* (2015) is a foldback narrative. Here, players have scope to follow their own paths, but only in-between narrative checkpoints. Once such a checkpoint is triggered, the player who might have been immersed in several side-missions at that point is folded back into the core narrative experience.

Television narratives can be serialised, with a main story arc that spans a whole season or series. They can also be episodic, where there is a consistent cast of characters, but each episode has its own arc. Like cinema, television viewers need to keep track of several characters, multiple plot lines, motifs, and thematic meanings. But they usually face the additional challenge of frequent interruptions – for commercials, week-long gaps between episodes, and months between seasons. Yet they manage to keep track of not only a single long-running narrative, but often several simultaneously thanks to skilful scriptwriting (Thompson, 2003, p. ix). Other particularities of television narrative can include seriality, widely distributed identification, and more plot lines. Where feature films usually have an A plot and B plot, a TV series can also juggle C, D, E, and F plots. TV shows also sometimes begin with a "cold open," a one to five-minute sequence before the opening credits which sets up the narrative and grabs the audience's attention.

Scott W. Smith (2016) observes that while movies usually provide closure, television is more likely to feature open-ended narratives, leaving content producers avenues for several years of additional storytelling. While a movie is usually less than 3 hours, a TV series can stretch over 100 hours. Where movies normally recount a once in a lifetime event, episodic sitcoms like *Cheers* and *Seinfeld* usually return to the status quo by the end of an episode. Generally, relationships between characters don't change much in episodic series, Homer and Bart have the same relationship they've had on *The Simpsons* (1989–) since the show's inception. Network shows often have an idealised life, such as the affluent families in *I Love Lucy* (1951–1957) and *The Fresh Prince of Bel Air* (1990–1996). In *Poirot* (1989–2013), the titular character neatly solves the crime in every episode. By contrast, movies aren't usually as idealised. Finally, writing features is generally considered a one- or two-person job while on (American) television, they normally use writers' rooms.[9]

Outside of screen narratives, the novel is also distinct in its processes of narration which need to be factored in when being adapted for the screen. For example, novels lend themselves to interiority while screen narrative relies on exteriors, the surface of things. Gaps and subtexts lend themselves well to screen narration, two characters can exchange an ambiguous glance in a movie or TV show while in a novel, readers will expect to be told what they are thinking. In addition, novels work in chapters, like block construction in screen narration, which is quite uncommon. Finally, a novel that takes 30 hours to read would need to be reduced to about 2 hours when adapted to film. This usually means pacing needs to be tighter and subplots might need to be axed for the screen. A movie is more like a novella, which takes an average of about 2 hours 45 minutes to read. Novels can take around 5–11 hours depending on length and speed of reading, more like a televised miniseries (Weiland, 2016).

The aim of this chapter was to provide a primer for the reader, an overview of key expressive variables in screen narration, historical developments in screen narration, and key distinctions between mediums. The chapters that follow will pick up on some of these themes in closer detail.

Notes

1 While the three-act structure was popularised in Field's book, the author accredits the concept back to Aristotle (Field, 2005, p. 65).
2 High-concept stories foreground dimensions of financial success in addition to the actual story. Justin Wyatt comments that critics "describe high concept as Hollywood crassly privileging business over any consideration of creativity or artistic expression" (1994, p. 14). Since Hollywood shifted the weight from the story to selling the story through its concept, "the term [has] gained such a negative connotation that high-concept is often associated with the most sensationalist material" (ibid.). Others view it more positively as a clear and succinct presentation of the story that is immediately available to both studios and audiences.
3 Linda Aronson (2010) expands on the concept of narratives that feature several equally important stories running simultaneously, proposing six different types. Three of them are linear, without time jumps (tandem narrative; multiple protagonist narrative; double journeys), and three feature time jumps (flashback narrative; consecutive-stories narrative; the fractured tandem). See also: *The Multi-Protagonist Film* (Maria del Mar Azcona, 2010) and *Altman and After: Multiple Narratives in Film* (Parshall, 2012).
4 The word "movement" is being used instead of an era because New Hollywood never took over the American film industry. Rather, it was a particular movement which would influence future generations. Top-grossing films of their respective years include conventional movies such as *The Love Bug* (1969), *Diamonds Are Forever* (1971), *The Towering Inferno* (1974), and *The Return of Pink Panther* (1975), none of which are considered New Hollywood (Thompson, 1999, pp. 4–5; Gustafsson, 2021).

5 See: *A Decade Under the Influence* (2003), along with Peter Biskind's *Easy Riders, Raging Bulls* and *The Last Great American Picture Show: New Hollywood Cinema in the 1970s* (Eds. Thomas Elsaesser, Alexander Horwath, Noel King)

6 To add nuance, note that while they marked a new breed of film, the blockbuster movies of the 1980s were not without precedent. David Bordwell (2008) observes that the "megapicture mentality" precedes the 1980s in movies such as *Gone With the Wind* (1939), *Duel in the Sun* (1946), *The Ten Commandments* (1956), *Ben-Hur* (1959), *Lawrence of Arabia* (1962), *The Poseidon Adventure* (1972), and *Superman* (1978).

7 The term independent film essentially means it was produced and distributed outside the major studio system, by independent entertainment companies. As such, *Teenage Mutant Ninja Turtles* (1990) and *My Big Fat Greek Wedding* (2002) are both, strictly speaking, independent films. However, the term is being used here in the way it is commonly understood.

8 See *Puzzle Films Complex Storytelling in Contemporary Cinema* (Ed. Warren Buckland); *Hollywood Puzzle Films* (Ed. Warren Buckland); Allan Cameron's *Modular Narratives in Contemporary Cinema*; Miklós Kiss' *Impossible Puzzle Films: A Cognitive Approach to Contemporary Complex Cinema*; Hollywood Puzzle Films; *Impossible Puzzle Films* (Eds. Miklós Kiss and Steven Willemsen).

9 For more on narration in television, see Kristin Thompson's *Storytelling in Film and Television*; Jason Mittell's *Complex TV: The Poetics of Contemporary Television Storytelling*; and Narrative Strategies in Television Series (Eds. Gaby Allrath and Marion Gymnich).

References

Adams, E. (2013). *Fundamentals of Game Design*. New Riders.

Aronson, L. (2010). *The 21st Century Screenplay: A Comprehensive Guide to Writing Tomorrow's Films*. Allen and Unwin.

Azcona, M. (2010). *The Multi-Protagonist Film*. Wiley-Blackwell.

Berliner, T. (2010). *Hollywood Incoherent: Narration in Seventies Cinema*. University of Texas Press.

Bordwell, D. (1985). *Narration in the Fiction Film*. Routledge.

Bordwell, D. (2000). *Planet Hong Kong: Popular Cinema and the Art of Entertainment*. Harvard University Press.

Bordwell, D. (2006). *The Way Hollywood Tells It: Story and Style in Modern Movies*. University of California Press.

Bordwell, D. (2007). *Poetics of Cinema*. Routledge.

Bordwell, D. (2008, November 20). It's the 80s, stupid. Retrieved 27 April 2023, from http://www.davidbordwell.net/blog/2008/11/20/its-the-80s-stupid/

Bordwell, D. (2016, January 9). Pick your protagonist(s). Retrieved 19 December 2022, from http://www.davidbordwell.net/blog/2016/01/09/pick-your-protagonists/

Branigan, E. (1992). *Narrative Comprehension and Film*. Routledge.

Buckland, W. (2014). Introduction. Ambiguity, Ontological Pluralism, and Cognitive Dissonance in the Hollywood Puzzle Film. In W. Buckland (Ed.). *Hollywood Puzzle Films* (pp. 1–14). Routledge.

Carroll, N. (2013). *Minerva's Night Out: Philosophy, Pop Culture, and Moving Pictures*. Wiley-Blackwell.

Elsaesser, T. (2004). American Auteur Cinema: The Last – Or First – Great Picture Show. In T. Elsaesser, A. Horwath, & N. King (Eds.). *The Last Great American*

Picture Show: New Hollywood Cinema in the 1970s (pp. 37–69). Amsterdam University Press.

Field, S. (2005). *Screenplay: The Foundations of Screenwriting* (3rd ed.). Delta.

Gunning, T. (1986) The Cinema of Attractions: Early Cinema, Its Spectator, and the Avant-Garde. *Wide Angle*, 8, 3–4.

Gustafsson, F. (2021, February 19). New Hollywood and the box office. Retrieved 27 April 2023, from https://fredrikonfilm.blogspot.com/2021/02/1970s-and-economics.html

Ince, S. (2006). *Writing for Video Games*. Methuen Drama.

Murphy, J.J. (2007). *Me and You and Memento and Fargo: How Independent Screenplays Work*. Continuum.

Parshall, P. (2012). *Altman and After: Multiple Narratives in Film*. Scarecrow Press.

Smith, S.W. (2016, February 16). Film vs. TV Writing (10 Differences). Retrieved 19 December 2022, from https://screenwritingfromiowa.wordpress.com/2016/02/16/film-vs-tv-writing-10-differences/

Snyder, B. (2005). *Save the Cat! The Last Book on Screenwriting You'll Ever Need*. Michael Wiese Productions.

Staiger, J. (2005). The Hollywood Mode of Production to 1930. In D. Bordwell, J. Staiger, & K. Thompson (Eds.). *The Classical Hollywood Cinema: Film Style & Mode of Production to 1960* (pp. 88–244). Routledge.

Thanouli, E. (2009). *Post-Classical Cinema: An International Poetics of Film Narration*. Columbia University Press.

Thompson, K. (1999). *Storytelling in the New Hollywood: Understanding Classical Narrative Technique*. Harvard University Press.

Thompson, K. (2003). *Storytelling in Film and Television*. Harvard University Press.

Thompson, K. (2005). The Formulation of the Classical Style, 1909–28. In D. Bordwell, J. Staiger, & K. Thompson (Eds.). *The Classical Hollywood Cinema: Film Style & Mode of Production to 1960* (pp. 245–472). Routledge.

Vogler, C. (2007). *The Writer's Journey: Mythic Structure for Writers* (3rd ed.). Michael Wiese Production.

Weiland, K.M. (2016). *Creating Character Arcs: The Masterful Author's Guide to Uniting Story Structure, Plot, and Character Development*. PenForASword Publishing.

Wyatt, J. (1994). *High Concept: Movies and Marketing in Hollywood*. University of Texas Press.

PART I

Convention, Deviation, Evolution

2

ENJOYING CLASSICAL HOLLYWOOD STORYTELLING

Todd Berliner

We might assume that people enjoy narrative cinema because they like watching good stories, but a good story hardly accounts for the pleasures of narrative. *The Maltese Falcon* from 1931 has a story practically identical to that of the famous 1941 John Huston remake, yet few movie fans have even heard of the first movie, whereas the remake—which tells the same story in a different way—ranks among Hollywood's most celebrated productions. The pleasures of narrative come not just from good stories but from good storytelling.

Storytelling—or, more technically, "narration"—is the process of selecting, arranging, and rendering the events of a narrative, stimulating spectators to perform cognitive activities (Bordwell, 1985: p. xi). Narration arouses what we could describe as a guided act of imagination in which the audience mentally constructs a story based on plot cues from the work of art.

To understand the aesthetic pleasure of storytelling, we must draw a common distinction between "plot" and "story" (what the Russian formalists called "syuzhet" and "fabula"). Whereas "plot" denotes the artwork's presentation of narrative events, "story" denotes *all* narrative events, including events presented in the plot and events we infer. We construct the story by mentally linking plot events. So, if the plot has presented narrative events out of chronological order, then, to construct a coherent story, we rearrange the events chronologically in our mind. If the plot has left out key story information, we attempt to fill it in. In short, *narration* is the process by which an artwork's *plot* stimulates the perceiver to mentally construct the *story*. The aesthetic pleasure of storytelling derives from the mental activity that narration arouses, the result not of watching stories but of constructing them in our minds.

DOI: 10.4324/9781003197911-4

Hollywood cinema generally makes the spectator's process of story construction fairly easy. Most aesthetic commentary about Hollywood storytelling has focused on its unity because narrative unity enables spectators to readily connect plot events. Narrative unity stimulates the calm pleasures associated with easy understanding, making Hollywood cinema accessible and spontaneously pleasing for mass audiences. Easy understanding, however, does not fully account for the intensity of the aesthetic pleasure people often derive from Hollywood storytelling. Cognitive challenge, by contrast, can lead us toward more exhilarated aesthetic pleasure. In Hollywood storytelling, that challenge comes from disunities in the plot that make it more difficult for a spectator to construct a coherent story. Narrative disunity makes storytelling more demanding, as well as more cognitively exciting and interesting. So, for a full account of the aesthetic pleasure of Hollywood storytelling, we must account for the pleasures afforded by both narrative unity and narrative disunity.

Toward Narrative Unity

A unified narrative develops according to an internally consistent story logic, the work's narrative properties connected and interrelated to form a seemingly organic whole. The principle of unity in art dates to Plato and Aristotle and has governed much criticism of the arts. A disunified narrative, by contrast, contains gaps, ambiguities, improbabilities, incongruities, or other impediments to coherent storytelling. We expect disunity in surrealist and other avant-garde narratives, but, when it comes to classical narrative forms like Hollywood cinema, we generally expect to find unity.

David Bordwell (2006) has argued that by 1917 the American film industry had already adopted a firm set of practices for promoting narrative unity, practices that persist in contemporary American cinema (pp. 4–17). Indeed, many film commentators regard unity as a chief organizing principle of mainstream filmmaking. V. F. Perkins (1993) says that a film's credibility "depends on the inner consistency of the created world ... [which] must obey its own logic. There is no pretext, whether it be Significance, Effect or the Happy Ending, sufficient to justify a betrayal of the given order" (p. 121). Advice from Hollywood screenwriting manuals invariably accords with Perkins's observations on the importance of unity. "Everything in the story should contribute to its structural unity," Lewis Herman (1963) writes, an admonition echoed in manuals dating back to 1917 (p. 39. cf. Ball, 1917: pp. 38–40; Cowgill, 1999: p. 80).

Unity makes Hollywood storytelling easy to understand. Hollywood narration creates clear linkages between plot events by means of *causality*, the principle that one event brings about another. A classical story connects events not arbitrarily (x *and* y), not chronologically (x *then* y), but rather causally (x *therefore* y). Causality makes narrative connections tight and logical. According to Seymour Chatman (1978), causally linked events are "hinges" in a narrative structure and "cannot be deleted without destroying the narrative logic" (pp. 45–48, 53–56). One screenwriting manual says flatly, "There should be nothing [in a screenplay] which is not clearly caused by what precedes and nothing which is not clearly the cause of what follows" (Cowgill, 1999: p. 2; cf. Marion, 1937: p. 91).

Causality organizes virtually every aspect of a Hollywood narrative. Even disaster films, designed to exploit audience's attraction to the spectacle of stars and destruction, fasten scenes of spectacle by means of tight causal linkages. Shoddy workmanship, revealed at the beginning of *The Towering Inferno* (1974), sets in motion a fire that consumes the building, which traps guests at a gala event, which prompts a series of dazzling rescues (x therefore y therefore z). We call Hollywood narratives "linear" because each event leads to another in a sequential progression toward closure when the cause–effect sequence completes its course.

Noël Carroll (2004) attributes Hollywood cinema's "easily graspable clarity" in part to a question-and-answer structure that he calls the "erotetic model of narrative" (p. 487). Carroll argues that later events in Hollywood movies answer questions posed by earlier events. An early scene in *Make Way for Tomorrow* (1937) shows two ageing parents informing their adult children that they have run out of money and are losing their home. The scene poses the question, "Where will the parents live?" The answer comes later in the scene: The children decide, reluctantly, to share the burden of housing them by splitting them up, which poses other questions, "How will the children and parents react to the new arrangements?" Later scenes answer that question by depicting the children's difficulties adjusting, their resentments toward their parents, and the parents' disappointment in their children. By the end of the film, when the narration has answered our questions, we feel we have reached total understanding.

Bordwell (1985) has identified other components of Hollywood narration that enhance narrative unity. Hollywood movies typically contain two interconnected plots, one involving heterosexual romance and the other something else (work, war, etc.). Hollywood's dual plot structure promotes narrative parallels and encourages spectators to unite disparate plot elements, particularly at the moment of climax when plotlines resolve at the same moment through the same set of character actions (pp. 157–158). Both plotlines may resolve successfully, both may resolve unsuccessfully, or one may resolve successfully and the other unsuccessfully, but plotlines resolve interdependently. In *Groundhog Day* (1993), both plotlines resolve successfully and simultaneously when Phil (Bill Murray) escapes an eternity of Groundhog Days by becoming a man that Rita (Andie MacDowell) would fall for. In the end of *I Am a Fugitive from a Chain Gang* (1932), failure in one plotline means failure in the other: James Allen (Paul Muni) must live as a criminal on the run and never see his beloved Helen (Helen Vinson) again. In *The Maltese Falcon* (1941), success in one plotline means failure in the other: Sam Spade's (Humphrey Bogart) success at solving his partner's murder means sending the woman he loves to jail. In all such scenarios, spectators can readily unite the two plotlines because the films have created causal linkages between them.

Other components of Hollywood narration further contribute to narrative unity and easy understanding. A goal-oriented protagonist, struggling to overcome obstacles, motivates narrative progress and reinforces causal connections between scenes. Deadlines and definitive resolutions contain the narrative by finishing it off. "The ending becomes the culmination of the spectator's absorption as all the causal gaps get filled" (Bordwell et al., 1985: p. 17). Bordwell (1985) notes that Hollywood movies clearly demarcate scenes according to Aristotle's unities: the unity of time (scenes have a continuous duration), space (a definable locale), and action (a distinct cause–effect phase) (p. 158). Together, the foregoing principles make it relatively easy for the spectator to connect a movie's disparate plot elements.

Bordwell accounts for spectator *comprehension* of Hollywood narration, but how do we explain spectator *enjoyment*?

The unity of classical narration enables Hollywood spectators to conjoin different segments of a movie into a cohesive whole. Hollywood plots tend to avoid ambiguity, weak causal connections, narrative detours, and plot information extraneous to the story's causal progress, excluding the noise that makes ordinary experience so much more distracting and stressful. Indeed, the Hollywood plot has been streamlined to facilitate straightforward momentum, storylines delineated, and distractions minimized. Consequently, our understanding of the story pops into view without much effort or confusion. Drawing on Monroe Beardsley's (1981) description of aesthetic unity, we can say that a classical narrative is *complete* ("it has all that it needs") and *coherent* ("it all fits together") (pp. 192–194). Actions in Hollywood movies, Carroll (2004) says, "evince visible order and identity to a degree not found in everyday experience. This quality of uncluttered clarity gratifies the mind's quest for order" (p. 492). The question-answer model of narration, he adds, has "an extraordinary degree of neatness and intellectually appealing compactness" (p. 495). When endings link with beginnings by means of an unbroken causal chain, the spectator feels the satisfaction that comes from drawing a line of connections between plot segments. In the end, the film rewards our investment in the fate of the characters with a definitive conclusion that satisfies the desire for complete understanding and closure, putting our emotions at rest.

Causality, erotetic narration, and a commitment to narrative clarity make the spectator's process of constructing a coherent story relatively undemanding. The notion that spectator enjoyment results from classical Hollywood narration's "easily graspable clarity" finds support from empirical studies in psychology demonstrating that easy understanding correlates with positive aesthetic evaluation for most people. According to the Processing Fluency Theory of aesthetic pleasure, advanced by psychologists Reber et al. (2004), properties that ease our understanding of an artwork also increase our pleasure in it. When narration eases understanding, the studies predict, then movies become spontaneously pleasing.

The Limitations of Clarity, Accessibility, and the Processing Fluency Theory

Clarity, causality, and erotetic narration alone do not explain the enjoyment of classical Hollywood narration. If they did, then spectators would find all Hollywood movies enjoyable since all follow a question-and-answer storytelling model and make narrative events clear and easy to connect. Clarity may explain the "widespread engagement" of Hollywood cinema, just as Carroll (2004) argues, but it neither adequately explains what Carroll terms "intense engagement" nor does it explain viewer preference for one Hollywood movie over another (p. 486).

In Carroll's account, we should expect spectators to respond most intensely to those movies that have the clearest plot connections and the most accessible plot patterning. His theory, therefore, cannot explain why mass spectators do not engage more intensely with extremely clear and accessible films, such as *Paw Patrol: The Movie* (2021) or other films that appeal to toddlers. Such films rarely attract adult audiences beyond parents with their children. Nor can his theory explain the power of relatively challenging Hollywood narratives, such as *The Big Sleep* (1946), *The Killing* (1956), *2001: A Space Odyssey* (1968), *The Godfather, Part II* (1974), *Blade Runner* (1982), *The Matrix* (1999), *Kill Bill: Vol. 1* and *Vol. 2* (2003 and 2004), and *Inception* (2010). Although wedded to classical storytelling principles, such films challenge efforts to construct a coherent story. The films do not pose as many challenges as *Last Year at Marienbad* (1961), nor have they earned the box office of *Titanic* (1997), but they demonstrate less "easily graspable clarity" than typical Hollywood movies, yet masses of people have found them intensely engaging.

Clarity accounts for the mass accessibility and inherent pleasingness of Hollywood storytelling but not the exhilaration people feel when watching Hollywood movies they love. In short, unity and processing fluency tell only half of the story. Intense engagement results when Hollywood movies *strike the right balance* between easy understanding and cognitive challenge. Sometimes audiences, even mass audiences, want something less immediately pleasing and more persistently interesting.

Hence, although we have, from film studies, a theory of unity in Hollywood storytelling and, from experimental psychology, empirical studies that testify to the pleasure of narrative unity, we need a theory that accounts for the aesthetic pleasure afforded by disunity in Hollywood storytelling. We need, in other words, a more complete theory of the aesthetic enjoyment of classical Hollywood narration, one that accounts for pleasures afforded by complexity, novelty, ambiguity, inconsistency, incongruity, gaps, and other narrative properties that make Hollywood movies more disunified, dynamic, and difficult to process. In this chapter, I present such a theory and support it with film examples and empirical research, particularly research in the areas of insight and incongruity-resolution. The theory sets out to explain the ways in which Hollywood movies generate exhilarating aesthetic experiences by combining the classical model of storytelling with strategic breaches of narrative unity and story logic.

Toward Narrative Disunity

We should think of narrative unity and disunity not as all-or-nothing aesthetic properties but as a continuum. All Hollywood movies, no matter how unified, contain some measure of disunity, if only through the narrative gap that results from delaying resolution. The unity-disunity continuum, moreover, does not inhere entirely in the movie since it is determined in part by the subjective experience of individual spectators. Spectators experience a lot of narrative unity when they easily conjoin plot elements within the artwork. Spectators experience a lot of narrative disunity when they struggle or fail to make plot elements cohere.

Citizen Kane (1941) offers a notorious example of narrative disunity. In the film's first scene, Kane utters "Rosebud" on his deathbed, initiating the characters' search to discover the word's meaning. Astute filmgoers, however, have noticed that no one could have overheard Kane utter "Rosebud" because he said it alone in his bedroom. The violation of story logic, inasmuch as spectators register it, creates an aesthetic defect potentially so damaging that, when asked about it, Orson Welles reportedly considered the problem and said finally, "Don't you ever tell anyone of this" (quoted in Ryan, 2009: p. 66).

Because of the threat narrative disunity poses to the credence, causality, and reliability of Hollywood narration, commentators since the 1920s have admonished screenwriters to avoid illogical or implausible events (Marion, 1937: p. 124; Palmer, 1924: pp. 69–70; Vale, 1944: p. 39; White & Stock, 1948: p. 27). "Writers should be picky regarding logic and credibility," one screenwriting handbook says, "otherwise, the story will be riddled with gaps, improbabilities, illogic, and similar dents in believability" (Lucey, 1996: p. 91). Narratologist Marie-Laure Ryan (2009) regards faulty logic either as an aesthetic deficiency or, at best, as an excusable "trade-off" for an otherwise worthwhile narrative situation. Plots with faulty logic, Ryan says, "make the sophisticated reader groan" (pp. 56, 68).

I nonetheless propose that disunities in a narrative, even story logic violations, add aesthetic value to Hollywood narration, provided resolution seems tangible or somehow within reach. Spectators need not actually resolve a disunity, but as long as they feel *capable* of resolving it, then narrative disunity will tend to exhilarate aesthetic experience. If spectators remain motivated to continue the search for understanding, then plot disunity will invigorate spectators' cognitive engagement: the more plot disunity, the more effort required to construct a coherent story. Indeed, artworks that merely *present* stories—without stimulating us to *construct* stories—give our minds too little to do. Disunity makes story construction more athletic, increasing the potential for exhilaration in our aesthetic response.

Film scholars and authors of screenwriting manuals have not fully recognized the role that disunity plays in the aesthetics of Hollywood narration. Bordwell goes furthest toward explaining the value of disunity when he discusses narrative devices that complicate the viewer's experience. "Retardation devices," Bordwell (1985) says, "can introduce objects of immediate attention as well as delay satisfaction of overall expectation" (p. 165). The plot's rapid rhythm, he notes, impedes reflection and boredom, and the variety of scenarios presented in a typical Hollywood movie prevents narration from becoming monotonous (p. 165). These devices ensure that a Hollywood movie has more than one note—that within its highly unified framework, the plot creates sufficient delay, momentum, and diversity to maintain spectator interest.

But we still do not understand the aesthetics of disunity in Hollywood narration. How does narrative disunity exhilarate our aesthetic response? What thinking processes are engaged and what makes them enjoyable? When does disunity detract from our enjoyment and when does it add aesthetic value to Hollywood narration? I want to answer these questions by explicating the following hypothesis: *Provided story resolution remains tangible, even through fuzzy reasoning, narrative disunity within a classical Hollywood framework adds variety to the filmgoing experience; stimulates imagination, curiosity, free association, and creative problem-solving; and liberates our thinking from the burdens and limitations of good sense.* My hypothesis challenges the commonsense assumption that aesthetically successful classical Hollywood narratives show extremely high levels of unity and obey strict story logic. I hope to demonstrate that such narratives show a moderate level of disunity and may outright *violate* story logic. Skilled Hollywood storytellers can use apparent flaws in an otherwise unified narrative to a film's aesthetic advantage. As long as spectators retain confidence in the potential for understanding, then disunity in Hollywood narration will lead spectators toward *exhilarated pleasure.*

Disunity, Abduction, and Insight

To understand the pleasure of disunity in Hollywood narration, we must understand the mental processes at work when encountering information that seems somehow surprising, inexplicable, or out of place. Such an encounter stimulates a "fuzzy" type of reasoning that philosophers sometimes call *abduction*—or what Peter Lipton (2004) has called "inference to the best explanation." Abductive reasoning involves pondering problems and conjecturing an explanation. With abduction, someone observes a surprising fact (e.g., My car door has a huge scratch) then creatively infers a plausible cause (That juvenile delinquent next door must have keyed it). Abduction accounts for how people form hypotheses about the world based on hunches, and philosophers, such as Charles Peirce (1998), have argued that abduction explains how creative scientific discoveries take place.

Logicians regard abductive reasoning as "fuzzy" because it leads to inexact or unreliable conclusions. *Deduction*, by contrast, denotes "crisp" reasoning. With deduction, conclusions necessarily follow from general principles, as in the syllogism: (1) All women are mortal, (2) Beyoncé is a woman, (3) therefore, Beyoncé is mortal. *Induction* is the process of inferring probable causes through testing and scrutiny. Scientists work inductively when they test hypotheses. Abduction, by contrast, is just a guess.

Although abduction can easily lead to false inferences, it also enables creative connections unavailable through more strict sorts of reasoning. Making connections through abduction does not demand rigor or scrutiny. The process enlists our imaginations most of all: It relies on our ability to form new concepts, uninhibited by practical constraints.

Cognitive psychologists use the term *insight* to describe the "aha" moment when someone suddenly understands something. With insight, a creative solution suddenly comes into consciousness as we understand relationships among elements in a new way or break free of unwarranted assumptions (Mayer, 1992; Smith et al., 1995). Researchers have reproduced insight experimentally. In a classic study, Maier (1931) placed subjects in a room with several objects and asked them to tie together two pieces of string hanging from the ceiling. The strings, however, fell too far apart to hold at the same time. The solution came to those who thought to tie an object to one string in order to create a pendulum motion. Most people failed to see the solution, unless the experimenter prompted insight by "accidentally" brushing against one of the strings while leaving the room.

Although the underlying cognitive mechanisms of insight remain mysterious, research suggests that solutions to "insight problems" (like the string problem) occur instantaneously, rather than incrementally, and that insight relies on unconscious thinking processes unlike those required to solve "non-insight problems" (like algebra) (Bowden et al., 2005; Knoblich et al., 1999).

For instance, people can generally predict how they will solve an algebra problem and how long it will take, but they have no idea how or when they will solve an insight problem (Metcalfe & Wiebe, 1987). The answer just comes to them all of sudden. More like free association than crisp reasoning or intellectual scrutiny, insight demands imagination. Abundant scientific evidence supports the existence of this moment of sudden apprehension, and further evidence testifies to the pleasures—joy, satisfaction, and other positive emotions—that attend it.[1] Indeed, although my hypothesis concerning the pleasures of narrative disunity may contradict common sense, my point about insight is extremely intuitive. We have all enjoyed the moment when disconnected information suddenly fits.

So let's note the key features of insight: It involves unconscious problem-solving, it requires cognitive effort, it can be prompted, it relies on imagination, it happens unconsciously and instantaneously, it is prone to error, and it creates pleasure. Such features make insight an important area for understanding how people process disunities in narratives, since insight enables us all of a sudden to connect narrative information that does not easily fit together or that may not fit together logically at all. Studying moments in which storytelling induces insight can therefore help us understand some of the pleasures of narrative.

Given our understanding of disunity, abduction, and insight, I suggest that the process of making sense of a disunity in a narrative follows three stages:

1 The narration cues the perceiver to form a hypothesis about a story.
2 The narration surprises the perceiver by presenting plot information that the hypothesis cannot explain.
3 Using abductive reasoning, the perceiver tries to improvise a new hypothesis that connects plot information and restores consistency to the perceiver's beliefs.

Stage three marks the thrilling moment of insight when we break free of our current beliefs, and suddenly the improbable, the inconsistent, the inexplicable, or the unimaginable becomes reality.

But what makes insight pleasurable? The most illuminating scholarship on that question comes from humor and laughter studies, which offer the most comprehensive body of research—and perhaps the only empirical research—on the pleasures of narrative disunity. Let's examine some of that research.

Incongruity-Resolution, Pleasure, and Free Play

Most scholars of humor and laughter ascribe to some version of Incongruity Theory. The theory dates to Aristotle's *Rhetoric*, but Kant, Beattie, Schopenhauer, and others further developed it. The theory holds that humor results when someone suddenly recognizes a pattern violation. Laughter, as humor researcher John Morreall (1983) describes it, is a "reaction to something that is unexpected, illogical, or inappropriate in some other way" (p. 15).

Psychologists James M. Jones (1970), Thomas Shultz (1976), and Jerry Suls (1972) elaborated Incongruity Theory. Their "incongruity-resolution" theories propose that humor arises when the perceiver meets with an incongruity and feels motivated to resolve it. The perceiver laughs when suddenly apprehending the solution to a humorous kind of "insight problem." Consider the Woody Allen joke, cited by Suls (1972), in which a group of prisoners escape, "twelve of them chained together at the ankle, getting by the guards posing as an immense charm bracelet." When listening to the joke—as with almost all jokes that we would regard as narratives—our minds follow the three-stages that mark an encounter with narrative disunity.

1 The narration cues the perceiver to form a hypothesis about a story. *The prisoners will find a clever way to escape the chain gang.*
2 The narration surprises the perceiver by presenting plot information that the hypothesis cannot explain. *Posing as jewelry could never succeed because the prisoners are obviously too big.*
3 Using abductive reasoning, the perceiver tries to improvise a new hypothesis that connects plot information and restores consistency to the perceiver's beliefs. *Prisoners chained at the ankle, on second thought, have an appearance oddly similar to a very large charm bracelet, so their ruse could conceivably work.*

Although we do not really, rationally believe that such a ruse could work, the joke enables a fuzzy kind of resolution the moment we find a connection within the incongruous information (chain gangs/charm bracelets). Humor encourages us to entertain playful connections between disparate story elements, freed from the limitations of logic and scrutiny. Humor offers our minds a vacation from logic and scrutiny, replacing them with free play.[2]

Like jokes, the arts enable patterns of thinking that would be dysfunctional in real world situations. The arts remove the burdens and limitations of good sense and instead encourage guessing, free association, and creative insight—mental activities that, when unchecked by scrutiny and reason, might lead to false inferences, incomplete knowledge, or unrealistic beliefs. Liberated from the risks associated with casual, illogical thought, we feel free to think in ways that high-stakes reality inhibits. Under the security of the artistic context, we are let loose for cognitive play.

I introduce Incongruity-Resolution Theory here because it helps us understand how our minds respond to and enjoy the disunities we encounter in Hollywood narratives. Although it may seem strange to think of jokes as equivalent to extended narratives, we engage in the same cognitive processes when we recognize a pattern violation in either one. Indeed, most jokes *are* narratives. If a narrative, as many narratologists define the term, is a series of events in cause–effect relationship (Chatman, 1978: pp. 45–46; Richardson, 1997: p. 106), then the brief joke, "A skeleton walks into a bar and orders a beer and a mop," is as much a narrative as *The Brothers Karamazov*. A disunity, whether in a joke or in an extended sequence of events, motivates the same abductive search for connections. And if we find a connection, we experience the same thrill of insight.

Finding a connection may result in mirth and laughter or merely the delight of connecting inconsistent plot information. "We enjoy incongruity in other ways than by being amused," Morreall observes (1987, p. 204). Recall that the standard tropes of both humorous and non-humorous literature— rhyme, metaphor, metonymy, paradox, puns, oxymorons, irony—encourage us to find a connection between inconsistent things. Whether we consider disunities prompted by jokes, word play, or Hollywood narratives, the process of searching for resolutions has the same potential to inspire insights and playful mental associations, freed from the burdens of logic, scrutiny, and good sense.

A Hollywood whodunit, for example, typically reveals the *least* likely character as the murderer, the one we never considered (hence, "the butler did it"), surprising us and also enabling us to see an intriguing correctness and inevitability in events that previously seemed unimaginable. When, at the end of *Murder on the Orient Express* (1974), we learn that all of Hercule Poirot's (Albert Finney) suspects committed the murder together, it seems at first incongruous (because it violates expectation, realism, and whodunit tradition) and perfectly correct (because Poirot had, in traditional fashion, already demonstrated that each suspect had a motive). Aha.

Screwball comedies often bring together mismatched characters: a rich heiress and a working man (*It Happened One Night* [1934], *Holiday* [1938]), a stuffy intellectual and a sexy vamp (*Ball of Fire* [1941]), a stuffy intellectual working man and a ditsy rich heiress (*Bringing Up Baby* [1938]). The mismatch creates a disunity in the narrative (Those two could never be right for one another) and violates our expectations about suitable couples. However, the mismatch also enables us to find oddly appropriate connections between potentially incongruous plot information. Encouraged by the conventions of the screwball genre, viewers hypothesize a story logic that enables them to conceive of the improbable match as appropriate. Indeed, part of the interest and delight of such films comes from witnessing the inevitable union of characters who seem so wrong for one another. One can imagine an incongruity so pointed as to prevent resolution—say, a screwball romance between Joseph Goebbels and Gertrude Stein. However, highly inappropriate partners, such as the those in *The Ghost and Mrs. Muir* (1947), *Harold and Maude* (1971), and *Edward Scissorhands* (1990), although they strain reason and probability, enable imaginative resolutions that logic, scrutiny, and the practicalities of the real world would tell us are irresolvable.

Disunity, Imagination, and Cognitive Play

Research suggests that pleasure in humor correlates positively with the degree of disunity, provided some form of resolution remains tangible. Jones (1970) found that one group's rating of the funniness of cartoons correlated directly with another group's rating of the cartoons' degree of incongruity. Deckers and Buttram (1990), Hoppe (1976), and McGhee (1976) each found an "inverted-U" relationship between incongruity and humor, such that humor increased relative to the degree of incongruity and then began to decline. This research suggests that the greater the strain on our ability to resolve disunified information—so long as the strain does not overburden our efforts at resolution—the greater we enjoy it. Indeed, experimental psychologists have found that people prefer artworks that offer greater difficulty, provided the works do not overwhelm their ability to cope (Hare, 1974; Silvia, 2005). Greater levels of disunity warrant more imagination and effort, and the result can be exhilarating, as we try to unite properties that impede resolution but that nonetheless offer the prospect of resolution. Psychologists Armstrong and Detweiler-Bedell (2008) argue that an encounter with a disunified object excites a free play of ideas, as we reach for new understanding. "In ordinary cognition," they write, "a person smothers uncertainty with a familiar concept to avoid confusion. During free play, a person contemplates a novel stimulus, while holding prior understandings at bay, to expand his or her knowledge structures" (p. 320). The effort to understand a disunified object exercises our cognitive agility and creative problem-solving capacities.[3] If logic and practical reasoning cannot help us understand an object, then imagination and free association might.

But do all of these encounters with disunity—in jokes, whodunits, and Hollywood romances—amount to the same thing? We would not call the disunities in whodunits and screwball comedies violations of story logic. Indeed, those genres motivate certain conventional kinds of disunity. Still, from the viewpoint of a perceiver attempting to understand a disunified narrative, all such encounters excite the same cognitive activity. Whether experiencing jokes, whodunits, screwball comedies, or any other narrative, aesthetic pleasure intensifies, I propose, whenever the perceiver discovers a connection that repairs a breach in the story logic.

Finding unity in the mismatched romantic partners of screwball comedies poses only moderate challenges, but some disunities—such as the one in *Citizen Kane*—seem utterly irresolvable. An irresolvable disunity, once perceived, will readily damage a classical narrative, just as Ryan suggests. *Citizen Kane*'s failure to offer a potential resolution to its narrative inconsistency accounts for why critics regard it as a flaw. But suppose *Citizen Kane* had enabled in viewers a moment of insight. Suppose, for instance, that Raymond's flashback had shown the butler at Kane's bedside, inviting us to suddenly improvise a new hypothesis—that Kane's loneliness had distorted the initial scene of his death. In that case, the inconsistency could have been a source of aesthetic pleasure, rather than an aesthetic flaw.

Twist Films, Mysteries, and Convoluted Narratives

As a counterexample to *Kane*, consider *The Sixth Sense* (1999), which generates a narrative disunity when it reveals that a primary character has, in fact, been a ghost for most of the movie. The revelation briefly ruptures story logic, until we repair the rupture and restore coherence to the story, tying together the strings of the narrative in a new way. Judging from reviews and online commentary, the moment of insight, when we reimagine the entire story through the lens of a new hypothesis, creates tremendous excitement. Such "twist films" offer paradigmatic examples of the pleasures of incongruity-resolution in Hollywood narration because they work just like jokes.

Incongruity constitutes one form of narrative disunity in Hollywood storytelling. Another is a narrative gap—a break in the cause–effect chain that makes it more challenging for spectators to construct a coherent story. We encounter moderately challenging narrative gaps in all sorts of Hollywood genres, including gangster (*The Godfather, Part II*, 1974), horror (*The Shining*, 1980), science fiction (*Blade Runner*, 1982) and especially mystery films (*Vertigo*, 1958). Films with noticeable gaps generate curiosity by withholding crucial causal information, prompting spectators to try to repair the break imaginatively. *And Then There Were None* (1945) withholds from us the knowledge that one of the apparent murder victims faked his death. We eliminate him from our list of suspects yet have difficulty forming a coherent story because the remaining suspects also seem innocent. Narrative gaps establish an atmosphere of mystery and create intriguing puzzles for spectators to solve. The gaps motivate a search for understanding, and plot cues guide the search by manipulating our abductive reasoning processes.

The process of abduction creates pleasure only as long as we retain confidence in the possibility of story coherence. The search for meaning rests on the assumption that meaning exists. Once we give up that assumption, the search stops. Hence, the existence of meaning matters less than the assumption of its existence. Under normal circumstances, Hollywood mystery films fill in key narrative gaps, but sometimes they don't, and they don't have to. Indeed, the most certain way to sustain an audience's search for meaning is to make meaning impossible to find. The notorious example from classical

Hollywood is *The Big Sleep* (1946), with its perhaps irresolvable puzzle of double-crosses, cover-ups, and murders. "I never figured out what was going on," Director Howard Hawks told an interviewer, "After that got by, I said, 'I'm never going to worry about being logical again'" (quoted in McBride, 1982: p. 9). Movies like *The Big Sleep* invite us to use abductive reasoning to make sense of a plot that logic and scrutiny would not help us understand and might even prevent us from understanding.

Ambiguity and narrative convolution also afford enjoyable forms of disunity. *The Game* (1997), *Fight Club* (1999), *Vanilla Sky* (2001), *The Prestige* (2006), *Duplicity* (2009), *Source Code* (2011), *Looper* (2012), *Cloud Atlas* (2012), *Interstellar* (2014), *Arrival* (2016), *Tenet* (2020), and many other recent films have together formed a popular trend of puzzle films in New Hollywood narration, although studio-era films sometimes explored similar convolutions. The big caper movie *The Killing* (1956), for instance, puts scenes out of chronological order and contains other convolutions that make story construction more strenuous. Consider the convoluted progress of the shotgun that Johnny (Sterling Hayden) smuggles into a racetrack where a heist will take place. Johnny first brings the gun in a guitar case to his hotel room (Figure 2.1), where he later transfers the gun to a flower box (Figure 2.2), puts the flower box in a bus-station locker (Figure 2.3), and puts the key to the locker in the mailbox (Figure 2.4) of another caperist, Mike (Joe Sawyer), who picks up the key (Figure 2.5), uses it to retrieve the gun from the bus station (Figure 2.6), and puts the gun in another locker at the race track (Figure 2.7) where Johnny, after staging a distraction, picks it up again (Figure 2.8). The convolutions complicate the caper and inhibit viewers from questioning why Johnny didn't simply give Mike the gun (or the key) sometime earlier. In fact, the movie never explains why Johnny must arrange for Mike to obtain the gun at all, if Johnny will only pick it up again himself later on at the track.

Although scholars might regard Hollywood cinema as "excessively obvious" (Bordwell et al., 1985: p. 3), movies such as *The Big Sleep* and *The Killing* make comprehension difficult when their disunities jeopardize, or flat out violate, story logic. Would these narratives offer more aesthetic pleasure if they ultimately made better sense? I think they would not. If *The Big Sleep* and *The Killing* resolved all of their gaps and mysteries, they would surrender some of the qualities that make the films persistently interesting. The moment a plot makes perfect sense, it sacrifices the atmosphere of mystery and labyrinthine complexity so central to mystery films and convoluted narratives. "Nothing in the world is as dull as logic," Hitchcock was fond of saying (quoted in Naremore, 1993: p. 181). Mystery and narrative complexity sustain our interest in such films, as well as our sense that their stories contain difficult problems that demand attention and thought.

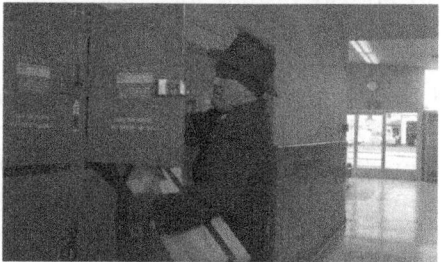

FIGURES 2.1–2.8   The convoluted progress of a shotgun in *The Killing* (1956).

Confronted with a mass of plot information that context says must make sense, spectators likely have a persistent feeling that more remains to be understood than their minds can readily grasp. For Armstrong and Detweiler-Bedell (2008), that feeling defines "exhilarated pleasure," which results, they say, from the prospect of "understanding particularly challenging stimuli when the potential to realize such understanding … is tangible but distant" (p. 312). Humor researcher Neil Schaeffer (1981) describes encounters with incongruity similarly: "In the after-experience of incongruity, we know and feel that something significant has occurred in our mind, but we do not know exactly what it is. We have a tense notion that we know more than we know, and we preserve this uncertain feeling as a means of arousing and sustaining our curiosity for the search" (p. 10). The surprising popularity of writer–director David Lynch—and his persistent ability to raise substantial budgets for projects with deeply convoluted, gappy, and ambiguous narratives—testifies to the aesthetic value and commercial value of films that keep understanding "tangible but distant." Even after Lynch's narratives have concluded, they linger because some of their plot elements do not obey story logic and remain mere potentials for understanding. Some spectators find Lynch's films too disunified, but for spectators engaged by them—spectators willing to persist in the search for understanding—Lynch's films offer exhilarated pleasure.

Because a classical foundation stabilizes Hollywood cinema, Hollywood films can still show a moderate level of narrative disunity without alienating a mass audience. Because they remain fixed to classical storytelling principles, films such as *The Big Sleep* likely retain an audience's trust in their underlying coherence. I still have not entirely figured out the story of *The Big Sleep*, but each time I encounter the movie I persist in a secret mad hope that this time I will. The search for story coherence endures because of the mere prospect of understanding. If that prospect is ever permanently ruined, then *The Big Sleep* would become an aesthetically damaged narrative. But as long as understanding remains "tangible but distant," then the guessing will continue. The film's atmosphere of mystery and complexity persists as long as reason does not clear things up and ruin the mood.

Conclusion

According to the theory of storytelling aesthetics presented here, storytelling creates pleasure by cuing spectators to mentally resolve disparate plot information. Hollywood generally makes resolution fairly easy by using time-tested storytelling principles, particularly classical principles of unity and causality, that ease mental activity and satisfy the desire for complete understanding. Easy resolution makes Hollywood movies spontaneously pleasing for mass audiences. However, Hollywood movies also exhilarate aesthetic experience by making plot resolution moderately difficult. The pleasures of narrative exhilarate when cognitive activity is athletic and resolution distant but still tangible. Using abductive reasoning, viewers engaged by such films seek to unify plot information, repair gaps and inconsistencies, and sort out convolutions. As long as a movie does not violate our trust in its underlying coherence or put so much strain on our cognitive resources that we give up the search for understanding, then aesthetic pleasure will likely intensify with the degree of difficulty at resolution.

This theory helps explain why a good story does not automatically translate into aesthetic pleasure. The aesthetic pleasures of narrative rely on good story*telling*—the process by which an artwork cues spectators to construct a story mentally. By complicating the spectator's story construction processes, a film can intensify that pleasure. Consider how much less pleasurable *Memento* (2000) would be if it told its story in chronological order. A chronological *Memento*, which one can find on DVD, eliminates the challenge of constructing a coherent story out of non-chronological segments. The chronological *Memento*, which tells the same story as *Memento*, is a dull movie.

Talented Hollywood filmmakers find inventive ways to disunify narratives and challenge spectators' story construction processes, while still retaining spectators' trust in a film's underlying coherence: ambiguous protagonists in *The Searchers* (1956) and *Chinatown* (1974), convoluted and improbable events in *North by Northwest* (1959) and *Magnolia* (1999), divergent plotlines in *Grand Hotel* (1932) and *Nashville* (1975), causal gaps in *Vertigo* (1958) and *2001: A Space Odyssey* (1968), stories told in non-chronological pieces in *A Letter to Three Wives* (1949) and *Annie Hall* (1977), and thwarted narrative expectations in *Mildred Pierce* (1945) and *The Prestige* (2006). Such films challenge our ability to construct coherent stories out of disunified plots. But as long as the films have not made the process too onerous for us—as long as resolution remains tangible enough that we persist in our search for understanding—then the films have enabled in us exhilarating moments of imagination, insight, and free play.[4]

Notes

1 For studies of the pleasures of insight, see Jung-Beeman et al. (2004: pp. 500–510) and, in Sternberg and Davidson (1995), chapters by Gick and Lockhart (1995: pp. 197–228), Gruber (1995: pp. 397–432), and Seifert et al. (1995: pp. 65–124).
2 Neil Schaeffer (1981) calls laughter "a vacation from the workaday economy of the mind" (p. 22). Laughter, he says, enables creative processes normally inhibited by "our practical investment in the process of reason" (p. 24).

3 Zenasni et al. (2008) found that creative people better tolerate ambiguity, a finding that suggests that creative mental activity may enable people to cope with disunity.
4 This chapter is a revised version of a chapter from *Hollywood Aesthetic: Pleasure in American Cinema* (Berliner, 2017: pp. 51–71), reprinted by permission from Oxford University Press.

References

Armstrong, T. & Detweiler-Bedell, B. (2008). Beauty as an emotion: The exhilarating prospect of mastering a challenging world. *Review of General Psychology*. 12 (4), 305–329.

Ball, E. H. (1917). *Cinema plays: How to write them*. London, UK, Stanley Paul.

Beardsley, M. (1981). *Aesthetics: Problems in the philosophy of criticism*. Indianapolis, IN, Hackett.

Berliner, T. (2017). *Hollywood aesthetic: Pleasure in American cinema*. New York, NY, Oxford University Press.

Bordwell, D. (1985). *Narration in the fiction film*. Madison, WI, University of Wisconsin Press.

Bordwell, D. (2006). *The way Hollywood tells it: Story and style in modern movies*. Berkeley, CA, University of California Press.

Bordwell, D., Staiger, J. & Thompson, K. (1985). *The classical Hollywood cinema: Film style & mode of production to 1960*. New York, NY, Columbia University Press.

Bowden, E. M., Jung-Beeman, M. & Kourios, J. (2005). New approaches to demystifying insight. *Trends in Cognitive Sciences*. 9 (7), 322–328.

Carroll, N. (2004). The Power of Movies. In: Lamarque, P. & Olsen, S. H. (eds.), *Aesthetics and the philosophy of art: The analytic tradition*. Malden, MA, Blackwell, pp. 485–497.

Chatman, S. (1978). *Story and discourse: Narrative structure in fiction and film*. Ithaca, NY, Cornell University Press.

Cowgill, L. J. (1999). *Secrets of screenplay structure: How to recognize and emulate the structural frameworks of great films*. Los Angeles, CA, Lone Eagle.

Deckers, L. & Buttram, R. T. (1990). Humor as a response to incongruities within or between schemata. *Humor*. 3 (1), 53–64.

Gick, M. L. & Lockhart, R. S. (1995). Cognitive and Affective Components of Insight. In: Sternberg, R. J. & Davidson, J. E. (eds.), *The nature of insight*. Cambridge, MA, MIT Press, pp. 197–228.

Gruber, H. E. (1995). Insight and Affect in the History of Science. In: Sternberg, R. J. & Davidson, J. E. (eds.), *The nature of insight*. Cambridge, MA, MIT Press, pp. 397–432.

Hare, F. G. (1974). Artistic Training and Responses to Visual and Auditory Patterns Varying in Uncertainty. In Berlyne, D. E. (ed.), *Studies in the new experimental aesthetics: Steps toward an objective psychology of aesthetic appreciation*. Washington, DC, Hemisphere, pp. 159–168.

Herman, L. (1963). *A practical manual of screen playwriting*. New York, NY, Meridian.

Hoppe, R. A. (1976). Artificial humor and uncertainty. *Perceptual & Motor Skills*. 42, 1051–1056.

Jung-Beeman, M., Bowden, E. M., Haberman, J., Frymiare, J. L., Arambel-Liu, S., Greenblatt, R., Reber, P. J. & Kounios, J. (2004). Neural activity when people solve verbal problems with insight. *Public Library of Science: Biology*. 2 (4), 500–510.

Jones, J. M. (1970). Cognitive factors in the appreciation of humor: A theoretical and experimental analysis. Unpublished doctoral dissertation, Yale University.

Knoblich, G., Ohlsson, S., Haider, H. & Rhenius, D. (1999). Constraint relaxation and chunk decomposition in insight problem solving. *Journal of Experimental Psychology: Learning, Memory, and Cognition.* 25 (6), 1534–1555.

Lipton, L. (2004). *Inference to the best explanation.* 2nd ed. New York, NY, Routledge.

Lucey, P. (1996). *Story sense: Writing story and script for feature films and television.* New York, NY, McGraw-Hill.

Maier, N. R. F. (1931). Reasoning in humans. II. The solution of a problem and its appearance in consciousness. *Journal of Comparative Psychology.* 12 (2), 181–194.

Marion, F. (1937). *How to write and sell film stories.* New York, NY, Covici Friede.

Mayer, R. E. (1992). *Thinking, problem solving, cognition.* 2nd ed. New York, NY, Worth Publishers.

McBride, J. (1982). *Hawks on hawks.* Berkeley, CA, University of California Press.

McGhee, P. E. (1976). Children's appreciation of humor: A test of the cognitive congruency principle. *Child Development.* 47 (2), 420–426.

Metcalfe, J. & Wiebe, D. (1987). Intuition in insight and noninsight problem solving. *Memory & Cognition.* 15 (3), 238–246.

Morreall, J. (1983). *Taking laughter seriously.* Albany, NY, State University of New York Press.

Morreall, J. (1987). Funny Ha-Ha, Funny Strange, and Other Reactions to Incongruity. In: Morreall, J. (ed.) *The philosophy of laughter and humor.* Albany, NY, State University New York Press, pp. 188–207.

Naremore, J. (ed.) (1993). *North by northwest.* New Brunswick, NJ, Rutgers University Press.

Palmer, F. (1924). *Author's photoplay manual.* Hollywood, CA, Palmer Institute.

Peirce Edition Project (ed.) (1998). *The essential Peirce: Selected philosophical writings, volume 2 (1893–1913).* Bloomington, IN, University Press.

Perkins, V. F. (1993). *Film as film: Understanding and judging movies.* New York, NY, Da Capo.

Reber, R., Schwarz, N. & Winkielman, P. (2004). Processing fluency and aesthetic pleasure: Is beauty in the perceiver's processing experience? *Personality and Social Psychology Review.* 8 (4), 364–382.

Richardson, B. (1997). *Unlikely stories: Causality and the nature of modern narrative.* Newark, NJ, University of Delaware Press.

Ryan, M-L. (2009). Cheap plot tricks, plot holes, and narrative design. *Narrative.* 17 (1), 56–75.

Schaeffer, N. (1981). *The art of laughter.* New York, NY, Columbia University Press.

Seifert, C. M., Meyer, D. E., Davidson, N., Patalano, A. L. & Yaniv, I. (1995). Demystification of Cognitive Insight: Opportunistic Assimilation and the Prepared-Mind Perspective. In: Sternberg, R. J. & Davidson, J. E. (eds.), *The nature of insight.* Cambridge, MA, MIT Press, pp. 65–124.

Shultz, T. R. (1976). A Cognitive-Developmental Analysis of Humour. In: Chapman, A. J. & Foot, H. C. (eds.), *Humour and laughter: Theory, research and applications.* New Brunswick, NJ, Transaction Publishers, pp. 11–36.

Silvia, P. J. (2005). What is interesting? Exploring the appraisal structure of interest. *Emotion.* 5 (1), 89–102.

Smith, S. M., Ward, T. B. & Finke, R. A. (eds.). (1995). *The creative cognition approach.* Cambridge, MA, MIT Press.

Sternberg, R. J. & Davidson, J. E. (eds.). (1995). *The nature of insight.* Cambridge, MA, MIT Press.

Suls, J. (1972). A Two-Stage Model for the Appreciation of Jokes and Cartoons: An Information-Processing Analysis. In: Goldstein, J. & Paul McGee, P. (eds.), *The psychology of humor: Theoretical perspectives and empirical issues.* New York, NY, Academic Press, pp. 81–100.

Vale, E. (1944). *The technique of screenplay writing.* New York, NY, Crown.

White, M. & Stock, F. (1948). *The right way to write for the films.* Kingswood, UK, A.G. Elliott.

Zenasni, F., Besançon, M. & Lubart, T. (2008). Creativity and tolerance of ambiguity: An empirical study. *The Journal of Creative Behavior.* 42 (1), 61–73.

3

AMERICAN INDEPENDENT CINEMA

Geoff King

Feature-length American independent cinema is, primarily, a narrative-based form, one that involves the telling of a story of some kind. Stories can be told in different ways, however, and can figure more or less largely in the overall mix. A particular version of narrative structure has become dominant in the mainstream, especially in Hollywood and its imitators: a form known generally, if often somewhat loosely, as 'classical' Hollywood narrative. One of the key identifying features of many American independent films is the extent to which they depart from the familiar conventions of the classical Hollywood variety. Some independent features are marked by their lack of strong, forward-moving narrative drive, opting instead for more relaxed or decentred structures akin to those associated with some forms of international 'art' cinema. Others are more complex than the typical Hollywood narrative, which usually revolves around a small number of major strands. Independent films of recent decades include several varieties of intersecting, multi-strand narrative.

A total abandonment of narrative is sought in some avant-garde or experimental films. These have, in some cases, influenced more accessible independent features, but it is rarely if ever the case that narrative is entirely absent in the more commercial/industrial independent sector. It is usually a substantial presence, in one form or another. Certain aspects of 'classical' narrative structure remain central to many independent features, even when others are undermined, minimalized, or complicated. In narrative terms, as in many others, indie cinema tends to occupy a place closer to Hollywood than to the outer experimental margins, although a range of alternative approaches has been explored, including some quite significant departures. This chapter will consider a number of alternative strategies employed by independent filmmakers, examining the extent to which they challenge the Hollywood

DOI: 10.4324/9781003197911-5

norm at a formal level and the consequences this might have for the viewing experience.

The Moments Between: Decentred, Downplayed or Fragmented Narrative

Two skinny boys, an adolescent and one who appears pre-teen, cruise the fictional small-town streets of Xenia, Ohio, armed with B-B guns, in search of cats to kill and sell into the local restaurant trade to fund their glue-sniffing habit. Three sisters, two teens and one younger, hang out together in various largely aimless activities, their own black cat initially surviving a close encounter with the preceding characters. The two groups form what might loosely be described as two main polarities in writer-director Harmony Korine's first feature *Gummo* (1997). Only loosely, though. *Gummo* is one of a number of independent features that largely abandons any conventional sense of linear plotting. Developing or sustained narrative drive is replaced by a more fragmentary portrait of an assortment of dead-end lives in a community of the disaffected and/or disadvantaged. A rationale for this approach is provided in the form of a framing device: home-video-style footage and voice-over commentary refer to a tornado that struck the town a few years previously, contributing, it seems, to the desolation of the place and its inhabitants, a device used by Korine to justify the presentation of a selection of individual scenes rather than the development of a strong narrative line.

For the unsuspecting viewer of *Gummo*, a number of narrative expectations are undermined. After the initial tornado-era video footage, the film opens, over the credits, with images of a young boy dressed in shorts and pink rabbit ears, playing on a footbridge, pissing and dribbling onto the cars driving below. He might be expected to be the main – maybe even the title – character, but he is not. Bunny Boy (Jacob Sewell) turns up on several more occasions during the film, but as a marginal figure (among marginals), whose presence and behaviour are as unexplained as his attire. The next few scenes introduce the two boys, Tummler (Nick Sutton) and the younger Solomon (Jacob Reynolds), and the three girls, Darby (Darby Dougherty), Dot (Chloe Sevigny) and Helen (Clarissa Glucksman). Some kind of coming-of-age narrative might be anticipated, even if an offbeat one. Or we might expect some form of romantic or sexual union to occur, or to be attempted, between some or all of what appear to be the male and female principals. No such expectations are fulfilled, however. They tend to be either ignored (in most cases) or deliberately subverted. The only resemblance to a conventional youth-dating-movie moment, for example, occurs in a very early scene in which Tummler is 'making out' with a girl in a wrecked car in a junkyard, only to inform her, deflatingly, that she has a lump in her 'titty' (she is seen again, much later, informing her family that she has to have both breasts removed).

The presence and activities of the two main groups of characters knits *Gummo* together, to some extent, but into a fabric that is far from narrative led. The focus of the film slides in and out, tracing some connections between the main protagonists and a range of other figures, represented directly or alluded to, sometimes in brief voice-over commentaries and grainy video footage. The major dynamic is as much centrifugal as centripetal. Korine has just established what appears to be the narrative centrality of the two boys, and has introduced the girls, and connected the two groups via their cat, when we shift, seemingly arbitrarily, to a sequence featuring two skinhead brothers said to have murdered their parents. Next, we are given video footage of a young girl, accompanied by a voice-over in which she (presumably) talks about having been sexually abused by her father. The film continues in this vein, in some cases bringing its gallery of minor characters (including some non-actors with disabilities) into contact with those who take relatively central stage, but quite often not doing so, and in no sense offering an impression of overall narrative progression or forward momentum. There is an absence in many instances of any classical-style continuation or closing of incidents or character-material left dangling in prior scenes. A viewer coming to *Gummo* armed with the classical schemata might spend some time trying to identify an overarching narrative thread or a central enigma, in keeping with canonic expectations, only to find that the central enigma lies partly in the lack of any such ruling plot device.

Korine's next feature, *Julien Donkey-Boy* (1999), is more closely focused than *Gummo*, but exhibits many similar qualities. The organizing principle is a single family, that of the schizophrenic title character, Julien (Ewen Bremner), rather than a community, although the family group is equally damaged: Julien himself, his pregnant sister, Pearl (Chloe Sevigny), a would-be-wrestler brother, Chris (Evan Neumann) and the raving authoritarian father played by the German director Werner Herzog. *Julien Donkey-Boy* begins with what proves to be a narrative red herring. Blurry opening video images of a skater – a motif repeated throughout the film – give way to a sequence that culminates in Julien drowning (we are led to assume) a young boy. This is a powerful moment, an arbitrary and disconnected act (the boy is pushed under the water because he declines to give Julien a turtle he has found in a pond). In a conventional dramatic narrative, we would expect consequences, or at least an arc of suspense (will he be found out, what will happen?), especially in the case of so dramatic an event positioned in the privileged opening moments during which major plot premises are often established. In this case, though, there is nothing. The incident remains isolated, just one moment in a film filled with digressions, like *Gummo*, in which the emphasis much of the time is on the scene playing rather than its place in any more than a loose accumulation of scenes. There is a degree of narrative progression in some respects, including something like a climax, in which Pearl falls while ice-skating, the unborn baby dies and Julien takes the foetus from the hospital, carries it home by bus and lies with it under his bed-clothes, as if himself returned to the womb. But many scenes are digressions, or would be if there were a more solid central narrative core from which to digress: sequences, for example, in which the father, variously, rambles, expounds and berates, sometimes alone, sometimes aiming his complaints at members of his family, especially Chris.

Gummo and *Julien Donkey-Boy* received very mixed critical notices, including many attacks for both the nature of the material presented (the alleged 'exploitation' of disabled non-actors and the 'anti-social' behaviour of the central characters, especially in *Gummo*) and the absence of conventional narrative development. There is a considerable logic to the departure from linear narrative, however. In *Julien Donkey-Boy*, the fragmented structure might easily be understood as part of the figuration of the disintegrating mental state of the title character, even if the material is not presented as a manifestation of his subjectivity as such. More generally, in both films, the lack of classical plotting seems entirely appropriate to the subject matter: a portrayal of lives that are essentially directionless, lived without the contrivances of conventional-mainstream narrative arc. This is one of the major justifications available to filmmakers who depart in this way from dominant or classical narrative form: a claim to the status of something more closely approximating the reality of the lives of most people and especially, perhaps, those on the socio-economic margins. There is, very clearly, a politics to this. To impose the usually affirmative Hollywood arc onto such material – to portray characters as heroically lifting themselves out of their difficulties, triumphing through adversity and so on – is to impose a typically American-capitalist ideological framework, rooted in the notion that America is a society in which even those from the lowest reaches can achieve the dream of prosperity. Without being overtly critical-political in emphasis, the implicit message of *Gummo* and *Julien Donkey-Boy* puts the lie to such illusions.

What is involved here, to use an analytical tool from Russian Formalist criticism, is a different form of 'motivation', a different rationale or justification for material presented on-screen. Motivation according to the expectations or requirements of narrative is known as 'compositional' motivation. Certain events occur, and might be anticipated, precisely because they are what is expected according to the schemata of canonic/classical narration. An obvious example would be the Hollywood happy ending, which might often make little sense other than in terms of familiar compositional motivation, or the eruption of some threatening or destabilizing event in the midst of the equilibrium portrayed in the earlier stages of any kind of action-adventure film. One alternative to compositional motivation that plays a large part in some independent films is motivation according to verisimilitude, or realism. Material 'makes sense' because of its claims of proximity to the way things are in the outside world, rather than the extent to which it accords with the dominant conventions of fictional narrative. The two are often viewed as diametrically opposed: the extent to which material is motivated by verisimilitude is often understood as precisely the extent to which it departs from canonic forms of narrative, and vice versa.

Films such as *Gummo* and *Julien Donkey-Boy* are certainly not unshaped reflections of reality, in their narrative or any other dimensions; that is not a claim Korine or many other independent filmmakers would make. *Gummo* and *Julien Donkey-Boy* offer a mixture of the seemingly 'real/authentic' and the 'poetic/impressionist', their basis of organization owing as much to montage or collage as to narrative or story. They remain constructs, even if constructed according to principles different from those associated with the commercial mainstream. It can be argued that they are relatively closer to, or more adequate evocations of, a particular kind of reality, however, in that the degree to which an artificially heightened narrative frame has been imposed is greatly reduced. 'Real life' is a complex phenomenon, and not something experienced entirely in the raw, as it were, purely, immediately and without the imposition of meaning-generating frameworks. There is a widespread human-cultural tendency to read narratives and other metaphorical or mythic frameworks into our lives, to shape perceptions of experience, both at the time of experience and in retrospect. The fact remains, though, that the lives of very few individuals accord with the kinds of plottings and character developments found in the classical Hollywood narrative model. The events of life tend not to have clear-cut beginnings, middles and ends, as Korine suggests, beyond the minimal biological framework of birth, life and death. Life tends, on the whole, to be rambling and without a great deal of tightly structured development. It just 'goes on', most of the time, rather than being subject to a regime of interlocked and forward-moving dynamics or moments of major crisis. Dramatic developments prompting equally dramatic responses are not the norm. One of the major appeals of classical Hollywood narrative as a form of fantasy-entertainment is precisely its distance in this and other respects from the texture of life as it is generally lived.

Hollywood-style narrative might be characterized as a heightened portrayal of aspects of very particular lives, in very particular circumstances – with most of the dull bits left out. Leaving the dull bits in, or building films around successions of 'dull' bits, has been one persistent tendency in the independent sector. [...] The classical Hollywood narrative model is one in which characterizations, events and other details are to a large extent subordinated to, or composed of, their place in the narrative design. In its ideal form – however, rarely that might fully be realized – every component would be locked securely into place, performing a narrative function (which might include establishing a particular mood required by the plot as well as more obvious story-development-related material). Nothing, or at least nothing of substance, is meant to be arbitrary or unmotivated. In independent features – or other alternatives to the Hollywood model – qualities such as arbitrariness or less focused narrative might be considered to be virtues, characteristics of a form in which the impression is given that individuals exist or things happen in their own right rather than in a context in which they are expected to 'lead' explicitly somewhere or become cogs in a linear-narrative-led machine.

Classical narrative usually establishes a clear hierarchy between moments that are presented as more or less important. The rhythms of narrative structure move between heightened, key moments of development ('plot points' as they are termed in screenwriting manuals) and action, and the balance provided by quieter or more discursive periods. It is the heightened moments or major plot points that are discarded or downplayed in some independent features, leaving a more even, de-dramatized or rougher structure of events. Points of dramatic crisis might arise more abruptly and not be subjected to the kind of reconciliation or closure typical of the Hollywood model.

One of the distinguishing qualities of Jim Jarmusch's *Stranger than Paradise* (1984) is the sense that nothing much ever seems to happen. The principals Willie (John Lurie), his visiting Hungarian cousin Eva (Eszter Balint) and friend Eddie (Richard Edson) hang out, largely aimlessly, in locations ranging from Willie's New York apartment to a Florida beach. A typical example is a single-shot sequence in the apartment in which Willie and Eddie sit drinking beer from cans and say nothing, a shot held for nearly a full minute. Much of what occurs in the film is not so much understated as unstated. A year after Eva moves on to stay with her aunt in Cleveland, a decision by Willie and Eddie to visit is made obliquely: in one scene, Willie talks about borrowing a car and getting away from the city; in the next, they are driving and he is asking whether Eddie thinks the car will make it to Cleveland. A decision to move on to Florida, with Eva, instead of returning home, is made in a similarly arbitrary manner, for which no preparation is made. Despite all the miles covered, in a series of uneventful car-interior scenes, the dominant sense is of an absence of change. 'You come to someplace new and everything looks the same', as Eddie observes in a snowbound scene in Cleveland, the truth of his words for the viewer demonstrated in a later scene in Florida in which an overexposed background of sand and sea creates a similarly whitened-out effect.

Jarmusch's next feature, *Down by Law* (1986) features another prominent elision: the three principals escape from prison, but exactly how is glossed over and undepicted. One of the appeals of this style of filmmaking is the emphasis it places on aspects of life that are usually edited out in the interests of speed and economy of narrative movement. In *Night on Earth* (1991), for example, Jarmusch constructs an entire feature through a series of taxi rides, events that are not usually seen as significant. As Jarmusch puts it:

> [I]n a film when someone takes a taxi, you see them get in, then there's a cut, then you see them get out. So in a way the content of this film is made up of things that would usually be taken out. It's similar to what I like about *Stranger than Paradise* or *Down by Law*: the moments between what we think of as significant.
>
> *(Jarmusch, quoted in Keogh, 2000, p. 127)*

The main focus of the films of John Cassavetes, often seen as a pioneer of the later independent cinema from the 1980s onwards, is on the delineation of character rather than plot. If the classical Hollywood narrative style tends to be relatively lean and linear, with the emphasis on forward momentum, that of Cassavetes and many of his successors is broader and thicker in texture, particularly in the rendition of character and performance. Characters tend to be more complex or ambiguous, defined less in terms of clearly established goals or morality than is usually the case in Hollywood. An absence of unambiguous moral tone is one of the strengths of Korine's *Gummo*, as well as being one of the prime sources of criticism from some sources. How, exactly, are we meant to take characters such as Tummler and Solomon? For some critics, habits such as killing neighbourhood cats, sniffing glue and turning off the life-support system of the grandmother of one of their contemporaries, make them suitable only for condemnation and, with them, the filmmaker himself. The film takes no clear line. By giving them a relatively central place, it might be assumed to be celebrating as well as documenting their activities, but no very strong lead is provided. A sequence such as the break-in that culminates in what amounts to the murder of the grandmother sounds shocking, but the act itself is conducted in what might be seen as a spirit of kindness and release as much as coldness or malice. Tummler and Solomon might well be judged as victims of their own squalid circumstances.

The point, though, is that the film leaves such questions open. The characters just 'are', essentially; they do what they do and viewers are left to come to their own conclusions. This is not a quality usually associated with the Hollywood mainstream, the productions of which tend to display clear-cut, often Manichean, oppositions between those established as good or evil.

The films of Cassavetes devote large amounts of running time to the more overt exploration and laying bare of character, through extended acts of foregrounded 'performance', as might be expected of the work of an actor-turned-director. Centre stage in a film such as *A Woman Under the Influence* (1974) is taken by the performance of Gena Rowlands in the title role. Narrative here emerges from character and character relationships, rather than vice versa. Events seem to develop more organically, out of the situations in which characters are found, rather than being imposed artificially from less plausible-seeming outside intrusions. The focus generally is on relatively 'ordinary' characters in 'ordinary' situations, rooted in their life worlds rather than 'ordinary characters in extraordinary circumstances' – a Hollywood model given explicit voice in a reference to the protagonists of Spielberg's *Close Encounters of the Third Kind* (1977) – or extra-ordinary characters in the kinds of situations that might be normal in their worlds (police officers, secret agents, space travellers and so on).

Another option is to give a low-key, 'ordinary' quality to the lives of characters who occupy worlds that are usually depicted in Hollywood in a heightened or salacious manner, the classic example of which is Lizzie Borden's *Working Girls* (1986), a portrait of women working in a New York brothel. *Working Girls* uses a 'day-in-the-life' structure, an ideal framework within which to provide a 'slice of life' that has some shape without the imposition of any grand narrative design. The whole point of the film is to emphasize the mundane quality of the life, as one among other ways in which women are exploited.

Narrative structure is not abandoned in any of these examples, although its forms and sources may be variable. The films of Cassavetes and Korine are constructed through a balance between pre-established structure and improvised performance. Cassavetes' films are usually scripted narratives rather than works of improvisation, although suggestions from performers are often integrated into the script during periods of rehearsal. *Gummo* was scripted in advance but in an episodic manner, with the emphasis on individual scenes that were only subsequently worked into a sequence (Macnab, 2000, p. 196). In the case of *Julien Donkey-Boy*, improvisation played a larger role, the script outlining the general thrust of what might happen in scenes but without much in the way of pre-determined dialogue (Kim, 1999). Downplayed or low-key narrative can also be combined with more conventional frameworks, as suggested by Jarmusch in the case of *Stranger than Paradise* and *Down by Law*, each of which conforms to an overarching structure of three acts followed by a coda (Keogh, 2000, p. 129).

If some independent films depart substantially from the Hollywood norm, with fragmented, oblique or minimal narrative development, others do so in more subtle or nuanced fashion. This is one of many respects in which the distinction between independent and mainstream is often relative rather than absolute, embracing gradations of difference. An 'indie' impression might be created through a relative resistance to familiar narrative cliché or a relaxation rather than a halting of linear narrative dynamics. When Greg Harrison sought industry funding for his rave subculture feature *Groove* (2000), for example, he came under pressure to add conventional plot elements to the account of one night's experiences at an unlicensed rave. 'They wanted to add a gun [to the story] or have someone die of a drug overdose, but that wasn't the film I wanted to make' (Harrison, quoted in Gore, 2001, p. 3). To make the film his own way, without the imposition of such devices, Harrison had to make it independently on a low budget. *Groove* is far from being an obscure or 'arty' film, in its approach to narrative or in any other dimensions. It has very accessible and commercial dimensions, especially to an audience attracted by the music and general youth-culture ambience. It is a clear illustration, however, of how formal qualities, such as narrative can be shaped quite directly by industrial imperatives: in this case how a particular approach to narrative, even if not a radical one, necessitated recourse to an independent mode of production.

Many more independent features could be cited in which, without greatly radical formal innovation, narrative is downplayed or displaced, slower-paced or de-melodramatized. Such strategies reduce the potential for lapses into sentimentality in examples such as Allison Anders' portrait of two sisters coming of age with their hard-pressed mother in a trailer park in *Gas, Food, Lodging* (1992). In their major relationship scenarios, films such as these are conventional enough, but they are structured to resist the kind of heightened melodramatic dynamics that would be expected in more mainstream, Hollywood equivalents. It is a question of focusing on something closer to the rhythms and textures of ordinary life. Each is organized around key, life-changing experiences for the central characters. These are not handled as obliquely as in some of the examples cited above, but neither are they given the full Hollywood treatment. In these and other examples, narrative drive, enigma and climax often take second place to the establishment of character and dialogue of a quirky or offbeat character.

If the oblique style of Jarmusch can be seen as motivated in part by verisimilitude, as a tribute to the low-key and unspoken nature of much of what goes on in real life, it is also a heavily stylized minimalism that draws attention to itself as a formal-artistic device. Digression as a mark of stylization is also found in the films of Quentin Tarantino, especially in the character/dialogue-based riffs around various issues of popular culture found in *Reservoir Dogs* (1992) and *Pulp Fiction* (1994). In one sense, again, this could be seen as making a claim to a degree of verisimilitude. Hitmen such as Vincent (John Travolta) and Jules (Samuel L. Jackson) in *Pulp Fiction* might be just as likely to engage in trivial discourse about items such as the merits of various types of burger, before and during their work, as anyone engaged in more humdrum activities. Inserting such material, incongruously, into this context gives the very fictional world of such characters some grounding. But it is also a stylistically motivated flourish, a marker of the distinctive presence of the director (and, as such, a valuable tool in his establishment of a marketable identity). The same can be said of the offbeat and often stylized dialogue and characters found in the work of other notables in the indie scene, including figures such as Joel and Ethan Coen and Hal Hartley. Relatively low-key, fragmented or disjointed narrative need not be the product of commitment to notions of quotidian authenticity, as is the case in a film such as *Working Girls*. It can also be a licence for enjoyably unfocused romps such as the Coen brothers' *The Big Lebowski* (1998), the kidnap/ransom plot at the centre of which is largely an excuse for an assortment of eccentric digressions. The fragmentary narrative style and imagery of Korine is another example of an approach that combines elements of motivation by claims to both verisimilitude and the poetic-artistic.

Tangled Webs: Multi-Strand Narrative

If some independent features play down narrative, reducing or undoing its classically smooth and driving qualities, others increase its presence through the use of strategies to link or combine a multiplicity of different narrative threads. A number of approaches can be identified. In some cases, a complex web of narrative strands is woven, more or less easy to untangle. Different narrative elements can be closely tied together, or their relations left implicit or uncertain. The same action might be viewed from different perspectives or re-enacted in different circumstances. More work is often required from the viewer in such cases than would usually be expected in Hollywood, a process that also tends to increase consciousness of the process of narration itself. A film that offers a point of transition between examples included in this and the previous section is Richard Linklater's *Slacker* (1990), another of the landmark indie films of the early 1990s. *Slacker*, in its portrayal of an assortment of eccentric characters in the director's hometown of Austin, Texas, certainly belongs to the school of decentred and downplayed narrative, but it also offers an example of a novel approach to the linking of its numerous components. The narrative line, as far as it can be described as such, is passed along from one character to the next. In one typical sequence, near the start, an arrested youth is taken from his doorstep to a police car. Two others comment as they pass by, one carrying a guitar case. Cut to the latter busking. A girl puts in a coin, and we follow the girl. She goes into a coffee shop, where we pick up a group of youths talking at a table. The camera follows one as he goes outside, and is joined by another as he walks down the street. So it goes on.

    Slacker is comprised entirely of micro-narrative fragments. The structure is different from that of *Gummo*, in which certain elements can be described as *threads*, in that their character groupings and activities are revisited on numerous occasions, even if others remain entirely fragmentary. *Slacker* has a principle of unity much like that of *Gummo*, however: the evocation of a particular kind of community, in this case mostly college and post-college young people talking and hanging out around the vicinity of the Austin campus. There are similarities in the obsessions shared by some of the characters, especially in the realm of assorted rambling conspiracy theories. The structure is one of repeated short ends, linked clearly enough one to another through the passing-on of the line (compared with the abrupt leaps of *Gummo*), but in a pattern that displays no sign of progression (it does not prove to be a 'round' format, in which a return is made to characters introduced at the start). There is a logic to this, as in the case of *Gummo* and *Julien Donkey-Boy*, that might be described as a 'thematic' source of motivation. The structure of *Slacker* is appropriate to the evocation of a landscape in which many characters are tied up in worlds of their own quirks, concerns, obsessions and theories, largely disconnected from others (there is much talk, but often 'at' rather than 'to' the addressee). Self-conscious allusion to the narrative format is also made, including the ramblings of the character played by the director himself, about splitting and parallel realities. A quotation is read aloud from James Joyce's *Ulysses*, a reference to one individual imagining himself the first but always being the last term of a preceding series (in this case, the lovers of Molly Bloom), and the comment towards the end that 'the underlying order is chaos'.

The effect of interwoven multi-strand narrative structure is often to defer the process of narrative progression in each thread and, in some cases, to create a proliferation of material that can reduce narrative clarity. Developments in one strand tend to be put on hold and left dangling for longer than is usual in the classical format, except at moments in which one or more strands cross or are tied together. A certain degree of shifting from one narrative strand to another is familiar in the dominant Hollywood-style model, but some independent features go further in the multiplication of threads that can be more or less neatly brought together to form a unified fabric. The effect created can be one of confusion for the viewer, the result of a lower degree of narrative communicativeness, especially during the earlier stages, in which connections between an array of sub-narratives might not yet have been established or become apparent. Three good examples, each of which offers a slightly different emphasis, are *Short Cuts* (1993), directed by Robert Altman, *Happiness* (1998), directed by Todd Solondz, and Paul Thomas Anderson's *Magnolia* (1999). Each offers a balance between centrifugal and centripetal tendencies; between a diversity of narrative components, on the one hand, and a number of linking devices and thematic continuities, on the other.

The least integrated of the three in terms of explicit narrative connections is *Short Cuts*, reflecting, perhaps, its source in material from a number of separate short stories by Raymond Carver. Its multi-strand style is also a long-standing Altman trademark, his best-known earlier example of the format being *Nashville* (1975). *Short Cuts* offers a mosaic portrait of life in the Los Angeles area, featuring at least 20 principal characters. The narrative style is restless, moving swiftly from one component to another. Characters and relationships are no sooner established, briefly, in the opening moves, than we switch to others. Any sense of sustained narrative focus is constantly undermined in the early part of the film, in which, on first viewing, it can be difficult to keep a sense of which characters are which and what, exactly, is the nature of some of the relationships sketched on-screen. This can create a sense of discomfort that goes against the Hollywood norm; it is not always immediately apparent who is who and what is what in the very opening stages of Hollywood films, but clarification is usually provided sooner rather than later. Two main devices are used in the opening and closing scenes of *Short Cuts* to create a sense of unity, at least at the level of the geographical (and, by implication, social) community. The fast-moving credit and immediately post-credit sequences, a point at which fragmentation of narrative focus and potential disorientation for the viewer are at their highest, are tied together through the presence of a flight of helicopters spraying the area with chemicals to protect against an outbreak of medfly. The closing stages are linked through the eruption of an earthquake, a succession of scenes depicting its impact across a variety of narrative components. These are marked as somewhat arbitrary devices, however, in a feature that does not seek to offer any single focal point or intersection for the multitude of narrative threads but that captures, as Jonathan Romney puts it, 'the cellular essence of LA, as city in which separate zones, separate homes, are linked by highways' (2000, p. 169).

Some narrative threads in *Short Cuts* intersect, with one or other components, but in only a partial and limited overlap between the separate elements of what remains closer to the structure of a patchwork quilt. Links in the diegetic world (the fictional universe on-screen) are in some cases supplemented through formal devices imposed by the filmmaker. One example follows an incident in which a young boy, Casey Finnigan (Lane Cassidy), is hit by a car driven by a character from another narrative thread, Doreen Piggot (Lily Tomlin): a random (literal) collision of two narrative elements. Back home the boy's mother, Ann Finnigan (Andie MacDowell), allows him to fall asleep, and into a coma. She telephones her husband, Howard (Bruce Davison), a television news commentator, at work. Howard tells her to take the boy to the emergency room, an ambulance visible and audible on a monitor behind him. An overlap of sound places the call of the siren over the scene at home, where Ann attempts to wake Casey and give him a glass of milk. She puts the glass down at the bedside. The camera moves in on the milk as she sits Casey up, increasingly desperate. Cut away to the image of a glass of milk on a television screen. It is knocked over, a voice-over intoning that 'accidents happen every day', and we realize that we are now at the Piggot home, where Doreen comments – ironically, for the viewer – on what a close call the incident had been for the boy. This is a very slick sequence, characteristic of many in the film, and very different from the resolutely un-slick style of the films of Harmony Korine and the other examples cited in the first part of this chapter. Considerable effort is made in *Short Cuts*, *Happiness* and *Magnolia* to *orchestrate* the different narrative components, a narrative style that shares with Hollywood a commitment to the production of a smooth and glossy finish, even if at a level of narrative density or complexity untypical of the mainstream.

Stronger diegetic connections between narrative elements are offered in *Happiness* and *Magnolia*. *Happiness* is organized around the lives of three sisters, their parents, and others who come into their orbit, although this is not apparent from the start. The film begins in the story of one sister, the inaptly named Joy Jordan (Jane Adams), breaking up at the end of what appears to be the latest in a series of failed relationships. It then switches to that of Bill Maplewood (Dylan Baker) and it is only several scenes later that we find out that he is married to Joy's sister, Trish (Cynthia Stevenson). In between, we are introduced to the third sister, Helen (Lara Flynn Boyle), although the relationship is not made clear at this stage. As is the case with *Short Cuts* and *Magnolia*, the viewer has to work harder than is the norm in Hollywood to trace the nature of the relationships that exist between characters established in separate narrative threads. The mutual implications and resonances of events in different parts of the narrative weave gradually become increasingly clear as films such as *Happiness* and *Magnolia* progress. The diegetic structuring principle of *Magnolia* takes longer to establish than that of *Happiness*, although some connections are made from the start.

The ubiquity of television, drawn upon on occasion in *Short Cuts*, is used as a major linking device in *Magnolia*. The opening image of the narrative-proper is one of the main characters, the male sexual-assertiveness guru Frank T.J. Mackey (Tom Cruise), appearing on-screen in an advertisement for his latest book. The ad is showing in an empty living room, then in the background at a bar, where another of the principals, later identified as Claudia (Melora Walters), is picked up by a stranger. Back at her apartment, as they make love, a TV show is profiling Jimmy Gator (Philip Baker Hall), the presenter of a long-running children's quiz show. That Claudia is Gator's daughter will only be established much later (unless the very sharp-eyed viewer recognizes her in a photograph during the early sequences); and, later still, the fact that her hatred of him, manifested when he visits her the following morning, is the result of apparent sexual abuse when she was a girl. We then see Gator and a woman we might assume (rightly) to be his wife, at an unidentified location (probably a hospital; we learn later that he has been diagnosed with inoperable cancer). Cut to them arriving home – and entering the room in which the television was initially playing – where the Gator profile is focusing on the current child-prodigy performer, Stanley (Jeremy Blackman). Cut to Stanley at home, rushing to get to school. Shift to archive footage of his predecessor, Donnie Smith from 1968, playing on the Gator household television, and on to the hapless 'Quiz Kid' Donnie Smith today

(William H. Macey). Television screens continue to play an important role in the creation of smooth continuity between segments throughout much of the film, particularly during the broadcast of an episode of Gator's show, 'What Do Kids Know?', which forms one of the central narrative episodes. The opening movement of *Magnolia* is completed with the introduction of the viewer to the other principals: the household of an elderly dying man, later identified as Earl Partridge (Jason Robards) – who turns out to be the father of Frank Mackey – including his nurse Phil (Philip Seymour Hoffman) and his much younger wife, Linda (Julianne Moore); and a relationship-hungry cop, Jim (John C. Reilly), who will form an alliance with Claudia.

This is a breathtakingly fast and fluid example of initial multi-strand narrative exposition, the effect increased through the use of highly mobile camerawork and emphasis-creating zooms, introducing all the major characters in a sustained sequence of about six minutes. 'What Do Kids Know?' proves to be a link between all of these components, although it is nearly two hours into the film before the closing credits reveal the show to be 'A Big Earl Partridge Production', thus including the Partridge contingent in its orbit. The fluid style of *Magnolia* has something in common with *Short Cuts*, as does its use of environmental factors as another form of organization and linkage.

Chapter headings in *Magnolia* are supplied by titles giving weather conditions ('Partly Cloudy. 82% Chance of Rain', 'Light Showers. 99% Humidity. Winds SE 12 MPH', 'Rain Clearing. Breezy Overnight') that reflect something of the rising and falling dramatic arc that flows across the various narrative components. Heavy rainfall in the central portion of the film is both a temporal continuity device, establishing a clear sense of simultaneity, and expressive of the emotional outpourings it contains. *Magnolia* climaxes, very much like *Short Cuts*, with a freak of nature, in this case, a deluge of frogs, the moment of impact of which is traced across the various narrative strands.

Restless camera movement, including rapid whip-pans both across and between scenes in the more heightened instances, impose a formal design across the different narrative strands of *Magnolia*, but the strongest unifying device in this dimension is provided by music, including a number of songs by Aimee Mann. The introduction sequence described above owes much of its impression of unity to its accompaniment by the song 'One', with the strong thematic resonance of its refrain 'One is the loneliest number'. A line of building tension and expectation is sustained in large parts of the film through the use of a simple, insistent and repeating strings theme, a device that enables the film to keep all of the major narrative components rapidly intercut in a state of close-to-crisis for remarkably sustained periods. The use of music is at its most overt in a sequence in which, in turn, Claudia, Jim, Gator, Donnie, Phil and Earl, Linda, Frank and Stanley sing along, in lip-synch, to Mann's 'Wise Up', a highly unconventional and non-naturalistic usage. This, and some of the other, more 'showy' devices, here and in *Short*

Cuts, can be said to be motivated artistically, as much as in compositional terms, as demonstrations of the virtuoso use of cinematic technique to keep so many narrative balls in the air. There is a compositional logic to the 'Wise Up' sequence, in the sense that it marks a particular point of emotional development in each strand, but the device exceeds purely compositional bounds.

The structure of multi-strand narratives such as *Short Cuts*, *Happiness* and *Magnolia* can also be understood in terms of claims to the status of verisimilitude, like the more downplayed narratives considered earlier. They depict a wider canvas of life than is usually found in the more conventional or classical Hollywood format, coming at least relatively closer to the dense complexity of real life. At the same time, this might easily be read in more 'artistic' terms. If classical Hollywood narrative has some features in common with the short story, especially in the delineation of character, these films are more 'novelistic' in scope, displaying complex structure and a wider array of characters. The move from one format to the other is most explicitly traceable in *Short Cuts*, the individual segments of which are based on short stories and could in some cases, separated out, have provided the scale of material suitable for a more conventional feature. The thematic resonances of these films also have more in common with their literary/novelistic equivalents than with the stuff of dominant Hollywood narrative.

Loneliness and alienation, and attempts to forge connections, are pervading themes of *Short Cuts*, *Happiness* and *Magnolia*, material that is entirely appropriate to their principles of narrative design. Characters are separated from one another in their lives, in many instances, as are the narrative components they inhabit. Where narrative strands are brought together, relationships can be established in some cases – the fragile but promising relationship of Claudia and Jim in *Magnolia*, for example – if not in others. *Magnolia* has a narrative and emotional impetus that moves, generally but far from absolutely, towards degrees of reconciliation between those previously alienated, a respect in which it is relatively closer to what might be expected in a Hollywood feature. The same cannot really be said of *Happiness*, even if most members of the central extended family are together for dinner at the end. Relationships remain brittle all round and Bill Maplewood is absent, facing prosecution for serial acts of child sexual abuse. Many potential connections prove abortive. Typical of the style of *Happiness* is the almost entire failure of some characters to appreciate either the fragile nature of their own existence (Trish's smug assessment of the virtues of her life, in a scene that immediately follows one in which we see her husband masturbating with the aid of a kids' magazine) or the hurtful impact of their comments on others (Trish, again, trilling away to Joy that she never thought she would amount to much, insensitively mistaking for the truth Joy's claim to be happy and, in the process, hammering nails into the coffin). Connections, where they occur in these films, are the product of chance as much as goal-directed design on the part of characters, an issue highlighted in a prologue sequence in *Magnolia* that documents three purportedly real cases of unlikely coincidence.

Repetition or reworking of events from different perspectives or shifted into different contexts is another strategy adopted by some multi-part narratives in the independent sector, examples including Jarmusch's *Mystery Train* (1989) and *Night on Earth* and Hal Hartley's *Flirt* (1995). *Mystery Train* and *Night on Earth* are exercises in simultaneity, the events of their different components occurring in parallel. *Flirt* is more radical in its approach, reenacting the same basic relationship-narrative scenario, with some variations, in three different international settings. Each of these films draws attention to its narrative strategy, inviting viewers to look for narrative overlaps and patterns.

A more radical toying with different threads, and with the basis of narrative structure as a whole, is found in *Adaptation* (2002), an independent production given studio distribution by Columbia. *Adaptation* is a highly self-reflexive sequel to *Being John Malkovich* (2000) (from the same writer and director team), in which the central character is the screenwriter Charles Kaufman (Nicholas Cage), agonizing over the adaptation of a book to the screen. Kaufman begins with a characteristically indie-screenwriter stance, resistant to the imposition of any Hollywood-style devices – guns, drugs, character arcs or the learning of 'profound life-lessons' – on the material. His position is set up explicitly against that of the mainstream, the latter represented by the popular seminar run by the real-life screenwriting guru Robert McKee (Brian Cox). Both Kaufman and the film we are watching play with a number of different points of narrative focus (often expressed in briefly inserted and rapidly cut or fast-motion stylized routines), before eventually settling on the subject known best to the writer: himself. At this point the film goes into reflexive overdrive: Kaufman dictates into a tape recorder a scene about himself dictating a scene about himself into a tape recorder. A conversation with McKee leads Kaufman to inject doses of conventional drama into his script, according to the axiom that you cannot lose if you wow the audience in the end. The film shifts as a result into a denouement filled with sex, drugs, kidnap, attempted murder and moments of self-illuminating character insight of the kind against which the screenwriter had previously railed.

How devices that call attention to the narrative process are used and understood depends very much on the way individual features are positioned in the independent marketplace: at the more art-house/specialized end of the spectrum, in which case they might be more likely to be designed to raise questions about various aspects of the nature of experience or its mediation; or at the more commercial/exploitative end, where visceral effects and showmanship might play a larger role (as, for example, in *Pulp Fiction*). *Adaptation* has a foot in each camp, as both an explicit deconstruction of mainstream narrative design and as a narrative game in which the viewer is encouraged to take pleasure in the style and verve with which it eventually flips its own structure inside out. These are relative tendencies, however, within the indie landscape as much as between the independent sector and Hollywood. Similar arguments can be made to understand independent features that go further into the realms of narrative complexity or enigma. These include the reverse order of the main narrative of Christopher Nolan's *Memento* (2000), a strategy motivated subjectively by the fact that an injury has left the protagonist with no short-term memory, and radical and largely unexplained character-identity reversals in David Lynch's *Lost Highway* (1997) and *Mulholland Drive* (2001).

An Alternative Narrative Mode?

The point to be made here is that departures from the dominant classical Hollywood form of narrative of the kind outlined in this chapter should not just be defined negatively, as denials, disturbances or subversions. They also constitute an alternative narrative mode in their own right, even if one that contains a number of variations and does not have exact boundaries. A narrative mode, as defined by David Bordwell, is 'a historically distinct set of norms of narrative construction and comprehension' (1985, p. 150). The classical Hollywood variety is one narrative mode to which a number of alternatives have been offered, including art-cinema narration. The mode or modes found in American independent features lies somewhere between the two, including various forms and degrees of downplayed or more complex narrative.

Not all independent features depart substantially from the more familiar and dominant classical Hollywood narrative mode, however. The aim of this chapter has been to highlight differences more than similarities but it is important to remember that these tend to be relative and variable rather than absolute. Some independent features are quite conventional in their narrative approaches and the gap between the more unconventional films and work of a genuinely radical or avant-garde cast remains a substantial one even if relatively distinctive narrative structure is a key defining component of many.[1]

Note

1 This chapter is abridged, revised and reprinted by permission from *American Independent Cinema* (King, 2005: pp. 59–104). © Geoff King, 2005, American Independent Cinema: Indie, Indiewood and Beyond, I.B. Tauris, an imprint of Bloomsbury Publishing Plc.

References

Bordwell, D. (1985). *Narration in the fiction film*. Routledge.
Gore, C. (2001). 'Still Indie Indies', *Hollywood Reporter*, March.

Keogh, P. (2000) 'Home and Away', in Hillier, J. (ed.), *American Independent Cinema: A sight and sound reader*. British Film Institute. pp. 125–130.

King, G. (2005) *American Independent Cinema*. I.B. Tauris.

Kim, E. (1999). *Improvisation Drives Julien Donkey-Boy*. [online] hollywood.com. Available at: http://www.harmony-korine.com/paper/int/hk/improvisation.html [Accessed 4 February 2023].

Macnab, G. (2000) 'Moonshine Maverick', in Hillier, J. (ed.), *American Independent Cinema: A sight and sound reader*. British Film Institute. pp. 194–199.

Romney, J. (2000). 'In the Time of Earthquakes: Robert Altman and Short Cuts', in Hillier, J. (ed.), *American Independent Cinema: A sight and sound reader*. British Film Institute. pp. 165–170.

4

INTERVIEW: DAVID J. GREENBERG

Can you put your finger on what it is you want to give your audiences when you write a story? Entertainment? Emotional catharsis? Moral instruction? Something else?

First, as a writer-for-hire as opposed to someone who sits around and comes up with stories, I am obligated to satisfy the person who hired me. If someone wants a basic, romantic-comedy, I will write a rom-com and, if they want a slasher movie, I will write that. Now, I will say that my philosophy is that a movie should do more than merely entertain, it should provoke and enlighten. Whenever possible, I try to promote my own agenda, outlook or opinion on things but in a subtle, not heavy-handed way.

In Michael Ondaatje's book *The Conversations*, he paraphrases Robert Bresson by commenting "a film is born three times – in the writing of the script, in the shooting, and in the editing" (2002, p. 16). Based on your experience as a writer and director, does the film die at these transition points?

If the question is "does it die in writing, producing and editing" my answer is, in a best-case scenario, "no." Yes, I have had good screenplays that were really badly produced and so, in that respect, yes, they died. In general, I would say that the process is usually one of evolution and, hopefully, the story evolves in the process.

Allow me to provide the original Bresson quote: "My movie is born first in my head, dies on paper; is resuscitated by the living persons and real objects

DOI: 10.4324/9781003197911-6

I use, which are killed on film, but, placed in a certain order and projected onto a screen, come to life again like flowers in water."

Okay, I do get what he is saying but I would never put it that way. We all do the same thing, more or less, but everyone has different terms for each part of the process. I don't think in terms of things dying but more in terms of morphing and evolving.

Do you ever watch a movie or TV show and think "how did the writer(s) do that?" If that has happened, can you offer an example?

After watching Season Two of HBO's *Silicon Valley*, I got sort of depressed because, if I am being honest with myself, I do not think I am capable of work on that level – smart, savvy, well-plotted, and really funny. Thankfully, people in my circle were quick to remind me that the show is not the result of one person's work, it is a team effort.

Presumably, you know a poorly written show or movie when you see it. What are the typical or most common signs?

Reliance on tropes, cliches, lack of originality in plot, character and dialogue.

Books and classes on screenwriting are sometimes described by working writers as constraining. Was there ever a book or a particular idea you discovered during your education that has always stuck with you as useful?

Alternative Screenwriting by Jeff Rush and Kan Dancyger is not just my favorite book on screenwriting, it is one of my favorite books, period. Not a specific concept per se but just an acknowledgment of and awareness that not everyone believes in conventional three-act structure as the gospel truth; that most Best Screenplay or Best Adapted Screenplays Oscars do not follow three-act structure. After years of reading (or trying to read) the classic texts on screenwriting that prescribe certain beats on certain pages in a really rigid manner that I always found off-putting, Alternative Screenwriting showed me that there is more than one way to tell a story onscreen and that it was okay to break the so-called rules the book is subtitled "Successfully breaking the rules."

Rush and Dancyger demonstrate the conventional approaches to story structure in a screenplay and then, much like the title suggests, provide alternative approaches. For me, one of the biggest takeaways was the example of Woody Allen's *Crimes & Misdemeanors* (1989), a film that I loved and one that was instrumental in my decision to pursue screenwriting. The authors point out that the film is actually made up of two stories, a murder mystery and a romantic comedy, both with beginning middle, and end that intersect at the climax of the film. What struck me most was their point that both stories flip genre conventions – the bad guy in the murder mystery gets away with his crime and the lead in the rom-com does not get the girl.

Did *Alternative Screenwriting* offer any insights on working with protagonists that stuck with you?

At the time of my first reading of the book, I had been struggling with a screenplay that was a semi-finalist for the prestigious Sundance Writers Lab. In the book, they ask "What happens to your screen story when the main character is more passive, more voyeur than participant?" and the screenplay I was working on confronted this very question. My protagonist was passive and everyone told me that this was something one could not do in a screenplay but, in my gut, I knew it would work and *Alternative Screenwriting* was the only source of encouragement.

Flash-forward many years and I was writing what would become my feature debut, *Stomping Ground* (2016). Emboldened by what I read in the book, I wrote a screenplay where the inciting incident happens offscreen, before the movie begins and, in a radical departure from convention, the incident is a completely conscious choice made by the protagonist/antagonist, not something that happens to him involuntarily but something he does with intention. Nobody grows or changes for the better in the story. In the end, the "good" guy, the voice of reason, winds up being a rather complicated character whose intentions are not always as altruistic as one might think. *Alternative Screenwriting* opened my mind to be able to see things in a new way and feel comfortable breaking the rules.

As a teacher, what are the principles or tools with which you would like your students to step out from your classes? In other words, what kind of film writing would you like young screenwriters to engage with in the future, given the obstacles and constraints you know they will encounter?

One of the key concepts I stress is that students need to be aware of the realities of being a working screenwriter. Ninety-four percent of all screenwriting jobs are assignments, jobs for hire where a writer is given the job of writing something for someone else, not seeing their own wildly original vision hit the screenplay. So ego-management, collaborative skills, working as a team member, being able to give and receive constructive criticism; negotiating and compromising are big parts of being a professional writer.

On the other side, as someone who is most comfortable in the low-budget indie film world, I stress the idea that, given the technological advancements that have continued to democratize film production over the past thirty years or so, my students are quite likely to attempt their own feature film production. It is incredibly important for them to set realistic goals for these productions, meaning that they are not likely to have a budget anywhere close to a million dollars or more, so they need to know how to conceive of productions for low budget, reverse engineering their stories so that they fit the tight parameters with which they will mostly like work within.

5

COMPLEX FILM NARRATIVES

Diegetic Fictionalization in Christopher Nolan's
Fantastical Puzzle Film Cycle

Miklós Kiss

Puzzle Films in Context: Historical, Narrative, and Cognitive Approaches

From around the mid-1990s, mainstream Hollywood cinema has embraced more experimental approaches to its long-established and solidified "classical narrative" forms and rules. A fresh tendency has seemed to emerge through a handful of films injecting generic fictions and their traditional storytelling constraints with novel and, at the time, rather bold narrative creativity—practices that were thought to be exclusive to (post)modern literature and art cinema, and techniques that, in turn, also inspired new types of stories to be told. The success of pioneering early indie films, like Quentin Tarantino's 1994 *Pulp Fiction*, Alejandro Amenábar's 1997 *Abre los ojos* (*Open Your Eyes*), Tom Tykwer's 1998 *Lola rennt* (*Run Lola Run*), or Christopher Nolan's 2000 *Memento*, triggered a wave of films, marking out a clear trend that has remained an enduring current over the subsequent decades. Trailblazers, like Richard Kelly's 2001 *Donnie Darko*, earned cult status or were repositioned as trendsetters, such as David Lynch's 1997 *Lost Highway*, opening the gate to a mainstream phenomenon culminating in bigger (budget) productions like Duncan Jones' 2011 *Source Code*, Rian Johnson's 2012 *Looper*, Doug Liman's 2014 *Edge of Tomorrow*, or Denis Villeneuve's 2016 *Arrival*, just to name a few.

Probably the most notable and insistent director within the current, Nolan has brought the trend to the blockbuster level. His 2006 *The Prestige*, 2010 *Inception* and 2014 *Interstellar* concluded, somewhat naturally, in his highly intricate *Tenet* in 2020, pushing the nexus between narrative experimentation and mainstream popularization to its limits. Parallelly, serial fiction

DOI: 10.4324/9781003197911-7

in television has witnessed a similar development: Mark Frost and David Lynch's 1990–1991 *Twin Peaks* and, later, J. J. Abrams, Jeffrey Lieber and Damon Lindelof's 2004–2010 *Lost* paved the way towards increasingly intricate narrative innovations within the mainstream, resulting in an abundance of variously challenging shows—for example, from Lisa Joy and Jonathan Nolan's 2016–2022 *Westworld*, through Baran bo Odar and Jantje Friese's 2017–2020 *Dark*, to Frost and Lynch's "batshit crazy" (Mittell 2022) 2017 *Twin Peaks: The Return*—all of which were long unimaginable for the medium of television.

Without wanting to provide an excessive exploration of the various social and cultural aspects of the reasons behind the emergence and endurance of the trend (see these, in more detail, in Manovich 2001; Kinder 2002; Johnson 2006; Mulvey 2006; Cameron 2008; Ang 2011; Kiss 2012; Mittell 2015; Kiss & Willemsen 2017), I will only briefly highlight two contextual factors that played a key role. Firstly, most of these formally innovative and mentally challenging films capitalized on the novel affordances of *technological advancements*: while, for example, analogue (VHS) and later digital (laser disc, DVD, Blu-Ray, and VOD) consumer-friendly and consumer-accessible time-shifting technologies have given agency and (inter-)active control to viewers in their hermeneutic quests, widespread access to broadband internet has provided a communication channel and interactive platform for participatory engagement and collective intelligence. Filmmakers frequently design their narrative experiences in ways that take advantage of viewers' increasing familiarity with and use of these technical goods:

> For example, doppelgänger and other schizophrenic stories and their corresponding narrative modes – multilinear, forking-path or loop – are said to be prompted by our customary practice of digital lossless copying, our familiarity with hyperlink and database logic, the habitual virtualisation of our selves through varied avatars on videogame and other online platforms, and our routine in the creation and maintenance of different social media profiles to express the diversity of our *multiple characters*, both professional and private.
>
> *(Kiss & Willemsen 2017: 14)*

Secondly, afforded by these technological developments, new *economical demands* emerged within the industry. Television programmes and movies that encouraged, if not demanded, multiple viewings were favoured. The arrival of specialized, 24/7 broadcasting television channels preferred more sophisticated shows that gratified their new model of "Most Repeatable Programming". Television's "MRP model has infiltrated Hollywood" (Johnson 2006: 163), resulting in an increasing abundance of films with "rewatchability value", luring viewers to either return to the box-office, buy the film as a physical medium, or rent it at a streaming provider. Instead of determining whether these technological advances and their resultant economical shifts *reflected* (Everett 2005), *encouraged* (Johnson 2006), were *answered by* (Buckland 2014) or *extended in* (Cameron 2008), *feedbacked* (Hayles & Gessler 2004), *set the stage for*, *impacted*, or merely *coincided with* (Mittell 2015) the emergence of the trend—that is, instead of further investigating the trend's contextual aspects—let me get back to, and put under an analytical loupe, the film-texts themselves.

What is common and most remarkable in these films and television shows is their various experimentations with storytelling techniques and, often as a result of these, entanglements of storyworlds. This prominent creative reoccurrence, manifesting in non-linearity and inversion (e.g., in *Memento*), forking paths (Spike Jonze's 2002 *Adaptation*), networks (Alejandro G. Iñárritu's 2006 *Babel*), multiple embedded storylines (*Inception*), alternative futures (Jaco Van Dormael's 2009 *Mr. Nobody*), perplexing metalepses[1] (Quentin Dupieux's 2014 *Reality*), and other formal-structural kinds of playfulness, has been recognized relatively early and labelled by scholars as "puzzle" (Bordwell 2006; Klinger 2006; Mittell 2006; Panek 2006; Buckland 2009), "modular" (Cameron 2008), or, essentially, as "complex" film narratives (Staiger 2006; Simons 2008).

Early theoretical reflection attempted to channel this emerging stream and its new terminology of *simple*, *complex*, and *puzzle* narratives into more general currents of *classical* (Bordwell et al. 1985), *post-classical* (Wyatt 1994; Thanouli 2006, 2009), or even *post-post-classical* modes of cinematic narration (Elsaesser & Buckland 2002). Film scholars hold different opinions over whether contemporary complex films fully deconstrue the rules of classical film narration or mostly just offer playful variations of well-established strategies. On the one hand, David Bordwell and Kristin Thompson see puzzle films as "unconventionally conventional" (Bordwell 2012) and "complicated rather than complex" (Bordwell & Thompson 2019: 61), and, by that, somewhat downplay the trend's innovations as mere intensifications of still-prevailing classical norms and rules (see also Bordwell 2002a, 2002b)—a "creative renewal within flexible but firm limits" (Bordwell 2006: 103). On the other hand, scholars like Allan Cameron and Warren Buckland "disagree with Bordwell's contention that 'offbeat storytelling' has become 'part of business as usual' in Hollywood" (Cameron 2008: 5) and assert that "the majority of forking-path/multiple draft/puzzle films are distinct in that they break the boundaries of the classical, unified mimetic plot" (Buckland 2009: 5). For Buckland, puzzle plots extend "far beyond" the Aristotelian complexity concept (on which tradition Bordwell's classical norms are based), representing a distinct "third type of plot that comes after [the simple and] the complex plot" (ibid.: 3). Puzzle films, Buckland argues, are "intricate in the sense that the arrangement of events is not just complex, but complicated and perplexing; the events are not simply interwoven, but entangled" (ibid.: 3). Without wanting to do justice to these claims and their resulting taxonomies, by seeing this development either as a trend or tendency, or rather as an altogether new narrative mode, one can realize that the set of films labelled as cinematic puzzles are too heterogenous (see the variety of films discussed in Buckland 2009 anthology) and, what is more, their excess of complexity that supposed to characterize and, thereby, justify a distinct and general category of "puzzle films" is often fairly limited.

Indeed, the complexity of puzzle films cannot be described by only studying these films' formal aspects; the trend's idiosyncrasy could be better tested by taking account of the actual effects they evoke in their viewers too. *Simple*, *complex*, or *puzzle* films should not be studied and classified only by the extent to which they complicate the relationship between their stories and storytelling modes, or through close narrative and stylistic analyses that can lead to arguments for their interrelation, in terms of classical and (post-) post-classical modes of representation, but also (or even especially) by the differences in the actual viewing experiences they offer. According to this distinction, the essence of narrative complexity does not lie in a variety of formal structures mapped by narratologists' descriptive methods, but in a degree of sensed mental confusion—i.e., hindrance in viewers' comprehension and meaning-making routines—explained by *cognitive poetics* (Stockwell 2002; Tsur 2008). Such a cognitive approach colours existing taxonomies, differentiating movies in regard to their relative complexity: that is, their ability to cause various states of cognitive puzzlement and trigger diverse mental responses in their viewers. In all, beyond merely focusing on the striking formal-structural experimentations visible on the surface of the film text, one also needs to concentrate on "what really matters": that is, on the intricate "mind games" (Elsaesser 2009) puzzle films play with their audiences.

The Puzzling Effects of Manipulating the Narration and the Narrated

For the above reasons, the understanding of the functioning of puzzle films demands an explanatory nexus that brings together narrative and cognitive approaches. Close analyses of film-textual triggers and their effects on the viewing experience are particularly pertinent in regard to complex narratives of which film-texts are innovatively experimental and whose effects result in stimulating mental challenges. Therefore, connecting formal and experiential dimensions—that is, itemising the different storytelling strategies of puzzle film narratives and revealing how these play on viewers' cognitive processes and routines—is the ambition of this section. The goal is to provide an insight into how complex narrative features evoke certain psychological and aesthetic responses in their viewers.

Complexity—a sense of temporary or lasting cognitive puzzlement regarding comprehension and meaning-making—can be prompted through a range of manipulations across many parameters of cinematic narratives. Puzzle films experiment with a variety of key *narration* features, such as (1) the segmentation of the telling, (2) disruption of story-logic, (3) manipulation of the plot's communicativeness, and (4) playing games with characters' points of view and focalization. These manipulations go hand-in-hand with complex situations in the *narrated*, like (I) deviations of diegetic chronology, (II) presentation of overwhelmingly complex stories and character relations, (III) implied instability in character-continuity, or (IV) creation of openly incongruent diegetic worlds. Let me take a closer look at these recurring manipulations of complex storytelling and storyworlds, couple them with their cognitive effects, and test their functioning through some concrete film examples.

Manipulations of *narration*—that is, with the way stories are told—include the following strategies:

1 Probably most frequently, but at least most noticeably, puzzle films experiment with the segmentation of the telling of their stories. Non-linear, inverse, or (multiple) embedded plot trajectories may result in a challenging experience through problematizing viewers' habitualized reliance on narrative linearity and its natural chronology. Dismantling narrational chronology often requires extra concentration from viewers, activating an increasing reliance on their working memories, retrospective reading, and other mental reorganization efforts. If piecing together a shattered narrative has cognitive costs, then why do filmmakers put their viewers into such a position? Why are stories not always told in chronological order? The reason, in Joseph D. Anderson's words, lies exactly in the effort of the viewing process: "in some cases stories may create a more dramatic effect, greater emotional impact if rearranged" (Anderson 1998: 149).

   Indeed, viewers' mental investment against drastic disruptions of the chronological order of the presented events might pay off, either for the aesthetic or emotional experience of the film at hand. Concerning aesthetic payoffs, viewers' confrontation with the partly inverse chronology of *Memento*'s plot, for example, might help their identification with the film's protagonist, Leonard Shelby, by bringing their experiences close to that of the character's anterograde amnesia. As for emotional upshots, in Gaspar Noé's rape-revenge horror *Irréversible* (*Irreversible*, 2002), changing the chronological order between beautiful and repulsive moments has a clear impact on the way audiences' emotions develop during their viewing: by revealing a relationships' horrible end in advance, and then only showing its lovely beginning at the end of the film, the audience is denied any emotional change (that would have happened in a chronological version)—instead, the grim experience is established early on and kept throughout. Although emotionally less demanding, François Ozon's 2004 inversely told marriage drama *5 × 2* achieves the same effect.

2 Disruption of story-logic, often a consequence of a non-linear narration, is another commonly used technique in contemporary puzzle films. While a disordered narrational chronology does not necessarily hinder comprehension—as the unproblematic understanding of flashbacks or flash forwards in classical narratives proves—disruption in the logical order of telling a story has more serious consequences on viewers' meaning-making. In the process of classical storytelling, as it is elsewhere put, "chronology is often subordinated to narrative logic; what should be shown first for the sake of the story trumps the chronological order of events. The 'right order of time' is subservient to the 'right order of events'" (Kiss & Willemsen 2017: 38).

Playing on such a rational rule of thumb, puzzle films do not only put off the right order of time, but often also entangle the right order of events. They either disorder their chronology without justifying it with some causal necessity in the story, or simply mess up causality altogether. In complex films, the restoration of a broken link between causality and chronology is often withheld or outsourced to the viewers, requesting their contribution to solve the film's puzzle. For example, on the one hand, in *Memento*, the reversed chronology that inverts the film's causal chain moderately challenges viewers without confusing them. The partly inverse plot, moreover, is justified by the film's strategy of facilitating viewers' identification with the protagonist. On the other hand, in more experimental "multiple-plot" films, like Tom Tykwer and the Wachowski's 2012 *Cloud Atlas*, the wrinkles of the disjointed causality cannot simply be ironed out within the story, thus inviting viewers to come up with more extra-diegetic inferences about the reasons behind such loose continuity and permanency among the film's actions and characters.

Full and irreparable disruption of story-logic might trigger viewers to switch their interpretative frame from the classical to the art-cinema narrative domain, where causality is not a must and its absence does not necessarily need to be justified. For this reason, movies like Alain Resnais's 1961 *L'année dernière à Marienbad* (*Last Year at Marienbad*) should not be mistaken with contemporary puzzle films. *Marienbad* does not only withhold, delay, or outsource the restoration between chronological or causality aspects, but entirely disallows—if not intentionally works against—our chances of fixing these unambiguously: "Films like Resnais's *La Guerre est finie* and Ruiz's *Mysteries of Lisbon* … don't need to keep spelling out and providing alibis for their formal strategies. In these films, it takes a while for us to figure out the shape of the game we're playing, and sometimes we just can't" (Bordwell & Thompson 2019: 62).

3 Feelings of puzzling complexity can also be achieved through the strategic manipulation of the plot's communicativeness. In Bordwell's definition, "the degree of communicativeness can be judged by considering how willingly the narration shares the information to which its degree of knowledge entitles it" (Bordwell 1985: 59). Hence, communicativeness with regard to complexity does not refer to the quality or even veracity of the information provided, but to the quantity of the information being suppressed. A strategic selectiveness from the available information the narration holds, or rather, withholds from the film's knowledge (Ibid.: 57–58), often becomes the source of complexity. Complexity, in this case, is not about departing from veridical information (or "lying"), but only about withholding crucial information.

Suppressiveness can be employed to mislead and, potentially (but not necessarily), confuse the viewers. For example, while there is nothing confusing in the strategic and rather consequential suppressiveness of Bryan Singer's 1995 *The Usual Suspects* (except, perhaps, for its ending's brief moment that could be better described as surprising), the holding back of key information in Duncan Jones' *Source Code* causes the film to play a mind game with its confused audience throughout most of its running time (the ending's twist works less as a surprise than as a revelation: a quasi-scientific explanation, based on the theory of "envatment" and its idea of brain simulation, that rationalizes the film's multidraft narration and, in so doing, brings some alleviation to the perplexed audience).

4 The distinction between the quality and quantity of information that the narration is holding or withholding brings me to highlight the final narrative strategy that elicits viewers' puzzlement through playing games with characters' point of view and focalization. High narrative communicativeness might particularly result in viewer confusion if the trustworthiness of the verbose communicator and, therefore, the veracity of the extensively communicated is questionable. An oversharing of false information (false to the storyworld), facilitated by storytelling techniques, is often utilized as a complexifying manipulation in puzzle films. Dubious and, consequently, confusing diegetic information provided by either deliberately lying or unconsciously fallible characters is not these characters' "fault" but part of the narration's cunning puzzle game plan.

Malcolm Rivers' (Pruitt Taylor Vince) split personality disorder in James Mangold's 2003 *Identity* or Soo-mi's (Lim Soo-jung) schizophrenia in Jee-woon Kim's 2003 *Janghwa, Hongryeon* (*The Tale of Two Sisters*) are all concealed by the narration's various strategies, such as seemingly unmotivated non-linear plot segmentations or hidden shifts of focalization, resulting in unmarked subjective realism. Unlike other unreliable twist movies, such as Alfred Hitchcock's 1950 *Stage Fright* or M. Night Shyamalan's 1999 *The Sixth Sense*, in which the film's confusion is being avoided and, certainly, delayed until the brief moment of the final twist (in fact, an unobstructed supply of misleading information is precisely a pre-requisite for maximizing the effect of these films' twists), *Identity* and *The Tale of Two Sisters* fall under the earlier—cognitively—defined category of complex films: their narrative non-linearity and disguised focalization, filtering the diegetic reality through these characters' mischievous or innocently frail mental views and presenting these as confusingly objective realities, bring about a complex narrative that is puzzling *throughout* most of the viewing experience.

Up until now, I described complex formats of *narration*, such as (1) the segmentation of the telling, (2) disruption of story-logic, (3) manipulation of the plot's communicativeness, and (4) playing games with characters' points of view and focalization. The following points (I–IV) represent manipulations of the *narrated*—that is, when complexities arise from spatially or temporally unnatural disruptions in the storyworld (compared to our natural real world and its mimetic diegeses in fiction):

I Puzzling effects can be achieved through deviations of diegetic chronology. Unlike non-linear storytelling that complexifies the experience through disordering the ordinary sequentiality of the telling, in achronological storyworlds non-chronology is an intrinsic feature of the narrated fictional diegesis. Intricate time travel (e.g., Terry Gilliam's 1995 *12 Monkeys*), tangled multiple universes and complex parallel metaverses (e.g., the tangent universe in *Donnie Darko* or the alternate universe in J.J. Abrams, Alex Kurtzman and Roberto Orci's 2008–2013 television series *Fringe*), confusing time-based loops (e.g., Christopher Smith's 2009 *Triangle*) and other strange and impossible storyworld temporalities provide challenging experiences through their deviations from viewers' real-world and embodied experiential backgrounds.

While both achronological storytelling and achronological storyworlds function through non-linearity and deal with time, I have, in previous work (Willemsen & Kiss 2020), proposed to distinguish between the cognitive effects of the complexities that either come from manipulating the arrangement of information (the plot) or from a fictional unnaturalization of the diegetic world (the story). While a complex experience in the case of non-linear storytelling results mainly from an increased cognitive effort required by a chronological (re)ordering of the non-chronologically presented events, achronological storyworlds (and their various forms of diegetic time structures that are phenomenologically non-experienceable thus non-relatable) elicit puzzling effects through undermining core processes of viewers' mental, situational, or event model formation (Johnson-Laird 1983; Van Dijk & Kintsch 1983; Zwaan 1999, respectively), thus problematizing the very parameters by which spatiotemporal connections between narrative events can be established (Willemsen & Kiss 2020).

Either way, concerning strategies of both achronological storytelling and achronological storyworlds, one can observe a trade-off that compensates for each of these strategies' complexifying effects and thus maintains these films' cognitive manageability; as much as disrupted narrative segmentation often works with perfectly chronological stories, achronological diegetic worlds are frequently presented by following a single focalizing character's trajectory throughout. Films that do not conform to these "unwritten rules" but combine achronological storytelling with achronological storyworlds—like Shane Carruth's 2004 *Primer* or Michael and Peter Spierig's 2014 *Predestination*—present intense (if not impossible) challenges to their viewers' attempts of meaning making.

II Viewers' confrontation with overwhelmingly dense stories and their complex web of character relations can be a source of a puzzling experience too. Diegetic understimulation (or under-determined narration)—in which essential story elements are either absent or minimal and stretched out to form a loose causal chain—is of less concern here due to their different perceptual, emotional, or interpretive challenges that typically belong to art-cinema narratives. On the other hand, diegetic overstimulation, eliciting viewers' cognitive overload, may result in meaning-making difficulties that characterize contemporary complex cinema.[2]

Overstimulatingly dense stories overwhelm viewers with their endless storylines, excessive number of events and countless characters. For example, Tomas Alfredson's 2011 *Tinker Tailor Soldier Spy* or Stephen Gaghan's 2005 hyperlink movie *Syriana* overstimulates us by providing an "overabundance of facts" (Chisholm 1991: 392) in their stories. These films' "detail overload" (ibid.) can either inspire viewers to allocate more cognitive resources—in the form of an intensified reliance on their attention and working memory—in order to keep track with their complex stories (as Alfredson's film may require), trigger some "forensic" (Mittell 2009) activities, such as rewatching the film or going online to read others' explanations, or allow for a frame switch through which viewers, while stepping off from the film's cognitive treadmill, look at the overwhelming experience not as a puzzle to be solved but as an allegorical illustration of the complexity of the story it aims to tell (in this way, the somewhat desperately confusing experience that *Syriana*'s extremely tangled representation elicits can be seen as the "point" of the film, confronting the viewer with the desperate image of the extremely tangled global oil politics without compromising such a serious problem through forcing it into some simplistic representation).

III Various forms of (implied) instabilities of character-continuity—character splittings, doublings and multiplications—are often not triggers of complexification in themselves but, in fact, come into existence as confusion-eliciting consequences of the above-listed manipulations of the narrated. Doppelgängers, like Jess (Melissa George) and her fight with her own infinite reincarnations in *Triangle*, or Hector (Karra Elejalde) and his attempts to outsmart his other selves of Hector 2 and Hector 3 in Nacho Vigalondo's 2007 *Los cronocrímenes* (*Timecrimes*), appear as inevitable outcomes of fictional diegetic worlds characterized by non-chronological and other fantastical non-natural features. Spatiotemporal loops caused by time traveling (as in *Looper*) or transgressions between alternative universes (presented through flash-sideways in the final—sixth—season of *Lost*) "naturally", and for sure logically, result in diegetic characters' encounters with other version(s) of themselves. Such encounters are not only confusing for the diegetic characters, but also mind-bending for the viewers. Violating our real-world frames and universally shared principles of "mutual belief" (Walton 1990) and "minimal departure" (Ryan 1991), doppelgänger scenarios force us to reconsider one of the strongest existential beliefs about our own singularity and uniqueness, and moreover, require us to sort out the paradoxical scenarios that result from such diegetic and existential confrontations.

While, in most of the cases, character multiplications appear as fictional facts that come from following the logic of these fantastical storyworlds (if we could go back in time, we would "inevitably" meet our younger selves or ancestors), in some other fictional occasions the confusion arises from uncertainty about the diegetic reality-status of the presented double. For example, in Denis Villeneuve's 2013 *Enemy* viewers' confusion comes from the ambiguity concerning the diegetic actuality of Adam and/or Anthony (Jake Gyllenhaal). Villeneuve's film adaptation turns José Saramago's 2002 novel *O Homem Duplicado* (*The Double*) into a puzzle. *Enemy* exchanges the single supernatural impact that comes from Saramago's biological anomaly of presenting an "existing double" (a fact in the novel's fiction) for an uncanny complex enigma in the film, challenging both Adam and/or Anthony and the viewers through facilitating a careful balance among at least two interpretive possibilities: instead of being a supernatural or magical realist tale of a real character duplication (à la Saramago), the film is most likely a subjective realist story in which either Anthony is Adam's frustrated hallucination or Adam is Anthony's guilt-ridden projection.

IV Slightly related but distinct from the third and fourth aspects of narrative strategies facilitating viewer puzzlement through concealed unreliability (either through the telling's withholding of information or by its high communicativeness of untrustworthy falsities), confusion can also surface

from an open communication of a diegetic world's inherent incongru-
ence. Some puzzle films create, as Umberto Eco would put it, "impossible
possible worlds" (Eco 1994: 77): i.e., "storyworlds that are seemingly
coherent and in compliance with the logic of generic and real-world laws,
but which, amidst this seeming coherence, also host narrative elements
that will strike viewers as remarkably dissonant (with regard to both the
internal laws of the storyworld and our sense of real-world logic)" (Kiss
& Willemsen 2017: 85).

Transforming the spatial logic of the famous "Penrose steps" (referred
to and, in fact, reconstructed in Nolan's *Inception*) or Maurits Cornelis
Escher's perplexing works (see Ryan 2013 analysis of Escher's 1956
lithograph *Print Gallery*) into diegetic three-dimensional spaces, impossible possible storyworlds in puzzle films elicit effects comparable to the
experiences we have when we look at these artworks. They cause intense confusion and force viewers to come up with creative hypotheses
to explain how such uninhabitable and impossible spaces, in terms of
real-world experientiality, can still form a coherent spatiotemporal universe within their fiction, in which characters' actions and reactions can
unfold in a seemingly continuous causality. Time-based loop narratives,
such as *Triangle* and *Looper*, metaleptic puzzle films, like *Adaptation* and
Reality, or stories preying on quantum theory, like James Ward Byrkit's
tellingly titled 2013 *Coherence*, earn part of their engaging potential by
inviting viewers to take up the challenge and somewhat integrate these
films' incompatible spatial building blocks into a comprehensively coher-
ing diegetic structure.

(For a detailed embodied-cognitive explanation of what allows viewers
to make sense of strange and impossible storyworlds and temporalities, see
Willemsen & Kiss 2020; as to how they experience the confrontation with
such complexities' emerging effects, see Ros & Kiss 2018; and regarding the
subsequent question of what audiences can ultimately do with such unnatural and impossible experiences, see Alber 2009, 2013; Kiss & Willemsen
2017: 111–118.)

Diegetizing the Narration into the Narrated: Christopher Nolan's Fantastical Puzzles

Memento's very first scene, in which Leonard Shelby (Guy Pearce) kills Teddy
(Joe Pantoliano), is played in reverse as the time of the scene runs backwards.
The first shot of the film presents us with a gruesome photo, showing a dead
man soaked in blood, undeveloping and *subsequently* sliding *into* a Polar-
oid camera which *then* goes off with a flash in Leonard's hands. Then, in
a steady montage, we see blood streaming backwards, an empty gun shell,

blood-covered glasses, and the victim we know from the photo. Suddenly, a gun jumps *into* Leonard's hands, *after* which, out of the victim's head, a bullet shell explodes into the gun. Teddy, with his glasses flying back on, comes *back* to life, turning and shouting at Leonard: *!oN*. The function of this technical-aesthetic choice is to warm up the viewer for the film's non-linear storytelling technique, which oscillates between linear and inversely told plot-bits: a choice that in 2000—a relatively early moment of the com-plexity trend—was just as much stylistically bold as dramaturgically neces-sary for the contemporary audiences, unprepared for such narrative trickery. The technique of literal reversion returns some 20 years later in Nolan's *Tenet*; however, this time, the function of the scene changes considerably: *Memento*'s viewer-conditioning gimmick turns into an inherent diegetic fea-ture of *Tenet*'s fantastical world. As Nolan has put it in an interview,

> I had this notion of just a bullet getting sucked out of the wall and into the barrel of a gun. It's an image that I had in *Memento* ... I always harbored this ambition to make a film where the characters had to deal with the physical reality of that.
>
> *(Khal 2020)*

Highlighting the significant difference in the functioning of time reversion in these films helps me in formulating a proposition by which I claim to discern a pattern in the dramaturgy of Nolan's fantastical puzzle films. I see *literaliza-tion*, or more precisely, *diegetic fictionalization* of various complex narration techniques into the narrated fictional world as a recurring creative strategy that does not only characterize but fully defines his puzzle film cycle, consist-ing of *The Prestige, Inception, Interstellar*, and *Tenet*. I will briefly go through these films, one by one and in chronological order, and highlight the various manifestations and puzzling effects of this recurring strategy. However, I start with a somewhat surprising absentee of this series: *Memento*—a film that, while it undoubtedly offers a unique puzzling experience, should be excluded from this list as its production followed a rather traditional course of fitting a narrational form to a pre-existing story (and not the other way around).

Memento's plot composition experiments with a non-linear segmentation of its told story (thus falling under the first of the above-listed aspects of nar-rative manipulation). The reason (or excuse) for the film's sawtooth narra-tion, alternating between linear and inverse scenes, is "to put the viewer in the same condition as the main character, sharing his anterograde amnesia, the impossibility of making new memories" (Ghislotti 2009: 90). Certainly, the in-verse plotline's function is to help viewers in their identification with Leonard; however, the experience of narrative inversion is clearly not the same as—only comparable to—one's suffering from short-term memory problems.

This is because, while both narrative and psycho-physiological conditions disrupt causality, what inversion means for us is "only" a prioritization of *effects* and a delaying of access to their *causes*. For Leonard, who is living in a permanent present of *effects*, there's no access to (short-term) *causes* at all, on which hopeless condition he is desperately trying to compensate by collecting—that is, fabricating—"facts" through photos, notes, and tattoos.

Even though the film qualifies as a puzzle narrative, inviting the viewer to team up with Leonard in piecing the story's scattered fragments together, it isn't guided by the creative filmmaking strategy that I claim to see as recurring in Nolan's ensuing puzzle film cycle. In fact, according to the film's production history (Mottram 2002), *Memento*'s development followed a rather traditional screenwriting trajectory in searching for a fitting narrational form that could support an original story. Telling a story about an amnesiac protagonist (written by the director's brother, Jonathan Nolan) compelled the subsequent screenwriting process of finding a fitting narrative form (by the director himself), by which viewers could approximately take the distorted perception of the protagonist and therefore make the puzzle operable.

All things considered, in *Memento* there is no diegetic fictionalization; on the contrary, the film was built in a conventional sequentiality originating in a *content* that is in need of a fitting form to be able to elicit a functional *effect*. For similar reasons, neither Nolan's 1998 feature debut *Following* nor his 2017 *Dunkirk* should be seen as part of the writer-director's puzzle film cycle, as these films' complexity, although fully motivated in their particular stories, remain on the level of the storytelling (achronological narration doses a story to maintain its mystery and maximize the surprise effect of its twists in *Following*; crosscutting supports the suspense by bringing three parallel storylines that unfold at different speeds into a joint climax in *Dunkirk*). It seems as if Nolan's creative strategy of literalization needs to reach out to the domain of the fantastical to become operable.

The Prestige, adding exactly such a fantastical element, is Nolan's first puzzle film that originates from the creative idea of diegetic fictionalization of a narrative feature. Since this film, just like *Memento*, is also an adaptation of an original novel, written by British writer Christopher Priest in 1995, it is necessary to acknowledge that the idea behind such dramaturgical creativity is essentially Priest's merit. Either way, the creative concept of a narrative feature's diegetic fictionalization becomes a recurring method in Nolan's subsequent original screenplays.

Beyond some less-substantial differences in the framing of the story, both the book and its film adaptation are about a bitter rivalry between two nineteenth-century magicians, Robert (in the book, Rupert) Angier (Hugh Jackman) and Alfred Borden (Christian Bale), over the perfection of the ultimate magic trick "The Transported Man". The novel's epistolary narration is translated into a doubled focalizer structure in the film, alternating between the perspectives of Angier and Borden on the history of their competition and ensuing enmity. Being bright magicians in the hands of Priest and Nolan, they aren't only tricking their diegetic audiences or each other, but us extra-diegetic viewers too. Their best magic tricks do not occur on stage but through their strategic bluffs and lies: in narrative terms, through their untrustworthiness and unreliability. Such narrative unreliability, facilitated thus by focalization through untrustworthy characters (aspect 4 in the above list), combined with a non-linear segmentation of four timelines (aspect 1) and high suppressiveness in the telling (aspect 3), together, (science-)fictionalize the film's genre.

This delicately withheld genre shift, switching from period drama to science–fiction by introducing the process of teleportation, not as a magician's illusion but as a fantastical feature in the diegetic reality (aspect III), brings about a solution to the film's puzzle in a switch from the film's illusory doubles (Borden and his secret identical twin Fallon) to real doppelgänger double figures (Angier's clone-multiplication as the side-effect of his actual teleportation). The challenge for the viewer is to recognize and embrace this genre switch; that is, to realize that these stage magicians aren't even that brilliant without the real teleportation machine invented (in the diegetic fiction) by Nikola Tesla (David Bowie), allowing Angier to come up with his "New Transported Man" "trick".

All in all, *The Prestige* cleverly plays with and, when it finally changes its genre, ultimately reverses the interpretive ambiguity of Villeneuve's *Enemy* back into a clarity that characterizes Saramago's original fiction. Presenting a clear but fantastical solution, the film earns its *prestige* when the apparently realist period drama's puzzling unreliability resolves in a fantastical turn of the introduction of the biological anomaly of real character doubling.

Inception's original story was written by Nolan himself. This is the first time since *Following* that he is directing his own story, from which creative method he won't look back up until, and including, his latest *Oppenheimer*, premiering in 2023 (with the sole exception of his 2012 franchise film *The Dark Knight Rises*).[3] While such a clear shift towards personal projects could probably be best described by pointing out a successful filmmaker's progress to economic independence, here, I aim to highlight the recurring creative aspect that this change towards more authorial control has brought about. By that, *Inception* could be seen as the first clear example of the manifestation of the productive idea—the diegetization of narrative features into a fiction's narrated world—which will characterize his coming fantastical puzzle films.

The film introduces a fictional world in which Dom Cobb (Leonardo DiCaprio) and his team are hired by business magnate Mr. Saito (Ken Watanabe) to "incept" an idea into the subconscious of Robert Fischer (Cillian Murphy), the would-be heir of a powerful conglomerate and, thus, rival of Saito's corporate interest. The team, secretly joining him in a long-haul flight, sedates Fischer and enters into his dream. To keep their operation unnoticed and, by that, avoid any suspicion about the origin of the planted idea, they create a less-suspicious multiply embedded dream labyrinth, ultimately extending its levels to four layers "deep", among which they move in and out, or rather, up and down.

As I have outlined elsewhere, in *Inception* "Nolan 'diegetises' the narrative feature of the embedded structures' metaleptic transgressions" (Kiss 2012: 37). He explores the inherent potential of narrative features like embedded storytelling and metalepsis, the latter of which is a transgressive and ontological intrusion between conventionally well-sealed embedded story-levels (see, e.g., Genette 2004; Pier 2005, 2013; Wolf 2005; and also, my first footnote), and transforms these into some fictional features and physical laws of his built diegetic world. Making the process of inception a scientific possibility in the film's fantastical reality, Nolan fictionalizes the storytelling strategies of narrational embedment and metalepsis, appearing in the film as complex transgressable dream-within-a-dream layers, architected by Ariadne (Elliot Page as Ellen Page) and criss-crossed by the film's characters.

Notably, this diegetic fictionalization of a narrative feature, which here manifests as a "literalization of the metaleptic logic", means that the film doesn't actually present any metalepses as narrative tropes. There is no real transgression between embedded narrative levels, at least there's none in narratological sense, because the film's embedment is only illusory as being part of the fiction: it is not narrative but diegetic, i.e., it is part of the diegetic fiction between its uppermost reality-level (the long-haul flight between Sydney and Los Angeles) and lower "hypodiegetic" layers (Ariadne's dream-design). Speaking of complexity, describing it as a sum effect of a diegetic fictionalization of the above-listed narrational aspects, the film's puzzling challenge comes from its narrative's non-linearity—crosscutting among and even within four alternating strands, plus dropping a hard-to-place conversation between a hazy Cobb and an aged Saito at the beginning of the plot (all these fall under aspect number 1)—combined with a gradually emerging uncertainty about Cobb's lucidity—that is, about the narrative's subtle undermining of its own reliability (aspect 4)—which results in the much-discussed ambiguity of the film's final shot concerning the reality-status of the diegesis' uppermost level.

Interstellar, co-written with his brother Jonathan, is the next in Nolan's personal film projects that fits into his gradually shaping creative filmmaking pattern. The film guides us to a dystopian near-future of an imminent climate catastrophe, where mankind's only survival hope lies in a space mission led by a group of astronauts searching for a habitable planet as an alternative to the dying Earth. Following a series of adventures and confrontations with a variety of obstacles, their leader, Joseph Cooper (Matthew McConaughey), finds himself in a black hole called Gargantua. Speeding through it, he enters the "tesseract"—a kind of window through which the natural unity of spatiotemporality is rearranged—allowing Cooper to coexist in his own present and past, and, by that, to deliver an important message, at two different moments in the past, to his daughter Murph (Mackenzie Foy and Jessica Chastain).[4]

The film's complexity does not really stem from the difficulties that come from its extensive efforts to maintain scientific accuracy in this fiction, but from yet another literalization of narrational features that set the diegetic stage and invent science-fictional laws to the unfolding events. While, according to Bordwell and Thompson, "the principles of astrophysics and the conventions of science fiction motivate some storytelling innovations" (Bordwell & Thompson 2019: 49), looking at the recurrence in Nolan's artistic inventiveness, I would add: innovations in storytelling principles motivate a novel configuration between the film's science and fiction, i.e., between the story's accuracy to astrophysics and the convention of time-travel in the sci-fi genre.

The particular narrative technique that converts into a key feature in *Interstellar*'s narrated story is "crosscutting"—an editing technique that alternates between two or more lines of action, happening in different places but (usually) occurring simultaneously in time. In its typical cinematic appearance, "a crosscut sequence presents a variation in *rate of change* between the story lines. One line of action often seems to move more slowly than another" (ibid.: 22). In Bordwell and Thompson's illustrative example, derived from D. W. Griffith's crosscutting innovation, "the villains are inches away from breaking into the cabin/the hero is miles away/the villains are almost inside/the hero is just arriving" (ibid.: 37).

Such narrational "cheat", on the one hand, is a standard tool of dramatization and thus does not disrupt viewers' general feelings about the simultaneity of the alternating actions. On the other hand, such temporal disparity can be deliberately reflected upon, as Nolan does here, by turning it into the physical rule of the fiction's fantastical storyworld. This idea, although only as an arbitrary rule, is already present in *Inception*, with the embedded dreams having their own "clock", with time slowing down the deeper (in terms of levels) characters descend. Using the 1:20 ratio of Cobb's calculation, a ten-hour flight on the uppermost reality level allows for spending about a week in the first dream level, roughly half a year in the second, and almost ten years in the third. In *Interstellar*, the idea of time-disparity returns as a time dilation in the storyworld—this time even scientifically justified, showing its central role in the story (see Nobel laureate in Physics and *Interstellar*'s scientific advisor Kip Thorne's astrophysical explanation in Thorne 2014).

The consequences of the diegetic literalization of crosscutting's inherent effect—that is, the rule according to which time is running at different speeds on different planets—becomes the central source of the film's emotional drama. The storyworld's natural law, according to which one hour spent on an interstellar planet lasts seven years on Earth, does not only cause a devastating delay in the reunion of Cooper and Murph, but also allows for Murph to grow up and become a scientist, who is now able to decipher her father's encrypted communication from the tesseract. The time-disparity between father and daughter totals around 84 Earth years: Cooper skips 23 Earth years on Miller's planet, 51 while entering the black hole, and naturally ages another ten years during the entirety of his mission, including the time he spends in hypersleep.

All in all, *Interstellar*'s hermeneutic challenge does not (only) result from its scientific complexity (the same story could be told through a more straightforward modern physics-influenced "actualist" fiction: see Strehle 1992), but (more) from a complex diegetic fictionalization of the traditional narrative feature of crosscutting between spatially parallel but, time-wise, simultaneous actions (an intensified playfulness with aspect 1 in the above list), resulting in a fantastical fiction with deviated diegetic chronology (aspect I) and apparent character multiplication (aspect III).

Tenet's bullet, blasting back into the Protagonist's (John David Washington) revolver is unlike *Memento*'s—only aesthetically motivated—reversed gunshot. *Tenet*'s inverted bullet is part of the diegetic possibilities that the fiction's fantastical physical laws allow. In such a dystopian reality, scientists invent the ability to reverse entropy in objects and in people. Russian oligarch Andrei Sator (Kenneth Branagh) plans to use the consequence of this invention—which, from the film's chronological point of view, is experienced as some kind of "traveling back in time"—to start World War III. Without further explanation, following the above consecutive inventory of creative techniques, it must now be clear what Nolan, once again, is doing here: he takes a narrational technique, this time inversion (a specific category within aspect 1), and turns it into a physical law of his unfolding fiction.

The narrational inversion's diegetic fictionalization combined with the narration's suppressed communicativeness, mainly about the Protagonist's associate Neil's (Robert Pattinson) identity, plans and actions (aspect 3), and then all this being told in a non-chronological order, results in a level of complexity with which most of the film's (intended mainstream) audiences are unable to cope. The sum consequence of establishing a bi-directional world hosting an already rather dense story—turning the film's narrative into a palindromesque "temporal pincer" of a part-chronological, part-inverted diegetic chronology (aspect I), in which characters meet and even fight with their own backward-moving inverted selves (aspect III), and where the Protagonist and the inverted Neil have already met in Neil's past, thus in the Protagonist's future—is that it becomes a cognitively unmanageable hermeneutic challenge for most of the film's overstimulated audiences (aspect II).

Piecing Puzzles to Form a Pattern: A "Nolanesque Auteurism"

Complexity is trending in contemporary narrative cinema, where it should be understood more as a cognitive effect than a narrative feature. A mental hindrance on one's hermeneutic efforts of creating explicit or referential meanings, however, does not simply fall from the sky, but is triggered by various manipulations of some familiar (known from viewers' classical narrative literacy or real-life experientiality) aspects of the narration and the narrated.

Through a particular and recurring manipulation that brings narration and the narrated into a specially motivated nexus, Christopher (and Jonathan) Nolan's cinema seem to mark out a distinct pattern within the trend, that derives from his (their) consequently applied creative idea that I have called the *literalization* or *diegetic fictionalization* of a narrative feature into the narrated story. Overall, I agree with Bordwell and Thompson's conclusion, who, through a discernment of similar consequentiality in Nolan's writing and filmmaking practice, defined a "Nolanesque auteurism". Indeed, the writer-director's signature method is his recurring "formal project": through "an urge to explore a specific set of storytelling techniques (…) Nolan zeroes in, from film to film, on a few narrative devices" (Bordwell & Thompson 2019: 6). My contribution to this insightful observation is thus a specification of what exactly he is doing with those storytelling techniques and narrative devices, and by that, distinguishing his fantastical puzzle film cycle. As earlier observed, remarkably, only the oeuvre's fantastical fictions fit the claim and support the forming pattern: even though *Following*, *Memento*, and *Dunkirk* all represent clear formal-structural experimentation with some puzzling effects, their complexity remains on the level of narration. On the other hand, as I have argued throughout, Nolan does not only select narrative techniques to play with and ultimately design some novel *narrational* forms (as he does, for example, in *Memento*) but also exploits the inherent creative potentials of these techniques by turning them into some fantastical laws of his *narrated* storyworlds. Certainly, this method is not his invention; as we have seen, similar diegetization propels Priest's original novel *The Prestige*, as well as other imaginative science-fiction stories (for example, Villeneuve's *Arrival* and its fictionalization of flash-forward-based non-linearity into the film's storyworld, resulting in the protagonist's fantastical "clairvoyance", comes to my mind). What makes the Nolanesque auteurism, however, is a consequent fascination with and consistent utilization of this particular method's creative potential.

Notes

1 The concept of "metalepsis" was introduced by Gérard Genette in his 1972 Discours du récit, defined as "any intrusion by the extradiegetic narrator or narratee into the diegetic universe (or by diegetic characters into a metadiegetic

universe, etc.), or the inverse [...], [that] produces an effect of strangeness that is either comical [...] or fantastic" (Genette [1972] 1980: 234–235). Specifying the options of such violations of distinct narrative levels, Marie-Laure Ryan distinguishes between unintended, covertly "unnatural" level-contaminations, that are mere "rhetorical metalepses", and deliberate, overtly playful transgressions that are "ontological metalepses" (Ryan 2006: 247). "The one based primarily in the (rhetorical) effects produced by representation through discourse or other semiotic means, the other in the problems of logical paradox encountered by modern science" (Pier 2011: 3). Rhetorical metalepses, on the one hand, do not aim at breaking the immersion; they are, according to William Nelles, "unmarked" (Nelles 1992: 93) or, for Genette, "ordinary and innocent" (Genette 1980: 235). On the other hand, ontological metalepses are "marked" (Nelles 1992: 93) and "'genuine' type[s] of metalepses" (Wolf 2005: 89), which overtly foreground their stories' fantastic or metafictional quality. By laying bare their fictionality, ontological metalepses establish fictional transgressions between otherwise well-separated story levels. Genette's example is Cortázar's *Continuity of Parks*, in which short story the protagonist is apparently threatened by a fictional character from a book he is reading. Formal-narrative experimentations of contemporary complex films embrace ontological metalepses, utilizing the concept's potential for devising either logical paradoxes or fantastic, metafictional and other puzzling scenarios (see later in my discussion of *Inception*).
2 This important distinction is based on our utilization (Kiss & Willemsen 2017: 140–182) of Bordwell's four-tier definition of cinematic meanings (Bordwell 1991: 8–9), in which we describe puzzle films as movies that mainly hamper comprehension of the *explicit* and *referential* levels, unlike most of the art films, which mainly trigger *implicit* and *symptomatic* types of meanings.
3 The writing of this chapter closed in June 2022.
4 The term "tesseract" is coined by mathematician Charles Howard Hinton in his 1884 article "What is the Fourth Dimension?". Hinton's notion of tesseract led to the discovery of non-Euclidian concept of spacetime, implying access to multiple spaces (simultaneously) and times (from the same location). In *Interstellar*, the tesseract is a grid-like structure, constructed by humans from millennia in the future, presenting time as a spatial and physical dimension.

References

Alber, Jan 2009. 'Impossible Storyworlds – And What to Do With Them', *Story-Worlds: A Journal of Narrative Studies* 1: 79–96.
Alber, Jan 2013. 'Unnatural Narratology: Developments and Perspectives', *Germanisch-Romanische Monatsschrift* (special issue, ed. Ansgar Nünning) 63 (1): 69–84.
Anderson, Joseph D. 1998 [1996]. *The Reality of Illusion: An Ecological Approach to Cognitive Film Theory*. Carbondale, IL: Southern Illinois University Press.
Ang, Ien 2011. 'Navigating Complexity: From Cultural Critique to Cultural Intelligence', *Continuum* 25 (6): 779–794.
Bordwell, David 1985. *Narration in the Fiction Film*. Madison, WI: University of Wisconsin Press.
Bordwell, David 1991 [1989]. *Making Meaning. Inference and Rhetoric in the Interpretation of Cinema*. Cambridge, MA: Harvard University Press.
Bordwell, David 2002a. 'Film Futures', *SubStance* 31 (1): 88–104.
Bordwell, David 2002b. 'Intensified Continuity: Visual Style in Contemporary American Film', *Film Quarterly* 55 (3): 16–28.

Bordwell, David 2006. *The Way Hollywood Tells It*. Berkeley, CA and Los Angeles, CA: University of California Press.

Bordwell, David 2012. 'Tinker Tailor: A guide for the perplexed', *Observations on Film Art*. 23 January. Available online at www.davidbordwell.net/blog/2012/01/23/ tinker-tailor-a-guide-for-the-perplexed (retrieved 6 December 2021).

Bordwell, David, Janet Staiger and Kristin Thompson 1985. *The Classical Hollywood Cinema*. London, UK: Routledge.

Bordwell, David and Kristin Thompson 2019. *Christopher Nolan. A Labyrinth of Linkages*. Second edition, Madison, WI: Irvington Way Institute Press.

Buckland, Warren 2009. 'Introduction: Puzzle Plots', in Warren Buckland (ed.) *Puzzle Films: Complex Storytelling in Contemporary Cinema*. Oxford, UK: Wiley-Blackwell, 1–12.

Buckland, Warren 2014. 'Introduction: Ambiguity, Ontological Pluralism, and Cognitive Dissonance in the Hollywood Puzzle Film', in Warren Buckland (ed.) *Hollywood Puzzle Films*. London, UK: Routledge, 1–14.

Cameron, Allan 2008. *Modular Narratives in Contemporary Cinema*. Basingstoke, UK: Palgrave Macmillan.

Chisholm, Brad 1991. 'Difficult Viewing: The Pleasures of Complex Screen Narratives', *Critical Studies in Mass Communication* 8 (4): 389–403.

Eco, Umberto 1994 [1990]. *The Limits of Interpretation*. Bloomington, IN: Indiana University Press.

Elsaesser, Thomas 2009. 'The Mind-Game Film', in Warren Buckland (ed.) *Puzzle Films: Complex Storytelling in Contemporary Cinema*. Oxford, UK: Wiley-Blackwell, pp. 13–41.

Elsaesser, Thomas and Warren Buckland 2002. *Studying Contemporary American Film*. London, UK: Arnold.

Everett, Wendy 2005. 'Fractal Films and the Architecture of Complexity', *Studies in European Cinema* 2 (3): 159–171.

Genette, Gérard 1980 [1972]. *Narrative Discourse*. Ithaca, NY: Cornell University Press.

Genette, Gérard 2004. *Métalepse. De la figure à la fiction*. Paris: Seuil.

Ghislotti, Stefano 2009. 'Narrative Comprehension Made Difficult: Film Form and Mnemonic Devices in *Memento*', in Warren Buckland (ed.) *Puzzle Films: Complex Storytelling in Contemporary Cinema*. Oxford, UK: Wiley-Blackwell, 87–106.

Hayles, N. Katherine and Nicholas Gessler 2004. 'The Slipstream of Mixed Reality: Unstable Ontologies and Semiotic Markers', in *The Thirteenth Floor, Dark City*, and *Mulholland Drive*', *PMLA: Publications of the Modern Language Association of America* 119 (3): 482–499.

Hinton, Charles Howard 1884. 'What Is the Fourth Dimension?', *Scientific Romances* 1: 1–22.

Johnson, Steven 2006 [2005]. *Everything Bad Is Good for You*. London, UK: Penguin Books.

Johnson-Laird, Philip N 1983. *Mental Models: Towards a Cognitive Science of Language, Inference, and Consciousness*. Cambridge, UK: Cambridge University Press.

Khal 2020. "It's Tricky': Christopher Nolan Assembles the 'Tenet' Puzzle.' *Complex*, December 14. Available online at https://www.complex.com/pop-culture/2020/12/ christopher-nolan-tenet-interview?utm_campaign=musictw&utm_source=twitter. com&utm_medium=social (retrieved 6 December 2021).

Kinder, Marsha 2002. 'Hotspots, Avatars, and Narrative Fields Forever – Buñuel's Legacy for New Digital Media and Interactive Database Narrative', *Film Quarterly* 55 (4): 2–15.

Kiss, Miklós 2012. 'Narrative Metalepsis as Diegetic Concept in Christopher Nolan's *Inception*', *Acta Film and Media Studies* (5): 35–54.

Kiss, Miklós and Steven Willemsen 2017. *Impossible Puzzle Films. A Cognitive Approach to Contemporary Complex Cinema*. Edinburgh, UK: Edinburgh University Press.

Klinger, Barbara 2006. *Beyond the Multiplex: Cinema, New Technologies, and the Home*. Berkeley, CA and Los Angeles, CA: University of California Press.

Manovich, Lev 2001. *The Language of New Media*. Cambridge, MA: MIT Press.

Mittell, Jason 2006. 'Narrative Complexity in Contemporary American Television', *The Velvet Light Trap* 58: 29–40.

Mittell, Jason 2009. '*Lost* in a Great Story: Evaluation in Narrative Television (and Television Studies)', in Roberta Pearson (ed.) *Reading Lost*. London, UK and New York, NY: I. B. Tauris, 119–128.

Mittell, Jason 2015. *Complex TV. The Poetics of Contemporary Television Storytelling*. New York, NY: New York University Press.

Mittell, Jason 2022. 'How Not to Comprehend Television: Notes on Complexity and Confusion', in Steven Willemsen and Miklós Kiss (eds.) *Puzzling Stories: The Aesthetic Appeal of Cognitive Challenge in Film, Television, and Literature*. New York, NY and Oxford, UK: Berghahn, 259–277.

Mottram, James 2002. *The Making of Memento*. London, UK: Faber and Faber.

Mulvey, Laura 2006. *Death 24x a Second. Stillness and the Moving Image*. London, UK: Reaktion Books.

Nelles, William 1992. 'Stories within Stories: Narrative Levels and Embedded Narrative', *Studies in the Literary Imagination* 25 (1): 79–96.

Panek, Elliot 2006. 'The Poet and the Detective: Defining the Psychological Puzzle Film', *Film Criticism* 31 (1–2): 62–88.

Pier, John 2005. 'Metalepsis', in David Herman, Manfred Jahn, and Marie-Laure Ryan (eds.) *Routledge Encyclopedia of Narrative Theory*. New York, NY: Routledge, 303–304.

Pier, John 2013. 'Metalepsis', *The Living Handbook of Narratology*, 13 March. Available online at http://lhn.sub.uni-hamburg.de/index.php/Metalepsis.html (retrieved 21 June 2022).

Ros, Veerle and Miklós Kiss 2018. 'Disrupted PECMA Flows: A Cognitive Approach to the Experience of Narrative Complexity in Film', *Projections* 12 (1): 71–96.

Ryan, Marie-Laure 1991. 'Possible Worlds and Accessibility Relations: A Semantic Typology of Fiction', *Poetics Today* 12 (3): 553–576.

Ryan, Marie-Laure 2006. *Avatars of Story*. Minneapolis, MN: University of Minneapolis Press.

Ryan, Marie-Laure 2013. 'Impossible Worlds and Aesthetic Illusion', in Walter Bernhard and Werner Wolf (eds.) *Aesthetic Illusion in Literature and Other Media*. Amsterdam and New York, NY: Rodopi, 131–148.

Simons, Jan 2008. 'Complex Narratives', *New Review of Film and Television Studies* 6 (2): 111–126.

Staiger, Janet 2006. 'Complex Narratives, an Introduction', *Film Criticism* 31 (1–2): 2–4.

Strehle, Susan 1992. *Fiction in the Quantum Universe*. Chapel Hill, NC and London, UK: The University of North Carolina Press.

Stockwell, Peter 2002. *Cognitive Poetics: An Introduction*. London, UK: Routledge.

Thanouli, Eleftheria 2006. 'Post-Classical Narration: A New Paradigm in Contemporary Cinema', *New Review of Film and Television Studies* 4 (3): 183–196.

Thanouli, Eleftheria 2009. *Post-Classical Cinema: An International Poetics of Film Narration*. London, UK: Wallflower.

Thorne, Kip 2014. *The Science of Interstellar*. New York: W. W. Norton and Company.

Tsur, Reuven 2008. *Toward a Theory of Cognitive Poetics*. Brighton, UK and Portland, ME: Sussex Academic Press.

Van Dijk, Teun and Walter Kintsch 1983. *Strategies of Discourse Comprehension*. Academic Press.

Walton, Kendall 1990. *Mimesis as Make-Believe: On the Foundations of the Representational Arts*. Cambridge, MA: Harvard University Press.

Willemsen, Steven and Miklós Kiss 2020. 'Keeping Track of Time: The Role of Spatial and Embodied Cognition in the Comprehension of Non-linear Storyworlds', *Style* 54 (2): 172–198.

Wolf, Werner 2005. 'Metalepsis as a Transgeneric and Transmedial Phenomenon', in Jan Christoph Meisler, Tom Kindt, and Wilhelm Schernus (eds.) *Narratology Beyond Literary Criticism*. Berlin and New York, NY: Walter de Gruyter, 83–107.

Wyatt, Justin 1994. *High Concept. Movies and Marketing in Hollywood*. Austin, TX: University of Texas Press.

Zwaan, Rolf A. 1999. 'Five Dimensions of Narrative Comprehension: The Event-Indexing Model', in Susan R. Goldman, Arthur C. Graesser, and Paul van den Broek (eds.) *Narrative Comprehension, Causality, and Coherence: Essays in Honor of Tom Trabasso*. Mahwah and London, UK: Lawrence Erlbaum Associates Publishing, 111–134.

PART II

Art Cinema

6

REALISM, TIME, AND AMBIGUITY

Narration in Art-Cinema

Paul Taberham

Art cinema has been described as "a diffuse, heterogeneous label that applies to many historical periods and types of filmmaking" (Buckland, 2020, p. 81), a "mongrel" defined by "impurity" (Galt and Schoonover, 2010, p. 3), and "capacious enough and flexible enough" to tolerate different styles and audiences (Forbes and Street, 2000, p. 40). Responding to David Bordwell's influential article "The Art Cinema as a Mode of Film Practice" (1979) which identifies key narrational traits of art cinema that distinguish it from classical narration (i.e., Hollywood and other popular forms), Eleftheria Thanouli claims that art cinema is too heterogenous to be cast as a cohesive paradigm of narration (2009, p. 1).[1] In *Theorizing Art Cinemas: Foreign, Cult, Avant-Garde, and Beyond* David Andrews favours Steve Neale's "more supple" (2013, p. 174) article "Art Cinema as Institution" (1981) which frames the field in terms of its sources of finance, circuits of production, distribution, and exhibition, its relationship to the state and the discourses used to support it (Neale, 1981 [reprinted 2002], p. 103) rather than its narrational strategies. Andrews adds "art cinema is a dynamic, global category that theorists must come to grips with somehow. But they can't do so through a *unified* theory of art-cinema narrative" (2013, p. 174 [italics added]).

As Geoff King notes (2019, p. 9), any thorough account of art cinema needs to acknowledge both the institutional factors and the textual qualities. But despite its institutional dimensions and textually amorphous character, this chapter will illustrate how there are narrational strategies that can be identified which make the field distinct from mainstream cinema, and these can be explained through a *non-unified* theory of art-cinema narrative. The proposal will be advanced that there are three principal, interconnected modes of art cinema narration which cover much (though not all) of the

DOI: 10.4324/9781003197911-9

field. They will be called realist art cinema, slow cinema, and the film enigma, with most films operating somewhere on a continuum between these modes. Before explaining these terms in detail, existing research by David Bordwell, András Kovács, and Paul Schrader will be outlined before my own observations, which stem from their insights.

The goal of this chapter, then, is twofold. The first is to acquaint readers with existing ideas about art cinema. Since it is intended as a survey, critical remarks will be light touch. The second goal is to offer the aforementioned modes as a response to previous accounts.

There is a wider debate about whether a commercial/art cinema dichotomy is too simplistic. Geoff King's *Positioning Art Cinema: Film and Cultural Value* (2019) explores the question of what qualifies as art cinema, claiming that it has no single definition although there are recurrent tendencies. Directors such as Béla Tarr and Michael Haneke are granted "heavyweight" status as producers of particularly challenging films, while others work with popular genres, such as Pedro Almodóvar (melodrama) and Johnnie To (crime films). In this chapter, the parameters for membership as an art film are not stringent, and so there will be examples that could be considered borderline cases, indie movies, cult movies, and outliers. All examples are included in the spirit that they would be putatively understood as art cinema or draw from that tradition, and are spaces where "indigenous cinema[s] can develop and make [their] critical and economic mark" beyond Hollywood's domination (Neale, 1981 [reprinted 2002], p. 104).

Art cinema is being defined here as a category rather than as a genre for two reasons.[2] First, genres generally work with consistent themes—gangster films are normally about the price of criminal success, screwball comedies feature odd couples and romance movies feature star-crossed lovers. In addition, certain genres aim for a particular emotional effect, such as comedy, tragedy or horror movies. Iconography normally tells you what genre a movie is (spaceship, saloon, ballgown, or trilby hat). While genres shift over time, there is still a consistent thread. No such consistencies exist in art cinema.

Generally, art cinema sits within the realm of psychological or social drama, but it does draw from genre conventions on occasion. They can either be outright genre movies, or they can use genre as a point of departure where conventions can be negated or challenged (King, 2019, p. 212). *Eyes Without a Face* (1960) and *Repulsion* (1965) are horror movies. *Smiles of a Summer Night* (1955) and *Playtime* (1967) are light comedies, while *Songs from the Second Floor* (2000), *The Lobster* (2015), and *Parasite* (2019) are dark comedies. *Seven Samurai* (1954), *Léon: The Professional* (1994), and *Oldboy* (2003) are action movies, while *Breathless* (1960), *Branded to Kill* (1967), and *Hana-Bi* (1997) are crime movies. *La Jetée* (1962), *Alphaville* (1965), and *Solaris* (1972) are sci-fi, and *Umbrellas of Cherbourg* (1964) and *Dancer in the Dark* (2000) are musicals. *W.R.: Mysteries of the Organism*

(1971), *In the Realm of the Senses* (1976), and *Titane* (2021) are erotic films. All are united under the umbrella term "art cinema" (or arthouse cinema), despite working with genre conventions.

There is less consensus as to how a screenplay should be written in art cinema when compared to mainstream cinema. Testament to this, consider the abundance of screenwriting manuals available for mainstream ventures which focus on motivated protagonists overcoming obstacles, such as Syd Field's *Screenplay: The Foundations of Screenwriting*, Robert McKee's *Story: Substance, Structure, Style, and the Principles of Screenwriting*, and David Trottier's *Screenwriter's Bible: A Complete Guide to Writing, Formatting, and Selling Your Script*. By contrast, no such equivalents exist for budding art cinema screenwriters. While this chapter won't remedy this absence, it will sketch out some of the key traits that generally distinguish art cinema narration from more mainstream movies.

The Bordwell Version

The first major statement on narration in art cinema remains the most influential: David Bordwell's aforementioned "The Art Cinema as a Mode of Film Practice," which was first published in the journal Film Criticism. He frames art cinema as a distinct mode of filmmaking that crystallised after World War Two, a result of Hollywood's decline in dominance and the flowering of various New Waves across Europe. It features a set of formal conventions which include a definable set of reading strategies and viewer expectations (Bordwell, 1979 [reprinted 2007], p. 152).

Focusing mainly on European art cinema of the 1950s and 1960s, Bordwell defines art cinema according to seven main characteristics: a loose cause-effect logic, three types of realism, two types of authorial expressivity, and ambiguity. Paraphrasing Warren Buckland's useful summary (2020, p. 85) of Bordwell's original article, these characteristics can be outlined thus:

Cause-Effect Logic

1 Art cinema defines itself against the continuous, unified cause-effect logic of classical narrative by loosening this logic and emphasising episodic structure.

Realism

2 Objective realism (a): location shooting with available light and *temps morts*.
3 Objective realism (b): the story world is complex, conflicting, and unpredictable, just as our own lives are.

4 Subjective realism: characters are psychologically complex and may suffer from "realistic" problems, such as feelings of alienation. They also lack clearly defined traits, motives, and goals but are likely to be highly articulate about their psychological states. They might drift aimlessly and unlike classical narration, the reaction is privileged over action.

Authorial Expressivity

Unlike mainstream movies, the director does not conceal themselves from the storytelling. The art film is to be read as "the work of an expressive individual" (Bordwell, 1979 [reprinted 2007], p. 155) This can mean two different things:

5 Unique stylistic signatures (e.g., camera angles, editing style, camera movements) can be attributed to the director.
6 Distinctive plot structures (how is the story being told? Why in this way?) which the literate viewer will recognise from the director's other works and will have already developed the appropriate viewing strategies.

Ambiguity

7 Realism and authorial expressivity are incompatible since realism derives from an effort to capture the world as it is, while authorial signatures require creative intervention. This contradiction is resolved through making the films ambiguous and open-ended. Either the world the characters inhabit is ambiguous, or their internal psychology is, or the director's creative input creates ambiguity.

This chapter on formal conventions, alongside Steve Neale's "Art Cinema as Institution" published in the journal *Screen* has been the most widely cited and influential text about art cinema. Despite this, Bordwell has stated that he has refined this original article with more informative texts since then (2007, p. 158), notably with *Narration in Fiction Film* (henceforth *NiFF*), where he expands art cinema narration into three distinct modes, called art-cinema, historical-materialist film, and parametric narration.

Additional key principles of traditional art-cinema narration are added to the original account. For example, deadlines as a temporal motivation of the plot don't tend to feature, but radical temporal manipulations might be applied. Genre conventions are usually avoided, but overt political didacticism is more likely to feature. There is an increased use of chance as a motivation, such as random encounters between characters, and open endings sometimes feature. There is also greater interpretive ambiguity, with use of mental states such as subjective realities, dreams, memories, and fantasies that may feature. Symbolism might also feature over realist imagery, challenging viewers to make sense of the ongoing narration.

Put concisely, historical-materialist cinema can be understood as a form of filmmaking with strong didactic principles that sought to offer a lesson about the world instead of mere entertainment (a *roman a thèse*). In addition, characters become prototypes (representatives of a broader social class) instead of individual protagonists furnished with complex psychology. Classical norms of space and time are defamiliarised in historical-materialist cinema, and there is a liberal use of montage editing with a faster cutting pace than the Hollywood convention of the time. It also self-consciously interrogates cinematic conventions. Historical-materialist cinema is principally located in Russian cinema from 1925 to 1933, though it later bore an influence on the French New Wave, and its use of montage editing came to influence cinema more generally.

Parametric narration is less historically located than historical-materialist films, and appeals instead to "isolated filmmakers and fugitive films" (1985, p. 274). Usually, the style of a film (cinematography, mise-en-scène, editing, sound design) guides our experience of the plot (events as they are presented in the film), which in turn shapes our broader construction of the story (events seen and inferred, in chronological order). By contrast, parametric narration places equal importance on style as it does on plot, with a small set of stylistic devices recurring systematically that are subtly decorative. The style of the film does not change to fit the demands of the story—rather, it is given equal weight to the storyline instead of working in service of it. The word "parametric" derives from the parameters directors choose to work within. Robert Bresson, Carl Dreyer, Yasujirō Ozu, and Kenji Mizoguchi are presented as key exemplars of this approach.

At the time of writing NiFF, Bordwell had about 45 years of art cinema history to draw from if we take post–World War II Italian neorealism as the starting point. Today, another 40 years have elapsed and the landscape has shifted. As he notes in his afterword to a reprint of "Art Cinema as Mode of Film Practice" in *Poetics of Cinema* (2007, pp. 158–169), European figures such as Ingmar Bergman, Federico Fellini and Michelangelo Antonioni belong to a specific historical period of art cinema rather than epitomising the field today. Other national cinemas have emerged since then, such as Hong Kong New Wave, New Iranian Cinema, and New Mexican Cinema. Movements such as *cinema du look* and Dogme 95 ran their course, and Indie cinema, which treads an aesthetic and institutional line between art house and the mainstream emerged. Some art cinema conventions such as the open endings eventually bled across into blockbuster movies. In addition to all this, the emergence of videocassettes, DVDs, Blu-ray, and streaming services like The Criterion Channel, Mubi, and Kanopy have broadened access to world cinema and allowed repeated viewings.

Bordwell returned to this subject in 2012 with the blog titled "How to Watch an Art Movie, Reel 1," offering an informal primer in art-cinema comprehension strategies.[3] It is more journalistic in tone than the previous publications as a blog rather than an academic piece, but some of the earlier ideas are expanded on. He explains that art films "cultivate *intrinsic norms*, storytelling methods that are set up, almost like rules of a game, for the specific film. In a way, every film [trains its spectator]" (Bordwell, 2012). Intrinsic norms are contrasted with *extrinsic* norms, filmmaking conventions of genre, structure, style, and theme which audiences will be familiar with through years of cinema viewing. Both art cinema and ambitious Hollywood movies try to update their traditional intrinsic norms. It is possible for intrinsic norms to eventually become extrinsic norms through repetition and normalisation. For instance, a flashback was traditionally marked by dissolves, wobbly music, or voice-over comments signposting as such. In the 1960s, art film directors developed other techniques to denote flashbacks such as a switch to black and white, an abrupt switch to an out-of-context scene, or slow motion. Soon, these intrinsic norms were copied and normalised by Hollywood, becoming extrinsic conventions.

Experienced art cinema viewers will already tacitly understand the various viewing strategies and formal features that are typical of art cinema, but they are explicitly coaxed out by Bordwell in the aforementioned blog. He observes that formal details are paramount—the way in which the story is presented is as important as what is presented. Art films might rework familiar story actions, but transform them through narrational choices (e.g., suppress some information) or shoot the action in an unusual way. As such, they heighten our awareness of both ordinary life and the conventions of art. In addition, there will always be some images, sounds, or scenes that resist easy sense-making. Information flows differently in art cinema too—exposition can be left to the imagination, so the viewer must be prepared to fill in a lot and expect to occasionally be wrong. While Hollywood tends to apply *redundancy*, sharing important story points multiple times, this is less common in art cinema. We may also need to research outside the film to understand the context of the story, and they sometimes need to be watched two or more times to be fully appreciated.

Since some art films are quite laconic and economical in expression, Bordwell comments that patience is often required. Physical space isn't just used as a neutral container for the clash of characters pursuing their goals. Instead, blocks of space contain moments that function like descriptive passages in a novel, we might be invited to see spaces in terms of their abstract design. Instead of revealing character through conflict, in many art films "character is revealed—or kept under wraps—through *routines*. This strategy puts an emphasis on what the person is like when not grappling with problems—on what we might call their enduring natures, or [...] their essential mystery" (ibid.). Art films also present life as one thing after another, not necessarily one thing *because of* another. Parallels matter more than causality in many art films, and they may give us nascent conflicts that are never developed or paid off. Mimicking real life, characters may come and go without preparation and chance events may divert the plot.

This account echoes Bordwell's original 1979 article in the sense that it offers a consortium of traits one will typically find in art cinema to varying degrees. But the elements detailed here are not to be understood as a checklist that needs to be met for membership as an art film. As such, I would suggest that David Andrews' charge that Bordwell casts art cinema as a form that can only be narrated in a single way (2013, p. 174) as a misconstrual. Rather, his account should be understood as what is known in philosophy as a cluster concept, which is defined by a "weighted list of criteria, such that no one of these criteria is either necessary or sufficient for membership" (Matthen, 2010).

To date, Bordwell's account of narration in art cinema remains the most useful, given its abiding influence. However, we can ask if there are trends in art cinema narration which can be categorised in a way that helps viewers locate shared features and commonalities. Bordwell's distinction between realist art cinema, historical-materialist narration and parametric narration points the way. But realist art cinema is exceedingly broad, while parametric and historical-materialist narration is very narrow. As such, the next section will look at two different theories that offer alternative typologies of art cinema.

Alternative Accounts

The following concepts presented by Paul Schrader and András Kovács offer additional useful theories of art cinema which can productively co-exist with Bordwell's original formulations, overlapping with one another in places. We can begin with Schrader's typology, featured in the edition of *Transcendental Style in Film: Ozu, Bresson and Dreyer* published in 2018. He divides art cinema into three types: the surveillance camera, the art gallery, and the mandala.

The surveillance camera is defined by the absence of editorial judgment or statement. It focuses on quotidian, day-to-day reality with minimal human intervention. As Schrader concisely puts it, "Turn the camera on, let it record" (2018, p. 25). *Umberto D* (1952) is cited as an early pioneer of this approach, though *Jeanne Dielman, 23, quai du commerce, 1080 Bruxelles* (1975) (henceforth *Jeanne Dielman*) offers a clearer example. Films with extended walking sequences also lean towards the surveillance camera, such as Rossellini's *Viaggio in Italia* (1954), Antonioni's *L'Avventura* (1960), and Gus Van Sant's *Elephant* (2003).

Works that follow the art gallery tradition break into three different iterations: dream cinema, structural cinema, and abstract cinema. Dream cinema
is characterised as a collage of associative imagery connected to surrealism
and its subsequent offshoots, as seen in the work of Jean Cocteau, Jean Epstein, Germaine Dulac, Maya Deren, and Sergei Parajanov. In structural cinema, films pursue a predetermined path as seen in the works of Michael
Snow, Hollis Frampton, and Ernie Gehr. Abstract cinema includes non-
figurative work as seen in some of the films by Walther Ruttmann, Oskar Fischinger, Norman McLaren, and Jordan Belson. All three iterations of the art
gallery, according to Schrader, take pure light and colour as their endpoint
(ibid., p. 29).

The mandala leads the viewer into a meditative state, a "cinema of inaction" (ibid., p. 30) using the medium to evoke a feeling of quietude. Bresson
is taken as an early pioneer in taking inaction as a cinematic tool, though
subsequent films took it to greater extremes, such as Andy Warhol's *Empire*
(1964), Abbas Kiarostami's *Five Dedicated to Ozu* (2003), Michelangelo
Frammartino's *Le Quattro Volte* (2010), and James Benning's *Twenty Ciga-
rettes* (2011) Films that observe to the point of trance. The endpoint of the
mandala is silence, like the rock garden or flower arrangement that can be
meditated upon for hours.

Within Schrader's formulation of these three strands, there is a "Tarkovsky Ring" which splits the surveillance camera, art gallery and mandala
in two. Directors in the inner circle produce films for commercial theatrical
release, while directors outside the circle make films for festivals and galler-
ies. For the surveillance camera (minimal intervention or judgment), Chantal
Akerman and Gus Van Sant are inside the ring, while Ben Rivers and Wang
Bing are outside. For the art gallery (surrealist and abstract), David Lynch,
Sara Driver, and Parjanov are inside the ring, while Stan Brakhage and Nath-
aniel Dorsky are outside. For the mandala (inducing a meditative state), Carl
Dreyer, Nuri Bilge Ceylon, and Robert Bresson are inside the ring, while
James Benning and Ben Stamper are outside.

One of the key virtues in Schrader's model is that it splits "slow cinema"
into two distinct branches with the surveillance camera and mandala. The
flexibility of placing individual artists between poles is also valuable, rather
than boxing filmmakers into specific categories. For example, Kelley Reich-
ardt sits between the surveillance cam and the art gallery, while Alexander
Sokurov sits between the art gallery and the mandala.

An issue with the model arises from Schrader's claim that his model represents filmmakers who "broke free from the iron nucleus of narrative" (ibid.,
25). This suggests that the very centre of his model is narrative, and the further a filmmaker strays from the core, the further they drift from narrative.
As such, Yasujiro Ozu is close to narrative on the mandala line, Robert Bresson is further, and Apichatpong Weerasethakul is further still having passed

outside the Tarkovsky ring. James Benning is at the extreme end. This warrants further unpacking, if he is claiming the filmmakers are on a continuum with Ozu being about 90% narrative, Bresson being 50%, Weerasethakul being 30% and Benning at 0%. Is narrative and non-narrative to be understood as twin poles on a continuum instead of binary opposites? Don't Ozu, Bresson, and Weerasethakul's films remain decidedly narrative, given that they feature psychologically defined agents moving between causally linked events? In addition, his placement of David Lynch along the same art gallery line as Stan Brakhage, Tony Conrad, and Nathaniel Dorsky is surprising in its broad strokes, given his perceptive distinction between two different types of slow cinema.

For a more comprehensive typology of art cinemas, consider András Kovács' formulation which explores the field within Europe from 1950 to 1980 in relation to modernism, which was published 11 years prior to Schrader's model. Paraphrasing the influential art critic Clement Greenberg, at its core, modernism can be defined simply as "the aesthetic self-criticism of art" (Kovács, 2007, p. 12). Elaborating on this, he defines the three main principles of modern art as abstraction, reflexivity, and subjectivity. Kovács comments that the traits responsible for the modernist effect in narration are "*ambiguity* of the interpretation, the spectator's conscious intellectual *involvement* in the plot construction, and the *subjective* character of the story" (ibid., p. 62). In addition to this, he makes the important distinction between classical and modernist art films, emphasising the ambiguity of modernist films. He comments, "Classical art films make narration a multilayered, complex system, and the modernist art film makes this complex system essentially ambiguous or even self-contradictory" (ibid., p. 64). By reflexivity, he means that while cinema ordinarily conceals its own process of production, reflexive art draws attention to that process.

From here, Kovács goes on to identify four major trends in European art cinema during the modernist period: minimalism, naturalism, ornamentalism, and theatricality. Each category is broken into smaller subdivisions, acknowledging further the creative idiosyncrasies of individual auteurs. Prudently, Kovács notes: "Not all these tendencies were equally strong or influential in all periods during late modern cinema. As is often the case with matters of art historical categories, one can find only a few emblematic, clear cases of a given paradigm; most of the time we must suffice with mixed or transitory cases" (ibid., p. 140).

Offering a category that is comparable to Schrader's surveillance camera and mandala, Kovács defines *minimalism* as a "systematic reduction of expressive elements in a given form" (ibid.), a cinema of restraint. It provides a rich experience by paring back expressive elements instead of redundantly insisting on a given dramatic effect through music, colour filters, exaggerated performance, or conspicuous cinematography. This style was originally typified by mid-twentieth century directors like Carl Dreyer, Robert Bresson, Yasujiro Ozu, and Michelangelo Antonioni, though it has since seen a more recent resurgence with directors, such as Jim Jarmusch, Bela Tarr, Aki Kaurismäki, and Abbas Kiarostami.

Minimalism breaks into three categories. *Metonymic minimalism* (epitomised by Robert Bresson) makes extensive use of offscreen space, features highly elliptical narratives, and a "radically dispassionate" acting style (ibid., p. 141). *Analytical minimalism* (seen in Antonioni's work from 1957 to 1966) features "austere compositions associated with long takes and in some cases complicated and long camera movements" (ibid., p. 149), drawing the viewer's attention to their experience of time. Geometrical compositions tend to feature, and characters can be seen wandering landscapes in isolation, paralleling their state of mind. *Expressive minimalism* featured most prominently in Ingmar Bergman's work from 1961 to 1972. Like Bresson and Antonioni, Bergman reduced expressive formal elements during this period, making closed-situation dramas within bare and confined landscapes. But his work is different to the other two auteurs in that his style remains highly expressive, with abundant use of close-ups, expressionistic lighting, and more overtly dramatic performances (ibid., p. 142) (see Figure 6.1, Bergman's *Winter Light*, 1963).

FIGURE 6.1   Bergman's Winter Light, 1963.

The second trend, *naturalism* derives from the origins of most national art cinemas following World War II, notably Italian Neorealism, though Kovács comments that most of the European "new cinemas" debuted to some extent with a return to the representation of real-life experience. There are two sources of the naturalist style: socially committed neorealism and ethnographic documentary. In both forms, the naturalist film style "reminds the viewer of real-life experiences, either by the characters' natural way of acting and talking or by giving the image the style of a cinéma vérité documentary or newsreel (e.g., shaky handheld camera movements, wide-angle lenses, random panning around as if looking for a subject, characters communicating directly with the camera)" (ibid., p. 168). *Umberto D.*, *Saturday Night and Sunday Morning* (1960) and *The Sun in a Net* (1963) all fit this category. Even though the naturalist style heralded modern post-World War II art cinema, it is not to be identified with modernism proper (i.e., abstraction, reflexivity, and subjectivity) since narration is concrete, unambiguous, and non-reflexive in this form (ibid., p. 168).

Drawing together ancient culture with modernist aesthetics, *ornamentalism* is split into two forms: *folkloric* and *mythological* ornamentalism (ibid., p. 175). As the name suggests, the two principal sources for this style of cinema are national folklore and religious or mythological stories. Prototypical films include Pier Paolo Pasolini's *Oedipus Rex* (1967), Fellini's *Satyricon* (1969), Sergei Parajanov's *The Color of Pomegranates* (1969), and Miklós Jancsó's *Electra, My Love* (1974). While the visual style is more lavish than minimalism and naturalism, the ornamental style is not merely decorative. Instead of representing physical reality, surface details are intended to "convey some deeper meaning; they are meant to represent some kind of 'inner reality' and express fantasy, emotions, or a psychological state of mind allegedly inexpressible by elements of surface reality" (ibid., p. 175). Like Schrader's art gallery, oneiric, and surrealistic elements dominate ornamentalist films, they can be understood as representing the world of traditional mythologies as an unconscious mental structure that underlies "the cool, alienated, and technological surface of the modern world" (ibid., p. 182).

Finally, there is *theatrical* cinema, which gets its name from late modernist theatre conventions. Key characteristics of this approach include an unnatural and exaggerated acting style that emphasises artificiality rather than psychological realism, along with unnatural expressive lighting and artificial looking sets (ibid., p. 192). Kovács observes that in *Last Year at Marienbad* (1961), "all the characters talk and move as they were depicting a seventeenth-century French classical drama where gestures are overdramatized and symbolic at the same time. [...] the characters of *Marienbad* are pure artificial creatures with no reference to any kind of social or existential reality" (ibid., p. 193). *Fellini's 8½* (1963) also merges reality, memory, and fantasy, and both use high-contrast lighting and artificial acting styles, and overtly artificial costumes and sets (ibid., p. 194). The difference is that where *Fellini's 8½* drifts between fantasy and reality, *Marienbad* is entirely a mental projection.

Kovács' typology remains a valuable and perceptive system for categorising modernist European cinema within his chosen period of 1950–1980. In relation to the focus of this chapter, it is not a theory of narration as such, rather it identifies recurring themes and stylistic choices. The typology also narrows its focus to European cinema over a 30-year period. None of these are shortcomings of the theory itself, but they served as a motivator to see if I could formulate a broader model that covers art cinema from its origins in the 1940s up to the present day, covering a wider range of nationalities.

A New Model

Up to this point, Bordwell's realist art cinema, historical-materialist cinema, and parametric form have been surveyed, along with Schrader's surveillance camera, art gallery and mandala, and Kovács' minimalism, naturalism, ornamentalism, and theatricality. The goal was not to evaluate the relative merits of each model, but rather to acquaint the reader with each one and establish them in a context for my own model that will follow.

The model I formulated in Figure 6.2 connects back to Bordwell, Schrader, and Kovács' insights, offering a non-unified theory of art cinema narration. It is designed to be broad enough to encompass the social realism of *Bicycle Thieves* with the quiet contemplation of *Alice in the Cities* and the mysteries of *Last Year in Marienbad*.[4]

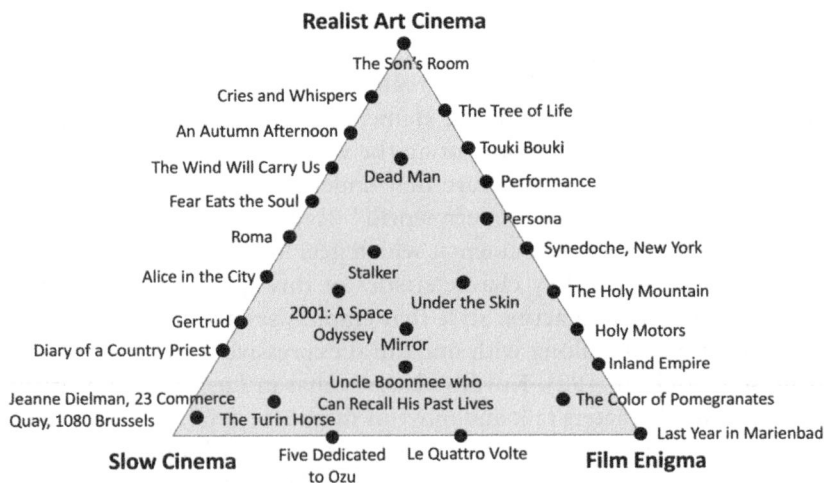

FIGURE 6.2   Most arthouse cinema (or movies influenced by that tradition of storytelling) sit on a continuum between three poles: Realist Art Cinema, Slow Cinema, and the Film Enigma.

The model comprises three poles: realist art cinema, slow cinema, and the film enigma. Realist art cinema can be identified primarily through traits already detailed in Bordwell's original 1979 article: a loose episodic structure, and revealing characters who are not pursuing a clearly defined goal, but experience various kinds of challenges. If the challenges are on an emotional level, such as *Cries and Whispers* (1972) or *Breaking the Waves* (1996), it is a psychological drama. If the challenges highlight a social problem such as *Rome, Open City* (1945), or *I, Daniel Blake* (2016), it is a social drama. It is common for realist art cinema to play a balance between the social and the psychological (social problems inevitably lead to psychological difficulties, and sometimes vice versa). The pacing is generally steady in realist art cinema as opposed to the more reflective pacing of art cinema, and the story (the sum total of events seen and inferred) is easy to discern from the plot (what we are shown, in the way we are shown it). In other words, ambiguity is downplayed, and viewer comprehension is not strained. This overlaps with Kovács' naturalist strand of art cinema.

The other two modes connect more directly to modernism, as it is cast by Kovács. The second is related to Bordwell's parametric form, along with Kovács' minimalist film and Shrader's surveillance camera and mandala, but will be called slow cinema—a term that has gained a wide currency in the last decade and has become the focus of a range of academic studies.[5] It picks up on aforementioned concepts, such as *temps mort*, a laconic style, patience being required, and space being used as an object of interest in and of itself instead of simply being a container for human interactions. In its purest form, there is less focus on characterisation or inner psychology and greater emphasis on the experience of filmic time.

The third mode which doesn't already have a name will be called the film enigma. This picks up on Schrader's art gallery and Kovács' ornamentalism and theatrical cinema, as well as Bordwell's identified techniques, such as ambiguity and resistance to sense-making, challenging viewer comprehension, unique stylistic signatures, and subjective realities. Like slow cinema, in its purest form it is light touch in its use of characterisation.

What are the key narrational strategies in these three modes? I suggest that realist art cinema emphasises internal psychology and emotional or social problems. Slow cinema reduces the speed of information flow, offering fewer story details for the viewer to follow. The enigma leaves informational gaps which are never explained or resolved, either by strategically withholding information or because they don't have a concrete meaning. The further a work pulls towards slow cinema and the enigma, the less emphasis is placed on character psychology and social concerns. Instead, they move more towards the evocation of mood, offering a more ethereal experience and are motivated in part by artistic self-investigation.

In Figure 6.1, film placement is subjective. Reiterating Kovács' prior comment, art historical categories most examples of a given paradigm are mixed or transitory, and there are few emblematic cases. As such, the most films are placed somewhere on a continuum instead of operating within a triangular Venn diagram since that would imply definite cut-off points between modes. Most films favour one mode over another, and some sit between all three.

There is space for variation between these three poles. *All About My Mother* (1999) and *Kes* (1969) could have equally been placed as archetypal classical art films alongside *The Son's Room* (2001) despite the fact they are tonally and stylistically distinct. But all putatively fit within a tradition of classical film art, directed by auteurs, featuring a readily comprehensible narrative and a pacing that would not put much of a strain on the average viewer. Likewise, there is much to distinguish *Last Year at Marienbad* from *The Color of Pomegranates*, but both could be described as evocative over concrete, poetic, and mysterious. The same principle applies to *Jeanne Dielman* and *The Turin Horse* (2011) as slow films despite their stylistic distinctions.

Realist Art Cinema

Since realist art cinema narration has already been outlined, we do not need to dwell on it again in detail. As stated, it can be distinguished from classical narration by its loosened cause-effect logic, emphasising an episodic structure and chance encounters. Mundane reality can feature, and the story world is more multifaceted than typical Hollywood fare in which good and evil are often easy to distinguish. Stories centre around ordinary people instead of archetypes (e.g., the mad scientist, renegade cop, Victorian schoolmarm), and the literate viewer will often recognise distinguishing stylistic or thematic flourishes which featured in the director's other works. Protagonists generally lack a clearly defined goal, and we are usually more focused on them and who they are, over what obstacles they are trying to overcome. Overt moral judgments on the events onscreen are often avoided. To clarify, the overriding sense of realism in this type of film does not come from the sense that we are watching a fly-on-the-wall documentary—behaviours and events are still streamlined, and dialogue isn't completely naturalistic. As Noël Carroll observes, movies (both arthouse and mainstream) reorganise and construct "actions and events with an economy, legibility, and coherence" that surpasses real life and intensifies our engagement with the screen (1996, pp. 86–87). Nonetheless, conventions of art cinema pull us closer to daily experience than what viewers are accustomed to in popular cinema.

Character-based emotional upheavals often feature, such as feelings of alienation during childhood and adolescence, as seen in *The 400 Blows* (1959), *Kes*, *Fish Tank* (2009), and *Blue is the Warmest Color* (2013). Or it can feature the fallout following sickness or death in the family, such as *All About My Mother, The Son's Room, Amour* (2012) and *Manchester by the Sea* (2016). Characters can be highly articulate about their emotions, as found in Ingmar Bergman's chamber dramas, or lacking self-knowledge, they can fall from grace such as Holly (Sissy Spacek) in *Badlands* (1973), Antoine (Jean-Pierre Léaud) in *The 400 Blows* or Bess (Emily Watson) in *Breaking the Waves*. They can lean towards slow cinema like *Cries and Whispers* and *Roma* (2018), or they can be highly phrenetic like *A Woman Under the Influence* (1974) and *Festen* (1998). As already noted, they can be either psychological dramas, or social dramas such as *Bicycle Thieves* and *Kandahar* (2001). Kovács comments:

> In classical art films the story is usually developed from the conflict between a particular character and a generally specified environment. The conflict cannot be eliminated by resolving a single well-defined problem. The more complex the character, the less need to have one single causal starting point in the exposition. Development of the conflict may appear step by step as we learn more about the main character's persona. Rational problem solving is not the main motivation in art films of classical narrative form, which develop psychological motivations for the plot to explain why the character acts the way he does.
>
> *(2007, p. 65)*

Despite the typical absence of goals, realist art cinema can sometimes feature objectives although instead of a conventional resolution, they are more likely to end in failure, bitter-sweet success or are never resolved. In *I, Daniel Blake*, the titular character spends the movie trying to overcome the (intentional) bureaucratic inefficiency that has prevented him from claiming the employment and support allowance which he is entitled to. At the end, he suffers a fatal heart attack just before his appeal takes place. Overall, this may be taken as a tragic ending, although the movie closes with his funeral in which we see his core integrity continue to inspire those who knew him.

Unlike realist art cinema, the modernist impulse that Kovács outlines—art as "an aesthetic reflection on and a critique of its own traditional forms" (2007, p. 16) is clearer in the other two modes outlined here—slow cinema and the film enigma.

Slow Cinema

The core traits of slow cinema date back to the long takes, minimalist styles and de-dramatised narratives of Carl Dreyer, Yasujiro Ozu, Bresson, Antonioni, Tarkovsky, and Jancsó. More recently, the contemporary slow cinema movement from international directors such as Béla Tarr, Tsai Ming-liang,

Nuri Bilge Ceylan, Pedro Costa, and Theo Angelopoulos has been framed as a somewhat nostalgic and exaggerated revision of what the earlier directors did (Çağlayan, 2018, p. 9).

The term slow cinema was kickstarted by Nick James in the April 2010 issue of *Sight and Sound*, characterising the movement pessimistically as an act of passive aggression against Hollywood's increasing domination of the film industry, though it eventually became a cliché in its own right (James, 2010, p. 5). Despite James' criticisms, the movement now had a name and received wide critical attention. Jonathan Romney offered an influential definition, describing it as a "varied strain of austere minimalist cinema" that is designed to offer "a certain rarefied intensity in the artistic gaze, [...] a cinema that downplays event in favour of mood, evocativeness and an intensified sense of temporality" (2010, pp. 43–44). Geoff King refers to these bleak, minimalist films as operating on the "heavyweight" end of the art cinema spectrum which are often celebrated by journalistic and academic critics (2019, p. 80).

As it is implied on the table in Figure 6.1, slow cinema is not to be taken as a complete break from realist art cinema. Many films can be placed on a continuum between the two modes with both featuring loose, incidental structures. Wim Wenders' *Alice in the Cities* sits between the two modes, operating as a road trip movie "about traveling and observing; it is constructed from a series of low-key episodic events loosely linked together by a travel itinerary" (Buckland, 2020, p. 84) featuring dead time that creates "space for reflection rather than a relentless focus on action" (ibid., p. 86). Other films such as *Jeanne Dielman* are more extreme in their reduction of narrative details.

Key distinctions from realist art cinema are that it employs longer takes, slower narrative pacing, an increased focus on daily activities, and a reduced focus on psychological characterisation. The human condition in general is more the focus than the specific individuals populating the film. Those simple distinctions yield important consequences. Paul Schrader observes that while film techniques are usually about *getting there*—telling a story, explaining an action or evoking an emotion, by contrast the long take is about *being there*. Time isn't used as a vehicle to tell a story, time is the goal (Schrader, 2018, p. 8). Remedying the modern age when "we are already bombarded with, overwhelmed by, and perhaps even fed up with images that are saturated with details, texts, meanings, messages" (Çağlayan, 2018, p. ix), expanding on the gaps between narrative developments and emphasis on dead time fosters a "ruminative mode of spectatorship" (ibid., x).

As Emre Çağlayan explains, "the extended experience of duration enables the absorption of a mediated reality with a luxury that we no longer possess in our daily lives, and the films are in many ways *making* us look and listen— and the longer we do, the more differently we can see and hear" (ibid., xi). He also reframes boredom as a positive expressive tool, "In contrast to boredom's conventional handling as a negative emotion, slow cinema uses it as a formal strategy: these films demand patience, attention and imagination, and are designed to transform idleness and monotony into a productive and aesthetically rewarding experience" (ibid., xiii).

While slow cinema is typically associated with "a tone of quietude and reticence" along with "an aura of unexplained or unearned anguish" (Quandt, 2009, 76), other effects are possible. Directors Jacques Tati and Roy Andersson have made unlikely use of dead time as a comedic tool in *Playtime* and *Songs from the Second Floor*. *2001: A Space Odyssey* (1968) uses long takes to evoke the vast, barren vacuum of outer space while creating an increasingly tense atmosphere. American indie directors have drawn from the aesthetics of slow cinema to (paradoxically) explore movie violence, with *Dead Man* (1995) (a Western) and *Ghost Dog: The Way of the Samurai* (1999) (a crime film) by Jim Jarmusch, and Gus van Sant's *Elephant*, which is based loosely on the events of the 1999 Columbine High School shootings.

The Film Enigma

Unlike realist art cinema narration and slow cinema, the film enigma does not already have a name with a wide currency. Put concisely, this mode can be defined principally by its use of ambiguity as an expressive tool. Putting greater demands on viewer comprehension than other modes of screen narration, the relationship between scenes in the film enigma can be resistant to interpretation, and dialogue can be oneiric. Strategically omitting expositional information that would allow viewers to comprehend onscreen events and sometimes employing obscure symbolisms, the film enigma leaves the viewer to creatively interpret its meanings, research to find out the artist's original rationale, or settle into its mysteries and feel the movie intuitively instead of trying to consciously understand it.

The film enigma might be described as illuminating the borders of the unconscious, as Stan Brakhage once evocatively described Tarkovsky's work (Brakhage quoted in White, 2005, p. 69), but they are not as radical a departure from narrative form as works from the avant-garde such as Brakhage's own *Mothlight* (1963) or *Dog Star Man* (1964). In the film enigma, we follow discernible protagonists through a series of events. But instead of following a conventional cause–effect logic, links between scenes may be indirect or implied through symbolic, conceptual, indirect associations or dream logic (Buckland, 2020, p. 86). Events depicted can be unusual or impossible, and standard rules of space, time and causality can be disrupted. Like slow cinema, in its purest form there is a decreased focus on psychological characterisation.

Inland Empire creates mystery through an unusual juxtaposition of scenes early in the film, going from a radio play to a hotel room in Poland, to a rabbit sitcom on television, to a Hollywood film star's mansion. Buckland observes that when the viewer cannot discern a meaningful motivation for actions, events, and stylistic flourishes within the film such as *Inland Empire's* blurring of faces on one occasion, or the seemingly unmotivated shift between colour and black and white, one has to look outside the diegesis to understand motivation, such as marking the presence of an expressive voice (i.e., Lynch himself) (ibid., p. 91). Harking back to Bordwell's distinction between objective and subjective realism in art cinema, subjective reality is depicted as if it is objective: "the director outside the storyworld presents the character's subjective delusions as if they were actual" (ibid., p. 92). Ambiguity, then, can be attributed to the storyworld itself, to the characters within the film, or to the director.

The earliest films to fit this tradition would include quasi-narrative avant-garde shorts,[6] such as *The Seashell and the Clergyman, The Fall of the House of Usher* (1928), and *Un Chien Andalou* (1929). Maya Deren's psychodramas *Meshes of the Afternoon* (1943), *At Land* (1944), and *Ritual in Transfigured Time* (1946) are also notable early examples. But pioneering feature films made for a paying audience (inside the Tarkovsky ring, as Schrader put it) would include Luis Buñuel's *L'Age d'Or* (1930) and Jean Cocteau's *The Blood of a Poet* (1932). Cocteau continued his work with *Orpheus* (1950) and *Testament of Orpheus* (1960).

As the influence of surrealism faded, a new wave of modernist filmmakers began making radical formal experiments in the 1960s and 1970s. Atmospheric works like Resnais' *Last Year at Marienbad*, Herzog's *Fata Morgana* (1971), Tarkovsky's *Mirror* (1975), Parajanov's *The Color of Pomegranates*, and Rivette's *Celine and Julie Go Boating* (1974) were produced. Buñuel also continued with works, such as *The Phantom of Liberty* (1974) and *That Obscure Object of Desire* (1977). In the same era, modernist ambiguity and reflexivity blended with psychedelia and counterculture in Chytilová's *Daisies* (1966), Cammell and Roeg's *Performance* (1970), Russell's *The Devils* (1971), and Jodorowsky's *The Holy Mountain* (1973). The film enigma is flexible enough to include the visual essay *Sans Soleil*, animations *Tale of Tales* (1979) and *Paprika* (2006), and horror movies such as *Don't Look Now* and *Hausu* (1977).

Ingmar Bergman shifted from psychological chamber dramas dealing with human relationships to modernist narrative features in the early 1960s, such as the open ending in *Winter Light* (1962), locating his story in abstract time and space in *The Silence* (1963), and the self-reflexive, ambiguous *Persona* (Kovács, 2007, p. 63). All of these devices lean towards the film enigma. Bergman himself once described cinema as something which should speak to its viewers preconsciously, rather than as a simple medium to impart stories or moral messages, commenting "Film as dream, film as music. No art passes our conscience in the way film does, and goes directly to our *feelings*, deep down into the dark rooms of our souls" (Bergman, 1987, p. 73).

Like slow cinema, the film enigma may seem like a style of another age, though the spirit lives on with some of the work by directors, such as Leos Carax, Guy Maddin, and David Lynch. While *Last Year at Marienbad* and *The Color of Pomegranates* evoke an atmosphere of serene entrancement, Lynch's labyrinthine trilogy *Lost Highway* (1997), *Mulholland Drive* (2001), and *Inland Empire* uses ambiguity to invoke a sense of dread, much like *Persona* and *Don't Look Now*.

If realist art cinema captures the human experience in its multi-layered complexity and slow cinema offers the viewer space for quiet contemplation, what does the film enigma offer viewers in its mysterium? Torben Grodal calls it *saturation*, a tantalising-but-diffuse sense of being on the cusp of some profound insight. He comments that when a film offers a network of emotionally charged motifs which don't support a clearly discernible narrative, it produces a lyrical-associative atmosphere:

> The feelings evoked have moodlike qualities that I call saturated; they are strong but unfocused. There is no clear goal that might provide an outlet to such feelings through narrative action. [...] The feeling of deep ungraspable meaning need not correspond to deep, buried meaning in the film. Sometimes, indeed, the opposite is true. Lynch's or Resnais's films, for example, use all the mind's blind spots to send the viewer on a quest for meanings that can never be fully found because the images and scenes are underdetermined.
>
> *(Grodal, 2009, p. 149)*

Grodal's notion of saturation may sound pessimistic, as if narratives using the saturated effect are "all sizzle and no steak" with the empty promise of an eventual payoff that never comes. But if a comedy produces feelings of mirth, horror movies invigorate the senses and thrillers are exhilarating, why shouldn't we be drawn to films that evoke a sense of wonder?

He cites *Last Year in Marienbad* as a "prototypical art film" combining stylistic innovation with a claim to higher meaning (ibid., p. 207). Open endings are also core to the saturated effect. If works of lasting value linger in the mind, movies with ambiguous open endings like *Last Year in Marienbad*, *2001: A Space Odyssey* and *Picnic at Hanging Rock* (1975) are more likely to do so since they don't offer closure in the way mainstream narratives generally do (ibid., p. 211).

Like classical art narration and slow cinema, there are degrees of purity in this mode. *Last Year at Marienbad* might be the closest we have to an emblematic or quintessential example. By contrast, *Wings of Desire* (1987) sits between realist art cinema and the enigma, featuring both a clear narrative thread, and a mysterious atmosphere with poetic interludes. The saturated effect can intensify across the course of the movie, shifting from a linear story to something more poetic, such as *Synedoche, New York* (2008). Self-reflexivity can manifest through the film seemingly tearing or burning up on the projector (like *Persona*) or a camera pulling back to reveal the set where the film is being produced (*The Holy Mountain*).

For those who don't enjoy settling into the mysteries of an enigmatic film, there is the option of formulating interpretations of the otherwise inscrutable events. *Mulholland Drive* can be interpreted as the fever dream of Diane Selwyn (Naomi Watts), recounting her doomed love affair with Camilla Rhodes (Laura Elena Harring) embellished with her personal biases, neuroses, and revenge fantasies, her unconscious made concrete. We see what "really happened" in the final third of the movie, when we go inside the blue box. This isn't a canonical explanation (no such explanation exists) but viewing the film through this lens does provide a sense of cohesion, and one may speculate that Lynch had this in mind when he wrote the screenplay. Carax's puzzling *Holy Motors* (2012) can be broadly construed as a meditation on the demands an actor puts themselves through, though this is never spelled out.

Kovács offers a framework for understanding *Last Year at Marienbad*. He comments that where *Fellini's 8½* shifts between reality and fantasy, *Marienbad* features no distinction: "[it] is the story of the flow of memories and fantasies in a narrator's brain where there is no difference between layers of past, present, reality, and fantasy. Everything and everybody appears here as a creature of the narrator, and there is no distinction between events, places, and individuals having a real existence outside the narrator's mind and those fabricated entirely by him" (Kovács, 2007, p. 131).

There have been occasions where they are willing to share the rationale behind the onscreen events. When asked about the famous ending of *2001: A Space Odyssey* during an interview, Kubrick answered in earnest with some reluctance:

> I've tried to avoid doing this ever since the picture came out. When you just say the ideas they sound foolish, whereas if they're dramatized one feels it, but I'll try. The idea was supposed to be that he is taken in by god-like entities, creatures of pure energy and intelligence with no shape or form. They put him in what I suppose you could describe as a human zoo to study him, and his whole life passes from that point on in that room. And he has no sense of time. It just seems to happen as it does in the film. [...] when they get finished with him, as happens in so many myths of all cultures in the world, he is transformed into some kind of super being and sent back to Earth, transformed and made into some sort of superman. We have to only guess what happens when he goes back.
>
> *(Kubrick, quoted in Internet champ, 2020)*

Explaining away the hidden premises of a film enigma can reduce the sense of awe and wonder to something bland, or "foolish" in Kubrick's words. The saturated feeling (as Grodal puts it) risks being undermined. Also wary of explaining his films but being more guarded, David Lynch had the following exchange with Jason Barlow during a 2007 BAFTA interview:

Lynch: "Believe it or not, *Eraserhead* is my most spiritual film."
Barlow: "Elaborate on that."
Lynch: "No."

Despite these explications of *Mulholland Drive*, *Holy Motors* and *2001: A Space Odyssey*, not every film enigma should be understood as a safe to crack. A film might feature a hidden narrative or be guided by a broader concept rather than a cohesive story. But it might also be free-associative, with filmmakers allowing their untethered intuitions to run wild.

Closing Disclaimers and Future Directions

This chapter defended the idea that art cinema should not be defined exclusively by institutional factors, but rather narrational strategies can be identified which lean towards art cinema rather than mainstream cinema. The umbrella concept of art cinema narration, I have suggested, becomes more inclusive when it is divided into separate modes rather than being cast as one thing. Most films, it has been suggested, sit between the three poles of realist art cinema, slow cinema, and the film enigma. Films such as *Stalker*, *Dead Man*, *Uncle Boonmee who can See into Past Lives*, and *Under the Skin* sit somewhere between all three to varying degrees, combining a degree of characterisation with contemplative pacing and unexplained mysteries. Films that straddle all three modes could be broadly construed as 'classical art cinema'. In a future study, time should be spent exploring case studies in greater detail and with a greater focus on cinemas outside Europe and America.

Note that the model presented is not intended to be an all-encompassing theory of art cinema. Realism, time, and ambiguity are not presented as a checklist required for membership. Films such as *Battleship Potemkin* (1925), *F for Fake* (1973), and *Arabian Nights* (1974) are interesting because they don't fit comfortably in the model. None are ambiguous, slow, or focused on psychological realism. The same goes for films that straddle art and cult/grindhouse markets, such as *Irreversible* or *Titane*. Extreme cinema has existed as a cultural outlier to art cinema proper, and can be traced back to *Man Bites Dog* (1992), *Caligula* (1979), *Salo, or the 120 Days of Sodom* (1975), and *Pink Flamingos* (1972). Prior to this, extreme provocations only existed in experimental film (unconstrained by the Hayes Code[7]), such as *Flaming Creatures* (1963), *Window Water Baby Moving* (1959), and *Un Chien Andalou* (1929).

An additional clarification: not all filmmakers who lean towards the same mode share the same, homogenous purpose. The modes need to be malleable enough to accommodate a diverse range of filmmakers from a range of creative voices, this is the only way selected works of Ingmar Bergman and John Cassavetes can be placed together as realist art cinema directors, for example. They share narrational cornerstones, as do Ackerman and Tarr as Slow Cinema directors, but there are still a range of distinctions between the artists.

A topic that could be expanded on is what Bordwell calls this a game of form, where a film "initially trains the viewer in its distinctive storytelling tactics, but as [it] proceeds, those tactics mutate in unforeseeable ways" (2007, p. 165). For example, *2001: A Space Odyssey* switches from slow to enigma quite abruptly towards the end. *I'm Thinking of Ending Things* (2020) is mostly a realist art cinema chamber drama, but the end suddenly becomes pure enigma. *Persona* features an enigmatic prologue and epilogue, framing an otherwise traditional drama to something more ambiguous.

If a viewer takes a commitment to realism, contemplative pacing, and ambiguity as the core traits of art cinema, they will be well equipped to navigate the field as a whole. In addition, while narrational devices are more malleable than institutional factors in their establishment of an art cinema, they have worked together productively and remain inseparable.

Notes

1 Bordwell himself made this observation two years prior to Thanouli when reflecting on the original article. See Bordwell (2007, p. 158).
2 The term "mode" would have also worked, but I opted for category in this chapter to avoid confusion since three different modes (realist art cinema, slow cinema, film enigma) will be proposed within art cinema.
3 Jaime Rosales' *Sueño y Silencio* (2012) is used as a case study in the blog, but this will be skipped over for the sake of brevity.
4 *2001: A Space Odyssey*, *Dead Man* and *Synedoche, New York* are not generally conceived as Art Cinema proper, but draw from the conventions nonetheless.
5 *Slow Cinema*, edited by Tiago de luca and Nuno Barradas Jorge; *Tsai Ming-liang and a Cinema of Slowness*, by Song Hwee Lim; *Poetics of Slow Cinema* by Emre; and Mark Betz's "On Parametric Transcendence" in *Global Art Cinema* (Eds. Galt and Schoonover).
6 The concept of a quasi-narrative avant-garde film would benefit from some unpacking which will be resisted now in the interests of space. But essentially, it refers to films of an avant-garde persuasion (usually made on a low budget by an individual or small collective, evocative over concrete, attention is drawn to the materials used) which follows discernible characters through a series of events, unlike the non-figurative films of Oskar Fischinger, for example. For a more detailed discussion of avant-garde film and narrative, see Taberham (2018, pp. 25–66).
7 The Hayes Code was a set of industry guidelines that was enforced from roughly the mid-1930s to the late-1960s. It forbade depiction of various acts such as crime being portrayed in a positive light, nudity and sexual behaviour, mocking the clergy, and drug or alcohol consumption.

References

Andrews, D. (2013). *Theorizing art cinemas: Foreign, cult, avant-garde, and beyond.* Austin: University of Texas Press.

Bergman, I. (1987). *The magic lantern.* London: Penguin.

Bordwell, D. (1985). *Narration in the fiction film.* Madison: The University of Wisconsin Press.

Bordwell, D. (2007). *Poetics of cinema.* Taylor and Francis.

Bordwell, D. (2012). How to Watch an Art Movie, Reel 1. *Observations on Film Art.* 26 August. Available online at http://www.davidbordwell.net/blog/2012/08/26/how-to-watch-an-art-movie-reel-1/ (retrieved 3 May 2023).

Bordwell, D., Staiger, J. & Thompson, K. (1985). *The classical Hollywood cinema.* London: Routledge.

Buckland, W. (2020). *Narrative and narration: Analyzing cinematic storytelling.* New York: Columbia University Press.

Çağlayan, E. (2018). *Poetics of slow cinema.* Gewerbestrasse: Palgrave Macmillan.

Forbes, J. and Street, S. (2000). *European Cinema: An Introduction.* New York: Palgrave.

Galt, R. and Schoonover, K. (2010). Introduction: The Impurity of Art Cinema. In R. Galt and K. Schoonover (Eds.), *Global Art Cinema* (pp. 3–27). New York: Oxford University Press.

Grodal, T. (2009). *Embodied visions.* Oxford: Oxford University Press.

Internet champ. (2020, May 2). *Stanley Kubrick Explains the Ending of 2001 and The Shining.* [Video]. YouTube. https://www.youtube.com/watch?v=zaR2pJjL08g

James, N. (2010). Passive aggressive. *Sight & Sound.* 20 (4), 5.

King, G. (2019). *Positioning art cinema: Film and cultural value.* London: Bloomsbury.

Kovács, A. B. (2007). *Screening modernism: European Art cinema, 1950–1980.* Chicago: University of Chicago Press.

Matthen, M. (2010). Cluster Concepts. *It's Only A Theory.* 21 January. Available online at http://itisonlyatheory.blogspot.com/2010/01/cluster-concepts.html (retrieved 3 May 2023).

Neale, S. (2002). Art Cinema as Institution. In C. Fowler (Ed.), *The European cinema reader* (pp. 103–120). London: Routledge.

Quandt, J. (2009). The Sandwich Process: Simon Field Talks About Polemics and Poetry at Film Festivals. In R. Porton (Ed.), *Dekalog 3: On film festivals* (pp. 53–80). London: Wallflower Press.

Romney, J. (2010). In search of lost time. *Sight & Sound.* 20 (2), 43–44.

Schrader, P. (2018). *Transcendental style in film: Ozu, Bresson, Dreyer.* Oakland: University of California Press.

Taberham, P. (2018). *Lessons in perception: The avant-garde filmmaker as practical psychologist.* New York: Berghahn.

Thanouli, E. (2009). 'Art Cinema' narration: Breaking down a wayward paradigm. *Scope: An Online Journal of Film and Television Studies.* www.nottingham.ac.uk/scope/documents/2009/june-2009/thanouli.pdf

White, J. (2005). Brakhage's Tarkovsky and Tarkovsky's Brakhage: Collectivity, subjectivity, and the dream of cinema. *Revue Canadienne d'Études Cinématographiques/Canadian Journal of Film Studies.* 14 (1), 69–83.

7

INTERVIEW: IOANA URICARU

Could you please share with us a few words on how you developed your screenwriting style given that screenwriting manuals (with very few tentative recent exceptions) are geared towards a career in Hollywood?

I took, of course, screenwriting classes in film school (both in Romania and in the United States), and I read the basic books that deal with the craft – which are indeed, by and large, American books. I think I am very influenced by my Romanian background, by the books and the films and the plays that I absorbed in my childhood and teenage years, which are at the root of any idea or story I am compelled to work on. In terms of craft, I think what made the biggest difference for me were actually the books on directing actors by Judith Weston and her acting and script analysis workshops.

Your film *Lemonade* (Uricaru, 2018) deals with the increasingly delicate immigration issue in the United States. Unlike other films on the same topic, yours uses silence in a more subtle way than the obvious 'fill in the blanks' in commercial movies. In creating this film, what meaning did you attribute to the 'quiet' moments? What response did you anticipate the viewers would have?

I must say I haven't necessarily planned the silence(s); now that I'm thinking of it, I probably start with silence (as in no music and no dialogue) and then introduce dialogue when it feels necessary or organic. I'd love to be able to make a film without dialogue, not in the sense of a silent film, but maybe a film where actors speak an invented language and there's no translation, so

DOI: 10.4324/9781003197911-10

we can hear their voices and their intonations, but not pay any attention to the words themselves. As for music, I haven't yet used scoring in my films. Maybe that's why the silence gets noticed! What people do when there's silence is very important, and that goes for the relationships on screen as well as for the relationship between the audience and the film. To quote Mia Wallace in *Pulp Fiction*: (1994) you know you have something special when you can comfortably share silence.

We feel that we should provide more information about the motivation behind this question (without including this motivation in the printed interview): If I were to bring in a naïve viewer's experience, McCarthy's *The Visitor* (2007) seems to use silence as an apparent counterbalance to the featured drum beats. The viewers, therefore, know how to fill in the silent moments. Your film seems to give the viewers more degrees of freedom in interpreting the 'between the lines' silence.

How did your political and cultural background (being born in communist Romania) inform – or maybe hinder – your work as a visual narrative creator?

It's the most important factor of influence in my work, and in my life. For one thing, my relationship with cinema was completely shaped by its precious scarcity and its almost mystical status in a country that was in a kind of spiritual and emotional lockdown. The memory and awareness of growing up immersed in doublespeak, wrongthink, censorship, self-censorship, gaslighting, arbitrary exercises of power and so on, are probably to be found in the texture of everything I do.

You teach screenwriting at both introductory and advanced levels. From your college students' work, what do you think future screenwriting manuals should look like?

I found that the most useful things for students are practical exercises that are very clearly formulated, relatively small/contained in scope and revelatory of specific concepts. For example, write a one-page, two-character scene where the two characters have assigned, opposing objectives. This is a very basic beginner's exercise, but this kind of clarity can be very useful for an advanced-level exercise as well. It's not very easy to come up with these!

Some writers consider themselves 'plotters', planning the structure of the story from the beginning. Others are 'pantsers', writing by-the-seat-of-their-pants where little is planned in advance, they see where the process leads them. There are also 'plantsers', who combine both. Where do you see yourself on this continuum, if you do at all?

Definitely a plotter, up until act 3. An exciting script is one that could potentially go in different directions in act 3, so at that point, I like to try things out.

Could you share your main processes, from the initial spark of an idea to the final script?

That's an easy question! I keep a folder of potential ideas, most of them from the news or stories I heard from friends. From time to time I go through the folder trying to see if any of the notes in there jumps out at me or grabs my attention as having potential to grow into a story. If I pick one, I try to think of the story next. Is this initial idea or event the inciting incident? Or is it the end of the story? Or is it something that happened before the story even started? I go back and forth between potential protagonists and try to figure out the shape of the plot. This is a pretty fuzzy stage, when I'm actually waiting for the story to grab me, to reveal its possibilities. Many times I stop at this stage and the story never grows beyond it. If it does, it might turn into a treatment – and I have a folder of those too! In any case, I have to have some thematic clarity before I start writing scenes. And I usually have several scripts in different stages of growth, which helps with taking the edge – and the pressure – off.

Your screenplays deal with social issues and emotional conflict. What do you think your role is as a storyteller? Someone who offers emotional catharsis? An entertainer? Someone who brings our awareness of social problems to light?

I'm trying to build emotional experiences that hopefully make people ask questions, of themselves and of the world. I also have questions, so I think I'm inviting the audience to marvel together with me at what's going on in the world and between people and inside their minds. Hopefully, they will be intrigued and energized enough to keep thinking about it and come up with their own interpretations.

Lastly, as a screenwriter and director who engages in her art two very different cultures that she experienced directly, what insights would you share with other international filmmakers in America?

I'll pull in a bit of a cliché here, but everybody's experience is different. Moreover, filmmaking in the United States is a huge field: there's Hollywood and now the streamers who are also a kind of studio system, there's independent festival-bound filmmaking, there's microbudget filmmaking, there's low-budget genre filmmaking and niche, experimental, visual art-type work. It depends on what one wants: trajectories are different for somebody who wants to penetrate the studio system from somebody who wants to have fun and recoup their investment making low-budget horrors from somebody who wants to put out extremely personal, aesthetically bold content. But in any of these cases, the major difference from Europe is that the sources of funding are completely different and so is the value of various assets (the most obvious example being the importance of 'name' performers in the United States). So the first thing to do is learn the financial ropes and figure out if you can – and want – to do what it takes so you can make the kind of film you want to make.

8

PSEUDO-NARRATION IN JEAN-LUC GODARD'S LATE FILMS

András Bálint Kovács

Jean-Luc Godard has been widely considered the most influential and the most subversive among the great authors of modernist cinema. As one of his critics put it: "there is the cinema before Godard and the cinema after Godard" (Roud, 1968). The immense impact of his films on the evolution of modern cinema stems from the fact that his films were subversive within the boundaries of narrative art-film. Except for 12 years between 1968 and 1980, Godard's cinema can be considered as an oeuvre that moves away from the rules of this framework as far as it gets, yet not falling into the category of non-commercial experimental cinema. Here is what Godard himself says about his in-between position: "They say that I am an extremist; but, in fact, I am someone in the middle who always needs the two extremes, who has always liked the contrasts" (Godard, 1980). The key to this position is Godard's peculiar relation to narration.

The vast literature on Godard's cinema has mainly focused on distinguishing the unusual and peculiar ways in which Godard constructs his films from conventional narrative structure (e.g., see: Dixon, 1997; Emmelhainz, 2019; Silverman & Farocki, 1998; Wollen, 1972). For a long time, there has been a wide consensus about Godard's main technique consisting in simply moving away from and openly criticizing traditional forms of cinematic narration. This approach has found ample material in Godard's commentaries on his own films. One of the most widely cited comments to date seems to reveal Godard's relation to narration: "I don't really like telling a story. I prefer to use a kind of tapestry, a background on which I can embroider my own ideas. [...] I just write out the strong moments of the film, and that gives me a *weft*" (Godard, 2009) (my emphasis). In other words, for Godard narration seems to be just an auxiliary scaffold, which does not contribute to

DOI: 10.4324/9781003197911-11

the essence of his films. Narration provides only structural support for the web of ideas constituting the essence of his films. Based on this approach it seemed useless to focus on Godard's narrative technique as his films seemed to be impossible to be interpreted in terms of narrative devices. Terms like "montage", "collage", "essay", "anti-cinema", and "research" have been widely used in attempting to grasp the essence of Godard's peculiar technique distinguishing it from the narration (Dixon, 1997, p. 5). Very early in his career, Godard also emphasized the non-traditional character of his films: "If I analyze myself today, I see that in the essence, I have always wanted to make a film of research in the form of a spectacle" (Godard, 2006). Ultimately, this leads to the question of the identity of his films in terms of classical cinematic conventions. Here is what Godard said about *Deux ou trois choses que je sais d'elle* (1967): "In short, this is not a film. This is an attempt of a film, and it presents itself as such" (Godard, 1967). Obviously, when confronted with such statements by the author, critics did not have many incentives to analyze his films in terms of classical narration.

The first attempt to study Godard's cinematic form as a peculiar narrative technique rather than anything else was made by David Bordwell in his *Narration in the Fiction Film* (Bordwell, 1985). Bordwell criticized earlier critics for neglecting the narrative aspect of Godard's films and overemphasizing their non-narrative tendencies. Ideas cited above certainly contributed to this critical attitude inasmuch as Godard himself encouraged his critics not to look for the relevance of narration in his films. But Bordwell rightly pointed out that Godard's pre-1968 films were all fundamentally narratives. And the reason why the viewers struggle with understanding these films is precisely because the nature of their narration is unusual and unclear. However, the citations, digressions, reflections, and commentaries pervading his films can only be really understood in the context of the narrative, therefore, we have to study the nature of this peculiar kind of narrative. This is why Bordwell was not satisfied with the explanations referring to the form of "essay-film" or the form of the "critical semiotic analysis" that tries to avoid facing the difficulties Godard's narrative strategy imposes on the viewer. One can agree with Bordwell that interpreting the films of Godard based on idiosyncratic irregularities does not help much if one ignores the background from which these irregularities diverge. And this background is still classical narration. So, rather than trying to make sense of Godard's cinema as fundamentally non-narrative, one should seek to understand the specific narrative logic Godard employs in his films.

According to Bordwell, the source of the problems with Godardian narration is that he mixes "established narrational modes in disorienting ways" (Bordwell, 1985, p. 313). This entails that the viewer must quickly change interpretive frameworks more than once sometimes in a matter of minutes. The same film may start as a gangster movie, then jump into a propaganda film, then into an art-film in the style of Bergman, shifting into a Fellini style film, on to a television advertisement, or a documentary. Classical narration's space-time-causal logic in the order of shot sequences is often and regularly broken by connections of shots based on principles other than the space–time-causal one. One cut links two shots by their local and chronological relations, the next one is a metaphorical association, and the one after that is a juxtaposition based on thematic similarity. This is the peculiar editing system that made Godard state that "Two shots following each other, do not follow each other after all" (Godard, 1965). We should add: … in the same way they did seconds or minutes earlier. Not only must we keep different associative logics ready to use simultaneously, but we also have to find out which one to use in any given shot change. Yet, until 1968 all Godard films had a narrative framework in which identifiable characters were placed in a somewhat dramatic situation, performing goal-oriented actions, and where the film's ending situation was different from the initial situation. Within this framework, which is the minimal condition of a narrative, more or less fragmented scenes followed each other based on a variety of associative logics corresponding to fragments of different narrational modes.

Accepting Bordwell's idea that Godard's main narrative procedure in his early period is to juggle with various, even contradictory narrative modes in his films, I want to propose another account of Godard's peculiar narration that is more characteristic of his late period, even though it is firmly based in the techniques developed in his early period. The effect this formal system has on the viewer is an illusion of the traditional development of a narrative while in fact what the viewers see is only a series of seeds of possible stories, which become an atemporal variation of thematic and visual motifs. I still would not call it non-narrative, since it conveys the impression that some story must be hidden behind the apparently chaotic narrative fragments in the film, only it is impossible to decipher.

Back to Narration

Godard has stated several times in different interviews that *Sauve qui peut. (la vie)* (1980) was his second first film (Champlin, 1981). After 12 years of experimental/documentary/television production he went back to more traditional theatrical release feature films. In the critical reception the general view was that Godard had turned back to more traditional filmmaking, again confirmed by his own statement: "I rather have the impression of landing again in the beautiful country of narration, story, and narrative" (Godard, 2021). Bordwell saw in this "a regression". He considered Godard's films of the early 1980s seeming "to be almost completely assimilable to the art cinema's narrational mode" (Bordwell, 1985, p. 334). Compared to his films made in the 1970s, the new Godard films represented again character emotions, private lives, and relationships. They also lacked direct political commentaries, confusing edit sequences and harsh alienating effects such as actors facing the audience and delivering speeches. They seemed to represent mostly ordinary life situations with traditional cinematography, without too many self-reflexive visual effects, and without any apparent reference to different conventions of genres and narrational modes. And most importantly, they had an apparent, although not very transparent narrative development that made an initial dramatic situation progressively transform into another through actions and character interactions. Most of the dialogue contains reference to the characters' situations, and the order of the scenes is reminiscent of the unfolding of a linear and coherent storyline.

In the exposition of *Sauve qui peut.(la vie)* for example, Denise (Nathalie Baye) tells Paul (Jacques Dutronc) that their relationship is over, after which the film goes through scenes illuminating their situation and the nature of their relationship. We learn that Paul has an ex-wife and a little daughter whom he treats rudely and without much affection, and ends on a scene where Paul finally decides to see his daughter and ex-wife more often, but in that moment a car hits him, and his ex-wife and daughter walk away. It is a clear and linear storyline, even though the relative lack of redundancy between dialogues and scenes (the dialogues refer vaguely or not at all to the situation), and the highly elliptical scene and story construction (missing important information that could clarify the situation) make it hard to follow the narrative. Unusual, sometimes even astounding arbitrary events taking place in almost every scene contribute to this hardship. Early in the film, for example, when a woman shows Denise around a cow farm, suddenly, she pulls down her trousers and shows her naked backside to the cows. Or a little bit later, when Denise arrives at the railway station, we see two men nagging a woman, then violently slapping her face, and ordering her to "Make a choice", to which she answers: "I make no choice". In the meantime, a Formula 1 race car arrives at the parking lot, and the driver leaves the car. Then, when we see the woman already bleeding, suddenly all of them leave the scene. Episodes like that divert the viewer's attention from the main storyline which is very elliptical as it is. These episodes have the function to enrich a situation with possible associative pathways that bring the viewer's imagination away from the concrete story. Still, the basic elements of a storyline, such as recurring identifiable characters and locations, emotional interactions between characters, recognizable and changing interpersonal relationships, some reference to a background story in the dialogues, development of the scenes from an initial situation through cause-effect relations into a different ending situation are there in this film.

Later in this period, Godard's films evolved toward omitting even those basic elements, but instead of making this conspicuous and explicit, as in the 1970s, Godard created an ambiguous structure: a technique by which his films continued to appear to be fundamentally narrative while they were not. One can find no more references to various conventions of narrative genres in these films, so they cannot be explained by a constantly changing narrative scheme as in the case of his films in the 1960s.

The films later in this period, starting around the mid-1980s depict dramatic situations with characters expressing emotional states and personal relationships, but they are not developed into stories. Instead, for all the situations, Godard proposes multiple divergent associative pathways, which lead the viewer's imagination to different directions. Each of these directions offers the seeds of a possible virtual storyline, but in the end none of them will be developed. Most Godard films in this period have this structure. In the beginning there is an initial event creating a dramatic situation – a spy is dismissed in *Allemeagne neuf-zéro* (1991), Richard and Elena meet at the side of the road and fall in love in *Nouvelle vague* (1990), and the rest of the film seems to be the development of this situation. The films present a series of reactions to and a series of possible continuations of the initial dramatic state of affairs. Sometimes the possible continuations are just variations of each other.

For example, in *Nouvelle vague* we have two consecutive series of events, each with the same main characters both ending on a scene very similar to each other. But the main characters' behavior changes considerably from one series of events to the other (let alone the fact that he dies in the first and reappears alive in the second). Both series end with one of the main characters falling into a lake and asking for help. In the first one she lets him drown and he dies, in the second one he saves her, and she survives. In some films the variations of different series of events are organized in unrelated thematic episodes. In *Détéctive* (1985) five different situations are placed in one location, a hotel, but none of them are developed into a straight storyline. In *Soigne ta droite* (1987) we find three episodes that are not even connected by any means with each other. *Film socialisme* (2010) consists of three different parts. Two of them are fictional, and unrelated. One takes place on a cruiser, the other at a country gas station. None of them tells a linear story. The third part consists of different citations from films, documentaries, and television programs. Yet, identifiable but unrelated dramatic situations taking place all over the film, and the emotional acting style suggest to the viewer that behind this fragmented surface there are stories going on in the films, which are impossible to reconstruct.

This makes the narrative difficult or even impossible to follow but keeps the illusion of a narrative. Empirical research on psychology of narrative understanding suggests that viewers segment events in a film based on character constancy, space and time continuity (Cutting, 2014). Since in these films the characters, the time and the space remain identifiable, and coherent, its scenes constantly maintain the marks of a dramatic situation, which is supposed to have causal consequences, yet their consecution does not add up in a coherent storyline. Also, the narrative transformation, the difference between the beginning and the end, disappears. Very simply put: Godard pretends to tell a story by introducing a dramatic situation, and accumulating emotionally intensive moments, while in reality what we see is a series of fragments of different possibilities of developing alternative storylines. Several virtual stories start in a scene, but none of them unfolds entirely. As if Godard's scene construction was an illustration of what a character says in *Hélas pour moi!* (1993): "All of us are surrounded by invisible dreams".

The Key Role of the Dialogue

Elliptical dramatic construction whereby scenes do not follow each other in time-space continuity, and extensive use of dialogue most of the time unrelated to the situation, are the standard procedures to achieve the "late Godardian" effect.

From the point of view of dramatic construction, most Godard films are psychological or social dramas as are the majority of art films. This means that the narrative process is based on character interactions developing a psychological or social situation and follows the characters' mental or psychological changes caused by these interactions. Most of the time the dramatic situation is made clear by the dialogue that discloses the characters' goals, and describes their relationships to each other or to the exterior world. Therefore, dialogue is key to understanding this type of film. This is where Godard started to fragment his narrative structure in the mid-1960s, by introducing incongruency between the characters' lines and the concrete situation they were in. The result is that their dialogue provides very weak or no information at all about a possible development of a storyline. From the 1980s on, this continues to be his main procedure but in a more radical way than before.

Godard uses three main procedures to divert the dialogue away from the concrete situation. I will call the first *dialogue abstraction*, the second *counterpoint*, and the third: *parallel soundtrack*. Dialogue abstraction consists in starting a dialogue with a concrete reference to a situation but quickly transposing it into a symbolic or abstract level. For example, in the beginning of *Nouvelle Vague* (1990) Richard Lennox (Alain Delon) lies on the ground at the side of a country road as if hit by a car. A woman, Elena Torlato-Favrini (Dominiziana Giordano) driving by in a luxury car jams on the brakes to stop, backs up, gets out of the vehicle, and asks the man on the ground:

Elena: Are you hurt? You are hurt.
Richard: Who puts any value on a well-executed death? Even the rich, who can afford it, no longer bother. The wish to keep your death to yourself is rarer and rarer.
Elena: Are you in pain? Are you in pain? Are you in pain? How wonderful to be able to give what you don't have.
Richard: Miracle of empty hands.
Elena: Dolce miracolo.

During this last line all we see are the two hands, the man's and the woman's, their fingers lacing into one another.

This dialogue starts with a concrete reference to the situation. Richard's response still has some vague reference to their situation although it is not a real answer. Elena continues within the concrete situation, but suddenly she comes up with a line totally detached from it. Richard's response picks up already at this abstract level relating only to the word "miracle", which will be the link to Elena's final line, which is already in another language too. By the end of this short scene, we get far away from the situation of a supposed accident into a situation of a romantic relationship. By abstracting the dialogue, in a single scene roughly two minutes long, this is an extremely concise way of suggesting the story of a beautiful young lady stopping to help a man seemingly in trouble at the side of the road, and the two falling in love. By quickly getting away from the concrete situation through the dialogue Godard hints at an underlying story, but does not disclose it.

The first scene of the film is an example of a counterpoint. A gardener enters the frame on a tractor and stops. He gets off the tractor, grabs a broom and starts sweeping the road. While sweeping, he starts talking: "We've had no time to discover, like a lamp just lighted the chestnut tree in blossom or a few splashes of gleaming ochre strewn among the jade-green shoots of wheat". There is a clear contrast between the mundane activity of his everyday work and the poetic style of his text unrelated to his situation. The effect these procedures have on the viewers is that they lose the sense of the narrative direction of a given scene, which is usually assured by the connection between sound and image.

The third device, parallel soundtracks make the viewer listen to more than one dialogue or monologue simultaneously. This procedure alone can make the dialogue irrelevant in clarifying the situation, since the viewer simply cannot understand both texts at the same time, and it is very difficult to follow only one of them. If each of them lacks redundant information about the given scene it is impossible to figure out what exactly happens in the story, who the characters are, and what their roles are in moving the story forward.

In sum, from the point of view of his narrative procedures the main difference between Godard's first period (1960–1968) and third period (1980–) is this: in the first period his films were increasingly characterized by a single storyline meandering between different narrational modes, and intertextual references by loosely related scenes that nevertheless unfolded a linear story. In his third period, the individual scenes no longer develop a linear story only suggest multiple possible continuations containing, as it were, multiple seeds of different dramas. This is what I call *pseudo-narrative*.

The Pseudo-Narrative

The term and the concept "pseudo-narrative" is borrowed from T.A. Unwin's analysis of Charles Baudelaire's *Les fleurs du mal* (Unwin, 1991). The account Unwin gives of Baudelaire's technique is reminiscent of Godard's procedure in this late period. A strong cultural tradition of French poetry links Godard to Baudelaire, which makes this parallel appealing. Baudelaire has always been an important reference for Godard. He cited Baudelaire routinely in his writings, and in his films: in one instance he compared Truffaut to Baudelaire (Godard, 1984), in another while being interviewed, he declared that he lived like Baudelaire (Godard, 1998). Godard has had a peculiar relationship to literary texts. Very early in his career, around the mid-1960s, the abundance of literary citations became one of the most important signatures of Godard's style. Either the characters cited lines of poets, and novelists, or citations appeared as written inserts in the film. Dialogues and monologues in *Nouvelle Vague* (1990) consist almost exclusively of literary citations that Godard's assistant gathered in a file counting more than a 100 pages (Brody, 2008). Without any doubt, Godard knew Baudelaire's work as a poet and as an art critic very well, and Baudelaire's way of writing and thinking must have left traces in Godard's own relationship to art.

In Unwin's account, Baudelaire's *Les fleurs du mal* is constructed to give the reader an impression of a process that has a beginning and an end (as claimed by Baudelaire himself) (Baudelaire, 1991), but what the reader is confronted with is not a series of events, rather a series of "states of mind", "almost a suggestion of a series of events" (321). An important factor of this kind of pseudo-narrative is that it looks like presenting a temporal progression, while in reality it is not, as the "different dimensions of the poet's spiritual drama coexist, interlocking with and reflecting each other" (323). What is presented as a possible temporal development is in fact a mental journey, a route passing through different simultaneously coexisting aspects of a state of mind. Since causal and chronological systems do not organize this route, the journey gives the impression of "gratuitousness" of the individual items in this system. Hence the fragmented structure of this type of "narrative".

All these observations about Baudelaire's construction of his series of poems in *Les fleurs du mal* closely resemble the experience of the late Godard films. A dramatic situation in these films consists of fragments of characters' states of mind expressed in a sequential progression but this progression is just a temporal sequence of the presentation and does not correspond to a real temporal process where past, present and future observe any natural chronological order. When we enter a situation in a Godard film, every aspect of that situation is assumed to be simultaneously coexisting and present. He tries to express this simultaneity by breaking down the situation into seemingly gratuitous and mutually incompatible verbal and gestural fragments. "I cannot tell a story. I wish to restore everything, to say everything simultaneously" – says Godard (Godard, 2006). The films explore a situation fragment by fragment, where different aspects of the same feeling or thought are presented one after the other or very often at the same time.

Let's see an example of the pseudo-narrative scene construction from *Hélas, pour moi!* (1993) The scene is filled with dialogues and monologues, but they do not form a consistent whole, which could describe the scene as part of an unfolding logical chain. Only the coherence of the location and the behavior of the characters keep the scene together. Each shot represents the same place with the same characters, which assures the unity of the space and action. Each dialogue segment comes from a different point of view and leads to a different direction.

The scene starts in a black frame with a voice over of one of the characters:

Highschool student:	Are you the drawing teacher, Monsieur?
Vaché:	It's correct. Vaché Jacques.
Highschool student:	My dad says it's mandatory. I really need to take drawing lessons.
Vaché:	Mandatory for what?

Now we see the highschool student and Vaché at the back staircase of the bookstore

Highschool student:	To master the arabesque.
Vaché:	What have you been studying?
Highschool student:	I'm in my last year at Annemasse High School. I'm taking history.
Male voice (off screen):	Angelica!
Highschool student:	Right now, we are covering the French Revolution and World War I. In October we'll get to the Russian Revolution.
Off screen sound:	Can I borrow this?
Vaché:	Come see me once you've finished the Russian Revolution, Mademoiselle.
Simultaneous voices off screen:	Angelica ... Mademoiselle ... Marinette Duras ... Can I borrow this? ... Marinette Duras.

Cut to the inside of the bookstore.

Vaché:	Rafael again, Delphine?
Male voice (off screen):	Angelica!

Delphine (off screen):	I would like to know why Luther's soldiers …
Male voice:	Angelica!
Delphine (off screen):	… gashed these paintings with spears.
Vaché:	I'll tell you something, my dear …
Male voice (off screen):	Angelica!
Vaché:	They are the least Christian people among Europeans.
Sound off screen:	Why would the Church have chosen Italy if not to …
Male Student:	To organize and control.
Vaché:	Exactly.
Man entering the shop:	Good morning professor.
Vaché:	Or bookseller.
Man taking a book and leaving:	My wife will pay you tomorrow.
Female student:	This one or that one.
Male student:	I take these two.
Vaché:	89 francs.
Female student 1:	Maybe …
Female student 2:	Maybe what?
Female student 1:	I don't know.
Vaché (offscreen):	I'll tell you children. Painting will not reveal the path to the external vision of the universe.

Cut to a long shot of a park.

Female voice off screen (simultaneously):	Look, the women from Algiers.
Male voice off screen:	… in an almost jealous contemplation …

Cut back to the bookstore, Delphine reading a book in a high contrast lighting.

Male voice (cont'd):	… of human face and gestures.

From here on two monologues are heard simultaneously.

Male voice:	It's in the light that one should compose …
Vaché:	No, no, no, the painters won't reveal.
Male voice:	… to illuminate them
Vaché:	… the secret of suffering. It's for us to accept and understand …

Male voice:	... with the harmony of the most distant stars ...
Vaché:	. ... to look deep within ourselves to see if we have also loved.
Male voice:	... and the most stark darkness.

The scene is divided into three parts. It starts as a coherent dialogue between two characters who talk about the same thing: a drawing teacher and a student looking for a drawing teacher. But very soon, the scene will go astray from this line of development losing entirely the initial topic. The first part is the dialogue between a high school student and M. Vaché (Roland Blanche) about what the student is learning and wishes to learn. Here, the lines of the characters loosely relate to each other. The second part is within the bookstore introducing more characters. In this part different unrelated topics are discussed, some of which are related closely to the situation, some others not at all. Coherent dialogues consist of maximum two lines (e.g., Student: "I take these two", Vaché: "89 francs"), and the different dialogue fragments are interrupted by an unnamed man calling Angelica. It is as if we were in a crowded and noisy room listening to different dialogue fragments, but these fragments are presented as if they were parts of a coherent conversation. In part three, there are no more verbal exchanges. We hear two simultaneous offscreen monologues unrelated to each other, while watching Delphine reading an album of paintings.

A variation of different types of dialogue goes through the three parts but there is also a linear logic in this variation, starting with relatively classical dialogue but ending in simultaneous monologues entirely detached from the dramatic situation. This progression can be interpreted also as a mental journey into M. Vaché's inner state. He is the one who is present from the beginning to the end of the scene, so he could be called the protagonist of this scene. In the introduction he receives an assignment: to become the student's drawing teacher, which he declines temporarily by saying: "Come see me once you finished the Russian Revolution". This is an enigmatic and unexpected response, but it is the key sentence parts two and three will illuminate. Two themes, art and politics are juxtaposed and unexpectedly related in this conversation. In part two this relation is developed further by different topics (Raffaello, Luther and the control by the Church). In part three, Vaché's monologue explains what he meant when he told the student to come back once she is finished with the Russian Revolution: personal experience of history and politics is necessary to understand the suffering that the painters cannot reveal in their paintings.

One of the conventional functions of a dialogue is to explain a character's motivation, which contributes to the ease of understanding of the subsequent story events. In this sense this scene seems to be functional. But neither the concrete topic of this conversation nor Vaché, the main character of this scene returns in the rest of the film, so it cannot be interpreted in terms of character motivation, as the characters of this scene have no role in the unfolding of the narrative. Furthermore, due to the highly fragmented nature of the characters' lines and the lack of dialogue logic, no narrative development can be detected in a progression of the dialogues. The only detectable change taking place is that in the beginning, the characters' lines had more or less concrete references (drawing lesson), and in the end they have some abstract references (feelings about the relationship between painting and suffering). The viewer understands that there is some situation in this scene with constant characters, and the topics of the characters' lines seem to revolve around a somewhat coherent topic, which makes this scene look like an episode in a traditional narrative. What the viewer does not understand is how this scene contributes to the unfolding of a chronological and causal storyline. There is no reference to past or future events, no detectable change in the characters' situations from the beginning to the end, nor is there perceptible change in their states of mind. Nothing related to a causal or temporal logic leads from this situation to the next. This scene is vaguely reminiscent of a dramatic situation within a continuum of events, but in reality, it juxtaposes different fragments of mental states about a vaguely defined theme. It simply puts together a mosaic of a point of view about the relationship between art and history. There can be no hidden story found in this scene, nothing changes as a result of it.

These pseudo-narrative situations are assembled by pseudo-narrative frames. In *Hélas pour moi!* a man, Abraham Klimt (Bernard Verley) arrives in a little Swiss village, inquiring about a couple, Simon and Rachel. When a car mechanic asks him why he is looking for them, we hear this conversation:

Car mechanic:	Do they know you?
Klimt:	They will come soon.
Car mechanic:	Do they know you? Do they know you?
No answer.	
Car mechanic:	You should address them as "Monsieur" and "Madame" then, not by their first names. We are not characters in some novel.
Klimt:	Maybe you are! I heard that they have a story to sell.
Car mechanic:	Sir, you are buying stories?
Klimt:	Exactly.

It seems that Klimt is a writer, an editor or a producer who is interested in a story about Simon and Rachel Donnadieu, which is why he arrives to this village. And the exposition of the film promises to uncover this story. During the film, however, Klimt appears only a few times questioning the villagers, but all the exchanges he has with them are vague and contradictory, and no direct questions related to the "story" are asked. In the end he questions Simon himself, who tells him: "Nothing happened". Klimt could not reconstruct a coherent story from the different things he heard from the villagers. These are his last words about this investigation at the train station as he leaves the village: "There is nothing left to say about Simon and Rachel's life. The rest goes beyond the images and the stories". As he says that, a man approaches him trying to sell him various items from his suitcase, then he says: "Not beyond the images and the stories but this side of the images and the stories". To which Klimt responds: "Ha-ha! You may be right. My God, let who has never made a mistake …" The sentence is interrupted by the noise of a passing train and finished by two men throwing stones after the train and yelling: "… cast the first stone!" Not only is the difference unclear between the opening situation and the ending situation of the narrative frame (what Klimt found out about what), but his conclusion is also admittedly uncertain (is it or is it not possible to tell the rest in images and stories?). The narrative frame of the film is also a pseudo-narrative frame that pretends to represent a temporal progression of events (an investigation) while it makes all interpretation of the sequence of the events represented as a "story" uncertain.

Within the framework of this investigation, we see different scenes with Simon and Rachel suggesting that some story is being narrated. We learn that Simon, Rachel's husband left for a business trip. A little later, God disguised as Simon arrives and claims to have slept with Rachel. Rachel thinks that this was Simon himself but later on, she realizes that it was God. At the end, Simon tells Klimt: "It was me. I turned around". It remains unclear how the dramatic situation of God visiting Rachel and sleeping with her unfolds, and it is also unclear whether or not there was a dramatic situation at all or is this only what the villagers think. Klimt also firmly believes that "What happened was not ordinary". However, all we have are fragments of testimonies of the villagers and scenes that can be interpreted in many ways. Either Simon left and returned while Rachel and the others thought that he was God, or Simon left and God arrived in Simon's shape, and slept with Rachel who realized this only later. Whichever is the case, it is only a situation that can unfold in different ways, none of which is developed. Klimt is confronted with something that looks like a story, which he is unable to tell and the fragments of which he is unable to put together as a chronological and causal sequence having a beginning and an end. Not the least because the original situation is unclear. The uncertainty with which he arrives to this village is not dissipated by a bit when he leaves, so in the end nothing has changed. Fragments of memories, ideas, interpretations, events are put one after the other that are supposed to assemble a picture of an emotional situation that may or may not be developed into a story. The process the viewer sees is the process of this assemblage, which is suggested to hide a story somewhere but definitely not in the film.

Conclusion

From the point of the evolution of Godard's narrative procedures his third period, which is the longest, embracing more than 40 years, is similar to his first period in some respects, and dissimilar in others. At the beginning of both periods Godard's films respected at least the basics of classical narrative structures. In the first period it took about eight years, from 1960 until 1968, before Godard came to dismissing even the basic elements of classical narrative altogether. After 1968, in his second period, there is a sharp change leading to clearly non-narrative filmmaking, most of the time abandoning fictional dramatic situations (the main exception is *Tout va bien*, 1972). In the beginning of the third period (1980), Godard seemed to return to narration at least by restoring dramatic situations, and a narrative frame in his films. But again, only a couple of years later, from 1985 on, Godard's narrative mode took another turn. This time his films keep the fictional situations, do not mix different narrative modes and genres, the actors perform as if they were in a classical narrative in terms of emotional expression, but there is no linear or non-linear story development. The situations do not follow from each other, often in the same situation the characters do not respond to each other's lines, parallel monologues make narrative understanding impossible, and the narrative frame shows no difference between the beginning and the end.

This procedure is what I call a pseudo-narrative. It presents itself as if unfolding various dramatic situations in a chronology, but this chronology is simply the order in which the film represents fragmented acts, gestures, monologues, dialogues, closely or loosely related to the given situation, which itself does not progress in the film. Most viewers' impression of this structure is that they see a narrative they don't understand. However, these films do not contain stories with a beginning and an ending. They contain a variety of dramatic situations that could be developed into different storylines but all of them remain only potential or virtual in the imagination of the spectator. Understanding these films is not based on deciphering a narrative told in different narrational modes. Narrative is contained in them as multiple seeds provoking the spectator's fantasy to start out from a given situation and meander through different virtual paths possibly associated with this situation.

This technique is reminiscent of Baudelaire's construction of his volume *Les fleurs du mal*. This fragmented character is realized in Baudelaire's book as the series of individual poems, in Godard's films as a series of very loosely related individual scenes, and textual fragments in the form of dialogues and monologues, which are mostly literary citations. Therefore, it would not be too farfetched to interpret each Godard film after 1985 as *a collection of individual short poems expressing a variety of emotional attitudes related to some human, historical or political situation.* At the end, hopefully, the spectator obtains a complex, often contradictory impression of what it could be like to be in that situation.

Alain Delon's insight expressed in an interview made during the shooting of *Nouvelle Vague* is revelatory in this respect: "He is more a writer than a filmmaker" (Delon, 1989).

References

Baudelaire, Ch. (1991). In: Unwin (1991), p. 321.

Bordwell, D. (1985). *Narration in the fiction film*. Wisconsin University Press, p. 313.

Brody, R. (2008). *Everything is cinema: The working life of Jean-Luc Godard*. Holt Paperbacks.

Champlin, Ch. (1981) *Godard's second 'First Film'*. In: Los Angeles Times, January 22, pp. 1–3.

Cutting, J. E. (2014). Event segmentation and seven types of narrative discontinuity in popular movies. *Acta Psychologica*. 149, 69–77.

Delon, A. (1989). Un reportage diffusé le 23 octobre 1989 sur la TSR. https://www.youtube.com/watch?v=pXMwZTPoRpA (04:06).

Dixon, W. W. (1997). *The films of Jean-Luc Godard*. State University of New York Press.

Emmelhainz, I. (2019). *Jean-Luc Godard's political filmmaking*. Palgrave-McMillan.

Godard, J. L. (1965) Pierrot, mon ami. Les Cahiers du cinéma no. 171. October, 1965.

Godard, J.-L. (1967). Avant-Scene du Cinéma, no 70, May 1967.

Godard, J.-L. (1980). Interview in La Nouvel Observateur, October 20, 1980.

Godard, J.-L. (1984). In: Cahiers du cinéma, 1984 December.

Godard, J.-L. (1998). *Jean-Luc Godard par Jean-Luc Godard*. Cahiers du Cinéma, p. 16.

Godard, J.-L. (2006). https://laplumeetlimage.over-blog.com/article-bout-souffle-jean-luc-godard-82349640.html (accessed 2 August 2022).

Godard, J.-L. (2006). https://www.centrepompidou.fr/fr/programme/agenda/evenement/cc4zx9 (accessed 14 January 2022).

Godard, J.-L. (2009). Alex Munt: Retro-Modular Cinematic Narrative: Jean-Luc Godard's Masculin Féminin in the Digital Age. In: Jane T. and Gillian W. (eds.), *Countering narrative in art, theory and film*. Cambridge Scholars Publishing, p. 211.

Godard, J.-L. (2021). https://www.franceculture.fr/emissions/les-nuits-de-france-culture/la-nuit-revee-de-caroline-champetier-912-le-cinema-des-cineastes-jean-luc-godard-pour-sauve-qui-peut (accessed 26 March 2022).

Roud, R. (1968). *Godard*. Thames & Hudson Ltd. cited by Parkinson, D. (2015). https://www.bfi.org.uk/features/where-begin-jean-luc-godard-early-stuff (accessed 25 April 2023).

Silverman, K. & Farocki, H. (1998). *Speaking about Godard*. NYU Press.

Unwin, T. A. (1991). The 'Pseudo-narrative' of Les Fleurs du Mal. *Orbis Litterarum*. 46, 321–339.

Wollen, P. (1972). *Godard, counter cinema: Vent d'est*. Afterimage 4 Autumn, pp. 6–17.

9

DEFINING A LYNCHIAN NARRATIVE

Neil McCartney

This chapter will be carrying out a summary analysis of the films of David
Lynch. In doing so, I am throwing my hat into a crowded ring as I will be
contributing to an already popular, heavily researched and well-documented
area of film theory. Given the modest scope of this chapter, and within the
wider concept of telling stories through the moving image, this analysis will
focus narrowly on the question: what do we mean when we define a film
narrative as being 'Lynchian'? To have one's name adjectivised would imply
that there is broad agreement amongst scholars and critics that such a term is
viable purely because it is widely used. As such, I will use the term 'Lynchian'
as a framing device for my analysis of a filmmaker who has carved out a distinctive narrative style that at times defies conventional categorisation. For
those already familiar with the films of David Lynch, much of this chapter
will survey established knowledge and theories, but I will nevertheless try to
extend our understanding of his films within the context of narrative theory
in order to evaluate both the connotations of the term Lynchian and the extent to which it can be accurately applied to his film narratives as a whole.

There are a multitude of ways one can approach Lynch's work, and there
is no shortage of high-quality literature on this subject which considers his
work from a number of perspectives. In terms of narration and narrative
style in Lynch's films. Works like Michael Chion's *David Lynch* (2nd ed.,
2007) and Martha P. Nochimson's *The Passion of David Lynch: Wild at
Heart in Hollywood* (1997) are both extremely comprehensive in their analysis of Lynch's work. Working their way through each film chronologically,
both authors conduct detailed investigations into what makes the director's
output so distinctive. Situating their analysis within the relevant theoretical
and historical contexts, and bolstered with quotations from Lynch himself

DOI: 10.4324/9781003197911-12

(particularly in the case of Nochimson), each book serves as an ideal foundation for approaching Lynch's films. There are other works looking at more niche aspects of his work, as well as a glut of psychoanalytical and philosophical works that focus heavily on interpretation, particularly regarding those narratives that could be deemed oblique or puzzling. Beyond this, publications by Lynch himself are particularly illuminating and can serve as a very worthwhile alternative perspective for critical analysis. Alternative, that is, to works that perhaps focus primarily on production history or those that herald this or that 'definitive' answer to the meaning of a particular film(s).

Lynch's work is frequently described as blending surreal or sinister elements with mundane, everyday environments, and using imagery that evokes a dreamlike quality of mystery or menace. However, in certain respects, Lynch's work is quite conventional, relying on established tropes and genres, recognisable stars, and storylines that are – if stripped back to their synopses – reasonably simple tales. In the context of narratology and the accessibility of Lynch's films, it is clear that the director's work straddles a boundary between mainstream and art-cinema/avant-garde styles. Instead of an in-depth analysis of individual films, Lynch's work as a whole will be examined to look at key narrative features that can help us reach a clearer understanding of what (and if) one could call a Lynchian narrative.

One can gauge the consistency and critical usefulness of a term like 'Lynchian' by considering how it is used in theoretical discourse or audience reviews. In addition, we can look for consistent patterns or narrative features, taking an *auter* approach. With a filmography of ten features across 29 years (*Eraserhead*, 1977 – *Inland Empire*, 2006), Lynch's output appears relatively modest in terms of quantity. However, in terms of ambition and its impact on the landscape of film history, his influence is wide-reaching. Even for those who do not embrace *auteur* theory wholesale, the work of David Lynch contains strikingly distinctive features that are consistent across his output, which have allowed him to successfully carve out a narrative category of his own.

While the content of his films is varied, it is Lynch's visual flourishes and stylistic hallmarks that are often the principal identifiers for distinguishing his work. For instance, there is a recurrence of certain types of imagery; ringing telephones, smoke or steam, flickering light bulbs and other strobe effects like lightning, and sound effects like metallic clanging, throbbing hums and electrical fizzing, that suggest and evoke an industrial landscape or setting. In addition, his films often feature nightmarish scenarios and surreal, brutal imagery and violence, and storylines that vacillate between the bizarre, the everyday, and the supernatural. The characters in his films are frequently highly exaggerated in their bodily movements and vocal delivery, occupying an unnerving middle ground between comical and threatening. Thematically, there is a consistency of events and tone and areas of interest that the storylines appear to be focused on, such as women who are in danger, police procedures, questions over self-identity, mundane suburbia existing in parallel with a non-specific magical, fantastical realm. I use the term 'appear to be' since, as I will come onto shortly, narrative ambiguity is also an inherent feature of many of Lynch's films.

While Lynch's films arguably exist in their own standalone category, they also operate within a spectrum. *The Elephant Man*, for example, deals with dark subject matter by virtue of the real-life events upon which it is based, but it is also a commentary on morality and exploitation, and for the most part, behaves in a way that we might expect from a mainstream film narrative. *Blue Velvet* portrays dark, disturbing events but is still a somewhat conventional murder-mystery/private detective tale, albeit with the distinction of the lead being a youthful, amateur sleuth. But over the course of the running time, we are presented with a coherent progression of events displaying cause and effect linkage between scenes and time periods. Does this make these films any less Lynchian? If we considered them under the broad, popular understanding of the term, which conjures up adjectives like, 'weird, surreal, inscrutable, dark, erotic, magical', then yes.

This is where the concept of an *auteur* is problematised, as there a range of contributing factors that dictate the extent to which a director exerts control to the point where their signature hallmarks are abundantly clear. However, all of these films were directed by the same individual, so on a very basic level, they must qualify as Lynchian. But the Lynchian style can vary by a matter of degrees. There are motifs, themes, and subjects that are sprinkled throughout Lynch's films that make them characteristically Lynchian, and they are accentuated to a greater or lesser degree, depending on which film we are looking at. *The Elephant Man, Blue Velvet, Wild at Heart,* and particularly *The Straight Story*, have narrative structures and plot progressions that are accessible. They follow conventional narrative patterns, with only brief forays into the type of imagery and stylistic touches that might be considered more 'typically' Lynchian.

Twin Peaks: Fire Walk With Me, stands out as a feature that is rich with typically Lynchian features, but which is also inextricably linked to the TV series, co-created by Lynch and Mark Frost. A film that remains divisive, *Fire Walk With Me* essentially allowed Lynch to excise himself from the franchise and, arguably, provided some rewards/answers for its fans by serving as a prequel to the series. *Eraserhead*, Lynch's dark, semi-abstract, experimental debut, *Lost Highway, Mulholland Drive,* and *Inland Empire*, gravitate towards a more extreme, Lynchian-overdrive style of narrative. They contain highly unconventional character portrayals and character progressions, and could be grouped as a loose sub-set within Lynch's overall output.

Lost Highway's Moebius strip narrative structure can be contrasted with *The Straight Story*'s highly linear and causally connected chain of events. The latter is sometimes regarded as a response to the former following the frosty critical response by some who regarded *Lost Highway* as an impenetrable storyline due to its temporal impossibilities and multitude of narrative ambiguities (Berardinelli, 1999). *The Straight Story*'s title connotes several meanings; 'Straight' being the surname of the real-life individual portrayed in the film; he journeys to visit his brother along an almost unrelentingly straight highway; and the narrative design itself is highly linear (straight), depicting causally connected sequences and action in chronological order. Regardless of the motivations behind *The Straight Story*'s production, however, its linear and accessible narrative serves to blur the Lynchian label further by the fact that it is, by anyone's measure, a more simplified story than *Lost Highway*.

* * * *

The film *is* the talking.[1]

(David Lynch)

Lynch's more radical movies fundamentally challenge the concept of what it means to tell a story and, crucially, how it should be told. In David Bordwell's seminal essay 'The Art Cinema as Mode of Film Practice', he focuses on how the advancement of a clear, goal-oriented storyline is often subjugated in art cinema, favouring other aesthetic properties such as mood, atmosphere, performance, allegory, symbolism, and metaphor. That is not to say that mainstream films do not display all of these features, rather it is the delivery and narrative devices used that distinguish certain films and filmmakers as belonging to the art-cinema mode. In addition, the art-cinema canon contains films that foreground the artifice of what the viewer is experiencing and draws greater attention to the filmmaker's interventions and decision-making processes. Furthermore, in terms of narrative content and the clarity of events, Bordwell suggests that the slogan of the art cinema might be, 'When in doubt, read for maximum ambiguity' (2007, p. 156) – and a common, recurring, unavoidable topic that comes up when Lynch's films are being discussed is the search for narrative meaning.

Lynch is well-known for his reluctance, and at times refusal, to discuss and expand upon his own films. The quotation above – 'the film is the talking' – came from Lynch himself, illustrating his opinion that films are in themselves a finished article requiring nothing further to be added or subtracted – and that includes critical analysis and discussion (but here we are anyway!). He goes on to argue that any analysis will merely pale in comparison to the film (or other aesthetic product) being discussed and will add little or nothing to its overall effect on the viewer. In plain terms, we need not bother asking Lynch about meaning as it is all there in the film text. During the same interview, in relation to narrative content and subject matter, he echoes Bordwell by stating that 'the more abstract a thing gets, the more varied the interpretations'. There is no shortage of online debate or proponents of multiple theories claiming to have decoded or unlocked the meaning of Lynch's work, or a particular aspect thereof.[2] Indeed, professional critics themselves have also stepped into the trap of asking Lynch directly about the meaning of some of his films, only to come away none the wiser.

Taking a general perspective on how Lynch's work has been and continues to be received by audiences, a pervading response about some – although certainly not all – of his films is that they are confusing, frustrating, or seemingly devoid of meaning. This is observable across the spectrum of debates, from casual conversations to press reviews, from the plethora of online forums[3] to academic publications. I will not have the capacity here to go into the specifics of this debate as it pertains to individual narratives and storylines, however, what *is* pertinent is the fact that this debate exists at all. Since there is already literature on the interpretation of Lynch's films (see Chion, 1996), I will offer an observational analysis, rather than an interpretative one.

As viewers, we habitually build up coherence and understanding of a film storyline by drawing evidence from narrative events, retaining information for future reference, and relying on our familiarity with established cinematic cues to predict outcomes. In the list of Lynch's films that I termed a 'sub-set' – *Lost Highway, Mulholland Drive, and Inland Empire* – their storylines display plot progressions, location shifts, and alterations to characters that confound and disrupt the ways that we typically infer meaning and reconcile our expectations with what we witness. Within critical contexts, the term 'audience affect' or 'audience response' refers to a particular sector of critics and respondents to whatever film is being discussed.

To take one example: *Lost Highway* features Fred (Bill Pullman), who is arrested for murdering his wife and, in his prison cell on the first night after his conviction, he becomes a different person named Pete (Balthazar Getty). With the exception of one prison guard describing the strange occurrence as 'some spooky shit', no narrative explanations for Pete's appearance, or Fred's disappearance, are offered. Up to this point, we have seen little evidence in the narrative events to suggest that the storyline is introducing a science-fiction element, although there have been events that appear to defy the natural order of space and time consistent with surreal and supernatural narratives. However, although an apparent mutation has occurred, the context does not align with film narratives that overtly depict similar events and establish the unambiguously literal transformation that has occurred. For instance, *Lost Highway* does not display the sort of horror/science-fiction tropes such as those we are presented with in *The Thing* (John Carpenter, 1982) or deliver an explicit portrayal like the agonising metamorphosis in *An American Werewolf in London* (John Landis, 1981).

The late Roger Ebert (1997) made a rather casual dismissal of *Lost Highway* by commenting 'there is no sense to be made of it', and that, in his opinion, some of the narrative's irreconcilable ambiguities are a kind of joke being played on the audience. While I would not endorse such a critical response, I believe it is necessary to acknowledge an amorphous group of film viewers representing the corresponding audience for conventional, mainstream films that represent the 'average viewer'.

There is no homogeneity when we talk about 'viewer expectations' any more than there is consensus when we talk about viewers' tastes, preferences, sources of pleasure, or likely reactions. However, we may reasonably assume that viewers bring certain expectations to their experience of consuming a fiction film narrative and that these will incorporate a multitude of sub-assumptions such as a coherence of action, bodily continuity of characters, temporal markers, and clearly cued transitions between locations and time-frames. If these elements are blurred, deflected or confounded in some way, narrative coherence, and potentially viewer comprehension and enjoyment, break down – and in some of Lynch's films we can find instances of just that. By contrast, receptive viewers reach for alternative interpretative strategies that go beyond the literal or story-based level. When logical answers to what we see are elusive, a viewer may be inclined to interpret these events as symbolic and metaphorical rather than literal occurrences within the diegesis, particularly when consuming overtly art-cinema narratives.

Murray Smith comments that the avant-garde and art-cinema traditions have long been regarded as being particularly well-suited to analysing and illustrating aspects of (characters') subjective states, by acting as a 'metaphor for consciousness' through its tendency to place 'an emphasis on the rendering of subjective experience' (Smith, 2009, p. 45). The term 'dream logic' is often used to describe such sequences, depicting surreal imagery and events, as well as the way in which a film's structure, style or narrative progression appears to be governed by a loose, associative pattern rather than a classical narrative paradigm built around a goal-oriented protagonist operating in a classic three-act structure. In *Mulholland Drive* (2001), Lynch explores and builds on similar themes and ideas to *Lost Highway* and is something of a companion piece. Both storylines disrupt the conventions of character identities in similar ways – Fred/Pete has an equivalent alter-ego device in *Mulholland Drive* in the form of Diane and Betty. Similarly, both films heavily imply that a fugue state is at work and the seemingly distinct characters are actually fictional alternate selves created as a psychological refuge from trauma and guilt. Following on from there, Lynch delves even deeper into the fragility of personal/character identities with *Inland Empire* (2006) and the television series 'Twin Peaks: The Return' (2017), with the overriding use of dream-logic to guide their narrative structures and story progressions ensuring that unambiguous meanings and outcomes are hard to come by. Lynch's most recent work has challenged moving image storytelling conventions (along with acting performance, running time and shot length) in a way not seen since his debut, *Eraserhead*.

Obscured, evasive meanings, surreal progressions, and irreconcilable spatio-temporal events have become the predominant associations or connotations of Lynchianism, however, this is primarily due to the frequency of such narrative occurrences in Lynch's most recent work. In their study of the contemporary phenomenon of 'puzzle films', Miklós Kiss and Steven Willemsen state the following aim at the outset:

> What we aim to find out is *what such puzzling and enigmatic stories do and how viewers make them work* …. Ultimately, our questions are about what makes these stories *complex* beyond being simply *complicated*.
> *(Kiss and Willemsen, 2018, p. 3)*

This distinction is so simple and yet so far-reaching in terms of how a viewer might try to grasp and categorise a narrative, and thereby try to extrapolate why they may or may not find it cognitively challenging. The emergence of films such as *Memento*, *The Usual Suspects,* and *Fight Club*, to name a few, are the focus of Kiss and Willemsen's book, and they explore the distinction between 'complicated' and 'complex' narratives in detail. They also discuss the interplay between filmmaker and viewer, and the pleasure derived from deciphering the filmmaker's efforts to generate suspense by suppressing key narrative details and/or offering revised versions of events towards the conclusion of the film. However, in these examples there is a problem to be solved, a mystery to be unravelled, and part of the viewing pleasure is derived from either predicting the outcome or retrospectively exploring how the narrative hoodwinked the viewer.

By way of contrast, in *Dreams of Chaos, Visions of Order*, James Peterson sees the exercise of appreciating 'difficult' films as something to be learned and developed through repeated exposure. Peterson's argument is that a viewer's capacity to tolerate narrative paradoxes and inconsistencies is simply an issue of familiarity with avant-garde or, at the very least, non-mainstream stylistic features (1994, p. 38). As such, in this context, familiarity with other David Lynch films means that a viewer will anticipate and tolerate uncued tangents and narrative obscurity. If we are aware that many of his films set up intricate and frequently unsolvable puzzles then we may be ready and willing to embrace riddles and ambiguities, or actively anticipate them.

Editing plays a big part in shoring up a (sense of a) Lynchian narrative and underpinning a dream-logic structure. Inextricably linked to twists and turns of storylines and the introduction of bizarre events or behaviour, Lynch often favours an editing style that gives unclear indications about intervening action and the length of time that has elapsed between scenes. John Orr wrote in his review of *Inland Empire*:

> the meaning of the relationship *between sequences,* those notorious Lynchian non-sequiturs, is anybody's guess. In this respect, the film is tougher to read than any of its predecessors.
>
> *(Orr, 2009)*

By way of contrast, we can look briefly at one of the puzzle film examples cited by Kiss and Willemsen. In *Memento* (2000, Christopher Nolan), we are presented with an innovative reverse-chronology structure, which on an aesthetic level appears to be a challenging viewing experience given its highly unusual temporal design. By making the process of film viewing 'difficult' the viewer is made more conscious of the thought processes and techniques normally employed when following a conventional narrative – an effect perhaps comparable to asking someone to use their non-dominant hand to complete a simple everyday task. However, even though *Memento* displays a unique structure, stylistic choices and directorial decisions compensate for its unconventional structure to ensure that the viewer falls into step with its pattern so that overall comprehension is not lost. The narrative is meticulously organised so that there are overlaps of repeated action between each segment, to ensure that it falls on the side of 'complex' rather than 'complicated'. As such, despite its surface appearance, *Memento* demonstrates a design which is the antithesis of what Orr calls 'Lynchian non-sequiturs'.

We can deepen and expand this point further in the context of Lynch's work since Kiss and Willemsen's distinction raises a salient point in relation to one of his films which is sometimes dismissed as the anomaly – *Dune* (1984). This is the film that is most frequently cited as not only the least typical (or most un-Lynchian) of the director's work, but also one that is classified as a disappointment or 'failure'.[4] Regardless of one's personal opinion, *Dune* serves as an interesting counter-example to use against a prevailing critical reaction that Lynch's work is oblique and impenetrable. In the wider context of 'Lynchianism', *Dune* is interesting not simply because it appears anomalous amongst the director's other films (a large-scale, epic, studio-led, sci-fi blockbuster), and not even because it doesn't bear some of the stylistic hallmarks that we might refer to as Lynchian (which it does, such as its unnerving dream sequences, and the grotesque Guild Navigator that recalls the 'baby' in *Eraserhead*). The point of interest in the context of narratology is that the story of *Dune* is highly complex and involves a wealth of back-story involving galactic political struggles, and these operate both diegetically and allegorically on a multitude of levels. Frank Herbert's novel *Dune*, from which Lynch's film was adapted, is fiendishly complex and features a constellation of characters, planets, alien creatures, technologies, traditions, and mythologies. The world-building ability of prose is notoriously difficult to convert into a viable and enjoyable screenplay, and anyone familiar with the source novel will know that its storyline requires far more exposition than the most successful of Lynch's other films. By Lynch's own account, the production was a stressful and unrewarding process (Lynch and McKenna, 2019, p. 184). Lynch suffered from a toxic combination of studio pressures to deliver a mainstream blockbuster, and his own artistic sensibilities to deliver a detailed interpretation of the text that was true to his instincts and faithful to the source.

In relation to Kiss and Willemsen's 'complex/complicated' dichotomy, the source material for *Dune* would qualify as the former, but Lynch was at pains to make this complex array of characters and planets accessible to a mainstream audience. The storylines in Lynch's films that are considered inscrutable are often quite unconventional, at least in terms of their narrative components and scenarios. They often draw on recognisable genres such as film-noir, and mystery/detective/police procedural dramas, however, it is the way in which they are presented that creates a conflict with traditional conceptions of structuring film narratives. This presents a striking irony in that when dealing with an exceedingly complex story world such as that of *Dune,* Lynch strove to include as much detail as possible to achieve greater clarity. It would appear he wanted to do justice to the complex backstories of the novel but was very much an arthouse director operating in a big studio setting and these aspects were hard to reconcile. The studio pressures on Lynch and interference with the final cut were the primary reasons for *Dune's* incoherent storyline rather than any deliberate attempt on the director's part to challenge viewer comprehension or introduce ambiguity. In contrast, with a relatively simple premise such as that in, say, *Mulholland Drive,* he achieved significant amounts of narrative complexity, redundancy of storytelling, and a multiplicity of meaning, within a reasonably mainstream scenario. Regardless of the reasons, however, it is ironic that when adapting a complex source novel and striving for clarity and faithfulness to the text, Lynch's resultant effort is (respectfully) confused and confusing. In contrast, *Mulholland Drive, Lost Highway* and *Eraserhead*, which grapple with intense but comparatively 'human', everyday scenarios, are twisted into jarring, ambiguous, open-ended tales.

Concluding Remarks

By analysing Lynch's body of work, one can identify key tropes and recurring narrative features that populate most of his films. However, despite their recognisability there is surprising variation amongst them, and the fact that defining a Lynchian narrative (or Lynchianism in general) is not quite as straightforward as it seems, is entirely fitting. At times it is the appearance and performance of a character, at others it may be a jarring, unmotivated plot development, or perhaps a colour scheme rich with symbolism. We might associate a particular soundtrack or sound effect with a mood that could be considered Lynchian; it may be the unexpected intrusion of surreal events into an everyday scene or a tangential plot digression that is impossible to reconcile in both spatio-temporal and narrative contexts. It may be identifiable in all these elements but there is arguably no one defining feature (or even one standout film) that could be considered quintessentially Lynchian.

Certain films deviate and diverge in unexpected ways (unless, of course, as a seasoned Lynch enthusiast you are expecting them to do just that), at times appearing to follow narrative conventions before suddenly switching to a dream-logic pattern in which our assumptions about characters and storyline are thrown into disarray. As we have seen, however, this is not true of all his films, and it would be more accurate to say that they exist on a spectrum in which certain examples, or choice scenes that display a mainstream surface appearance fit the dictionary definition of a Lynchian narrative. *Wild at Heart* and *Lost Highway* were both adapted from novels by Barry Gifford and although the former frequently digresses into its dreamlike asides invoking the storyline and imagery of *The Wizard of Oz*, it is a far more conventional narrative than *Lost Highway*.

The fact that it is difficult to pinpoint exactly what constitutes a Lynchian narrative is perhaps the most fitting observation of all, so to refrain from imposing strict definitions and reaching an unambiguous conclusion is an appropriate way to end.

Notes

1 *Great Directors* (Angela Ismailos, 2009).
2 For example, see Arnzen (2008), Brek (2018), and Twin Perfect (2019).
3 One online author argues that the key to understanding Lynch's films is to be happy with not understanding them: 'a willingness to deal with confusion and to derive one's own meaning from what's transpired on screen is what Lynch has always tried to evoke in viewers' (Brek, 2018).
4 This is plainly a divisive and slightly lazy term that is used too frequently. I would qualify such an assessment as being seen through the lens of some Lynch fans on the one hand and studio expectations on the other – with both sides feeling disappointed. Michael Chion (1996, p. 77) expands in his companion to Lynch's work.

References

Arnzen, M. (2008) *David Lynch's Doppelgangers, the Popular Uncanny*. Available at: https://gorelets.com/uncanny/film/david-lynchs-doppelgangers/ (Accessed: February 4, 2023).

Berardinelli, J. (1999) *Straight Story, the, Reelviews Movie Reviews*. Available at: https://www.reelviews.net/reelviews/straight-story-the (Accessed: February 4, 2023).

Bordwell, D. (2007) *Poetics of Cinema*. New York, NY: Routledge.

Brek, M. (2018) *The Key to Understanding David Lynch is Being Okay with not Understanding David Lynch, Film School Rejects.* Available at: https://filmschool-rejects.com/understanding-david-lynch/ (Accessed: February 4, 2023).

Chion, M. (1996) *David Lynch.* BFI Publishing.

Ebert, R. *Chicago Sun-Times*, Thursday, February 27, 1997.

Kiss, M. and Willemsen, S. (2018) *Impossible Puzzle Films.* Edinburgh University Press.

Lynch, D. and McKenna, K. (2019) *Room to Dream: A Life in Art.* Canongate Books.

Orr, J. (2009) 'A cinema of parallel worlds', *Film International*, Vol. 7, Issue 1: 39.

Peterson, J. (1994) *Dreams of Chaos, Visions of Order.* Wayne State University Press.

Smith, M. (2009) 'Consciousness', in P. Livingston and C. Plantinga (eds.), *The Routledge Companion to Philosophy and Film.* Abingdon/New York, NY: Routledge.

Twin Perfect. *Twin Peaks ACTUALLY EXPLAINED (No, Really)* (2019) YouTube. Available at: https://www.youtube.com/watch?v=7AYnF5hOhuM (Accessed: February 4, 2023).

PART III
Alternative Media

10

TELEVISION NARRATIVE

Forms, Strategies, and Histories

Sean O'Sullivan and Robyn Warhol

Television blends many inheritances: the corporeal presence of theater, the imaginative immersion of the novel, the episodic structure of the short story, the intimacy and regularity of radio, and the technical language of cinema. Even the name—"television"—idiosyncratically blends the Greek word for distance and the Latin word for sight. Television's distinctiveness comes from its ability to draw on its predecessors while creating forms, combinations, and innovations that are recognizably televisual in their practices and effects.[1] Our goal in this chapter will be to identify the characteristics that have structured the organizational narrative patterns of the medium. Focusing on the strategies and effects most central to shaping our experiences of watching stories on TV, we consider both foundational and more recent versions of several core storytelling habits. We aim first to provide a narrative-centric vocabulary of televisual properties and options, and then to illustrate how they have been deployed in selected TV genres over the past 70 years.

Genre and expectation: Genre is one way to define the "strategies and effects most central to structuring our experiences of watching stories on TV," or the familiar arrangements that television has chosen to deploy, capturing our attraction through the comfortable and the known. The prominence of the genre, most especially in commercial television, derives from the need to keep audiences watching through advertising breaks and then—even more crucially—from week to week, and season to season. Many of these genres draw from the older artistic inheritances cited at the start of this chapter, but many are alterations or inventions made by television's unfolding discursive trajectory. The genre can exist at the level of story, of course—as in a police show. But it can also operate discursively through formal conventions—such as the half-hour episode length traditionally associated with comedy rather

DOI: 10.4324/9781003197911-14

than drama—or the kinds of actors that certain shows foreground—such as burly Italian-Americans in *The Sopranos* (1999–2007)[2]—or all the ways we are asked to engage the rules and latitude that a series makes prominent. There is inevitably recirculatory energy between genre and expectation: as producers inform audiences about what they "should" want, audiences inform producers about what they actually want, in a slightly drunken but clearly mappable collection of causes-and-effects (Altman, 1984). In many ways, the genre threshold has served as the point of commonality—and the point of departure—for each of the following sets of televisual characteristics that invite a narrative-theoretical approach.

Ratio and scale: Television storytelling is the art of parts, pieces, and fragments—working both as independent narrative units and as elements in larger organizational units. These parts can be "scenes" or "episodes" or "seasons," whose shapes and rhythms mold how we as viewers respond to moments, developments, and larger-scale narrative experiences (Newman, 2006).

Some of these parts may seem more marginal, such as a "cold open" or teaser scene that airs before the opening credits of an installment, or the recurring closing title music that signals a code of leave-taking. All these modules, however, matter to the distinctive methodology by which television draws us in. Two key deviations in 21st-century television from the medium's earlier practices are the relationship between the narratively local and the narratively global, and the relationship between the episodic and the serial (Feuer, 1986). If the local is a single story and the global is the entire universe of a show, the season in recent years has served as a crucial way of shifting our understanding of how the local and global operate; the 39-episode seasons of the police procedural *Dragnet* (1951–1959) in the 1950s created a very different sense of the ratio between the installment and our broader imaginative participation from the eight-to-ten episode norms of shows like *Stranger Things* (2013–). Influential narratives like *The Sopranos* drew critical attention to the varying dynamics between the serial (where installments are to-be-continued) and the episodic (where each episode has a beginning, a middle, and an end), presenting a creatively open range of options that constantly re-invent the part's connection to something beyond itself (Mittell, 2015).

Storyworld and style: Mayberry. Central Perk. Dunder Mifflin. Sterling Cooper. Winterfell. Sunnydale High School. Those familiar with these televisual locations will immediately be able to recall the unmistakable look and feel of each, as a place to which they are brought back week after week. The long reach of many television series creates this evolving connection to how a storyworld reaffirms its self-announcing physical properties every time that we reenter it. A storyworld is not just a stage set or even a group of sets; it is a grounded and revisitable virtual environment, created by the interplay of space, backstory, character behavior, history, social and psychological identities, and the consequent effect of viewer immersion (Harrigan and Wardrip-Fruin, 2009). Habit and ritual are among the most powerful elements of our bond with narrative television—how or when we watch, to be sure, but also the institutional storytelling practices that we associate not only with a particular series but with watching television itself (Jenkins, 2006). Style is the collection of aesthetic and practical choices that a show deploys for making that storyworld recognizable, using the cinematic language—camera, editing, and sound—to mold ways of seeing and hearing that embody the show's differentiated universe. Deviating from the physically and aesthetically known, some TV narratives—such as anthology series or more experimental shows—may deliberately refuse to be regularly recognizable; by playing with expectations about storyworld or style, these shows ask us to reconsider what makes any series a cohesive collection.

Representation and context: As one of the mimetic arts, television positions the "real world" as the referent for much of its programing, from presumably factual newscasts to fantasy shows like *The Twilight Zone* (1959–1964), where extraordinary things happen within recognizable televisual storyworlds. As TV rose to popular-culture dominance throughout the second half of the 20th century, the worlds represented in television shows powerfully influenced U.S. culture. Seductively idealized, gendered types (the always cheerful, industrious, and forbearing housewife; the strong, silent, self-sacrificing cowboy), not to mention egregious racial and ethnic stereotypes (the slap-happy Black sidekick; the nobly doomed or senselessly malicious Indian; the noisy, excitable Chinese man with big teeth and long pigtails) all burdened mid-century U.S. culture with damaging models for real women, men and children to aspire to or to shun.[3]

As the television industry gradually became more inclusive, so did TV storyworlds, positioning fictional television as an agent of social change (Sepinwall, 2013). It is hard to imagine how same-sex marriage could have become legal across the United States in 2015 without the normalizing influence of widely beloved shows featuring LGBTQ characters, such as *Ellen* (1994–1998), *Will and Grace* (1998–2006), and *Modern Family* (2009–2020). The enormous demand for new TV material brought on by the 21st-century proliferation of cable channels and streaming services has made room for show creators, producers and stars who represent the full range of U.S. genders, sexualities, races, and classes. In the Möbius loop linking the influence of televisual representation, the more diversely representative workforce in the TV industry, and the range of identity categories now represented on television, TV narratives shape and are shaped by the culture that produces and consumes them.[4]

Delivery and audience: If the narrative is an instance of "somebody telling somebody else for some purpose that something happened," the viewing audience is as integral to TV narrative as the production and distribution of shows (Phelan, 2010). In the broadcast era, television series followed lock-step schedules requiring viewers' presence in front of the TV set on a certain day at a certain hour every week. The television industry pitched its stories to an extrapolated audience based on Nielsen survey ratings representing a small subset of actual viewers. This imagined audience began to disperse in the 1970s, as subscriber-based cable networks gained traction. By the late 1990s, premium channels began pitching "quality TV" series which broadcast networks would have found too risky (or risqué) to produce, and in the early 21st-century video recording machines and DVD boxed sets made time shifting, binge watching, and re-viewing of favorite series possible. The advent of streaming services has rendered "appointment TV" a thing of the past, now that viewers can choose their own circumstances and devices for watching most television programs. Netflix altered the landscape further in 2013 when the premieres of *House of Cards* (2013–2018) and *Orange Is the New Black* (2013–2019) initiated the "season drop," where an entire slate of new episodes materialized at once, altering the established rhythms of weekly delay by which viewers moved from installment to installment; indeed, the entire baseline of an "installment" changed as a result (Warhol, 2014). The post-network burgeoning of channels consequently serves countless specialized audiences. Broadcast-era shows were intended to be intelligible to everyone, but TV series in the 21st century can address a more diverse set of viewers' identity positions, ideologies, and tastes (Spigel and Olsson, 2004). Individual shows may appeal to smaller subsets of the viewing public than broadcast programs were supposed to, but the pleasures they deliver to that tailor-made audience are arguably more intense.

The preceding ten terms provide a set of tools for identifying and then decoding how a television series chooses to present itself, episode by episode and season by season. The referents for each of those terms depend in part on the facts about how and when a given series was produced and distributed. As one example, consider *Gunsmoke* (1955–1975), the first show discussed below, as part of the paired illustrations that will take up the remainder of the essay. In terms of genre and expectations, *Gunsmoke* is a Western produced in an era when the genre was particularly visible on U.S. television, following the revival of the Western as a popular film genre in the 1940s; *Gunsmoke* in fact began as a radio drama that preceded and then ran concurrently with the television version for a few years, reflecting the multi-media manifestations of the genre at this moment in history. In terms of ratio and scale, *Gunsmoke*'s first season runs to 39 episodes—an almost unimaginable length in our era, but one that was quite typical at the time for all genres of TV series, before tapering off to 24 episodes in the 1970s, again reflecting industrial changes. The episodes were 30 minutes long from 1955 to 1961 before shifting to 60 minutes, with virtually no serial effects, beyond the audience's familiarity with the characters and vestigial awareness of preceding incidents. In terms of storyworld and style, the plot for each episode—as we discuss below—is generated by newcomers to Dodge City, Kansas, providing the temporarily new in an atmosphere dominated by regular characters oriented in established relationship to one other. In terms of representation and context, *Gunsmoke* provides a mid-20th-century depiction of the 19th-century American frontier, with familiar types articulating seemingly fixed roles of gender, race, and power with which the Western was long associated, at a broadcasting time when the furthest reaches of the frontier were finally closed: Alaska and Hawaii became the nation's 49th and 50th states in 1959, during *Gunsmoke*'s fourth season, and before the start of its fifth, respectively. And in terms of delivery and audience, each episode was aired with commercial breaks on Saturday nights by CBS, at a time when only two other networks (NBC and ABC) were in operation, resulting in vast audiences upward of 40-million people, far beyond the scope of today's multiply scattered viewing platforms. Even in that context, *Gunsmoke* had an especially large fandom, as ratings ranked it the #1 show in the United States from 1957 to 1961 and it remained as high as #7 until 1973.

We could, and most importantly *you* can provide the same baseline diagnosis for any television series. That array of information is vital to understanding the defining components of *Gunsmoke* as a narrative made for a specific medium, and to understand how that narrative was consumed at the time of its original airing—and can still be consumed on DVD or in syndication today, all 20 seasons' worth. For viewers and critics, the question then becomes how we want to examine specific aspects of the series, at either the microscopic level of an individual scene, or the macroscopic level of the series as a whole, or at any of multiple points and registers between those poles. We can consider the characteristics we find most worthy of study either in light of the show's own confines or in conversation with other shows that provide similar or perhaps contrasting narrative designs. For example, we might investigate how the significant alteration from half-hour episodes in *Gunsmoke*'s first six seasons to one-hour episodes in the subsequent seasons (or even the transition to color in the final nine seasons) altered or maintained elements of the series' narrative structure—including the pacing of the narrative, the use of the storyworld, and deployments of viewer expectations. More broadly, we might think about the long-standing dichotomy between the half-hour installments signifying "comedy" and the hour-long installments signifying "drama"—that has dominated U.S. television in particular, originally at the service of a programing grid beholden to the numerology of the clock. Movies, by contrast, typically run between 90 minutes and 130 minutes, and we don't automatically know the genre, or wider category of any particular film, based on time length alone. On TV through the 1970s, only anthological mysteries, such as *Columbo*

(1968–1978), provided episodes longer than 60 minutes, resulting in arrays of assumptions and conventions that transcend any individual series. We know that each episode of *Friends* (1994–2004) will squeeze all six principal characters into a node of stories lasting 30 minutes (with commercials); we also know that each episode of *Law & Order* (1990–2010, 2022–) will divide its hour more or less into an investigative half and a legal half, using the punctuation of advertising to organize its locked-in storytelling components. Matters of ratio, scale, expectations, style, context, and delivery (among other terms) all shape how *Friends* and *Law & Order* construct themselves, and how they are consumed by viewers. Noticing the choices, patterns, and situations of a series provides the initial array of data for probing the particularities of their effects.

The remainder of this essay will focus on the first of the ten terms that we provide: genre.

Genre is arguably the largest of these terms, synthesizing as it does issues of storyworld, style, representation, scale, and audience, helping to provide a framework for how a succession of series have brought together the constituent elements of television narration. Most importantly, genre allows us to move across television's historical span, to trace both the separations and continuities of the medium's principal storytelling apparatus across time. Within each category, we have juxtaposed a TV show from before 1970 with a show from the 21st century, in order to suggest how genres manage both to change and to stay the same over time. There are many narrative TV genres worthy of study, including the soap opera, the courtroom drama, the medical drama, "reality" TV, the made-for-TV movie, the sketch show, and the Saturday-morning cartoon, to name just a few. Our selection foregrounds not simply personal inclinations but genres that have functioned as key markers of the medium over many decades, and that remain as identifiable today as in the middle of the last century. With just one exception (*Black Mirror*), we have chosen U.S.-made series for their adherence to our chosen genres, but we offer these narrative-theoretical readings with the understanding that they are relevant across the TV spectrum.

The first three genres below—the Western, the police procedural, and the anthology series—demonstrate narrative processes and habits that bracket the development of television from its earliest days. The fourth and fifth permit a closer look at what is probably the most successful single genre in television history: comedy. We have split that genre into two parts to attempt not only to grasp the wealth of available examples but also to illustrate the double perspective with which this essay began—namely, television as an inheritor and television as an innovator. There is no more vivid evidence of television's innovative capacities than the sitcom, a genre that exists in no other preceding or concurrent medium. The "situation" of a set cluster of characters, delimited by specific, recurrent circumstances and behavior, shaped to provide laughs on a highly consistent schedule, and that reset with no linger-ing consequences from installment to installment, results from television's function as a machine that needs to keep disgorging congruous narrative pieces that we want to accumulate and live into. Shades of serialization have crept into this predominantly hermetic genre since the will-they-won't-they plots introduced by series like *Moonlighting* and *Cheers* in the late 1980s, but the basic infrastructure remains essentially unchanged. In juxtaposition, we also discuss a comedic genre that we call the "social comedy"—a category that, by explicit contrast with the sitcom, is a creature derived from the very long history of comedic expression in Western culture. While the Western, the police procedural, and the anthology show also draw from the pre-his-tory of the medium, in each case that history extends no further than the popular literature of the 19th century (in the case of anthology shows, via the form of print miscellanies). Social comedy, which collides amusement with cultural or political commentary, has been a mainstay of visual representa-tion for millennia; but often it was hidden, marginalized or handled with kid gloves by television comedy, for fear of causing offense to mass audiences, a crime of which the sitcom has long endeavored to stay clear. Social comedy reminds us that a television set, in its pre-digital incarnation, is the same elec-tronic box in the corner of the living room where—a few hours earlier or im-mediately following the narrative "prime time" from 8 to 11 p.m.—viewers would have learned about the contemporary, non-fictional world, including such momentous and long-running sagas as school desegregation, the civil rights and women's movements, and the Vietnam War.

The line between these comedic categories has often dissolved in the 21st century, as some recent series illustrates. *What We Do in the Shadows* (2019–) is grounded in an outlandish sitcom premise: four vampires sharing a house in unfashionable Staten Island. But the profusion of violence, pro-fanity, sexual dialogue, and death (and undeath) removes it from the safer contours of the sitcom in its classic state. *PEN15* (2019–2021) is set in the sitcom-ready confines of a public middle school at the turn of the last century; in this case, however, the two women showrunners play, in their thirties, ver-sions of themselves as teenagers among actual teenage actors. The deliberate awkwardness of adults and adolescents sharing the same physical and psy-chological space, conjoined with attention to matters of race, puberty, and the vulnerabilities of female bodies, make the social and the sitcom clash in almost every frame. *Heartstopper* (2022–), adopted from a webcomic, relies on the manifest formula of cinematic romantic comedy to depict the gradual coming together of two secondary school students. The students in question, however, are two boys, and matters of sexual orientation, body conformity, homophobia, ethnicity, and coming out are underlined in ways that make the challenges of living in the world much more present than sitcoms are usually willing to recognize, with their magically economy-free living circumstances.

Throughout all of the following studies, we aim to examine precisely these lines between the expected and the unfamiliar, the established and the disruptive, the inherited and the invented.

The Western

Gunsmoke (1955–1975)

While most TV westerns of the late 1950s–early 1960s feature regular characters who move around, *Gunsmoke* (1955–1975) prefigures *Deadwood* (2004–2006) by focusing on a single town. The storylines on *Gunsmoke* seldom originate with the show's regular protagonists. As with itinerant westerns like *Wagon Train* (1957–1965) and *Rawhide* (1959–1965), each episode introduces a set of new characters with a problem. These people, who live in the outskirts of Dodge City or are passing through, are beset with a moral issue: domestic abuse, a secret prison record, alcoholism, gambling, family cut-off or abandonment, racial persecution, a bad reputation that is undeserved, or plain old crime and mischief. All of them either reform through Marshal Matt Dillon's intervention, get killed, or "get out of Dodge," on Matt's orders or by their own choice. Whether they stay or go, viewers never see them again.

The one exception is Quint Asper (Burt Reynolds), a half-Comanche blacksmith who identifies as Indian but, over the course of some 50 episodes, gets assimilated into all-white Dodge City through Marshal Dillon's patronage. Quint's presence sparks numerous plots about anti-Indian racism, which is always condemned and resolved by the *Gunsmoke* regulars. In all the classic TV westerns, "Indians," as they are always called on classic Westerns (played, of course, by white actors in black braided wigs and dark makeup) are sympathetic characters so long as they live by white men's rules and treaties.

Classic TV western plots circle around the ways that rules, laws, morals, and social customs constrain the freedom the West was supposed to offer. Every traditional Western has its arbiter of the law, the hero, an unmarried man who is taller (Matt Dillon, played by James Arness, was 6′7″), braver, handsomer, wiser, more skilled with a gun, more reliable, and more efficacious than anyone else around. He may be the sheriff, the federal marshal, the bounty hunter, the hired gun, the trail boss, the wagon master or (like Lucas McCain in *The Rifleman* [1958–1963]) just the most responsible man in town. He holds other people's lives in his hands. He'd rather not kill anyone but will do it if he must to save his own or a bystander's life. He avoids showdowns and may get captured or injured himself, but he always wins in the climactic gunfight, ambush, skirmish with "Indians" or bandits, hostage situation, or chase scene. Sometimes he is a loner (the hired gun as in *Have*

Gun Will Travel [1958–1960], or the bounty hunter as in *Wanted Dead or Alive* [1958–1961]) but more often he has a comedic male sidekick who can help him out in a pinch, a little old man like the cooks on *Wagon Train* and *Rawhide*; or a man with an unusual characteristic like Chester (who limps) and, later, Festus (who has a bizarre way of speaking) on *Gunsmoke*; or an adorable little son like Mark on *The Rifleman*. The hero also has a sensible but emotionally vulnerable male friend (Doc on *Gunsmoke*, Micah on *The Rifleman*, Rowdy on *Rawhide*, Flint on *Wagon Train*). There's a lot of by-play between the sensible friend and the sidekick, with the sidekick defending himself against jocular verbal abuse, implausibly skirting the curses that TV censorship forbade.

The hero, the sensible friend or even the sidekick can have a romantic interest, but the woman—already married, or dying, or mixed-race, or doomed in some other way—comes and goes within one episode. Matt Dillon alone among TV western heroes has a consistent woman friend for whom he would do anything, Miss Kitty (Amanda Blake). Her costume, hairstyle and makeup connote Victorian brothel wear, but even though she owns a saloon with bedrooms upstairs, she never lets anyone touch her in a sexual way. Matt certainly never tries, never even kisses her on the cheek. They are like brother and sister, or like affectionate, respectful colleagues making Dodge City a safe place for white people to live. Based as it is on mid-century ideology about who counts as an American, this constellation of character types forms the deep structure for storytelling in classic Westerns.

Deadwood (2004–2006)

The HBO series *Deadwood* drew on many predecessors: the TV western of the 1950s and 1960s, whose episodic grounding in a recurrent set of characters established one of the key genres of the first decades of U.S. television; the "revisionist" cinematic western—like *McCabe & Mrs. Miller* (1971), directed by TV-western graduate Robert Altman—that disturbed norms of white male heroism and redemption; and, in a formal context, the "sonnet-season" series of the early 21st century that changed the U.S. television horizon through 12–13 episode uninterrupted seasons providing both a focused storytelling shape—compared to the 24-episode seasonal norm, scattered over nine months, of the late 20th-century—and boundless opportunities for invention—freed from the resistance to oddity and fear of audience alienation that ruled the networks (O'Sullivan, 2010). The first three sonnet-season series on HBO—*The Sopranos, Six Feet Under* (2001–2005), and *The Wire* (2002–2008)—altered television in disparate ways, providing *Deadwood* with a range of generative elements: from *The Sopranos*, a cutthroat antiheroic protagonist and discomfiting collisions of humor and violence that tested the limits of televisual comfort; from *Six Feet Under*, a recurrent recognition of human fragility, and the arbitrary methods by which we assign meaning to the unknowable, in perhaps futile hope of transcendent knowledge; and from *The Wire*, a vast array of characters that challenged the audience's ability to navigate individuals' fraught relationship to their circumstances. Eight people are killed in *Deadwood*'s pilot alone, requiring us immediately to manage information and the scope of the show's worldbuilding. One core difference between *Deadwood* and its three HBO predecessors was its focus on the start of something—the development of a Black Hills gold rush 1870s mining camp into a town—rather than on long-established (and gradually decaying) businesses, families, and environments. The series made explicit the parallel between building a physical 19th-century world and building a televisual world-space, with all the attendant fits and starts of potential, momentum, and the unexpected.

The sonnet-season format allowed each exponent to chart its own, often shifting, understanding of the tension between narrative freedom and narrative restriction. The traditional TV western emblematized that tension in its own idiom, juxtaposing the fantasy of freedom embodied in the American frontier and the necessity of resetting the drama after each episode. One restriction that *Deadwood* chose to embrace was Aristotle's long-standing diagnosis that "tragedy tends to fall within the single revolution of the sun"; by consistently limiting the events of each episode to one day, the show concentrated its attention on the dynamics that integrated multiple storylines. *Deadwood*'s synthesis of sonnet-season seriality with the classical emphasis on the day as the unit of plot created a unique distillation of storytelling intensity, simultaneously privileging the circumscribed and the consequential. But *Deadwood* also gloried, by contrast with that Aristotelian restriction, in a freedom of speech that few U.S. television shows had been able to achieve. Creator and showrunner David Milch explained the omnipresent and often baroque permutations of profanity, uttered by just about everyone in the camp, as an expression of the unfettered impulse to re-imagine: the characters, he said, "wanted a liberation from the restrictions of language just as they wanted a liberation from politics" (Milch 2006, 19). The western's long-standing antipodes of the wilderness and the garden became conjoined, the lawless territory now operating idiosyncratically as a site for cultivating the boundary-crossing words that connected people through a shared rejection of the expected.

The second and third seasons of the show are dominated first by the machinations and then the arrival of George Hearst—a figure of the Gilded Age "amalgamation and capital" that swept away the foundational illusions of frontier-town freedom and independence, which had themselves been derived from the exploitation of women as prostitutes and immigrants as disposable bodies. *Deadwood*'s wider engagement with economic and social consequence, by contrast with earlier TV westerns, mirrored a narrative investment in the consequences of serial accumulation as itself an engine that transforms improvisational events and discovers systems of meaning.

The Police Procedural

Columbo (1968–1978)

As a series, *Columbo* is preoccupied with technologies that were new and strange in the 1970s, such as mobile phones, answering machines, audio recording devices, video cameras, computers, and robotics. Lieutenant Columbo (Peter Falk) often remarks on these technological innovations, and when he does, they will invariably turn out to be the key to the killer's false alibi. Strictly episodic, *Columbo*'s formula turned out to be a kind of technology for establishing police-centered TV's genre norms before the 1980s, when the multiplot, multi-protagonist, serial *Hill Street Blues* (1981–1987) set a new pattern. Establishing the "open mystery" format for procedurals that would later be taken up by episodic series like *Law and Order: Criminal Intent* (2001–2011), the detective doesn't appear until after the crime has been dramatized, leaving the viewer in no doubt as to "who done it." The question is only "How will Columbo prove who did it?" In the tradition of Sherlock Holmes, Columbo solves one crime per episode through his pertinacious hunt for clues and his unique ability to interpret them. Columbo has no backstory, no story arc, no gradual development of personality because his series is not a serial.

But as a type, Columbo—and his generic descendants, the man-of-the-people detective of procedurals like *Law and Order* (1990–2010, 2022–) or cop shows like *Hill Street Blues* and *NYPD Blue* (1993–2005)—is the anti-Sherlock. Mumbling, shambling, under-dressed, married, middle-class, ethnic-Italian, and American, Columbo could hardly be more different from the articulate, genteel (Holmes's ancestors, Sir Arthur Conan Doyle's text tells us, were "country squires"), Oxbridge-educated bachelor detective. Over the ten seasons of the show's run, Columbo's character is established through repeated tics and taglines, such as referring to "the wife" or "Mrs. Columbo" (never seen during the series), whistling "This Old Man" when the case goes well, and continually popping back into a room to ask, "Just one more question, Sir." In some respects, Columbo is unique among TV detectives, such as his avoidance of the police station and his refusal to carry a gun. Atypically, Columbo is never in physical danger. But his ill-fitting raincoat alludes ironically to Jack Webb's natty trench coat on the 1967–1970 version of *Dragnet* (it seldom if ever rains in Los Angeles on either series) and would look right on Jerry Orbach's Lenny Briscoe (who has "shoes that are older" than his partner, "and maybe some ties, too") on *Law and Order*. Columbo's perpetual cigar smoking, beat-up gray Peugeot 403 convertible, and habit of breakfasting on hard-boiled eggs pulled out of his coat pocket help set the pattern for the slovenly detective who looks so incongruous, he must show his badge to be recognized as a policeman. With only wit and words as weapons, the Columbo type is the foil for arrogant killers who will overestimate their intellectual superiority, only to be driven by this incompetent-looking, relentless cop to confess.

Like later episodic procedurals, *Columbo* is set in a single city (though exceptional episodes take place abroad). Exteriors of Los Angeles are shot on location, and interiors are not constructed on sound stages, but shot in lavish Southern California homes, gardens, restaurants, clubs, and reception rooms where Columbo is a sore thumb among the well-heeled killer's peers. The detective cheerfully intrudes on these spaces of privilege, just as he pesters his suspect—who is always the killer—at home, at work, and at leisure. The killer is inevitably a wealthy and/or famous Los Angelino played by the top-billed guest star who is cast against type, usually a likable TV actor like Dick Van Dyke or Robert Culp, or else a late-career movie star like Janet Leigh or Ida Lupino. The plot of *Columbo* follows the detective's scrutiny of his suspect's psychology and of forensic details that have eluded other observers, especially the killer. As *Columbo* predates the era of serialized crime shows, viewers can expect perfect closure every time. Contrary to the idea that cliffhangers are what hook viewers into TV series, the genre of the episodic procedural demonstrates that the pleasure of watching a series can inhere as much in the predictable as in the surprising.

Mare of Easttown (2021)

As with *Columbo*, *Mare of Easttown* (HBO, 2021) is named after its detective protagonist. The resemblance between the two cops ends there. It's not simply that Mare Sheehan, an Irish Catholic born-and-bred Pennsylvanian played by Kate Winslet, is a different kind of investigator from her forebear; it's that the entire narrative infrastructure she inhabits represents a categorical alteration of the televisual landscape. While *Columbo* exploited episodic reinvention to the fullest—starting from scratch with a new methodical villain as the launch of each installment—*Mare of Easttown* exemplifies the serial turn that dominated "prestige" television in the first decades of the 21st century. The crime-drama interplay of episodic and serial began as least as far as back as the BBC's *Prime Suspect* (1991–2006), which extended the movie-length form of *Columbo* episodes into two two-hour installments, creating the barest of narrative gaps to open up an initial conversation between the hermetic efficiency of Sherlock Holmes and the potentially infinite sprawl of soap opera. By 2021, the vogue for "limited series"—typically six to ten episodes in length—had foregrounded a televisual form that bridges a serial paradigm with the promise of solution fundamental to the mystery yarn. "Mystery" is only half of the equation, however. Alfred Hitchcock distinguished mystery—where the audience learns information synchronously with the characters—from suspense—where the audience becomes privy to fragments of information that allow us to know, at least in part, facts not available to the full population of the storyworld, and often most especially the detective herself (Truffaut, 1985, 73). Choices of narrative focalization are crucial to all categories of storytelling; but they are especially fundamental to police shows, where data, behaviors, and their meaning define our experience. The first episode of *Mare of Easttown* is all mystery—even before the arrival of the first victim; but as the series unspools, the strategic, suspenseful disbursal of shards of information widens our perspective, while still delaying the payoff of explanation to the final installment.

The classical Roman poet Juvenal famously asked, "*Quis custodiet ipsos custodes*": who will guard the guardian themselves? This was not an operative concern with Columbo, whose scruffy, lovable demeanor ensured our confidence in his moral probity. But Mare Sheehan is aggressively unlovable, as her friends, relatives, and business associates never fail to remind us—her constitutional gruffness, drinking and vaping, and professional irresponsibility (including planting evidence to frame her daughter-in-law) designate her as a successor to the insalubrious cops of film noir and, more proximately, flawed female investigators like Jane Tennant from *Prime Suspect* (1991–2006) and Robin Griffin from *Top of the Lake* (2013–2017). Unlike those other two, Mare is imbricated in a familial community that she cannot escape—a structural belonging that can feel asphyxiating to her, and that is central for the viewer's narrative experience as we negotiate between her personal and ancestral history and the unfolding of the case. Burdened not only by her screwed-up present but by the faded glories of her past as a high school athlete, she lays out the conundrum to a male detective with whom she reluctantly works: "Doing something great is overrated—"cause then people expect that from you, all the time. What they don't realize is, we're just as screwed up as they are." The "they" in question are the citizens of Easttown, whose enmeshment in Delaware County exemplifies, in its particularity, the trend for unglamorous location shooting in such season-driven shows as *The Wire* (Baltimore) and the 2014 first version of *True Detective* (Louisiana); Kate Winslet's dedicated commitment to mastering the tricky "Delco" accent became a recurrent feature in discussions of the series, underlying the value ascribed to native granularity that has become a recurrent hallmark of a genre previously defined principally by puzzles and answers. Focused, serial immersion permits this newer iteration of the procedural to merge into messy communal environments, by contrast with the cleaner pleasures of *Columbo*'s discrete and intermittent visits.

The Anthology Series

Alfred Hitchcock Presents (1955–1962)

Rod Serling's *The Twilight Zone* (1959–1964) is often called the inspiration for *Black Mirror* (2011–, but *The Twilight Zone*'s formula was itself inspired by an earlier anthology series, *Alfred Hitchcock Presents* (1955–1962). Both *Twilight Zone* and *Alfred Hitchcock Presents* tell half-hour, character-driven stories; both employ dark humor to satirize modern morals and politics; both build suspense by limiting the viewer's knowledge to what the baffled focal character perceives; and both end every plot with an unpredictable twist explaining all that has come before. Their visual styles are similar, and both shows include an introduction and epilogue in which the host speaks directly to the camera about the week's story. But unlike the earnest Serling, Hitchcock is kidding around. After a title sequence displaying an obviously wrinkled piece of butcher paper bearing his caricature in silhouette,[5] Hitchcock makes jokes about himself, his show, and his archenemy, The Sponsor. The story Hitchcock presents may be funny, but—like Serling's—it is also creepy, scary, or disturbing. His silly addresses to the audience (including his censor placating explanations of how each murderer eventually had to pay for the crime) undercut the narrative tension the plays so expertly establish.

As in Hitchcock's films, that narrative tension emerges not so much from plot as from style. Though Hitchcock himself directed only a few episodes, other directors in the series adhere to the look of "the Master's" black-and-white films. Shot on a soundstage in high-contrast black and white, the elaborate sets and costumes are historically accurate, whether the era is Victorian, Gilded Age, or contemporary. Even when characters are shown in close-up, the meticulously detailed backgrounds remain distinct. The famed "Hitchcock shot" (a "dolly zoom" close-up signifying the subject's disorientation during the big reveal) is too large a camera effect to work on the small screen. In its place, the camera will often cut to a sharply defined closeup of the central character's shocked face against a suddenly blurred background.

The acting style falls just this side of melodrama, with extreme emotion written on the actors' faces. Hitchcock movies manage affect by alternating shots that follow the central character's misled gaze with tight close-ups of reactions on that same character's face, especially shock or fear. On *Alfred Hitchcock Presents*, however, the disoriented perspective is the viewer's. While making liberal use of shot-reverse-shot and close-ups, the camera frames the ensemble as if the observer were an invisible presence in the storyworld, looking on. These seemingly objective shots are sprinkled with extreme camera angles looking up at the characters from the floor, or down at them from just below the ceiling. In "Triggers in Leash" (1:3), two feuding cowboys in a restaurant agree to draw their guns when a cuckoo clock on a high shelf strikes noon. During the tense build-up, the camera alternates close-ups of each man's eyes with shots of the clock. Just before noon, Maggie the proprietor (Ellen Corby) removes a large crucifix from the shelf and crouches, as if in anticipation of the coming violence. In close-up, the clock stops. The camera shows all three characters from behind as they stand together, staring up at the motionless pendulum; then close-ups of each man's face; another close-up of the clock; and then a bizarre shot from the clock's perspective, looking down from the shelf on the three amazed, upturned faces below. The sequence ends by returning to the viewer's gaze at the three characters' backs. Maggie declares the occurrence a miracle, but the twist comes when we learn that the heavy crucifix was balancing a clock that wouldn't run unless the shelf was level. Mysteries inside the alternate dimension Serling posits before each episode of *The Twilight Zone* can find their solutions in the surrealistic realms of magic, fantasy, dreams, or science fiction, but in Hitchcock's more realistic storyworlds there is always a logical explanation.

Black Mirror (2011–Present)

Television depends on a productive exchange between meter and rhythm—between recurrent rules and imaginative variations that stretch those rules without breaking them. The anthology show, with its deep roots in the medium's history, has always operated as an intensification of the basic meter-rhythm dynamic, most visibly in the opposition between stark formula (such as Hitchcock's commentaries) and the disruptive scrapping of characters and backstories from one episode to the next. *Black Mirror* (2011–) thematizes that clash of the fixed and the improvisational through its framing of our historical moment—juxtaposing digital capitalism's sterile regulatory user-agreements with the seductive fantasy of the Internet as self-generated exploratory freedom. The show's technological parables tip toward the dystopic, illustrating the perils of surveillance culture, where the lure of instantly available knowledge typically results in unhappy comeuppance. The "black mirror" of the title refers to the smart phone's blandly reflective surface, whose rest state regularizes our relationship to our environment—until the device inevitably unleashes atomizing, alienating dysfunction upon us. *Black Mirror*'s title sequence is similarly stripped down—monochrome lettering introduces each episode name, hiding through sameness the Pandora's box to follow. The show's co-creator and chief writer, Charlie Brooker, once pitched the show through this televisual callback: "Just as *The Twilight Zone* would talk about McCarthyism, we're going to talk about Apple" (Brooker and Jones, 2018, 11). In this anthological iteration, the political is explicitly flipped into the personal and the commercial.

But *Black Mirror* isn't simply finger-wagging. The creative rhythm of the show celebrates a lush variety of speculative genre play, from social satire to

domestic elegy to prime-ministerial pig-fucking, in the show's infamous opening episode. If the anthology patterns of *Alfred Hitchcock Presents* were apparent in half-hour installments managed through metronomic adverting
breaks, the rhythmic flexibility of *Black Mirror* permitted episodes as differentiated in execution as the 42-minute amnesiac horror of "White Bear"
and the 89-minute futuro-procedural of "Hated in the Nation." And the
show's gestation enacted another version of meter and rhythm: the weekly
broadcast schedule during the first two seasons of U.K.'s Channel 4 three-
episodes-per-series ("series" is the U.K. term for the U.S. "season") yielded
subsequently to the scheduling vagaries of Netflix's streaming service,
where clusters of six episodes all dropped on a single day. This doubling of
narrative length now made the *Black Mirror* seasons more identifiable as
an unfolding object, putting the series in conversation with the "anthology
season" experiment pursued by the likes of *American Horror Story* (2011–)
and *Fargo* (2014–). These shows recalibrated the individual-vs.-collective
balance through rebooting their cast of characters each year, reconceptualizing the communal effects of anthologies. The 30-episode, self-replicating
seasonal sprawls of their 1950s and 1960s predecessors were now trimmed
considerably back to foreground different markers of storytelling and
authorship.

"You don't know who I am," says Yorkie (Mackenzie Davis) in the third-
season episode "San Junipero" to her would-be girlfriend, "and you don't
know what this means." That declaration likewise illuminates the anthology's tabula rasa approach; Yorkie and *Black Mirror* itself are both puzzles
of identification. We are required with each installment to figure out exactly
who a person is, and what things mean, the particular task of gleaning sense
from an anthology episode. More broadly, *Black Mirror* demonstrates a deep
commitment to one of television's most appealing features, its capacity to
build worlds from scratch. In the case of "San Junipero," the most beloved
episode of the series, we are slowly exposed to a world where matters of
sexual identity, race, disability, and ageing expand, over the course of an
hour of television, into a universe of experience, separate from the ruses and
game imbued in anthology's older strategies. And then the show starts all
over, ready for its next closed beginning.

The Sitcom

That Girl (1966–1971)

What is a "situation"? In terms of the half-hour comedy—perhaps the most
successful genre in the history of American television—a situation is a governing premise that seems to obliterate any interest in realistic representation,
at the service of a narrative formula anchored in a recurring cluster of quirky

types, beholden to a brisk, rhythmic joke delivery system framed through a multi-camera studio presentation and an instructive laugh track. Prominent subcategories of the situation comedy, or sitcom, include the domestic (such as *The Brady Bunch*, 1969–1974), the workplace (*Cheers*, 1982–1993), the fantastical (*Mork & Mindy*, 1978–1982)—or some combination of the three (*Bewitched*, 1964–1972). The rules of engagement of *That Girl* certainly made it reducible to the single-sentence descriptor required for the genre: young woman tries to make it as an actress in the zany world of 1960s New York City. But that synopsis obscures *That Girls'* rule-breaking dimension. While female characters and even producers were not previously unknown on the small screen—most prominently, Lucille Ball's *I Love Lucy* (1951–1957)—Marlo Thomas's position as a star/producer in her 20s, playing a single woman (Ann Marie) who would never marry over the show's five-year run (despite her faithful allegiance to long-time boyfriend Donald Hollinger, played by Ted Bessell) marked *That Girl* as a space for mid-century independence and liberation that would inspire most proximately *The Mary Tyler Moore Show* (1970–1977) and more distantly, Lena Dunham's *Girls* (2012–2017). The constitutional situation of a "girl"—perpetually on the cusp of growing up—provided the show with both fixed innocence and behavioral flexibility, both a rigid schema and an actual historical moment in which this version of comedy could flourish. As Thomas put it retrospectively: "I wasn't against comedy, or even low comedy, as long as it came out of the situation. It is called 'situation comedy' for a reason. The situation is real—then you can do whatever" (That Girl, 2006). The oxymoron enclosing the "real" and "doing whatever" speaks to the interplay of the grounded and the ridiculous on which the sitcom depends.

That interplay of the plausible and the unlikely was most vividly illustrated in *That Girl*'s weekly idiosyncratic deployment of a time-honored televisual device, the cold open—a one-to-two-minute pre-credits sequence that launches each installment. A soap opera will use cold opens to remind viewers of the most pertinent recent events, while episodic procedurals pivot to the opposite purpose of initiating a new storyline every time. Sitcoms such as the U.S. version of *The Office* (2005–213) typically exploit the cold open as a brief self-contained vignette from the show's world that may be completely disconnected from the upcoming installment. *That Girl* concocted a variation that signaled the series' commitment to absurdist theater alongside its willingness to serve televisual comfort food. Every half-hour started with a scene that anticipated the specific focus of the episode; and the scene always ended with someone pointing declaratively at Ann and shouting "that girl!" Ann would be caught in a freeze frame featuring a comic look of surprise, confusion, or pleasure, and then the unvarying credit sequence would begin. One such scene conveys improvisatory invention; two or three such scenes feel like planned goofiness; 136 iterations of "that girl!" over five seasons stage a spectacle of elaborated foolery manifesting pure delight in manic variation—including the time when an Italian tenor substituted the inevitable phrase with "quella ragazza!" On a story level, *That Girl* rewrote conventions about who could make a sitcom, and about what its protagonist could or should do; on a conceptual level, *That Girl* leaned hard into exuberant dallying with audience expectation. The baroque ritual of the show's cold opens embodied the institutionalized play that defines the sitcom as an art form.

Girls (2012–2017)

Girls is a half-hour HBO comedy series about the difficulties of "adulting," a term coined by the generation show-runner Lena Dunham represents. The opening scene of the pilot drives this home, as the parents of Hannah Horvath (played by Dunham, the star, writer, co-producer and sometime director of *Girls*) inform her that they are cutting off the allowance that enables her still to be working, two years after college graduation, as an unpaid publishing intern in New York City. Hannah, shocked, utters a whiny series of increasingly weak excuses for needing their money more than they do, while gobbling down an expensive dinner they are obviously paying for. It's a funny scene, but the "situation is real," as Marlo Thomas said about *That Girl*. Here the comedy arises from Dunham's deeply ironic take on the situations of contemporaries who share her own race (white), gender (cis), class (upper-middle), region (Northeast United States), and age (twentysomething). Without watching the writer/director's commentaries that HBO's streaming service runs after each episode of *Girls,* viewers could easily conflate Hannah and Lena, to assume the show has no more perspective on its bratty, self-absorbed young people than they have on themselves. Dunham-the-show-runner's incisive critiques of her characters' inability to connect with one another make it clear, however, that she is indeed the adult in the room, the woman who has more control over her series than Marlo Thomas could ever dream of having.

Like hundreds of female stars from Lucille Ball to Tiffany Haddish, Thomas knew how to work the power of her attractiveness to her comedic advantage. Pretty and model-thin, Ann Marie is the epitome of the to-be-looked-at subject of film and television's heterosexual male gaze. Hannah is emphatically not, which Dunham stresses by repeatedly appearing in unflattering outfits, without makeup, or naked. Dunham exercises her creative power by making us look at her anyway.

Concurrent sitcoms about girls—like *New Girl* (2011–2018) or *2 Broke Girl$* (2011–2017)—follow the classic sitcom formula more closely than *Girls*, which breaks with the four-camera, rhythmic-punchline style and follows a seemingly amorphous multi-plot structure. (There is no discernable story arc within or between seasons, although the series finale provides something like closure.) *Girls* looks more like an indie movie than a sitcom, with its vintage-furnished apartment sets and its long shots of characters walking down actual Brooklyn streets. Funny without being predictably jokey, *Girls* departs from the typical sitcom's tone, as well. The characters' predicaments can be frustrating, depressing—even disgusting, as when Hannah breaks her own eardrum with a Q-tip. Because this is HBO and not a broadcast network, the "girls" are continually having on-camera intercourse, whether straight, lesbian, kinky, promiscuous, or abusive.

For all its cynical insouciance about sex, *Girls*—like its serial-sitcom precursors *Cheers* (1982–1993), *Friends* (1994–2004), and *Sex and the City* (1998–2004)—can be romantic in a way that episodic 1960s sitcoms like *That Girl* never approached. In the Season 2 finale, Hannah, having broken up with Adam (Adam Driver in his breakout role), "accidentally" Facetimes him while descending into an OCD-induced panic attack. When he picks up, Adam has been trashing his apartment in frustration over a new girlfriend who found him scary in bed. Instantly focused on Hannah's need, Adam keeps her on the line as he sprints, shirtless, many blocks through the city to her apartment. The synthesized soundtrack rises, incongruously reminiscent of the theme from the 1981 dramatic film about heroic young men running, *Chariots of Fire*. Over the phone, Hannah repeatedly claims she doesn't need help, and Adam must kick her door open because she tells him to go away. Then comes the shot-reverse-shot of the romcom happy ending. "You're here," Hannah—crouched in fetal position—says in a tiny voice. "I was always here," Adam says as if it were obvious, lifting and holding her in his arms like a child. There's no girl-power here, no subversion of gender stereotypes or feminist resistance of traditional rescue plots. On the surface, the gender roles in *Girls* would appear not to have made much progress over those in *That Girl*. But Hannah is not Lena, any more than Ann is Marlo. The scene may infantilize Hannah, but it showcases Dunham's mature recognition that no girl is an island, entire of herself.

The Social Comedy

Room 222 (1969–1974)

The titles of many television comedies—like *That Girl* and *Girls*—invoke characters. This is hardly surprising, given how successful the medium has been at creating psychological and emotional attachments by artfully balancing combinations of fictional individuals. By contrast, *Room 222* and *Atlanta* are named after not characters but spaces, spaces that represent ideas or communities, as much as they do the individuals who populate those spaces. In the case of *Room 222*, the title refers to the instruction space belonging to Pete Dixon (Lloyd Haynes), the beloved Black teacher ensconced in an integrated Los Angeles high school in the wake of the 1964 Civil Rights Act. As timely as *Room 222* was, the series also gestured to a wider history of comedy than the "situation"-driven narratives that were taken for granted as half-hour television's natural environment. Comedy has a much longer cultural inheritance than the western, the procedural, and the anthology, which are all inventions no older than the late 19th century; comedy is as old as classical Athens and Jane Austen, and it has always celebrated the humor of domestic and sexual relationships, at the service of examining social customs with a broader remit than densely packed jokes. The early 1970s would see the advent of series like *All in the Family* (1971–1979) and its spinoff *Maude* (1972–1978), both the fruits of creator Norman Lear's commitment to bringing debates over racism, class conflict, the feminist revolution, and newly legalized abortion into small-screen homes. In a different vein from the loud interventions of Lear's series, James L. Brooks' debut show *Room 222*, and his immediate follow-up *The Mary Tyler Moore Show* (1970–1977), explored group dynamics more through harmony than conflict. The premise of Blacks and single women in leadership positions foregrounded comedy as an engagement with collective values, just as centrally to 1970s clashes as *Lysistrata* and *Pride and Prejudice* had been to their eras.

For all that, comedies are supposed to be funny. That seemingly non-negotiable condition remained uppermost in the minds of the ABC executives who green-lit *Room 222* as a fully integrated half-hour show; chuckles and guffaws were going to be the price to pay for high-minded, progressive ambitions. Those executives stubbornly insisted on maintaining a laugh track over the first few installments—before giving up by the seventh episode, which like every episode to follow was uninflected by the canned sounds that had for decades schooled audiences in the frequency and patterns of the officially funny. *Room 222* didn't foreswear humor: the sweet-grumpy principal Seymour Kaufman (Michael Constantine) and the eager, bumbling student teacher Alice Johnson (Karen Valentine) provided the grace notes of lightness that modulated the lines between politics and entertainment. The term that best describes *Room 222*, whether the show was aiming for heavy or light, is "earnest"—a word most associated with the unamused Victorianism famously lampooned by another social jokester, Oscar Wilde. The earnest moral center of *Room 222* was aimed at asking its audiences to take the world seriously, while reflecting an open mind about whether seriousness was always the most fruitful way to approach the world. The protagonist of *Atlanta* is also, literally, Earnest—or, as he is more commonly known, "Earn"—and Donald Glover is likewise not averse to asking us to consider who we are and why we do what we do. *Room 222* was a modern (if not modernist) show, by contrast with the postmodern traps in which *Atlanta* is purposefully embroiled. Lloyd Haynes as Pete Dixon perfectly captures *Room 222*'s laid-back devotion to redrawing—not too drastically—the lines between story and experience, pushing against television's familiar resistance to muddled storytelling borders. Haynes's performance is among the most effortlessly casual impersonations in the history of American art, grounded in querying reflections and wry smiles, in ways that altered our expectations of the narrowness of television form.

Atlanta (2016–)

The storyworld of the social comedy *Atlanta* is emphatically Black. As did social comedies *Transparent* (2014–2019) for LGBTQ+ Los Angeles and *Jane the Virgin* (2014–2019) for Spanish-speaking Miami, *Atlanta*'s serial form undercuts TV's white mainstream by focusing on so-called minority experience in such matter-of-fact detail as to make it a new normal (Warhol, 1999). Through satire and parody, these contemporary social comedies display a high degree of self-consciousness about their status as television shows. *Jane the Virgin,* for instance, with its voiceover narrator and overwrought plots, hilariously imitates the *telenovelas* in which some of its characters appear, while at the same time tackling intersectional identities and immigration politics. In the tradition of social comedy, *Atlanta*'s creator, writer, and star Donald Glover (Earn) upends TV genres that reinforce Black stereotypes, establishing southern Black Americans at the center of *Atlanta*'s world.

For 21st-century viewers, Atlanta as a TV location connotes "reality" crime shows like "Cops" (1989–) where mostly white police roust out mostly Black suspects. Glover tackles this in the first-season finale, where Earn, Darius (Keith Glover), and Al (aka Paper Boi, the rapper, played by Brian Tyree Henry) sit in a car on a low-rent Atlanta residential street, waiting to meet a sketchy guy who has Earn's jacket (1:10). Al mutters, "This Negro stakeout shit shouldn't even take this long for no jacket." "*48 Hours.* All Black cast," muses Darius from the back seat. He interrupts himself to ask, "Does that even *work?!?*" As usual, stoner-savant Darius is confused. He means *The First 48*, one of the police-action reality series often shot in Atlanta neighborhoods just like this one. The very first scene of *Atlanta* (1:1) sets up this allusion, involving the three protagonists in a parking-lot shooting like the ones where young Black men are continually killing one another on those "reality" shows. *Atlanta* also parodies *The Real Housewives of Atlanta,* where nouveau-riche African American women rattle around in under-furnished mansions recently bought by their football- or basketball-player husbands. *Atlanta* satirizes that world in episodes like "Value" (1:6) and "Juneteenth" (1:9), juxtaposing the hard-working teacher Vanessa with Black women acquaintances who live on money they take from wealthy men. Those women's surroundings are glamorous, but *Atlanta* offers an alternative Black American reality through lingering, warmly lit establishing shots inside the modest, vaguely *Real Simple* home where Van lives with her little daughter and sometimes Earn. Even Al and Darius—who spend a lot of time acting like teenaged characters on Season 1 of *The Wire* (2002–2008), lounging on a broken-down sofa in a vacant lot, smoking weed—subvert TV clichés by co-inhabiting a comfortable-looking house that is relatively tidy.[6]

Atlanta's preoccupation with TV tropes adds up to a *mise en abyme* that can make pinning down its politics tricky. Of course, the least sympathetic characters are openly racist white people (the stunned look on Earn's face when an angry middle-aged white woman calls his conciliatory expression a "sharecropper smile" is unforgettable). One elaborately satirical episode (1:7) imagines a TV network addressed to a non-white audience that cares about what rappers think. It features a talk show where Al/Paper Boi is invited to argue with a white transwoman scholar about rap's endemic homophobia and misogyny. Interspersed with their surprisingly amicable discussion are segments of a very funny "special report" about a dark-skinned, straight-faced 17-year-old who identifies as trans-racial. "I'm a 35-year-old white man," he tells the interviewer. A *reductio ad absurdum* of the idea that gender and race are socially constructed, the episode doesn't argue that they're not. But Glover won't let his audience forget that the social circumstances his series is commenting on are at least as complicated as anything Jane Austen or Oscar Wilde ever laughed at.

Conclusion

While we find our pairings of TV series and of narrative concerns rhetorically pleasing, we hasten to acknowledge that the binary organization of our essay imposes a highly artificial order on the fields of media narrative and of television studies. Our schematic categories do not exhaust genre's potential at either the beginning or the end of the TV history we are delineating, nor can they account for all the generic variations that occurred between the 1970s and today. For us, the impetus behind a narrative approach is to find larger patterns among significant details, and the point of situated or contextual narratology is to connect stories to the material conditions from which they emerge. Our hope is that scholars seeking models for narrative analytical practice and writers considering the choices they must make in writing a TV screenplay will find something in our essay they can use in fleshing out the history we have only begun to sketch.

Notes

1 For a comprehensive account of distinctively televisual forms, see Thompson and Mittell (2020) and Butler (2010).
2 See Lotz (2014) for a behind-the-scenes history of how the anti-hero figure evolved in "quality TV" series such as *Mad Men, The Sopranos,* and *Breaking Bad.*
3 See Wanzo (2009).
4 For example, newly introduced controversies include color-blind casting (Warner, 2018).
5 Since Hitchcock started in the film industry as a title designer, the wrinkled paper—not replaced before Season 7—suggests a sly allusion to the supposed inferiority of TV as a medium.
6 This echoes the moment in *The Wire* (3: 12) when police officers inspecting deputy drug lord Stringer Bell's (Idris Elba) apartment are amazed at its modernist elegance. "Who the fuck was I chasing?" McNulty (Dominic West) whispers as he takes a copy of Adam Smith's *Wealth of Nations* down from Stringer's bookshelf.

References

Altman, Rick. "A Semantic/Syntactic Approach to Film Genre." *Cinema Journal* 23.3 (1984). 6.
Brooker, Charlie and Annabel Jones. *Inside Black Mirror.* New York: Crown. 2018.
Butler, Jeremy. *Television Style.* New York: Routledge. 2010.
Feuer, Jane. "Narrative Form in American Network Television." *High Theory, Low Culture: Analysing Popular Television and Film.* Colin MacCabe, ed., Manchester, UK: Manchester University Press, 1986, 101–114.
Harrigan, Pat and Noah Wardrip-Fruin. *Third Person: Authoring and Exploring Vast Narratives.* Cambridge: The MIT Press. 2009.
Jenkins, Henry. *Convergence Culture: Where Old and New Media Collide.* New York: New York University Press. 2006.
Lotz, Amanda D. *Cable Guys: Television and Masculinities in the 21st-Century.* New York: New York University Press. 2014.
Milch, David. *Deadwood: Stories of the Black Hills.* New York: Melcher Media. 2006.
Mittell, Jason. *Complex TV: The Poetics of Contemporary Television Storytelling.* New York: New York University Press. 2015.
Newman, Michael Z. "From Beats to Arcs: Toward a Poetics of Television Narrative." *The Velvet Light Trap* 58 (2006). 16.
O'Sullivan, Sean. "Broken on Purpose: Poetry, Serial Television, and the Season." *Storyworlds* 2 (2010). 59.
Phelan, James. *Narrative as Rhetoric: Technique, Audiences, Ethics, Ideology.* Columbus: Ohio State University Press. 2010.
Sepinwall, Alan. *The Revolution Was Televised.* New York: Simon and Schuster Gallery Book. 2013.
Spigel, Lynn and Jason Olsson, eds. *Television After TV: Essays on a Medium in Transition.* Durham: Duke University Press. 2004.
That Girl. Season 1 DVD. Shout Factory, 2006.
Thompson, Ethan and Jason Mittell (eds.). *How to Watch Television* (2nd edition). New York: New York University Press, 2020.

Truffaut, François. *Hitchcock*. New York: Touchstone. 1985.

Warner, Kristen J. *The Culture Politics of Colorblind TV Casting*. New York: Routledge. 2018.

Wanzo, Rebecca. *The Suffering Will Not Be Televised: African American Women and Sentimental Storytelling*. Albany: State University of New York Press. 2009.

Warhol, Robyn. "Making 'Gay' and 'Lesbian' into Household Words: How Serial Form Works in Armistead Maupin's *Tales of the City*." *Contemporary Literature* 40.3 (1999). 378.

———. "Binge Watching: How Netflix Original Programs Are Changing Serial Form." *Literatur in Wissenschaft und Unterricht* 47.1/2 (2014). 145.

11

THE WAY TOONS TELL IT

Animation's Narrative Strategies

Christopher Holliday

As both a creative medium and an industrial art form, animation accommodates a multitude of approaches, styles, practices, and techniques. This means that any broad generalisations made towards its leading narrative systems, or attempts to solidify or 'fix' into place its dominant strategies of storytelling, are necessarily contingent upon recognising its defining heterogeneity and diversity of image-making technologies. For Suzanne Buchan, animation holds many aesthetic intersections with other fields, disciplines, and platforms, leading to its status as an "aesthetic puzzle" (2013: 8) supported by "widely divergent pro-filmic materials (objects, drawing, sand, painting, puppets)" in ways that "determining a unifying feature applicable to all its forms is questionable" (ibid.: 3). Where narration's relationship to animated media production has proven particularly useful, however, is in cutting across such an expanding typology of animation's multivalent applications, materials, resources, and processes, making valuable discriminations about a medium that has become inescapable within our experiences of contemporary moving image culture. This action has, in turn, helped to identify the critical or practical utility of 'narrative' – defined here as the sequencing or chaining of events and actions into causal relations in service of a resolution – as a foundation upon which has rested several understandings of what animation is as a "visual construction of meaning" (Wells 2002: 7), and how it functions as an artistic practice.

Not all animation tells stories, of course, and many animators have shown how the effects of animation do not require a clearly defined 'story' to place or situate them. A narrative is an option, rather than a necessity, something that has been particularly evident throughout the medium's multiple experimental and avant-garde traditions at the hands of fine and abstract artists, who

DOI: 10.4324/9781003197911-15

have provided a counter history to the dominance of storytelling within the industrial parameters of Hollywood and more commercial modes of production. Yet the organisation of story continues to traverse animation's spectrum of forms and functions. The possibilities for narrative are traceable across its many creative applications that support its identity as an interdisciplinary art and craft and secure its place within a range of cultural, political, and aesthetic frameworks. Narrative is, for example, fully imbricated in the medium's ideological application as a tool for political sentiment and the ability of animators "to produce allegorical or satirical works critical of totalitarian regimes" (Moritz 1997: 38), just as storytelling can be used to define animation's relationships to other aesthetic traditions and its specificity against other art forms. Indeed, the medium's rich history of storytelling has prompted frequent looks inward at the stakes of narrative structure, with narrative largely conceptualised according to animation's specific formal properties and innovative techniques of production. Animation is certainly a medium that possesses "the capacity to create new modes of story-telling, often rejecting the notion of a plot with a beginning, a middle and an end, in favour of *symbolic or metaphoric effects*" (Wells 1998: 68). The aim of this chapter is therefore to map animation's many creative and aesthetic connections to 'storytelling,' and to reflect on how the qualities of animation can both enforce and confuse standards of narrative orientation. By examining the style and practice of narration as it has been understood within a cross-section of popular animated examples, this chapter argues that narrative remains a compelling subject for scholars of animation precisely because it necessitates an ongoing enquiry about what the medium's narrative distinctiveness might be, and why it remains so attractive to animators, artists, and storytellers.

Humorous Phases

The emergence of narrative in animation in the first two decades of the twentieth century stands as a potted history of the medium itself, one typically shaped around the activities of numerous pioneers who collectively helped to usher in and hone the craft of the medium's storytelling capabilities. The contributions of several prominent U.S. studios – including Barré, International Film Service, Van Beuren, Walter Lantz Productions, Fleischer and, most emphatically, Walt Disney – have regularly been used in wide-ranging histories of animation's evolution across Europe and North America to graph the progressive emergence of animated storytelling as the medium consolidated into a viable economic industry (Bendazzi 2015; Furniss 2017). The rise of studio animation – not just in the United States, but in France too with Émile Cohl's work at Gaumont and Pathé – provided a robust industrial backdrop for narrative development, particularly as many studios founded animation divisions (MGM, Warner Brothers) while others (RKO, Paramount) entered distribution deals with existing animation studios. For Kristian Moen, how-ever, it was in the cartoons produced at another New York-based studio, Bray – founded in 1912 by John Randolph Bray – that animation's narrative capabilities were best formulated between 1914 and 1920. Moen describes how with *Bobby Bumps and His Goatmobile* (Earl Hurd, 1916), the Bray Studios began to adopt "narrative forms associated with live-action film" (2015: 135) as part of their intermedial approach to cartoons that prioritised the "conventions of narrative film" (2015: 137).

Such discriminations regarding animation's progressive 'narrativisation' have held sway due to scholarly assumptions that have downplayed the in-fluence of story in the realisation of the very first animated cartoons. These assumptions have, perhaps expectedly, mirrored those emphatically made in relation to histories of live-action cinema, whose precarious relationship with narrative logic in the 1900s and early teens would be used by Noël Burch to discuss cinema's move from "primitive" to more "institutional" modes of "simple narrative linearization" (1990: 154). Indeed, Donald Crafton simi-larly details the "primitive narrative structures of animation" (1993: 9) in this early period, including the "basic narrative structure" (1993: 50) pre-sent in the "lightning sketch" films popularised by J. Stuart Blackton in the United States, but also Georges Méliès in France and Tom Merry and Walter Booth in the United Kingdom. Dating from the late-1890s, these "lighting sketch" cartoons were influenced by the staged magic acts of vaudeville art-ists, with many filmmakers moving into cinema from the vaudeville circuit to become the first screen animators (see Cook 2018: 65–94). Yet despite the creative possibilities enabled by the sudden movement of rudimentary two-dimensional drawn figures – alongside the recognition of animation's comic intentions and conventions drawn from other popular entertainment forms (the fairground, circus, and theatre) – Crafton admits that "early cinema in all its forms had a craving for narrative [and] dramatic situations" (1993: 35).

If this story of animation's ultimate 'acquisition' of narrative at the turn of the twentieth century sounds familiar, that is because it is. The medium's sup-posedly aspirational relationship to narrative places early animation firmly in the throes of Tom Gunning's now-canonical concept of the "cinema of attractions" which has located both an historical moment within the evo-lution of cinema – emphasising exhibitionist presentationalism rather than narrative absorption – and the formal properties of early film that engen-dered such modes of address. The identity of narrative as an extraneous di-mension to early film has certainly encountered resistance since Gunning's initial formulation, including how it underplays the role played by oral com-mentaries and verbal 'patter' as part of early exhibition programmes (see Musser 1994). Whatever narrative's ambivalent value, the animated medium cannot be refused a place within the same understandings of early cinema's spectacular potential. Most strikingly, the original publication of Gunning's "cinema of attractions" in 1986 notably coincided with the rise of computer animation, which became central to blockbuster filmmaking in the United States and the spectacular fantasies of the postclassical era. The rise of digital VFX technologies in the mid-1980s certainly shaped the "cinema of attractions" into a highly attractive scholarly proposition at a time when cinema's latest exhibitionist tendencies were being fuelled by the decentring of classical storytelling at the hands of digitally animated imagery. Gunning's reference to a "Spielberg-Lucas-Coppola cinema of effects" (1986: 70) during the climax of his article only strengthens the idea that the "cinema of attractions" had as much to do with the impact of 1980s computer animation as it did with distinctions between the Lumière Brothers and Méliès. Given animation's historical connection to modes of display and the fetishism of spectacle, it is telling, then, that Kristine Brunovska Karnick and Henry Jenkins confirm that rather than disappear, the spectacle-oriented "cinema of attractions" actually survived in certain filmmaking contexts, including "the avant-garde, the musical, animation and comedy" (1995: 65). This comment both weakens the critical tendency to overstate the historical disappearance and devaluing of spectacle at the expense of narrative, but equally identifies animation as a vital and ongoing site where spectacle and storytelling were always able to coexist.

There is, however, little mention of animation in Gunning's original 1986 "attractions" essay, aside from a brief reference to Méliès' 'trick' film *Le Voyage dans la Lune* (1902) that utilised stop-frame effects as part of its filmed magic. Yet having made the journey from vaudeville, the very first animators such as Cohl, Méliès, and Blackton were likewise not guided by "the mission of narrative" (Gunning 1993: 71), at least not in the traditional sense, that would drive Classical Hollywood's later narrative paradigm. Rather, they were invested in new purposes and impulses that derived from a broader fascination with the curious novelty of cinema's fascinating illusion. Malcolm Cook makes this connection between animation and attraction explicit, arguing that "early lightning cartoon films" – such as Blackton's trio of shorts *The Enchanted Drawing* (1900), *Humorous Phases of Funny Faces* (1906) and *Lightning Sketches* (1907) made at the Edison studio – adopted a "non-narrative, spectacular mode of address that supports Gunning's 'cinema of attractions' account" (2018: 16). Early animation (albeit named by trade and popular discourses at the time as the 'trick film') appropriately demonstrated a similar "lack of a concern with creating a self-sufficient narrative world upon the screen" (Gunning 1986: 65) by prioritising moments of spectacular engagement while simultaneously evidencing minimal narrative impetus. Yet animation's seeming "non-narrative" tendencies do not just signal how the performers' actions and timing were honed in theatre, but bear out a connection with the "affective energies and aesthetics of the circus" that would equally go on to influence the "clownish" visual trickery exhibited by the first animated films (Stoddart 2015: 3).

As a result, any shift by animation towards narrative evident in the playful line drawings of Blackton and his contemporaries should not be mistaken for a smooth teleological progression from spectacular inception to storytelling coherency, but as with many technological innovations it was a more chaotic process marked by the creative vibrancy of trials and errors with storytelling structures. Even the very discourse of subordination regarding animation's perceived rejection of narrative – as demonstrated by Gunning's account of plot's initial redundancy – might be challenged given Crafton's description of (admittedly "primitive") narrative structures in the very first cartoons. But by whatever methods narrative was negotiated and integrated by cinema's first animators, early animation was not just a benign "preparatory period for later film styles and practices, the infancy of an art form," and neither was it "imperfectly realized" and wrought with "immaturity," prior to the emergence of film's inevitable narrative purpose (Gunning 1993: 71). Animated cartoons held narrative in creative tension with spectacle, as embryonic storytelling structures shifted in both importance and prominence during animation's early years. Narrative was therefore never actively resisted by animation in the early 1900s, as storytelling was only ever one of the qualities that the first animated cartoons possessed.

Personality Traits

Even if animation's destiny as a storytelling medium remained somewhat fuzzy, the sharpening of narrative as an increasingly visible component of animated media and the arrival of "narrative integration" (what Charles Musser calls the "rise of story film" [1994: 365]) has remained a highly durable component of animation's chronology. Often attributed to the work of American cartoonist Winsor McCay as "the first 'classical' artist of American animation" (Bendazzi 2015: 36), the refining of a more narrative-driven style of animation certainly coerced cartoons more readily into a storytelling medium. There is evidently a distinction regarding the presence of story that separates the very first cartoons running to only a few seconds – including the undulating and illogical lines of Cohl's *Fantasmagorie* (1908) – from McCay's later *How a Mosquito Operates* (1912), *Gertie the Dinosaur* (1914) and *The Sinking of the Lusitania* (1918) (often celebrated as the first animated documentary), which combined the comedy of emergent "personality animation" (Wells 1998: 129–130) with more perceptible narrative structures across their extended running time.

Personality-centred humour within early animation fully supported the medium's broader move towards its perhaps predictable status as a narrative cinema. Whereas the cartoon's comedic beats had previously been "unallied to identifiable characters or set within a developing story" (Wells 1998: 129), it was McCay who ushered in new models of comic behaviour rooted in the pleasures of both storytelling and, crucially, anthropomorphism, which drew from the familiar "humanity" of characters as motivated, distinctive, and subjective individuals. The subsequent trials and tribulations of human-like anthropomorphs crafted narratives of drama and jeopardy, and allowed storytelling to become quickly assimilated into animation's formal repertoire via a style of humour "personalised by a comic character" who would effectively (and humorously) execute "narrational action" (ibid.). The stakes of the narrative-character relation closely mirrors the ways in which Hollywood live-action cinema was, again, similarly evolving the actions and crises of recognisable characters to undertake a shift from "drawn-out" incidental plots to "a compressed set of causes and effects" (Bordwell et al. 1985: 266). As in animation too, the dominance of vaudevillian characters and performance styles gave way to motivated characters that were "psychologically defined, with a range of personality traits from which actions could arise" (ibid.: 269). In the case of McCay, *How a Mosquito Operates* and the later *Gertie the Dinosaur* both construct characters identifiable as much through emotions (shyness, irritation, excitement) as through action (gesture, reaction, mannerisms). Regularly framed by explanatory live-action sequences in which the craft of animation took centre stage, McCay's animated films additionally marked a gradual shift away from the visibility of animated technology, displacing the trope of "self-figuration" that defined the aesthetic style of the "lightning sketch" cartoons (Crafton 1993: 11). Aylish Wood has argued that with McCay, "the hand of the animator [...] became opaque, out of sight behind the telling of the story" (2007: 18). Similar charges of narrative coherency might also be levelled at the work of Polish-Russian stop-motion animator Ladislas Starevich, whose puppet short *The Beautiful Leukanida* (1912) prioritised a "full view of the animation itself" (Wood 2007: 18) across its insect-themed love story.

   Chief among the early pioneers of narrative were undoubtedly Disney, whose aesthetic innovations central to a dominant "hyper-realist" visual orthodoxy and their institutionalising of modern technologies of representation (synchronised sound, rotoscoping, Technicolor, multi-plane camera) replaced episodic gags with the development of "dramatic structure" (Klein 1993: 50).[1] Such "narrative concerns" have been viewed as "crucial to the development of feature-length animation" at Disney (Langer 1990: 307), yet the studio honed storytelling throughout their shorter film programmes too. The *Alice Comedies* (1923–1927), *Oswald the Lucky Rabbit* (1927–) and, later, the *Silly Symphonies* (1929–1939), were, again, far from "imperfectly realised" experiments, but sophisticated testing grounds for more narrative-driven styles of animation. But while Richard Schickel argues that the Silly Symphony that pioneered the multi-plane camera, *The Old Mill* (Wilfred Jackson, 1937), "has no real plot" (1997: 196), Disney shorts have been increasingly understood as marking a departure from earlier "gag-centered cartoons" towards fantasy and fairy-tale narratives, thereby establishing the "narrative formulas that would make him the country's most influential fairy-tale entertainer" (Merritt 2005: 4). Prior to 1932 (when the Disney studio signed a contract with United Artists to replace their earlier deals with Celebrity Productions and Columbia Pictures), their involvement with fairy-tale storytelling structures had been largely parodies of Puss 'n Boots, Cinderella, and Jack and the Beanstalk, which were "turned into cartoon Laugh-O-grams back in Kansas City, [and] had been entirely limited to simple Jazz Age parodies stuffed with gags and puns" (ibid.). As Russell Merritt argues, "As a series of spot gags strung together by loosely constructed plot lines," such fairy-tale-inspired shorts were "indistinguishable from Disney's other silent cartoons" featuring Oswald and Mickey (ibid.). Disney's first run of "gag-centred" fairy tales were therefore built solely around slapstick comedy gags, comic scenarios, and generalised character goals, and did not display the complexity that Merritt attributes to their musical fairy-tale adaptations that would define their output from the late-1930s onwards.

Supported by an industrial workflow designed to enhance story development, the Disney studio moved Hollywood cel-animation headlong into feature-length and with it institutionalised a set of labour practices and production hierarchies that are still in operation today. By the time of *Snow White and the Seven Dwarfs* (David Hand, 1937) the very first feature-length cartoon – the now-lost cut-out animation *El Apóstol* (Quirino Cristiani, 1917) – had already been produced in Argentina, a film that nonetheless employed a "quite linear, albeit complicated" plot (Bendazzi 2015: 87). Lotte Reiniger's 62-minute silhouette *The Adventures of Prince Achmed* (1926) had also been noted for its adoption of the "narrative structures of plot-driven cinema" (Blattner et al. 2015: 11). But by "using the script and the storyboard as a choke point," Disney was able to take "control of the narrative" as the Story Department at the studio became "the chief organ of this management [...] at the very top of the hierarchical pyramid (Langer 1991: 7). Compared to Dave and Max Fleischer's rival Fleischer studio and its more "haphazard" and "impressionistic" approach to narrative and character (with their own Story Department not arriving until 1932) (Langer 1991: 7–8), Disney's practical emphasis on the "story point" in line with the traditions of "nineteenth-century drama" (Klein 1993: 51) positioned the studio away from both its competitors and the dominant traditions of "graphic narrative" (ibid.) that defined earlier animated cartoon production between 1928 and 1934.

As the earlier work of McCay (who would adapt his 1905 illustrated children's comic strip *Little Nemo in Slumberland* in 1911) had already made clear, these earlier "graphic narratives" were indebted to nineteenth-century illustration and an influential comic book style. From William Randolph Hearst's *Katzenjammer Kids* (1916–1918), *Krazy Kat* (1916–1940), and

Li'l Abner (1944) shorts produced by the Charles Mintz Studio (later known as Screen Gems) to Fleischers' adaptation of E.C. Segar's *Popeye the Sailor* (1933–1957) and Barré's *Mutt and Jeff* (1916–1926), several animated cartoons capitalised on pre-existing comic strip characters by converting them into cartoons as a way of constructing animation's earliest narrative beats. Mark Langer explains that many New York animation studios of the 1910s and 1920s were often founded by "practitioners of newspaper and magazine cartooning and illustration," including commercial illustrators such as Bray, McCay, Max Fleischer and Pat Sullivan, shoring up an East Coast " 'cartoony' style" of narration that countered Disney's West Coast evocation of classical cinema storytelling models (1990: 308). In this East Coast style popularised by Terrytoons and Paramount, the "artificiality of the characters and their drawn nature were emphasized through design, movement, and dialogue," while the narratives were "loose aggregations of illogical gags, or, as seen in the 'Popeye' series, ritualized through endless repetition" (ibid.: 308–309). A possibility enabled by duplicating cycles of action was that narrative often "existed as a simple illustration of the lyrics to a song" (ibid.), particularly in the case of the Fleischers' *Song Car-Tunes* (1924–1927) that pioneered the "Follow the Bouncing Ball" sing-along device used to lead theatre audiences, but also in the studio's later *Color Classics* (1934–1941) series that similarly explored the power of music to drive story and action. As a result, character "motivation and causality tended to be discarded in favor of dreamlike connections between events" (ibid.: 310) and the prioritising of musicality, though similar charges might be levelled at the animation of musical rhythms that defined the expressivity of Disney's earlier *Silly Symphonies*, as well as the *Merrie Melodies* series (1931–1969) made at Warner Brothers.

Precursors to the self-consciously flat, artificial style popularised by the Fleischers along the East Coast were Sullivan and Otto Messmer's *Felix the Cat* (1919–), alongside the impish Koko the Clown – main protagonist of the Fleischers' *Out of the Inkwell* (1918–1929) series – though later stars like Betty Boop (who debuted in 1930) would likewise spotlight animation's emphasis on the flexible protoplasmic instability of animated images over strict narrative coherency. Although there were "allusions to story" in many of the surreal Felix shorts, just as there were in the serial storylines of *Out of the Inkwell*, the narrative premise of many silent cartoons still remained overwhelmingly subordinate to "surface, rhythm, and line" (Klein 1993: 5). Indeed, the fact that Felix was a trickster character who lacked a "singular defining narrative" owed much to the eponymous feline's excessive bodily transformations and propensity for physical manipulation, with a vivid fluidity of design that meant his body, like the plots in which he featured, was likewise fragmented and "vaguely defined" (Telotte 2019: 172). Many of the Felix shorts do include basic problem/solution set-ups, whether improving business for a local cobbler and attempting to 'make it' as a film star

(*Felix in Hollywood* [1923]), sneaking into a gym to confront a bullying boxer (*Gym Gems* [1926]), surviving freezing temperatures in the shorts *No Fuelin'* (1927) and *Eskimotive* (1928), or even proposing marriage (*Futuritzy* [1928]). However, such story beats were not intended to control Felix's emotional arc but simply to demonstrate the attraction of his graphic form, often re-locating his malleable inked body into several loosely-connected comic scenarios and environments. As animation (including Messmer and Sullivan's Felix) entered the 1930s, storytelling and style continued to remain closely entwined. Langer describes how narratives tended to be "a loose series of gags or a simple premise" (1991: 11), a quality he attributes largely to the institutional division of labour. At the Fleischer studio, for example, the "narrative's genesis took place with the participation of the Animation Department" rather than Storytelling Department (even after the latter's founding in 1932), which created the conditions for narrative's subordination and its place "down the pyramid of authority" (ibid.: 8). However, the relationship between animation's pictorial form and storytelling would be sharpened over the next two decades by the arrival of the seven-minute narrative popularised during the Golden Age of North American cartoon production.

Order and Chase

In the hands of the animators at Hanna-Barbera, MGM, and Warner Brothers, it was the repeating structure of the 'chase' (in combination with the vaudevillian gag) that robustly patterned storylines as animation reached its first half-century. From the *Looney Tunes* (1930–1969) series to the cat-and-mouse Tom and Jerry cartoons first premiering in 1940, the chase emerged as the dominant narrative model, allowing for the tribulations of recurring characters to be mapped onto pre-defined story frameworks. Scott Bukatman argues that throughout Hollywood cartoons of the 1940s and 1950s, "Settings might change (Yosemite Sam might be a pirate instead of an outlaw), variations might be rung (Bugs and Elmer might be singing opera), but the themes retain their familiarity" (2014: 310–311). Such cycles of repetition structuring many Golden Age narratives positioned Hollywood animation of this period within the routinised labour and Fordist principles of manufacture associated with the U.S. studio system, while also suggesting an intensified economic viability to the kinds of ritualism for which animation was both already known and industrially set-up. Hollywood cartoons did draw from alternate comic influences and entertainment traditions as part of their emergent formal repertoire (despite the subversive stylistic and storytelling tactics of Tex Avery, Chuck Jones, and Friz Freleng at Warner Brothers), yet they were nonetheless combined with repeating narrative schema and character archetypes in ways that began to shape the Hollywood cartoon into the definitive studio product.

Despite the rehearsal of basic narrative situations with little variation across the frenetic *Looney Tunes* cartoons – leading to Bukatman's dismissal that "the narrative is hardly the thing" (2014: 310) – their unique storytelling structures have positioned them as the target of sustained narrative analysis. Mary Slowik argues that the "narratology" of the *Looney Tunes* engages the animal "fable form" through the anthropomorphic activities of characters such as Wile E. Coyote (hare) and the Roadrunner (tortoise). Slowik notes that the narrative "composition" of such shorts "mine[s] both the fable's antic possibilities and its narrative structures for a comic effect that in surprising ways complicates the thematic, synthetic, and ethical dimensions of this kind of animal storytelling" (2018: 152). The identity of the seven-minute cartoon and its popularisation of the 'chase' and the 'gag' was additionally supported by another form of repetition rooted in the very materiality of the medium. Earl Hurd, who patented cel-animation in 1914 (before he formed the Bray-Hurd Process Company the same year), inaugurated an industrialised mode of production that dominated the efficiency of studio animation until the popularisation of computer graphics in Hollywood during the 1980s. The ability for cels to be inked and painted, washed, and ultimately reused held clear narrative implications, as these material elements constituting U.S. cartoon production were central to its machine-like efficiency. Hannah Frank argues that in the Hollywood cartoon, its "basic parts were interchangeable" (2019: 1), and in the case of storytelling, this meant repetition beyond purely movement (walk, run) cycles of action and held character/bodily poses. The reuse of individual cels provided the conditions for the repetition of stories, with many studio-era cartoons repeating not just jokes and characters but narrative material too. Such narrative strategies yielded two outcomes: high-volume production, and an economy of expression achieved via repeatable storytelling formulae in the truest Hollywood sense.

The arrival of longform television cartoons in the 1950s further influenced animated storytelling by introducing another 'serial' mode of narration, albeit one that evoked the seven-minute cartoon's episodic Sisyphean cycles of action marshalled by a disruptive and fuzzy treatment of temporality. Jeremy G. Butler's historical account of "the narrative cartoon" explains that the very first series produced for television *Crusader Rabbit* (1950–1959) and *The Ruff and Reddy Show* (1957–1960) "quickly adapted to television's special demands" (2007: 359). The formula for such made-for-TV cartoons included a specific treatment of narrative and dramatic structure (alongside shifts in tone in accordance with network control and broadcast standards), which would position such shorts in opposition to those designed for theatrical exhibition (ibid.: 341). Butler notes that both *Crusader Rabbit* and *The Ruff and Reddy Show* had to accommodate "television's (commercial) interruptions and the need for segmentation," resulting in cartoons that were "compartmentalized into four-minute segments that could be combined in a single day's program or run separately on subsequent days" (ibid.). Perhaps expectedly, narrative became subject to similar industrial forces. Cartoons evolved a seriality that resisted self-enclosed or contained storylines and instead celebrated the inconclusive and the open-ended, inviting Saturday morning audiences to stay tuned between episodes (or, simply, just return after the commercial break).

Animation's newfound capacities for telling stories on the small screen held aesthetic implications too, as animators challenged the aggressive naturalism of feature-length Disney with a more modernist, abstract style of limited animation – as pioneered by United Productions of America (UPA) – that, in its economy of production, was highly conducive to television's rapid turnaround and broadcast contexts. Many "made-for-TV cartoons" offered "simple" and repeatable visuals meaning that dialogue came to "dominate the presentation of narrative, often duplicating what is presented in the image" (ibid.: 359). Television's dramatic serial structure was therefore well-matched by an economical style of animation predicated on flattened space and perspectives, boldly abstract backgrounds, and looser character designs. In their visual curiosity and stylistic experimentation, the "stripped-down" techniques germane to such long-form animation also appealed to the abstract and sculptural aesthetics of mid-century modernism, thereby positioning commercial animation firmly within "the design-based, architectural, and artistic currents" of postwar U.S. culture (Bashara 2019: 5). This popular "template for television animation," which included a mode of storytelling that allowed for "TV's interrupted and segmented form" (Butler 2007: 359) and a limited style (that cost substantially less than a theatrical cartoon), returned the Saturday morning cartoon not just to animation's familiar studio-era cycle of repetition, but even further back to the blocked panel-style of a comic book. It was not until Hanna-Barbera's *The Flintstones* (1960–1966) that serial television animation's "narrative propulsion" (ibid.: 342) was marked by a clearer resolution of the episode's narrative drama, and with it a move into prime-time network programming.

Narrative evidently played a central role in the evolution of animation in the United States context across the first half of the twentieth century, and the gradual development of associative relations and causality within its specific fictional realisms. However, the centrality of commercial production to definitions of animated narrative means that as recently as the 1980s, "the focus on the American, basically narrative cartoon" had resulted in only "passing reference" to European filmmakers Robert Breer, Len Lye, Norman, McLaren, and Hans Richter, and "none at all to Viking Eggeling or Oskar Fischinger" (Kawin 1981: 39–40). Vital inroads have been made to correct this dominant core-periphery model that has often guided national cinema discourse, which tends to formalise intuitive networks of power by circumscribing the central against the fringe or marginal. Such correctives to the geographies of animation have, in turn, usefully sharpened industrial and artistic divisions between mainstream or commercial studio cartoons and more independent modes of production (at the same time as such distinctions are becoming increasingly illusory and interdependent). The idea of 'narration' has therefore become a useful tool in thinking through how animation has been celebrated for carrying the weight of serious and significant subject matter (as in the animated documentary), but also to formally distinguish more 'orthodox' animated media from non-figurative 'experimental' modes that sit outside the domain of realist construction. Nicky Hamlyn and Vicky Smith make clear that there are vibrant "non-generic, non-narrative" traditions of animation that expand the medium beyond "conventional cartoons," often connected to the 'siting' of animation away from traditional theatrical exhibition (2018: 2). It is therefore not just the abstraction, non-continuity, and interpretive form of experimental animation that counters the verisimilitude of 'realist' representation – embodied by the overwhelming dominance of Disney's "hyper-realism" – but equally its lack of narrative whereby temporality, sequentiality, and resolution are openly challenged by more avant-garde, illustrative, and alternate modes of presentation.

Narrative Orthodoxies

The issue persists, however, that despite a longstanding scholarly investment in the history of (largely American commercial) animated cartoon production, and conclusions drawn around its "binary opposition between loose gag structures and more linear developed narratives," the range of narrative possibilities made available by the animated medium remain remarkably "undertheorized" (Neupert 2011: 93). Several practical manuals and animator 'how to' guidebooks have begun to more readily reflect on the armoury of storytelling "rules" and "inventive narrative techniques" that direct characters, dramaturgical situations, and events within animation, which may include "pacing, revelations, suspense, flashbacks, clues and so forth" but also elements of "design, sound, movement, lighting, costumes, camera work and editing" (Purves 2015: 62). Commercial animation certainly employs easily familiar narrative structures as part of its repertoire of storytelling. Norman M. Klein credits the cel-animated features of Disney with "rediscovering the principles of Aristotelian narrative" (1993: 50) involving exposition, rising action, climax, falling action and denouement – dimensions of story often anchored to the studio's engagement with the fairy-tale's fantasy archetypes. The three-act structure common to narrative fiction also defines most short and feature-length film narratives (including animation), just as "most American cartoons are built around carefully unified narratives motivated by clearly defined, goal-oriented characters and chronologically arranged actions that lead toward a strong thematic resolution and discursive closure" (Neupert 2011: 93).

There are certainly other models of narration in operation that help to map animation's persistent storytelling strategies. Several of Walt Disney's animated musicals, including *The Lion King* (Roger Allers & Rob Minkoff, 1994), *The Hunchback of Notre Dame* (Gary Trousdale & Kirk Wise, 1996) and *Mulan* (Tony Bancroft & Barry Cook, 1998), alongside the recent *Happy Feet* (George Miller, 2006) and *Ratatouille* (Brad Bird, 2007), have been targeted by screenwriter Blake Snyder's three-act 'Beat Sheet' given their shared structural implementation of a "Storybook Superhero" plots that offer "variations on the "chosen one" legend, but made palpable with funny songs and talking animals" (Snyder 2007: 250). As Snyder himself admits, "I'd start every screenwriting class with a study of animated movies" (ibid.: 258). The generic identity of several recent big-budget computer-animated features (particularly those produced at Pixar Animation Studios and DreamWorks Animation) also remain notably derived from the durable 'buddy movie' template, while the virtual production of three-dimensional computer animation (and the ability for digital models to be reused in much the same way as individual cels) has greatly informed the multiple "journey narratives" that pattern contemporary Blockbuster animated franchises (Holliday 2018: 41–62). Noël Carroll's definition of "erotetic narration" – based on "the relation of a question to an answer" (1988: 171) as part of Hollywood's narrative clarity – is also exemplified in the work of much commercial animation and its strategies of coherency and flow of information (many computer-animated features employ a first-person voiceover narration to establish protagonist point-of-view through their framing as an orator [Holliday 2018: 161]). However, Patrick Power cautions against the repeated industry application of "formulaic narrative structures" for animation, particularly "Joseph Campbell's a hero's journey in a fairy-tale setting [that have] lead to a lack of originality in narrative" (2009: 118). Whereas the acceleration of animated documentary thanks to films such as *Persepolis* (Marjane Satrapi & Vincent Paronnaud, 2007) and *Waltz with Bashir* (Ari Folman, 2008) has opened the medium to historical-biographical stories via new aesthetic forms of "narrative structure and mode of delivery" (Honess Roe 2013: 156), there is, for Power, still a lack of narrative expressivity "all too common in CG features" (2009: 118).

Despite this admission, many recent computer-animated films have begun to test animation's default narrative organisations in an era where storytelling is becoming altogether more complex, convoluted, and puzzling. Jack Halberstam identifies several computer-animated features that prioritise "disruptive narrative arcs," noting that "very few mainstream films made for adults and consumed by large audiences have the audacity and the nerve [...] to tread on the dangerous territory of revolutionary activity" (2011: 22). The "narrative world of anarchy and anti-familial bands of characters" is exemplified by the features of the Disney, Pixar, and DreamWorks studios, which use "fairly conventional narratives" as 'gateways' into intricate stories of anthropomorphic queer alliance (Halberstam 2011: 22). These commercial "Pixarvolt" films, as Halberstam terms it, are increasingly invested in a politics of failure, selfishness, humility, awkwardness, limitation, and the disorderly, which manifest in radical stories of rebellion that propose "an antihumanist understanding of sociality" (ibid.: 46). Whereas most animated films "are allegorical in form and adhere to a fairly formulaic narrative scheme" (ibid.: 29), contemporary animated features such as *Finding Nemo* (Andrew Stanton, 2003) and *Over the Hedge* (Tim Johnson & Karey Kirkpatrick, 2006) have become heightened political spaces where queer narratives of disruption, anti-capitalist critique, and community underpin the revolutionary actions of their respective anthropomorphic cast of rebellious animals.

Since the turn of the millennium, Hollywood animation has also begun to embrace more baroque storytelling traditions and strategies that emphasise intricacy, iteration, and multiplicity in the arrangement of narrative material. If the growing tendency of contemporary U.S. cinema is towards a "puzzle film" structure that ultimately "rejects classical storytelling techniques and replaces them with complex storytelling" (Buckland 2009: 1), then animated narratives have also begun to adopt the kinds of self-consciously tangled plots and narrative reorientations that have been variously understood by the terms "forking path" (Bordwell 2002), "multiple draft" (Branigan 2002), "database" (Kinder 2002), "modular" (Cameron 2008), "mind-tricking" (Klecker 2013), and "network" (Poulaki 2014). When taken together, such descriptors signal the narrative deceptions, confusions, contradictions, and puzzlements of a mode of narration that is "*complex* beyond simply *complicated*" (Kiss & Willemsen 2017: 7), while establishing precisely the style of convoluted storytelling frameworks from which animators have begun to borrow. The computer-animated film *Inside Out* (Pete Docter, 2015) – which takes place largely in the mind of 11-year-old protagonist Riley – might even be usefully framed according to the conventions of the "mind-game" film, a sub-category of the "puzzle film" in which there are "switches between epistemological assumptions, narrational habits, and ontological premises that draw attention to themselves, or rather, to the rules of the game" (Elsaesser 2009: 39).

The emergent 'multiverse' storytelling structure displayed by the recent *Spider-Man: Into the Spider-Verse* (Peter Ramsey, Bob Persichetti & Rodney Rothman, 2018) not only allows for simultaneous versions of intellectual property resources and media content to co-exist, overlap, and intersect, but also crafts a pluralistic arrangement of narrative material beyond its monomyth framework that derives its impact by foregrounding "the relationship between the temporality of the story and the order of its telling" (Kinder 2002: 6). Other popular animated films released beyond Hollywood have further suggested creative deviations from the linear Aristotelian narrative from which Classical U.S. cinema first developed its dominant storytelling model. Satoshi Kon's anime *Perfect Blue* (1997) and *Paprika* (2006) demonstrate "the complex and apparently messy narration" familiar from mainstream "puzzle" cinema (Lo-riguillo-López et al. 2020: 81); *The Illusionist* (Sylvain Chomet, 2010) draws upon the "mind-tricking narratives" and reflexive causality from art cinema (Klecker 2013: 141); and Danish animated documentary *Flee* (Jonas Poher Rasmussen, 2021) re-tells the journey of refugee Amin Nawabi as he leaves his home country and fiancé in Afghanistan via non-linear plotting and shifting temporalities that are facilitated by the highly flexible animated form.

There ultimately begins to emerge some broad narratological conditions that have influenced and guided an understanding of what makes an animated narrative (or, perhaps, a narrative 'animated'). At the same time, as Brian Henderson provocatively asks, "Is there such a thing as a cartoon narrative?" (1991: 155), a question that points directly to the challenges that emerge from any attempt to identify and isolate formulaic cartoon plotlines, repetitive chains of cause-and-effect, goal-oriented character action, and unified narrative arrangements for a medium that is produced, distributed, and exhibited in numerous contexts. However, to provide a more robust solution to animation's defining heterogeneity, numerous scholars have leaned into the medium's potential for non-mimetic and metaphorical symbolism as a way of identifying the distinctiveness of animation narratives across a spectrum of forms (see Wells 1998). In his writing on the medium's "narrative strategies" that "inform the ways that animation can 'tell the tale'," Wells outlines several storytelling devices that are germane to its narrative orthodoxies (ibid.: 68). These properties inform the durable storytelling frameworks, archetypes, and myths routinised by animators and screenwriters with formal qualities intrinsic to animation's creative form, which when fully exploited are able to threaten the codes of (live-action) narrative feature filmmaking. For Wells, such techniques of representation include:

- *metamorphosis* (shifts in formation via 'quick change' transformation)
- *condensation* (predominance of ellipses and elision to construct sequentiality)
- *synecdoche* (where the part represents the whole)
- *symbolism and metaphor* (suggestive graphic bearer of story meaning)
- *fabrication* (the "expression of materiality" achieved in stop-motion)
- *associative relations* (conjunction of images to craft narrative meaning)
- *sound* (contribution of sonic elements to visuals)
- *penetration* (the invocation of internal space, states or experiences)

Animation's ability to be understood as 'narrative art' according to these underlying principles is ultimately comparable to its vexed relationship with generic classification (see Wells 2002), whereby animation's exchange and involvement with existing narrative models (typically drawn from live-action cinema and longstanding literary traditions) gives rise to a set of specific organising structures, modes, and techniques that are rooted in both its conditions of production and stylistic affordances. This means that rather than simply adopt the storytelling codes and conventions from predominantly literary or live-action cinema models of narration, animation can and should be understood as creating its own storytelling tactics that are closely connected to its ontology and flexibility of form. Just as with animation's arrival in the early twentieth century, then, its ongoing propensity for 'narrative' has never been fully cleaved from its ability for spectacular trick effects and wondrous illusions. By virtue of its sustained involvement with animation's conjuring of life, the medium's spectacular storytelling capabilities and potential for "attractions" never completely disappeared under the weight of classical narrative structures, but instead became progressively knotted together with them.

"Plots? We Never Bothered with Plots"

Despite ex-Fleischer and Walt Disney studio animator Dick Huemer (who also worked at the Barré studio) claiming that many cartoon studios "never bothered with plots" (quoted in Thomas 1958: 15), narration is clearly central to the formation of what makes the animated medium identifiable across numerous image-making contexts. Animation's narrational strategies and storytelling capacities reach far into the critical, industrial, historical, and stylistic recesses of the medium, sitting at the nexus of animation as a social, technological, economic, and political practice. Indeed, while certainly not animation's default standard, narrative and storytelling continue to play a role in – among many other applications – the medium's much-theorised genealogies, influences, and precursors; identifying formal divisions between naturalism and abstraction; theories of adaptation and animation's durable connections to oral folklore and fairy tales; the medium's potential for commentary, critique, satire and parody; its pervasive function as a tool of public engagement; and its instructional or pedagogical affordances that have made animation a useful multimedia agent of learning. While this chapter has only been able to briefly sketch the approaches and concepts that have given rise to animation's style of narrativity, narrative has undoubtedly retained its critical currency in shaping how we understand the medium's popularity and pervasiveness as a highly creative form, alongside the various methods by which it effectively and innovatively tells its stories.

Note

1 Paul Wells (1998: 25) has identified Disney's "hyper-realist" style as the approximation of a particular kind of pictorial realism and graphic illusionism. Wells notes that in Disney's hyper-realist aesthetics, in the 'hyper-realist' text, the "design, context and action," the "physical laws," the sound deployed by certain characters and objects, and the "construction, movement and behavioural

tendencies of 'the body'" all correspond to their real-world counterparts. The more an animated film follows these conditions "the more hyper-realist it will seem" whilst "the more an animated film deviates from these conventions, the more it will demonstrate different kinds of approach and purpose," and thus is deemed to hold a more non-realist (non-hyper-realist) agenda (1998: 26).

References

Bashara, Dan. 2019. *Cartoon Vision: UPA Animation and Postwar Aesthetics*. Berkeley, CA: University of California Press.
Bendazzi, Giannalberto. 2015. *Animation: A World History: Volume I: Foundations-The Golden Age*. Boca Raton, FL: CRC Press.
Blattner, Evamarie, Bernd Desinger, Matthias Knop, and Wiebke Ratzeburg. 2015. "Preface." In *Animation and Avant-Garde: Lotte Reiniger and Absolute Film*, edited by Evamarie Blattner, Bernd Desinger, Matthias Knop and Wiebke Ratzeburg, 9–13. Tübingen: Stadtmuseum.
Bordwell, David, Janet Staiger, and Kristin Thompson 1985. *The Classical Hollywood Cinema: Film Style and Mode of Production to 1960*. London, UK: Routledge.
Bordwell, David. 2002. "Film Futures." *SubStance* 31, no. 1: 88–104.
Branigan, Edward. 2002. "Nearly True: Forking Plots, Forking Interpretations: A Response to David Bordwell's "Film Futures." *SubStance* 31, no. 1: 105–114.
Buchan, Suzanne. 2013. *Pervasive Animation*. London, UK and New York, NY: Routledge.
Buckland, Warren. 2009. *Puzzle Films: Complex Storytelling in Contemporary Cinema*. Oxford, UK: Wiley-Blackwell.
Burch, Noël. 1990. *Life to Those Shadows*. Trans. Ben Brewster. Berkeley, CA: University of California Press.
Bukatman, Scott. 2014. "Some Observations Pertaining to Cartoon Physics; or, The Cartoon Cat in the Machine." In *Animating Film Theory*, edited by Karen Beckman, 301–316. Durham, NC: Duke University Press.
Butler, Jeremy G. 2007. *Television: Critical Methods and Applications*. Mahwah: Erlbaum.
Cameron, Allan. 2008. *Modular Narratives in Contemporary Cinema*. London, UK: Palgrave Macmillan.
Carroll, Noël. 1988. *Mystifying Movies: Fads and Fallacies in Contemporary Film Theory*. New York, NY: Columbia University Press.
Cook, Malcolm. 2018. *Early British Animation: From Page and Stage to Cinema Screens*. London: Palgrave Macmillan.
Crafton, Donald. 1993. *Before Mickey: The Animated Film 1898–1928*. Chicago, IL and London, UK: The University of Chicago Press.
Elsaesser, Thomas. 2009. "The Mind-Game Film." In *Puzzle Films: Complex Storytelling in Contemporary Cinema*, edited by Warren Buckland, 13–41.
Frank, Hannah. 2019. *Frame By Frame: A Materialist Aesthetics of Animated Cartoons*. Berkeley, CA: University of California Press.
Furniss, Maureen. 2017. *Animation: The Global History*. London, UK: Thames and Hudson Ltd.
Gunning, Tom. 1986. "The Cinema of Attractions: Early Film, Its Spectator and the Avant-Garde." *Wide Angle* 8, nos. 3–4: 63–70.

Gunning, Tom. 1993. "'Now You See It, Now You Don't': The Temporality of the Cinema of Attractions," *The Velvet Light Trap* (Fall): 71–84.

Halberstam, Jack. 2011. *The Queer Art of Failure*. Durham, NC: Duke University Press.

Hamlyn, Nicky, and Vicky Smith. 2018. "Introduction." In *Experimental and Expanded Animation: New Perspectives and Practices*, edited by Nicky Hamlyn and Vicky Smith, 1–18. London, UK: Palgrave Macmillan.

Henderson, Brian. 1991. "Cartoon and Narrative in the Films of Frank Tashlin and Preston Sturges." In *Film/Cinema/Theory*, edited by Andrew Horton, 153–173. Berkeley, CA: University of California Press.

Holliday, Christopher. 2018. *The Computer-Animated Film: Industry, Style and Genre*. Edinburgh, UK: Edinburgh University Press.

Honess Roe, Annabelle. 2013. *Animated Documentary*. London, UK: Palgrave Macmillan.

Karnick, Kristine Brunovska, and Henry Jenkins. 1995. "Introduction: Funny Stories." In *Classical Hollywood Comedy*, edited by Kristine Brunovska Karnick and Henry Jenkins, 63–86. New York, NY: Routledge.

Kawin, Bruce. 1981. "Review: The American Animated Cartoon: A Critical Anthology." *Film Quarterly* 34, no. 4 (Summer): 39–40.

Klecker, Cornelia. "Mind-Tricking Narratives: Between Classical and Art-Cinema Narration." *Poetics Today* 34, nos. 1–2 (Spring Summer): 119–146.

Klein, Norman M. 1993. *Seven Minutes: The Life and Death of the American Cartoon*. London, UK and New York, NY: Verso.

Kinder, Marsha. 2002. "Hot Spots, Avatars, and Narrative Fields Forever: Buñuel's Legacy for New Digital Media and Interactive Database Narrative." *Film Quarterly* 55, no. 4: 2–15.

Kiss, Miklós, and Steven Willemsen. 2017. *Impossible Puzzle Films: A Cognitive Approach to Contemporary Complex Cinema*. Edinburgh, UK: Edinburgh University Press.

Langer, Mark. 1990. "Regionalism in Disney Animation: Pink Elephants and Dumbo." *Film History* 4: 305–321.

Langer, Mark. 1991. "Institutional Power and the Fleischer Studios: The "Standard Production Reference." *Cinema Journal* 30, no. 2 (Winter): 3–22.

Loriguillo-López, Antonio, José Antonio Palao-Errando, and Javier Marzal-Felici. 2020. "Making Sense of Complex Narration in *Perfect Blue*." *Animation: an Interdisciplinary Journal* 15, no. 1: 77–92.

Merritt, Russell. 2005. "Lost on Pleasure Islands: Storytelling in Disney's Silly Symphonies." *Film Quarterly* 59, no. 1 (Fall): 4–17.

Moen, Kristian. 2015. "Imagination and Natural Movement: The Bray Studios and the 'Invention' of Animated Film." *Film History* 27, no. 4: 130–150.

Moritz, William. 1997. Narrative Strategies for Resistance and Protest in Eastern European Animation." In *A Reader in Animation Studies*, edited by Jayne Pilling, 38–47.

Musser, Charles. 1994. *The Emergence of Cinema: The American Screen to 1907*. Berkeley, CA: University of California Press.

Neupert, Richard. 2011. "'We're Happy When We're Sad': Comedy, Gags, and 1930s Cartoon Narration." In *Funny Pictures: Animation and Comedy in Studio-Era Hollywood*, edited by Daniel Goldmark and Charles Keil, 93–108. Berkeley, CA: University of California Press.

Poulaki, Maria. 2014. "Network Films and Complex Causality." *Screen 55*, no. 3 (January): 379–395.

Power, Patrick. 2009. "Animated Expressions: Expressive Style in 3D Computer Graphic Narrative Animation." *Animation: an Interdisciplinary Journal* 4, no. 2: 107–129.

Purves, Barry J. C. 2015. *Stop-Motion Animation: Frame by Frame Film-Making With Puppets and Models.* London, UK: Bloomsbury.

Schickel, Richard. 1997. *The Disney Version: The Life, Times, Art, and Commerce of Walt Disney.* Chicago, IL: Ivan R. Dee Publisher.

Slowik, Mary. 2018. "The Animal Fable, Chuck Jones, and the Narratology of the Looney Tune." *Narrative* 26, no. 2 (May): 146–162.

Snyder, Blake. 2007. *Save the Cat! Goes to the Movies: The Screenwriter's Guide to Every Story Ever Told.* California: Michael Wiese Productions.

Stoddart, Helen. 2015. "The Circus and Early Cinema: Gravity, Narrative, and Machines." *Studies in Popular Culture* 38, no. 1 (Fall): 1–17.

Telotte, J. P. 2019. "Felix in – and Out of – Space." In *Comics and Pop Culture: Adaptations from Panel to Frame*, edited by Barry Keith Grant and Scott Henderson, 169–183. Austin, TX: University of Texas Press.

Thomas, Bob. 1958. *Walt Disney, the Art of Animation: The Story of the Disney Studio Contribution to a New Art.* New York, NY: Simon and Schuster.

Wells, Paul. 1998. *Understanding Animation.* London, UK: Routledge.

Wells, Paul. 2002. *Animation: Genre and Authorship.* London, UK: Wallflower Press.

Wood, Aylish. 2007. *Digital Encounters.* New York, NY: Routledge.

12

INTERVIEW: JOSH WEINSTEIN

Can you put your finger on what it is you want to give your audiences when you write a story? Entertainment? Emotional catharsis? Moral instruction? Something else?

Most of all, I just want to really entertain my audience and make them laugh. But to truly entertain people, that involves a number of factors – we always found on the Simpsons, that the more emotionally invested a viewer is in a story, the more they'll like the jokes as well. And that's just human nature. If you're deeply invested in a story, your emotions are likely to be heightened in a positive way (even if you're feeling sadness along with a character). And if I can bring a viewer along on a character's emotional catharsis – even if it's something small or within a sillier story – that seems like that's something really good for the viewer. To be sappy but honest, the best response I've ever gotten to something I've written or helped write is when someone tells me they cried at a certain moment. And I'm talking about a cartoon comedy.

When working on a television program, is there any room for your own creative voice? Or if you write as part of a committee which drafts and re-drafts the screenplay several times, does your own voice get filtered out to serve the higher collective voice of the show?

The best shows I've worked on (meaning the writers are also really happy working along with feeling the show is worthwhile and good) have worked as comedy communes. Yes, we need to steer our writing to the original voice of the show's creator, but it's this symphony of voices that builds a show. Though the Simpsons came from the brilliant mind of Matt Groening (and has been carefully shepherded by him ever since), first you had the creative voices of Jim Brooks and Sam Simon added to his and

DOI: 10.4324/9781003197911-16

then the whole original writing staff added their own unique voices to the equation and that's when the show really blossomed. The Simpsons rewrite room gave birth to many other writers' rooms that employed the same Democratic feeling – while some shows are very competitive among writers, on shows like the Simpsons (and the American "The Office", "King of the Hill", etc.), the writers are all working together with the idea that the best joke or the best story idea goes in the script and it doesn't matter who that pitch comes from, a junior writer or a senior writer, we're all in it together. Incidentally, there's another benefit to this communal process – when people are happier, they tend to be funnier.

I'd also say that when I hire writers to work on a show, I do look for writers who have distinct voices. If we can add a new type of comedy or a unique perspective to the show and it fits, that makes the show all the more rich and interesting.

Do you ever watch a movie or TV show and think "How did the writer(s) do that?" If that has happened, can you offer an example?

Yes. It happens with some of my favorite shows. My favorite show of all time is "The Mighty Boosh" – I've seen every TV episode and listened to every Radio episode and am truly an obsessive Boosh fanboy. And I am continually in awe of their genuine funniness but also their storytelling abilities, their ability to create insane yet relatable characters, etc. I don't know if I can ever be as funny as the Boosh people but I have hired some of them to work on our show Disenchantment and they bring to that the same delightful energy and comedy that I love so much on the Boosh. It's interesting to me, too, that they are all writers/performers. I think that brings a special energy to writing that we regular sat-in-a-chair writers just don't have. The Boosh is an example of a show where I will watch certain scenes over and over just to (A) be amused and laugh out loud but also (B) see if I can figure out what makes it so damn funny.

Presumably, you know a poorly written show or movie when you see it. What are the typical or most common signs?

I get bored very quickly. The same goes for reading a bad script. If I'm not drawn in by the story and characters, if I don't care what happens next, to me, that's a bad show or movie. Of course, people's opinions about TV shows and movies – especially comedies – can be very subjective and I'm sure I can love something other people may find horribly boring.

Books and classes on screenwriting are sometimes described by working writers as constraining. Was there ever a book or a particular idea you discovered during your education that has always stuck with you as useful?

I only learned one thing in University from one class, from one teacher – and that was the lesson to always write with your own voice. The rest I learned from working on the university's humor magazine (a lot of valuable skills are learned by writing and producing something in a group). Unfortunately, my university at the time (the 1980s) did not have a lot of the practical, hands-on writing courses that I see in universities now. I took one of the most popular Pay-To-Listen-To-Some-Supposedly-Great-Writing-Instructor-Spout-Platitudes-At-You courses and it was useless when it came to actually writing. There was one book, however, that was genuinely useful and highly practical and great – "Save The Cat". I've known other writers who also loved that book. Hopefully, this book is one of those good ones, too! Don't listen to my advice, though!

13

VIDEO GAME NARRATIVE

Concepts and Practices for Structuring and Infusing Story in Games

Dominic Arsenault

The birth of video games can be traced back to two distinct sociocultural contexts. The most well-known is the skill-and-reflexes arcade machines of the 1970s and 1980s, made famous in popular culture with *PONG*, *Space Invaders* and *Pac-Man*. Skill-based games also appeared in the more obscure and earlier context of mainframe computers in university and research laboratories, complemented with a second genre of strategy and adventure video games, like *Hamurabi* and *Colossal Cave Adventure*. In these games, players were offered descriptions ("You are standing at the end of a road before a small brick building."), made choices by typing instructions ("Go in"), and the machine relayed the results through text narration ("You are inside a building, a well house for a large spring. There are some keys on the ground here."). Text-based games and their progeny that would be called interactive fiction (IF) laid the foundations for narration and narrative in games, but the phenomenon vastly exceeds these preliminary steps. This chapter will expose three core concepts for understanding narration across the landscape of modern video games: the *narrative program*, or the ambitions and relationship between a game's story and gameplay; the *narrative structure*, or the way the events and story's interactive nature are laid out in the game; and *narrative infusion*, or the ways in which games include narrative materials outside a formal, "proper" story or narrative.

Fundamentals of Interactive Narrative Design

The typical way of achieving interactive storytelling lies in the branching narrative, where a game offers players predefined choices to make in the story. If every choice impacts the story, however, then an additional parallel storyline

DOI: 10.4324/9781003197911-17

must be crafted each time, which quickly becomes unmanageable. This calls for one of four solutions:

1 the story has a high degree of variability, but is short;
2 the story is long, but with few decisions to make;
3 the many choices offered do not significantly impact the story;
4 the many choices fold back into a limited number of main story branches.

These compromises all lead to a diminished sense of narrative agency or control over the story. But before we get to the structures of narrative in games, we must address a more fundamental issue: the essential opposition between games and stories. This was a key aspect of the ludology/narratology debate which took the center place in the early days of game studies (see Pearce, 2005, or Roth, van Nuenen & Koenitz, 2018), but also a core concern among game developers. Costikyan (2000, 45), for instance, claimed that "To the degree that you make a game more like a story – a controlled, pre-determined experience, with events occurring as the author wishes – you make it a less effective game. To the degree that you make a story more like a game – with alternative paths and outcomes – you make it a less effective story. It's not merely that games aren't stories, and vice versa; rather, they are, in a sense, opposites".

This tension between game and story is not unique to video games, but can be found in tabletop role-playing games (RPGs) that start with *Dungeons & Dragons* (Gygax & Arneson, 1974). Players sit around a table and are invited to imagine a fantasy world described through the words of the game or dungeon master, who acts both as narrator and referee. Players describe how their characters (whether an elf wizard, warrior, or cleric) act and react, and the dungeon master determines the consequences. Characters have various statistics to govern their actions, and the rules found in the voluminous books provide ways to resolve most typical situations, often with dice rolls and adjustments based on their attributes or skills. The dungeon master is the prime narrative designer, responsible for coming up with a quest and a general storyline for the party of characters according to their personalities and motivations, while ensuring the story will progress.

Sometimes (and oftentimes) the players will act differently from what the dungeon master expected, which requires adapting, improvising, or reorganizing events on the fly. Anything is possible, and when a player declares "I run away and leave the helpless villagers to die", the dungeon master can't just say "No" or "You can't do that". This would break the sense (or illusion) of immersion that everyone strives to maintain and the ludic contract at the core of role-playing games, that players are free to exert their agency. Of course, this contract is socially situated and negotiated, and players are expected to engage with the materials proposed by the dungeon master proactively and earnestly to make the story work, and not fight against or destroy it. They are meant to engage in the active creation of belief, as Murray put it:

> The pleasurable surrender of the mind to an imaginative world is often described, in Coleridge's phrase, as "the willing suspension of disbelief." But this is too passive a formulation even for traditional media. When we enter a fictional world, we do not merely "suspend" a critical faculty; we also exercise a creative faculty. We do not suspend belief so much as we actively *create belief*. Because of our desire to experience immersion, we focus our attention on the enveloping world and we use our intelligence to reinforce rather than to question the reality of the experience.
>
> *(Murray, 1997, p. 110)*

Maintaining the immersive illusion can be difficult around a role-playing game table seating people that look nothing like their imaginary world counterparts. Video games may have an advantage here by virtue of being audio-visual experiences, but they also face a much bigger challenge: there is no dungeon master pulling the strings of the narrative in real time and adjusting to the player's actions with the wit and flexibility of the human mind. Computers can't improvise or transform their planned events, at least not outside the procedural rules that humans have provided them through programing. They can't create new speech, characters, or environments, unless they can rely on robust programed subsystems to generate sentences, villagers, families, forests, or towns, which require linguistic, behavioral, geological, and urbanistic models and simulations – and even with all that, there would still be a lot missing to simulate a living, breathing world. Without free reign over these building blocks of stories, the narrative agency in video games can only exist as far as the narrative designers predicted or restricted (and as far as the game developers implemented the results of) the decisions players can make. There is always a risk that the interactive and narrative contents will clash in what game designer Clint Hocking (2007) called "ludonarrative dissonance", for example, by portraying a character as charming and heroic in the narrative while they murder hundreds of people gratuitously in the game because of a player's individual playstyle. Managing players' ludic freedom while ensuring the narrative remains relevant and impactful is the job of the game writer or narrative designer, who strives for ludonarrative *consonance* or *harmony* by structuring the authored contents of a story to mesh together with the player's agency so that they support each other, recognizing that the actions players undertake through their characters when they play a game form in themselves a certain kind of story.

Game writer Mary DeMarle's terminology (2004) is useful in describing these intersecting forms of storytelling. The actions performed by players, whether slashing with a sword, moving armies or selecting replies in conversation, build an "immediate-level" or low-level story, in the sense that every time a game is played, it unfolds differently. Though the details may differ, these actions will typically advance the "main", pre-scripted storyline – the high-level story. The fact that it is pre-scripted does not mean it is fixed; a game like *Red Dead Redemption* does feature a linear high-level story (peppered with a high number of low-level stories that emerge as players ride their horse, get ambushed, hunt animals, or explore the open-world environment), but one like *Mass Effect* offers different pre-scripted branches depending on player choices, delivering an interactive high-level story. DeMarle offers one more distinct term, interactive narrative, to account for games where player interaction does not impact the story itself, but the order in which the events are told or viewed (for instance, when players must accomplish a number of tasks in any order before the story can continue). This distinction is consistent with the concepts and terminology developed in classical narratology, whereby a "story" is a set of events happening to characters (fictional or real), and a narrative is "the textual actualization of story" (Ryan, 2006, p. 7), that is, a synthesis of both the story and the discourse that communicates it.[1]

Video Games and the Narrative Program

As video game writers, Dille and Zuur Platten (2007, pp. 19–21) distinguish between linear path, largely pre-scripted games as "writer-friendly formats", and open-ended or free-flow "sandbox" games, as well as role-playing games (RPGs) where players create their own character(s), as "writer-difficult formats" since many scripted events require providing a number of "alts" (alternatives) depending on whether a specific earlier event happened, which character is present, or what their current mood or state is. "Friendly" and "difficult" categories are helpful since one of the main problems we face when discussing games and narrative is that "video games" is a very large set, and many games have little or even no bearing on narrativity whatsoever. It is not that they fail to provide "good" high-level stories (which is a question of aesthetic merit), but rather that the experiences they seek to elicit essentially revolve around gameplay or low-level stories with a vague narrative background, such that there can be "too much story going on", detracting from the game's main objective. In other art forms, we typically have genre distinctions or other categories to account for these "narrative-detached" forms (i.e., poetry, dictionary or encyclopedia, abstract or experimental film and portrait painting, opposed to novel, biography, fiction film, and history painting). While shooters or sports games may have minimal "ornamental" high-level stories that function well enough to provide justification for the action, and RPGs typically feature sprawling epics, this kind of generalization based on game genre masks the many forms narrative can take in video games, and at worst, limits the possibilities for game creators when they are accepted as gospel. RPGs like *Darkest Dungeon* do not rely mainly on a pre-scripted story unfolding through the game, and sports games can have rich narratives, as evidenced by *Madden NFL 18*'s "Longshot" story mode that presents the tribulations of a quarterback trying to make it into the National Football League. We need some way to address this.

I propose the concept of *narrative program* to frame the degree of importance given to the narrative in a game, *narrative* being understood as the textual discourse (whether written, spoken or audiovisual) that presents a high-level story, and *program* as the series of events or activities planned by the game's creators for their players. The program is useful to describe in broad terms a game's ambitions for communicating a high-level story through a narrative, before we get into detailed analysis of structures, scenes or plot points. A game can be described in one of four degrees: *a-narrative*, *hypo-narrative*, *meso-narrative*, and *hyper-narrative*.[2] To evaluate what kind of program it offers, we need to ask questions on the importance it gives to the narrative:

- *Extensiveness*: Is there evidence of extensive work that has gone into the game's narrative? *Red Dead Redemption* has many cut-scenes[3] and long conversations as the characters travel between locations to establish the motivations and characterization of the protagonist John Marston, more than *Grand Theft Auto: San Andreas* did for Carl Johnson, and more than *Grand Theft Auto III* did for its unnamed protagonist.
- *Immediateness*: How much of the narrative experience are you missing if you watch someone else playing? Watching a video of someone playing *Uncharted* is clearly not a way to experience its action gameplay, but since the high-level story unfolds largely in pre-written cut-scenes, not much of the high-level narrative experience is lost, contrary to games like *Mass Effect* where much of the narrative is impacted by player decisions.
- *Compulsoriness*: Can you skip narrative segments, and if you do, how much of the experience are you missing? Can you progress through the game without paying attention to the story? Even though extensive work has gone into the writing of quests in *World of Warcraft*, players can skip through the text and get help from arrows, map trackers and pointers, along with bullet-point lists of tasks and steps to do.
- *Compellingness*: Is the game feeding your expectations and rewarding you for progress mainly through its narrative, its gameplay, or both equally? Would you keep playing if you lost interest in the narrative, or if you lost interest in the gameplay? It seems easy to imagine someone playing *Tom Clancy's Splinter Cell* for the pleasures and challenges of sneaking around and using gadgets even if they find the narrative cliché, heavy-handed or over-extended; conversely, it is hard to imagine someone persisting in playing *L.A. Noire* or *Heavy Rain* with this appreciation of their narrative,

since everything players do in these games has to do with advancing the investigation and the narrative.

A game's narrative being extensive, immediate, compulsory and compelling (or not) provides guidelines in attributing a narrative program. *A-narrative* games (the prefix *a-* meaning "not" or "without", denoting negation or absence) feature no high-level story at all, and thus no narrative. Abstract puzzle games like *Tetris* or *2048* are the prime examples of these, but we can also include for instance sports games played in single matches without an overarching narrative. *Hyper-narrative* games (the prefix *hyper-* meaning "over" or "above", denoting excess or exaggeration) occupy the opposite end of the spectrum and feature so much high-level story that it may be too much for some players; the story takes the center stage and commands attention, eventually overshadowing the game elements as gameplay becomes, in essence, the means toward the end of advancing the story. Text or graphical adventure games and visual novels are two genres that typically feature hyper-narrative games, but Gerstmann (1998) hinted at this when reviewing the stealth game *Metal Gear Solid*: "If Hideo Kojima, the game's producer, was so set on this type of cinematic experience, he should really be making movies instead of games". In recent years, many games, such as *Mass Effect* or *Final Fantasy VII Remake* have started offering a "story mode" difficulty setting, which essentially turns the game into a hyper-narrative experience.

Occupying a larger part of the continuum within the two extremes, we find our two last categories. In *hypo-narrative* games (the prefix *hypo-* meaning "under" or "beneath", denoting a lack or shortage) there is some narrative put forth, but it is lacking without the game segments; for instance, adapting it to a predominantly narrative form would require significantly expanding on the narrative elements. Some typical examples include Nintendo's *Super Mario Bros.* series, where each time Mario must rescue Princess Peach from Bowser; *Angry Birds*, where the pigs have stolen the eggs to be retrieved; and *DOOM*, where scientists on a research base in space opened a gate to Hell and demons are invading. There is no expectation for dramatic reversals, character growth, or intimate, introspective moments speaking of the human condition in these games; the high-level story acts as justification for the gameplay, perhaps providing some initial situation and perturbation that sets the course for action and one or two pivots whose function is to generate more gaming situations.

The final category of *meso-narrative* games ("middle" or "intermediate", denoting moderation or balance) is probably (or arguably) the largest; it includes all games where there is some equilibrium between the gameplay and the narrative, so that any of the two can't be readily dismissed as being subservient to the other, because they are both necessary and complementary in fleshing out the game experience. Admittedly, this is a very large category spanning a number of game genres from open-world games like *Grand Theft Auto* or *Assassin's Creed* to action-adventure games like *Uncharted* or *Metroid Prime*, and the range covers everything with slightly too much narrative to fall into the hypo-narrative space, up to everything that has not quite enough story to enter the hyper-narrative space.

As we are dealing with individual perceptions, we may very well assess that *The Legend of Zelda: A Link to the Past* has a meso-narrative program, while someone else would consider it as a slightly more detailed hypo-narrative variant of its predecessor, *The Legend of Zelda*. These disagreements are productive, as they force us to pause and reflect on what the game attempts to achieve with its narrative and that led us to our own point of view. The narrative program helps us account for all types of games, from those that eschew narrative to those who couldn't be understood without it. When a video game does present a narrative, however, many other concepts must be brought into play to understand how it is structured.

Structures of Interactive Narrative, from Branching Trees to Open-World Games

There is a sizable professional literature on interactive narrative, with books and articles dedicated to video games or interactive fiction (IF) by writers and narrative designers. I offer here a synthesis of a dozen or so authors who introduced a number of similar "interactive narrative structures", with flowcharts or graphs of nodes and links (see Table 13.1). As Wendy Despain (2008) explains, there is no fixed way to do so, in part due to games having such widely differing needs regarding narrative structure:

> These methods truly have no standard. (...) I've seen trees, webs, matrices, and spirals. Some writers say they can keep the narrative and all its branches straight just in their own head, but in game development you have to be able to communicate your vision to others, and sometimes there's nothing like a flow chart or diagram to get the point across.
>
> *(Despain, 2008, p. 17)*

Mary DeMarle and Richard Boon (both in Bateman, 2004) have laid out four types of narrative structures and three types of interactive story structures. Marie-Laure Ryan (2006, pp. 100–107), as an academic studying narrative in general rather than a game writer, charts a high number of structures by examining other adjacent practices like interactive fiction, multimedia CD-ROMs and websites alongside video games, which yields a broader but more complex model that requires some reductive adaptation when we focus on games. In contrast, by concentrating on video games, Steve Ince (2006, pp. 47–54) works out the narrative structure together with the gameplay structure, producing categories that can be more appropriate given that a number of games feature interactive gameplay segments but fixed cinematic sequences or cut-scenes to advance the narrative in a predetermined way, no matter how the player went about doing things in the game levels. More importantly, he notes that the structures are "not a definitive list", they can be mixed and hybridized, and "new structures are likely to emerge as we learn more about the possibilities that interactive storytelling offer us" (Ince, 2006, p. 54). Flint Dille and John Zuur Platten (2007) identify four types of branching narratives (where the story's main arc or *spine* is akin to the trunk of a tree, with various branches poking out according to a player's decisions) based on how clear-cut or diffuse the branches are, how far they stray from the story's spine, and how long they carry out their effects before merging back toward the spine. An additional category of "nodal storytelling" is provided to cover open-world games, where the story episodes are dispersed across different locations. Contributors to Despain (2009) discuss these realities in similar terms, while Sam Kabo Ashwell (2015) and Christina "Chride" Lassheikki (2021) approach branching narratives from the slightly different perspective of contemporary interactive fiction or CYOA (Choose Your Own Adventure) stories, such as *Counterfeit Monkey* by Emily Short (2013) or *Howling Dogs* by Porpentine (2012).

Table 13.1 presents the common basic structures of interactive narrative. I have elected to call these structures *primitives*, not as a value judgment, but rather as in the geometric primitives (sphere, cube, cylinder, cone, pyramid, and torus) that are the foundation for computer graphics. Just as 3D modelers will seldom use a single primitive and call it a day, game writers usually combine, extend, and reshape many of these primitives to structure the interactive narrative of a game. I provided a basic descriptor for each primitive, but I prefer (and suggest) referring to them by their associated Roman numerals. A quick look at the table will reveal how similar words are used in different contexts, making terms such as "parallel paths" or "story branch" confusing since we may not share the same terminology. They are organized in three groups governed by different metaphors, with one on each page. If we wanted to seriously model the "storyspace" or "chronotope"[4] of a given game, we could map out a detailed representation of their interactive narrative structure in a three-dimensional space, with each of these groups distributed across an axis. In practice though, the primitives function well as quick sketches that provide loose basic building blocks.

Figures I–IV are *temporal* and revolve around the metaphor of traveling a path. The episodes or story beats unfold in succession in the narrative (which usually means they unfold chronologically in the story, but not necessarily thanks to the twists and warps of narrative time, like flashbacks). *I (footsteps)* is simple linear events, each moment of interactivity leading to a narrative moment in preordained succession, so that we are walking along the

TABLE 13.1 Common structures of interactive narrative found across the professional literature on video game writing

Authors / Primitives	Bateman (2004)	Ryan (2006)	Ince (2006)	Dille and ZuurPlatten (2007)	Despain (2009)	Ashwell (2015) and Chride (2021)
Temporal I. "Footsteps"	Linear/ Continuous structure (Boon)	State-transition diagram	Linear story	Linear story	Linear structure (Wessman, Suckling)	Sorting hat
II. "Train"		Interplay of actual and virtual events	Linear gameplay, player-influenced story			
III. "Freeway"		Track-switching	Parallel story and gameplay			Parallel storylines (Chride)
IV. "Loop"		Network (looping chronologically)				Loop and Grow

(Continued)

TABLE 13.1 (*Continued*)

Primitives \ Authors	Bateman (2004)	Ryan (2006)	Ince (2006)	Dille and ZuurPlatten (2007)	Despain (2009)	Ashwell (2015) and Chride (2021)
Virtual						
V. "Vine"		Vector with side-branches		Critical paths	Main objectives and side-objectives (Saad)	Gauntlet, pruning branches (Chride)
VI. "Pruned tree"	Parallel paths (DeMarle)	Flowchart		Limited branching	Branching structure (Wessman)	Branch and Bottleneck
VII. "Shrub"	Branching story (DeMarle)	Tree	Branching story and gameplay	Open-ended branching		Time Cave

TABLE 13.1 (Continued)

Authors / Primitives	Bateman (2004)	Ryan (2006)	Ince (2006)	Dille and ZuurPlatten (2007)	Despain (2009)	Ashwell (2015) and Chride (2021)
Spatial	Domain structure (Boon)	Sea-anemone + Vectors			Hub and spoke (Wessman)	Spoke and hub
VIII. "Museum"	Gated story (DeMarle)	Serial Networks or Mazes		Funneling narrative (chokepoints)	"Pot-based" story (Suckling)	Quest or Open Map
IX. "Islands"	Contiguous structure (Boon)	Storyworld/ Network + Flowchart + Maze	Controlled branching story and gameplay	Nodal storytelling	Open-world structure (Wessman)	Open Map or Floating Modules
X. "Garden"						

footsteps left by the narrative designer. In *II (train)*, the narrative events are dispersed in the environment, which we traverse by sitting in a train. While the way forward is fixed and the general direction of the story is linear, we get to see different things – alternatives – depending on some initial choice(s) we made (aisle or window, front or rear car) that are quite removed from the consequences, so our impression of narrative agency is limited. Typically seen in interactive movies more than in video games, we can still find *II* in games where we must select our character's backstory or origins; in *Mass Effect*, some story episodes will vary depending on whether our character used to be a Spacer, Earthborn or Colonist. In *III (freeway)*, we advance through the narrative by driving a car in a multi-lane highway, which is linear, but we get to make small-scale decisions constantly. We may not know that the highway will split at some point in the future, but we can nevertheless evaluate our position within it as we steer toward one side or the other. This structure is favored in BioWare games, where we make choices and gain or lose points that steer our character between the Light side and Dark side of the Force in *Star Wars: Knights of the Old Republic*, the Way of the Open Palm and the Closed Fist in *Jade Empire*, or between Paragon and Renegade in *Mass Effect*, each choice cumulatively orienting the character toward one lane of the narrative over a long-scale, temporal process rather than a one-time decision point (which we'll see with the figures V–VII). *IV (loop)* is a structure that revolves around a cyclical process; as we repeat the same events (whether a day, a season, a year, or an attempt at achieving something), new events, characters or situations add something to the narrative. In *The Legend of Zelda: Majora's Mask*, we have three days before the world ends, and playing a song will take us back in time to the start of the 72-hour period. As we chart out more of the locations, events and characters' activities during these days, we uncover more episodes and progress in the narrative.

Figures V–VII are *virtual* and revolve around the widespread botanical metaphor behind "branching stories". The episodes or story beats are organized in alternatives that may or may not happen depending on our actions and decisions, and while not necessarily predictable or direct, we have some degree of narrative agency. In *V (vine)*, we follow a main stem toward narrative resolution, but we may choose to pursue some offshoot events along the way before returning to the main stem (a device found in many games in the form of "side-quests" that complement the "main quest", as when we decide to stop and help a lost traveler return home in *Red Dead Redemption 2* rather than pressing on to the next step of the main quest). In *VI (pruned tree)*, the decisions we make direct us along the branches of a tree of narrative possibilities. The branches of the tree are cut off or recombined along the way to keep the emergence of alternatives manageable, and the focus of the narrative remains along the main stem (the tree's trunk). In the opening scene to *Fahrenheit/Indigo Prophecy*, our character is unexplainably possessed and murders an innocent person in the toilets of a diner. We can escape by running away in a frenzy, discreetly leaving through the back door, or walking out; we may or may not wash our bloodied hands, bump into people confusedly, finish our meal, pay our tab or play a song on the jukebox, and we may return home by taxi or by subway. All these choices, however, do not explode into 16 different story branches, but are folded back into a single branch for the next episode, as detectives find clues pointing to our character, with the investigation being a little easier or harder depending on our prior actions. Without such management, we end up with *VII (shrub)* instead, which differs from the pruned tree by the unmanageable multiplication of its stems and branches, to the point that it is impossible to distinguish a "main" stem amid the lot. The shrub cannot grow too high without becoming a *VI*; 10 decision points between 2 alternatives that each lead to a different storyline will result in $2^{10} = 1024$ alternatives, a problem colloquially referred to as the "death tree". Even without modeling hundreds of storylines, it nevertheless illustrates the challenges posed by branching trees and narrative agency in video games: planning even two or three alternative storylines requires doubling or tripling the workload, for possibly small benefits (unless players are prepared to replay through the entire story again to see the different outcomes).

Figures VIII–X are *spatial* and revolve around the metaphor of organized spaces. The episodes and story beats are located or accessible somewhere in an environment under specific conditions, rather than occurring chronologically. In practice, we usually find hybrid or joint constructions; as seen in Ryan (2006), many open-world games will embed temporal structures (I–IV) into these spatial structures. *Grand Theft Auto* games may disseminate characters that give us missions all over the environment, but each of them typically offers a series of missions that develop a certain story arc over time. The *VIII (museum)* features a hub or central space that connects the various sub-locations (exhibits) hosting the events or narrative pieces. This is typically found in detective games like *L.A. Noire*, where we travel to different locations to gather clues or interrogate witnesses, returning in-between to our office to examine evidence or interrogate suspects. The *IX (islands)* model differs in that we must progress from each sub-location to the next by satisfying various conditions (typically, having experienced certain or all events), which unlock bridges to other islands – quite literally in *Grand Theft Auto III*: we begin in the Portland area and must complete all the missions there for a bridge to open to Staunton Island and more missions. Whereas *VIII* favors cycles and *IX* progression, *X (garden)* is less prescriptive: we can stroll, walk or run in a garden's alleys in whatever order we wish, even though some of the plots may be more organized than others. Such a structure works well in open-ended games like *The Elder Scrolls* series, where we may choose to wander around and resolve situations that occur around us, work for a guild, or pursue any number of quests in any order.

The ten primitives outlined above can be combined in various ways, and games will often tell their story through many such configurations. Player-characters may initially wander around a city of neighborhoods accessible from a home base (*VIII*), meeting two or three minor characters who provide them with optional side-quests (*V*) and a major character that offers quests chained as a string of pearls (*I*), perhaps with a major decision to make that offers two alternatives for the last of them (*VI*). When all quests are completed, the virtual lock on the city is lifted (for instance, players learn the identity of the evil leader), allowing players to leave that space and evolve in an open-world environment (*X*) filled with other quest-givers and other gated sub-locations (*IX*) such as cities, castles, or caverns, as they advance through the main quest (*V*). It is common to reserve an open-ended branching tree (*VII*) for a game's ending for instance, where the vastly different consequences are left up to the player's imagination, or as an inverted figure to reduce an enormous space of possibilities into a small number of branches by tallying up the choices made during the experience. Emily Short (2016) calls this latter small-scale structure the "Endgame Time Cave", lifting the term from Sam Kabo Ashwell (2015) who identified "standard patterns" in choice-based games as large-scale templates to describe their overall organization. In some cases where a game keeps a rather homogeneous structure throughout, a larger scale can be more practical than the small-scale structures I have outlined here. These two scales are not contradictory in any case, as we could describe Ashwell's standard patterns as principally revolving around some of the primitives outlined here: his "Time Cave" is based on *VII*, the "Gauntlet" on *V*, the "Branch and Bottleneck" on *VI* and *VII*, the "Quest" on *IX*, *V* and *VII*, etc. In time, we may analyze a given corpus of gameplay or narrative patterns within a range of titles and develop a repertoire of compound structures, typical assemblages of primitives that would help scaling the discussion around narrative structures with ever sharper focus.

Beyond Formal Narratives and Stories: Narrative Infusion in Video Games

While structures are important to conceptualize the architecture of choices in video games, many practitioners and researchers observe that narrative choice in games is fragile and complicated, and that achieving the *illusion* of agency is the real objective. Maurice Suckling and Marek Walton (2012, p. 85) refrain from exhaustive structure mappings and instead distinguish between *fractal* and *modular* game story structures, the former providing players with "choices that take the story and/or gameplay in totally new directions", the latter with "choices designed to give the illusion of choice and player agency but which, in reality, don't significantly change a story's main course". Clara Fernández-Vara (n.d.) proposes a taxonomy of narrative choices to address how games may (or not) allow "true" agency over the events. Choices can be:

- Unfair: "there's no way to know what the consequences will be". Open one of two doors without any contextual hint, behind which lie either horrible death or treasure.
- Fake: in *Dragon Warrior*, princess Gwaelin asks the player "Dost thou love me?", and if they answer "No", she replies "But thou must!" in an endless loopback until they select "Yes".
- Invisible: "choices that the player is making but they don't know it's actually a choice". In *Chrono Trigger*, you bump into a girl at the market and she falls down, but something shiny falls in another direction; if you go pick up the shiny thing before checking up on her, witnesses will testify to your greedy behavior during a court trial later on.
- Narratively weak: "the consequences are not very interesting". For example, choosing our weapon of choice in games typically has no impact over the narrative.
- Expressive: "doesn't really have consequences in the system, but it makes the players feel like they're in control and they can be themselves". Commander Shepard in *Mass Effect* can be male or female, and the choice does not change the story aside from romancing options. Even if they don't romance specific characters, players still feel that their choice of playing as either male or female Shepard does matter to them.
- Moral: choices are made with "very clear consequences – we are good or bad (or maybe neutral)", as in games that award points on a scale of "Good" to "Evil", seen in primitive *III – Freeway*.
- Dilemmas: "the kind of difficult choices that games should use more often. It's what "moral choices" pretend to be, but they're hard and they often make people feel bad". In the backstory to *Mass Effect*, the alien species of the galaxy uplifted a race of reptilian warriors (the Krogan) from their harsh home planet and gave them advanced technologies, making them the perfect army to battle out insectoid invaders. After disposing of the threat, though, the Krogan became the new threat, with their aggressive nature, 1,000-year lifespan and annual 1,000-egg laying reproductive rhythm fueling their rebellions. To neutralize their incredible expansion, another species unleashed upon them the genophage, a genetic infection that effectively sterilized them. As they play through the games of the *Mass Effect* trilogy, players are given the opportunity to spread a cure for this plague – a choice that is far more involved than the quick impression one may have reading this short summary, as players meet and talk with Krogans who, like anyone else, try to make the galaxy a better place and carve a future for their doomed species as best they can. It's up to the player to

make the decision, and the game presents the reasons and issues efficiently (you must have the conversation with your own Krogan crew member) to stage a real dilemma that's not reducible to strategic considerations (i.e., curing it or not will not grant game upgrades or rewards that could eschew the moral or ethical quandary).

The question of whether in-game player agency actually translates to agency over the narrative itself is usually approached through narrative structures and decision points where clear "interactive storytelling" moments happen. But there are more hands-off approaches to interactive narrative, through techniques and strategies that I describe as *narrative infusion*. By this term, I refer to the use of discrete and diffuse narrative elements or qualities that can be added to a game's components without changing their interactive nature. These may not be full-grown narratives in themselves, but provided the right narratively inclined player, they can blossom into full-bodied aromas and flavors that will render the game experience narrative[5] in the much broader scope of cognitive narratology advocated by Monika Fludernik (1996) and Marie-Laure Ryan (2006), which have both argued against the narrow definitions of narrative as a formal discourse relating past events, and in favor of an expansive definition of narrative as a pervasive phenomenon that is more or less typical and more or less constructed, opening the way, following Ryan (2006), for a trans-medial narratology.

There are many reasons for the need to adopt a wider view of narrativity than that of classical narratology to understand video games. Many of them feature a minimal story, but a richly detailed world in which the action takes place, and the narrative experience becomes one of discovering the history of this world and getting to know the factions and people inhabiting it more than experiencing a thrilling tale through scripted events. The example of the genophage from *Mass Effect* illustrates this, and in fact, the entire *Elder Scrolls* series was built on this premise, as Wendi Sierra (2020) explains. *The Elder Scrolls: Arena* and *The Elder Scrolls II: Daggerfall* present huge worlds of hundreds of thousands of square kilometers, with hundreds of towns and dungeons, non-player characters wandering around and dozens of houses lining the streets. These all contribute to the objective of simulating a *Dungeons & Dragons* role-playing game world: this is not your story and the world does not revolve around you, but this is a full-grown, autonomous world in which you are living out your own adventures. This highlights the spatial nature of video games and their reliance on world-building as much as storytelling, a phenomenon that has been studied by multiple researchers (see Wolf, 2012; Jørgensen, 2013, or more generally Boni, 2017). Multiplying cities and the scale of cities beyond shops and key story characters only, providing a calendar with weekdays and holidays, a day/night routine with shops closed at night, and citizens discussing current world affairs or rumors all provide infusions of narrativity, a sense that the world is more than a door-monster-treasure series of risks and rewards.

Video games are also particular among narrative media in their ability to include narrative materials outside the bounds of the main experience. Typically, we think of narrative elements as being "on-line" or "intra-diegetic", that is, located inside the game's main experience or world. In many games however, players discover additional story and contextual narrative elements (sometimes quite substantial) through a variety of channels that are more or less closely connected to the main experience. Typically referred to as "lore" or "flavor text", De Fault (2021) explains it as "additional information about a game's world which fills out the illusion of an expansive, lived-in fiction", exemplifying: "audio or text that comes along with collectables, such as audio logs and notepaper left behind in gaming's post-apocalypses, or Lara Croft's interpretation of an old coin she just found". Many meso-narrative games will use these additional channels as a way to infuse narrativity without forcing it upon players who may not be that interested in it. In *Assassin's Creed II*, an in-game encyclopedia (fed by an in-game character in the game's fiction) offers background information on monuments, locations, and characters that the player encounters through the adventure; in *BioShock*, players can collect and listen to the audio logs recorded by the various characters that have died (or will die shortly) in the collapse of Rapture, offering additional information on the utopian city and the factions and events that led to it. Creative director and writer Ken Levine explained that this approach, which he terms the push/pull narrative, allows the game to push to players only the essential information required to understand what's going on and progress, while allowing intrigued players to pull at the environment for additional storytelling materials (Burch, 2008). *Assassin's Creed II* and *BioShock* both offer narrative infusions to satisfy players seeking a hyper-narrative experience without deterring those content with a meso-narrative game.

De Fault also provides interviewed writer Casey Lucas-Quaid's examples of lore delivery: "weapon descriptions, level-select screens, narration voiceover, battle cries, and map annotations". The historical dimension and the diversity of platforms and contexts for video games, alluded to in this chapter's opening paragraph, also contributes to this, as many early video games relegated their story to the printed game manual, or even included pack-in comic books or novelizations that fleshed out the narrative beyond what their limited memory and technological restrictions allowed. These last cases are not exactly a form of transmedia storytelling, but rather a form of paratext storytelling,[6] as the manuals and "goodies" were included in the game's packaging rather than being separate, autonomous media objects. Game narratives can be found anywhere along the margins of games, or even wholly outside them. But even in-game narrative can take on many forms depending on which materials will be infused with narrativity.

Henry Jenkins (2004) argued that game designers may not be storytellers so much as narrative architects, rooting storytelling in video games' spatial nature. In this, Jenkins (and I) follow a cue from Don Carson (2000), who explained the principles of environmental storytelling used in the design of Disney Park attractions as *infusing* story elements into the space that guests walk or ride through. For Jenkins, video game players experience four types of spatial stories: evoked (seeing a lightsaber evokes the previously known *Star Wars* stories), enacted (broadly defined goals that can be carried out through the space; for instance, making it past a guard outpost in *Tom Clancy's Splinter Cell* will mean hiding in the shadows below, climbing up the visible pipe to the window, and knocking out the guard when he turns to the other side), embedded (as clues, elements or events placed through the environment that must be discovered or pieced together), and emergent (the events are not pre-scripted, but arise out of the interaction of rules to produce a story).

As spatial exploration is inherently non-linear, it naturally produces two distinct chains of events: the fixed high-level story from the game's narrative program, and the fluctuating low-level story of the player wandering around and accessing the objects or events in whatever idiosyncratic manner. Since information that is placed in an environment may be missed or overlooked by players, DeMarle advises carefully planning the delivery channels for narrative information, saving critical data for mandatory cut-scenes and making sure that environmental storytelling contains only supplementary information that won't hurt the baseline narrative if it's missed. Bateman (2004, pp. 85–102) frames spatial exploration as a tension between maintaining player freedom and narrative clarity, since an open world of possibilities comes with the risk of losing sight of what needs to be done for the narrative to progress. He shares two techniques to keep players on track: *breadcrumbing*, that is, placing multiple bite-sized narrative elements to guide players along a trail instead of condensing a narrative episode in a single location, and *funneling*, which is guiding wandering players back onto the trail of breadcrumbs. Characters are one efficient way to restrain player freedom or, in the words of Murray (1997), scripting the interactor: if the characters are infused with narrativity (with a personality and backstory), and the story is about them and their problems, then players will accept doing what they need or want to do, and mold their agency accordingly. This is why video games have tended to rely on story archetypes such as the Hero's Journey (originally theorized by Joseph Campbell, but popularized through Hollywood by Vogler (1992) when he was consulting for Disney), or Manichean storylines: they provide clear objectives and familiar contexts for players to drop in and act according to the needs of the story. This works wonders for hypo-narrative games, and meso-narrative games can use these archetypes as a baseline with varying levels of narrative infusion as supplements.

There are many exciting research and creation trajectories awaiting in games and narrative. For lack of space, this chapter has not touched on the dynamics of procedural narratives and story generation systems, which a number of games have been exploring for decades now, either as a way to supplement their pre-written program narrative with modular additions or randomized substitutions, or as the core principle of their experience entirely focused on immediate-level story. The question of characters continues to be debated: do we identify with them, control them, or do they become digital surrogate bodies, or prosthetic extensions of our cyborg selves? What are the mechanisms of operation for fully fleshed characters, created avatars, non-player characters, and silent protagonists? I have outlined a set of narrative programs, but it may be necessary to conceptualize sets of character programs as well, ranging from the a-characterized to the hyper-characterized. These could be completed with a set of diegetic programs too, from the a-diegetic to the hyper-diegetic game world, to assemble a complete Triforce of narrative data fueled by characters, plot, and world. But as any Zelda fan will realize, the Triforce itself is but a small part of the overall adventure that awaits…

Notes

1 For an efficient overview on narratology and its main concepts, I would recommend Marie-Laure Ryan's chapter "Narrative, Media, and Modes" from *Avatars of Story* (2006).
2 No relation with Katherine Hayles, Lev Manovich or Nitzan Ben Shaul's use of the term, which stems from hyperlinks and hypertext to make "hyper-narratives" database pieces loosely organized by links.
3 Cut-scenes or cinematics are non-interactive segments that advance a game's high-level story.
4 Interested readers will find plenty to read from various researchers (too many to provide a quick overview here) who have used this term from Mikhail Bakhtin (developed in his 1937 essay "Forms of Time and of the Chronotope in the Novel") to envision the joint space-time nature of video games, some of them specifically for in-game narrative, others for games in general.
5 See Roth, van Nuenen and Koenitz (2018) for an overview of the ludonarrative hermeneutic process through which players develop the "protostory" into "instantiated narratives".
6 The concept of paratext, developed by Gérard Genette in literary theory, has been used in game studies with differing implications; here I use it to mean the liminal documents and semiotic arrangements that surround a text and that help make it present (see Švelch, 2020), including title, packaging, manual, etc.

References

All online sources retrieved January 5, 2022.
Ashwell, Sam Kabo. 2015. Standard Patterns in Choice-Based Games. *These Heterogeneous Tasks*. Retrieved from https://heterogenoustasks.wordpress.com/2015/01/26/standard-patterns-in-choice-based-games/

Bateman, Chris (Ed.). 2004. *Game Writing: Narrative Skills for Videogames*. Charles River Media: Boston, MA.

Boni, Marta (Ed.). 2017. *World Building: Transmedia, Fans, Industries*. Amsterdam University Press: Amsterdam.

Burch, Anthony. 2008. GDC 08: Storytelling in BioShock. *Destructoid*, February 20. Retrieved from https://www.destructoid.com/gdc-08-storytelling-in-bioshock/

Carson, Don. 2000. Environmental Storytelling: Creating Immersive 3D Worlds Using Lessons Learned from the Theme Park Industry. *Gamasutra (Game Developer)*, March 1. Retrieved from https://www.gamedeveloper.com/design/environmental-storytelling-creating-immersive-3d-worlds-using-lessons-learned-from-the-theme-park-industry

Costikyan, Greg. 2000. Where Stories End and Games Begin. *Game Developer* Magazine (September), 44–53.

Chandler, Rafael. 2007. *Game Writing Handbook*. Charles River Media: Boston, MA.

Chride (Christina Lassheikki). 2021. Branching Narratives. Experimental article part of the Playable Concepts project, Aalto University. Retrieved from https://sites.google.com/view/branchingnarratives/#h.grwtn8yt3iyk

De Fault, Antony. 2021. Breaking the Lore. *Wireframe*, December 7. Retrieved from https://wireframe.raspberrypi.com/articles/breaking-the-lore

DeMarle, Mary. 2004. Nonlinear Game Narrative. In C. Bateman (Ed.), *Game Writing: Narrative Skills for Videogames*, Charles River Media: Boston, MA, pp. 71–84.

Despain, Wendy (Ed.). 2008. *Professional Techniques for Video Game Writing*. A K Peters: Wellesley, MA.

Despain, Wendy (Ed.). 2009. *Writing for Video Game Genres: From FPS to RPG*. A K Peters: Wellesley, MA.

Dille, Flint & John Zuur Platten. 2007. *The Ultimate Guide to Video Game Writing and Design*. Lone Eagle: New York, NY.

Fernández-Vara, Clara. (n.d.). Taxonomy of Narrative Choices. *Itch.io*. Retrieved from https://clarafv.itch.io/taxonomy-of-narrative-choices

Fludernik, Monika. 1996. *Towards a 'Natural' Narratology*. Routledge: New York, NY.

Gerstmann, Jeff. 1998. *Metal Gear Solid* Review. September 25. Retrieved from https://www.gamespot.com/reviews/metal-gear-solid-review/1900-2546002/

Gygax, Gary & Dave Arneson. 1974. *Dungeons & Dragons: Rules for Fantastic Medieval Wargames Campaigns Playable with Paper and Pencil and Miniature Figures*. TSR: Lake Geneva, WI.

Hocking, Clint. 2007. "Ludonarrative Dissonance in Bioshock: The problem of what the game is about." Retrieved from https://clicknothing.typepad.com/click_nothing/2007/10/ludonarrative-d.html

Ince, Steve. 2006. *Writing for Video Games*. A & C Black: London, UK.

Jenkins, Henry. 2004. Game Design as Narrative Architecture. In N. Wardrip-Fruin & P. Harrigan (Eds.), *First-Person: New Media as Story, Performance, and Game*, The MIT Press: Cambridge, MA, pp. 118–130.

Jørgensen, Kristine. 2013. *Gameworld Interfaces*. The MIT Press: Cambridge, MA.

Murray, Janet. 1997. *Hamlet on the Holodeck: The Future of Narrative in Cyberspace*. The Free Press: New York, NY.

Pearce, Celia. 2005. "Theory Wars: An Argument Against Arguments in the So-Called Ludology/Narratology Debate". *DiGRA 2005 Changing Views: Worlds in Play Conference Proceedings*. Retrieved from http://www.digra.org/wp-content/uploads/digital-library/06278.03452.pdf

Roth, Christian, Tom van Nuenen & Hartmut Koenitz. 2018. "Ludonarrative Hermeneutics: A Way Out and the Narrative Paradox". *International Conference on Interactive Digital Storytelling* (Lecture Notes in Computer Science), pp. 93–106. Retrieved from https://doi.org/10.1007/978-3-030-04028-4_7

Ryan, Marie-Laure. 2006. *Avatars of Story*. University of Minnesota Press: Minneapolis, MN.

Sierra, Wendi. 2020. *Todd Howard: Worldbuilding in Tamriel and Beyond*. Bloomsbury Academic: London, UK.

Short, Emily. 2016. Small-Scale Structures in CYOA. *Emily Short's Interactive Storytelling*. Retrieved from https://emshort.blog/2016/11/05/small-scale-structures-in-cyoa/

Suckling, Maurice & Marek Walton. 2012. *Video Game Writing: From Macro to Micro*. Mercury Learning and Information: Dulles, VA.

Švelch, Jan. 2020. "Paratextuality in Game Studies: A Theoretical Review and Citation Analysis". In *Game Studies*, 20(2). Retrieved from http://gamestudies.org/2002/articles/jan_svelch

Vogler, Christopher. 1992. *The Writer's Journey: Mythic Structure for Storytellers and Screenwriters*. Michael Wiese: Studio City, CA.

Wolf, Mark J. P. 2012. *Building Imaginary Worlds: The Theory and History of Subcreation*. Routledge: New York, NY and London, UK.

14

INTERVIEW: EVAN SKOLNICK

What are the key expressive possibilities in video game storytelling that are not available in television or cinema?

We're still continuing to discover the possibilities of video game storytelling, which is what makes it such an exciting place to be as a writer!

One of the cards that we can play in games that doesn't apply to TV or movies would be the complicity card. Because we can require the player to take certain actions in order to progress through the game, there are emotions we can attach to those actions which can feel very personal to the player. For example, we can make them feel proud for achieving something, or we can make them feel guilty for making a certain choice. The participatory nature of games opens the door to a number of emotional reactions we can evoke from our players that would be difficult or impossible to accomplish in a more passively experienced medium like film or television.

How do players identify with their video game protagonists differently to protagonists in movies and TV shows?

In most video games, the player is directly controlling one or more player characters. Because of this fusion of player and character, there is a much stronger connection than you're likely to see between a viewer and a film protagonist. In a movie or TV show, we might be rooting for the hero, but there is always this distance between us and them.

For example, in a movie we might see a case of dramatic irony, in which the audience knows something that the onscreen characters don't. This can generate incredible suspense, as per Alfred Hitchcock's classic example of the ticking time bomb under the table that the audience is aware of but the

DOI: 10.4324/9781003197911-18

characters sitting at the table aren't. Dramatic irony such as this is perfectly acceptable in a film, but in a game, this kind of disconnect would be problematic. The player with a character sitting at that table would expect to be allowed to have their character take action to notice and defuse the bomb! If you didn't allow the player to do something about the bomb, you would not evoke suspense; you would elicit extreme frustration and probably earn the player's ire.

Can you comment on the different types of storytelling required for different types of games, such as role-playing games, first-person shooters, car games and platform games? How, for example, was writing for *Star Wars: Battlefront* different to writing for *Cuphead*?

Some writing for games looks a lot like writing for more traditional forms like comics, books or movies. Cutscenes – the short animated sequences we often see in between active gameplay experiences – are essentially short films, and they're written that way, too. However, there are other types of game writing that are unique to the medium and will vary depending on the game genre as well as the particular narrative approach for that specific game.

The interactive nature of games and the desire to give the player a feeling of exploration and freedom within the interactive space often requires us to develop systems that will play dialogue that's dependent on what's actually happening (or not happening) in gameplay.

Some of this dialogue is what we would call scripted – meaning, it's using programmatic scripting to make something happen. Scripted dialogue usually happens the same way and around the same time every time you play the game. For example, as your player character turns a corner and sees a huge, ancient temple, they might always say something about the incredible sight, which reveals something about the temple, or themselves. If you played that level again, your character would say the same line when you turned that same corner, every time.

Then we have systemic dialogue, which is also triggered programmatically but requires a vastly more complex system – one which will be able to decide if and when to play lines depending on various factors that are dynamically happening in gameplay. If you've ever played a military first-person shooter, and one of your companions yells out, "I'm hit" after they take fire, that is a systemic dialogue (also referred to as "barks" because of their short, punchy nature). It will only happen under certain circumstances, and there will generally be an entire bank of variant lines intended to be played when (for example) this companion is shot. The system will randomly select one line from this list each time, so repetition is avoided. The need to write many variant lines for each type of bark is part of what can drive video game dialogue line counts into the tens or even hundreds of thousands.

Cuphead has almost no voiced lines, just onscreen text, so there was no need to write barks or design a complicated system that would figure out when to play them. Mostly I wrote the words in the storybook-like cutscenes, and the text-based dialogue from all the non-player characters you encounter on the island. As game writing jobs go, it was smaller-scope, straightforward work.

Star Wars: Battlefront, on the other hand, is a first-person military-like shooter which allows many players to participate at once. I wrote scripted lines to help the player understand mission objectives and phase changes, and I wrote many, many barks to account for the various happenings that could occur during the often-frenetic gameplay.

As with many first-person shooters, the game writer's worst nightmare is usually figuring out ten different ways for a soldier to say, "Reloading!"

What are the common errors screenwriters make when writing video games for the first time, when they previously wrote for television or cinema?

The most common misconception I see from writers from other visual media is that they think they're going to write a script or story which will then be handed off to a game development team to produce into a game. This is virtually never how it works in video games.

In fact, it isn't just that story isn't first in the process; story is also rarely considered the most important aspect throughout. Folks working on a movie production would probably all agree that they should be serving the story in everything they do. But in games, it's not story that's primary – it's gameplay. Story is in a support role, contextualizing and improving the gameplay experience. Failing to understand this crucial difference can cause all kinds of agita for the writer and the team they're trying to help.

Compared to the other art forms, video games are still young, and storytelling in video games has developed very quickly since the arrival of home consoles in the 1980s. Do you have any thoughts on where the medium could be headed in the next 20 or 30 years?

Back in 2008 I wrote a book chapter about the future of video game storytelling. In it, I predicted that artificial intelligence (AI) would someday allow for games that can truly react dynamically to player choices and actions, weaving and modifying story elements "on the fly" while still cleaving to proven narrative principles and structures. This would have the effect of allowing the player to do almost anything they could imagine without "breaking" the game or its story. Essentially I was envisioning an AI Dungeon Master. At the time, I guessed it would be many decades before this came to pass.

We're not there yet, but as I write this in early 2023, I must admit I'm shocked to see the seemingly sudden emergence of AI art and AI-driven natural language systems. And I wonder how much we will soon see handed off to these new tools. We seem to be on the cusp of creating digital helpers that will be increasingly capable of standing in for creative artists and writers, in some circumstances at least.

What effect this will have on our games, and on the video game industry as a whole, is yet to be seen. But if this type of AI starts getting really good at fabricating and executing narrative concepts in real time, it will affect not only video games but nearly all storytelling forms.

15

TRANSMEDIA STORYWORLDS AND TRANSMEDIA UNIVERSES

Jan-Noël Thon

Contemporary media culture is shaped by technological innovations and the sustained move of media conglomerates from vertical to horizontal integration. Among other things, this has led to the increased visibility of transmedial constellations that transgress the borders of both single works and conventionally distinct media, ranging from novel-based franchises such as *The Lord of the Rings*, *A Song of Ice and Fire/Game of Thrones*, or *Harry Potter/The Wizarding World* via comics-based franchises such as *Batman*, *Avengers*, or *The Walking Dead* and film-based franchises such as *Star Wars*, *Indiana Jones*, or *The Matrix* to television-based franchises such as *Doctor Who*, *Star Trek*, or *Lost* and video game–based franchises such as *Tomb Raider*, *Warcraft*, or *Halo*. While there are other aspects worth considering, these transmedia franchises tend to be most visibly defined by their representational functions.

Accordingly, a number of influential approaches to the study of transmedia franchises such as Henry Jenkins's concept of "transmedia storytelling" (see Jenkins 2004, 2006) or Lisbeth Klastrup and Susana Tosca's concept of "transmedial worlds" (see Klastrup and Tosca 2004; Tosca and Klastrup 2019) focus on the representation of characters, stories, and worlds across media forms such as novels, comics, films, television series, and video games—as well as on the various ways in which individual installments within transmedia franchises can more or less transparently refer recipients to previous and future installments of the franchise in question by "opening" or "closing" gaps in the narrative texture. The significant theoretical value of Jenkins's as well as Klastrup and Tosca's approaches notwithstanding, however, it seems that both the concept of "transmedia storytelling" and the

DOI: 10.4324/9781003197911-19

concept of "transmedial worlds" suffer from a largely unexamined commit-ment to what we could describe as the model of the "single world."

While such a model would, of course, be entirely appropriate in those cases in which transmedia franchises not just aim at but actually succeed in representing a "single world" as part of what Jenkins describes as the ideal of "a unified and coordinated entertainment experience" (Jenkins 2007, n.p.), on closer inspection, these cases appear to be rarer than we might initially assume. One way or another, it seems somewhat unsatisfying to base the analysis of transmedia franchises' narrative functions exclusively on the as-sumption that they ideally should represent a "single world," independently of whether we call that world a "story world" (Jenkins 2004, 124; see also Harvey 2015), a "transmedial world" (Klastrup and Tosca 2004, n.p.; see also Tosca and Klastrup 2019; Wolf 2012), or something else altogether. In-stead, it may be helpful to move from the model of the "single world" to a model of "multiple worlds," thus more explicitly acknowledging transmedia franchises' specific brand of narrative complexity.

Against this background, the present chapter explores how the theoretical framework of transmedial narratology can contribute to the development of a nuanced account of the complex arrangements of narrative works that characterize transmedia franchises. Aiming to complement rather than con-tradict existing approaches within current transmedia studies, transmedial narratology offers a theoretically and methodologically refined foundation upon which we can build in order to extend the existing tools for the analysis of transmedia franchises' narrative functions beyond the model of the "single (story)world" (see also Thon 2016 for a more detailed discussion of the aims and scope of transmedial narratology; as well as Thon 2015, 2018 for earlier versions of the argument presented here; and Thon 2019, 2022 for more on how the processes in question play out with regard to the intersubjective construction of transmedia characters).

The Concept of the Storyworld and Representational Correspondence across Media

While the concept of the storyworld has recently begun to gain currency within transmedia studies as well, it has been primarily developed within the field of narratology. Indeed, the history of the concept can be traced from Gé-rard Genette's "diegesis" (1988, 17) and Seymour Chatman's "world of po-tential plot details" (1978, 29) via the "fictional worlds" of possible worlds theorists such as Thomas Pavel (1989), Ruth Ronen (1994), or Lubomír Doležel (1998) to cognitive narratologists such as Marie-Laure Ryan (1991), Richard Gerrig (1993), or David Herman (2002). Despite a common concep-tual core, then, the various approaches to storyworlds that are located within different strands of narratological practice not only use a variety of terms to refer to them but also conceptualize them rather differently. Herman, for example, understands storyworlds as "mental models of who did what to and with whom, when, where, why, and in what fashion in the world to which recipients relocate" (2002, 9) or as "global mental representations" of "the world evoked implicitly as well as explicitly by a narrative" (2009, 107).

Yet, equaling storyworlds with their mental representations ignores that we usually presuppose some kind of intersubjective plausibility when we talk about what is represented by narrative works across different media forms. We can, in other words, construct more or less accurate or appropriate mental models of a given narrative work's storyworld. Of course, this does not at all mean that the ways we imagine a storyworld based on a given narrative work will be entirely alike, nor that they should be—but equaling the storyworld that a narrative work represents with the ways in which individual recipients imagine it rather obviously runs counter to how we usually talk about storyworlds, both as "mere" recipients and as academics. One way to solve this terminological problem within the context of transmedial narratology would be to distinguish between the medial representation of a storyworld as part of a narrative work, the mental representations of this storyworld that recipients build during the reception process, and the storyworld itself as an intersubjective communicative construct (see also the account of film characters as intersubjective communicative constructs in Eder 2008; as well as, once more, Thon 2016).

One of the advantages of a narratological perspective on transmedia franchises is that it provides a better understanding of the processes that underlie narrative representation and comprehension. While this chapter cannot discuss these processes in too much detail, it still seems helpful to mention two complementary principles that are generally taken to be relevant in this context. According to Marie-Laure Ryan, there is a *principle of minimal departure* at work during narrative meaning-making that allows the recipients to "project upon these worlds everything [they] know about reality, [making] only the adjustments dictated by the text" (Ryan 1991, 51). It is worth stressing, though, that recipients do not "fill in the gaps" from the actual world itself but from their actual world knowledge, and that, moreover, "[t]he frame of reference invoked by the principle of minimal departure is not the sole product of unmediated personal experience" but may include various forms of medial and generic knowledge, or even a specific "textual universe as frame of reference" (Ryan 1991, 54; see also the additional discussion of the "reality principle" and the "mutual belief principle" in Walton 1990, 155–169; as well as Ryan 2022).

Clearly, the principle of minimal departure is no less relevant in transmedia(l) contexts, as recipients will often draw on previously established specific "fictional world knowledge" when trying to comprehend a work that is part of a given transmedia franchise. Nevertheless, works that are part of a transmedia franchise can and usually will "depart" from what was previously established to be the case in that franchise's world(s), as well, ranging from "sloppy contradictions" (Jenkins 2006, 105) and minor changes of an established "worldness" (Klastrup and Tosca 2004) to more substantial cases of "retconning" (Wolf 2012, 213) and "reboots" (Wolf 2012, 215). While variations of the latter in particular may change the storyworlds established by previous entries in a transmedia franchise quite substantially—for example by casting the black actor Idris Elba as Norse god Heimdall in *Thor* (2011), or by reimagining the previously male team of parapsychologists as female in *Ghostbusters* (2016)—"reboots" will never change a storyworld "beyond recognition." Accordingly, even those (few) Marvel or *Ghostbusters* fans that did not appreciate the above-mentioned casting decisions will have had no trouble "filling in" a good number of "gaps" based on their previous fictional world knowledge (also see Blodgett and Salter 2018; Perkins 2020; Proctor 2017, for more detailed discussion of the reception discourse surrounding the *Ghostbusters* reboot).

Yet, despite the importance of the principle of minimal departure and the "filling in" of the "gaps" of narrative works for which it allows, some "gaps" can never be "filled" in an intersubjectively valid manner. The main reason for this is that recipients' world knowledge—whether historical or contemporary, nonfictional or fictional, universal or particular—can provide only comparatively general additional information so that they cannot conclusively infer the answer to specific questions such as "Does character X have a birthmark on their back?" if the narrative representation does not provide it. While recipients may *pretend* that storyworlds are complete in the process that Marie-Laure Ryan calls "fictional recentering" (1991, 24), most theorists of fictional worlds agree that represented worlds are *actually* incomplete (see also, e.g., Doležel 1998; Ronen 1994; Ryan 2022). This still holds with regard to the worlds represented by transmedia franchises, though "filling in the gaps" of a previously established storyworld is one of the core functions that new works being added to a transmedia franchise may fulfill.

Even with regard to the less extensive question of how storyworlds may be represented within the confines of a single work in a single conventionally distinct medium (see also, e.g., Rajewsky 2010; Ryan 2006; Thon 2014), however, it is also important to note that recipients routinely "ignore" some aspects of narrative representations in order to intersubjectively construct the storyworlds thus represented. Narrative meaning-making is based on an acute awareness of the intricacies of what Gregory Currie calls *representational correspondence*, a term designed to capture the general observation that, "[f]or a given representational work, only certain features of the representation serve to represent features of the things represented" (Currie 2010, 59). Particularly in cases where the assumption of representational correspondence becomes problematic, recipients will look for alternative *external explanations* related to hypothetical authorial intentions or established representational conventions before trying to imagine contradictory or otherwise problematic storyworlds based on a rigid insistence on *internal explanations*.

Kendall L. Walton pointedly describes this aspect of narrative meaning-making in terms of a *principle of charity*, stressing that, "if there is another ready explanation for the artist's inclusion of a feature that appears to generate a given fictional truth, it may not seem that [they] meant especially to have it generated. And *this* may argue against recognizing that it is generated" (Walton 1990, 183, original emphasis). Beyond readily apparent "sloppy contradictions" (Jenkins 2006, 105), these external explanations will often refer to medium-specific representational conventions, as the "distance" between a given narrative representation and what that representation represents can indeed be quite pronounced (see also Walton 1990, 181–182, for a famous discussion of the "distance" between the words of the Shakespeare character Othello and the words of the actors that play him; as well as Thon 2017 for a more in-depth examination of the application of charity across media; and Ensslin and Bell 2021, 19–48, for a recent critique of the underlying argument about "ignoring" contradictions from "unnatural narratology").

Take, for example, the audiovisual representation of Yoda in *Star Wars Episode V: The Empire Strikes Back* (1980), *Star Wars Episode VI: Return of the Jedi* (1983), and the original theatrical release of *Star Wars Episode I: The Phantom Menace* (1999), which evidently differs from the audiovisual representation of Yoda in *Star Wars Episode II: Attack of the Clones* (2002), *Star Wars Episode III: Revenge of the Sith* (2005), and *Star Wars Episode VIII: The Last Jedi* (2017). It amounts to a "silly question" (Walton 1990, 176; see also Currie 2010, 59), however, to ask for an internal explanation of these differences in Yoda's apparent appearance, as the film series' switch from using a puppet to using computer-generated imagery (CGI) in order to present the famous Jedi master readily provides an external explanation (which was further emphasized by the implementation of a CGI representation of Yoda in the Blu-ray release of *The Phantom Menace* [2011] and the combination of a puppet with CGI effects in *The Last Jedi*).

Likewise, it would be "silly" to ask for an internal explanation of the differences between the audiovisual representation of Albus Dumbledore in the first two feature films of the *Harry Potter* series (2001, 2002) and the corresponding audiovisual representation in its third through eighth installment (2004–2011), as the use of actors to represent characters is a core representational convention of narrative films, and the untimely death of actor Richard Harris, who was then replaced by Michael Gambon, provides a ready external explanation of these differences. This general principle also holds in cases where changes resulting from (re)casting decisions are more noticeable, as when Johnny Depp, who played the Dark wizard Grindelwald in *Fantastic Beasts and Where to Find Them* (2016) and *Fantastic Beasts: The Crimes of*

Grindelwald (2018), was replaced by Mads Mikkelsen in *Fantastic Beasts: The Secrets of Dumbledore* (2022). In both *Star Wars* and *Harry Potter/The Wizarding World*, then, the intersubjective construction of the serial storyworlds represented by the films entails applying charity in order to "ignore" at least some aspects of their audiovisual representation (for further discussion of the *Star Wars* and *Harry Potter/The Wizarding World* franchises, see, e.g., Guynes and Hassler-Forest 2017; Nardi and Sweet 2020; Proctor 2019; as well as Brenner 2015; Brummitt 2023; Firestone and Clark 2018).

It is, of course, also entirely possible for (series of) narrative works to provide internal explanations for these (as well as other) kinds of apparent contradictions. The need for such explanations can, once more, result from unforeseen developments impacting the production process, as when the Oracle's status as a program with clairvoyant abilities, the destruction of her "shell" by the Merovingian, and her subsequent restoration are used to offer an internal explanation for the effects of the recasting decision that became necessary after the death of Gloria Foster, who played the Oracle in *The Matrix* (1999) and *The Matrix Reloaded* (2003), and was replaced by Mary Alice in *The Matrix Revolutions* (2003). However, a much more salient case of this practice would be the BBC's long-running television series *Doctor Who* (1963–), which internally explains the regularly occurring changes of the actors used to represent its protagonist as the result of all Time Lords' capability for "regeneration," a process that transforms both their physical form and some aspects of their personality, and which has generated considerable publicity for the show both when it was announced that Jodie Whittaker would take over from Peter Capaldi as its first female lead in 2017 and when it was announced that Ncuti Gatwa would take over from Whittaker as its first black lead in 2022, which has since turned out to be following another stint of David Tennant in-between Whittaker's and Gatwa's portrayals of the Doctor (see Hills 2017 for some context; as well as, e.g., Evans 2011; Harvey 2015; Hills 2015 for additional discussion of the franchise).

In the absence of this kind of internal explanation, though, some degree of apparently contradictory difference in the audiovisual representation of a character tends to be "charitably ignored"—and this arguably also applies to transmedial representations such as those of Yoda in the *Star Wars* movies, the animated television series *Star Wars: Clone Wars* (2003–2005), the CGI feature film *Star Wars: The Clone Wars* (2008) and the CGI television series of the same title (2008–2014), the more recent CGI television series *Star Wars Rebels* (2014–2018) and the animated YouTube series *Star Wars Forces of Destiny* (2017), the various *Star Wars* comics, and the no less numerous *Star Wars* video games or to those of Albus Dumbledore in J. K. Rowling's seven *Harry Potter* novels (1997–2007), their eight feature film adaptations, and the various *Harry Potter* video games that, in turn, tend to base their audiovisual representations of Dumbledore on the way he is represented in the films (which yet again does not cause any particularly noticeable representational inconsistencies with Toby Finn Regbo's portrayal of the teenage Dumbledore and Jude Law's portrayal of the middle-aged Dumbledore in the *Fantastic Beasts* film series).

Just as the principle of minimal departure does not allow recipients to "fill in" every last "gap" that a given narrative work leaves in the storyworld it represents, however, so does the principle of charity not allow recipients to generally "ignore" all kinds of contradictions that these narrative works may "appear to generate." Indeed, it is quite frequently the case that narrative works successively represent situations that do not immediately "add up" to a noncontradictory storyworld without providing a plausible external explanation for these apparent contradictions, leading to various contemporary narrative works being best described as representing compounds of two (or more) noncontradictory storyworlds. While it seems generally helpful to conceptualize storyworlds as noncontradictory "by default" and analyze contradictory storyworlds as compounds of noncontradictory sub-worlds, then, it will have already become clear that this kind of "compounding" occurs on a significantly larger scale in many transmedia franchises.

Work-Specific Storyworlds, Transmedia Storyworlds, and Transmedia Universes

Whether a given franchise is conceived as transmedial from the beginning (as is, for example, the case with *The Matrix*) or expanded across media after an initial commercial success (as is, for example, the case with *Star Wars*), the narratological approach sketched above postulates that every narrative work that is part of the franchise represents a storyworld of its own, but, at the same time, establishes a relation between that storyworld and the storyworlds represented by the other narrative works that are positioned as part of the franchise. Instead of assuming that transmedia franchises generally represent a "single world," then, this perspective allows for a systematic distinction between the local medium-specific storyworlds of single narrative works, the glocal but noncontradictory transmedia (or, in many cases, merely trans*textual*) storyworlds that may be constructed out of local work-specific storyworlds, and the global and often quite contradictory transmedia storyworld compounds that may, for lack of a better term, be called transmedia universes (for further discussion of the rather contested terminology, see also, e.g., Harvey 2015; Packard 2015; Wolf 2012, 216–220; as well as, once more, Thon 2015, 2018, 2019).

Drawing on Henry Jenkins's discussion of "adaptation and extension" (2011, n.p.), Mark J. P. Wolf's discussion of "adaptation" and "growth" (2012, 245), and Marie-Laure Ryan's discussion of "expansion" and "modification" (2008, 385), we can then further ask to what extent two single narrative works within a transmedia franchise are defined, first, by a relation of *redundancy*, when one is aiming to represent the same elements of a storyworld that the other represents; second, by a relation of *expansion*, when one is aiming to represent the same storyworld that the other represents, but adds previously unrepresented elements; or, third, by a relation of *modification*, when one is aiming to represent elements of the storyworld represented by the other, but adds previously unrepresented elements that make it impossible to comprehend what is represented as part of a single, noncontradictory storyworld. While this rather basic distinction will not capture all the intricacies of transmedia universes, it still seems to be a helpful heuristic for the in-depth analysis of the interrelations between a given franchise's work-specific storyworlds.

Take, for example, the transmedia franchise *A Song of Ice and Fire/Game of Thrones*, which is based on George R. R. Martin's novel series *A Song of Ice and Fire* (1996–), but has since been developed to include not only the (initially) wildly successful HBO television series *Game of Thrones* (2011–2019) and its prequel series *House of the Dragon* (2022–) but also various comics and graphic novels, collectible card games, board games, pen-and-paper role-playing games, and video games (as well as a series of prequel novellas by Martin himself, an extensive companion book that he co-authored, a book of maps, and two collections of artwork). At first glance, the strong presence of Martin as the author of the franchise's "ur-text" (Jenkins 2007, n.p.) might suggest that its subsequent entries should generally be expected to be redundant adaptations of (specific parts of) the transtextual world over which Martin has exerted direct authorial control. Even if we accept that, say, Daniel Abraham and Tommy Patterson's comics series *A Game of Thrones* (2011–2014) is a largely redundant adaptation of the first novel (from which it has also borrowed its title), though, this evidently does not apply to many of the other entries in the franchise (see also, e.g., Schröter 2015 for further discussion of some of the video game adaptations).

While there are obvious differences in the ways that the novel series and the comics series present their respective work-specific storyworlds, these differences might arguably be "ignored" by reference to the diverging representational affordances and limitations of literary texts and graphic narratives. In the case of HBO's television series *Game of Thrones*, however, it would seem that no amount of charity will allow for the intersubjective construction of a storyworld sufficiently similar to that represented by Martin's series of novels in order to speak of a primarily redundant adaptation. While the television series does not simply "re-tell" the story originally told by the novels, then, it also quite clearly does not expand the storyworld represented by the novels in a noncontradictory way (despite ultimately "overtaking" the novel series). Rather, it takes certain elements and leaves others, changing and re-arranging them to an extent that it seems more appropriate to speak of a modification of the novel series' transtextual storyworld than of its redundant adaptation or noncontradictory expansion (even though the television series certainly also "re-tells" and expands on elements of the storyworld that is represented by the "ur-texts" of the novel series).

Much more could be said about the *A Song of Ice and Fire/Game of Thrones* franchise, of course (see, e.g., Carroll 2018; Frankel 2014; Larrington 2016; and the contributions in Gjelsvik and Schubart 2016), but the main point here is that transmedia franchises are often not appropriately described as representing a single storyworld, even though the work-specific storyworlds of the various works that are part of a given franchise may, to various degrees, add up to noncontradictory transmedia storyworlds. Indeed, while we can also find franchises such as *The Matrix* or *Halo*, which at least initially appeared to be primarily defined by an attempt at the noncontradictory expansion of a single transmedia storyworld (see, e.g., Atkinson 2018; Jenkins 2006, 93–131; Ryan 2015; as well as Harvey 2015, 93–115; Jaagola 2019; Rosendo 2015), it seems not uncommon even for comparatively small-scale franchises (in terms of storyworld "spread," not in terms of commercial success) to establish two clearly distinct storyworlds via a high-profile modifying adaptation, while still aiming at a further expansion of each of these storyworlds via works in other media (see also Parody 2011 for additional discussion of the role that adaptations play in transmedia franchises).

A particularly clear example of this would be the comics-based franchise of *The Walking Dead*, which, similarly to the novel-based franchise of *A Song of Ice and Fire/Game of Thrones*, has experienced significant commercial as well as critical success. At first glance, AMC's *The Walking Dead* television series (2010–2022) may appear to be a straightforward adaptation of Robert Kirkman's *The Walking Dead* comics series (2003–2019) and Telltale's *The Walking Dead* adventure game series (2012–2019) may, in turn, appear to be a straightforward adaptation of the television series, but the differences between the stories these series tell turn out to be quite striking and do, in fact, make a description of the television series' work-specific storyworld as a modification of the comics series' work-specific storyworld appear more appropriate. In contrast, Telltale's adventure game series takes even more liberties—including not just the use of video game–specific narrative affordances but also a change in the main protagonist—yet does so in a way that makes it appear as a largely noncontradictory expansion of the comics series' work-specific storyworld rather than as either a redundant adaptation or a contradictory modification of that storyworld (see also, e.g., Beil and Schmidt 2015; Ecenbarger 2016; Hassler-Forest 2014). And, last but not least, Terminal Reality's first-person shooter *The Walking Dead: Survival Instinct* (2013) is, perhaps, not a very well-made video game, but still manages to convey its aim to expand the work-specific storyworld of the television series rather than that of the comics series with sufficient clarity.

Again, there would be more to say about the various spin-off television series, the web series, the board games, the card game, and the other video games that have been published or gone into production since the commercial and critical success of AMC's *The Walking Dead* television series, but the general principle of storyworld interrelation should have already become clear. Indeed, it seems that both Telltale's *The Walking Dead* and Terminal Reality's *The Walking Dead: Survival Instinct* are authorized to expand the storyworlds established by the comics series and the television series, respectively. They are, in other words, what is commonly described as *canonical* expansions, which sets them aside from quite a large number of other works that could, at first glance, be comprehended as noncontradictory expansions of a previously established storyworld based on what they represent, but are not authorized to expand the storyworld in question, remaining *apocryphal*. The current proliferation of author collectives and licensing practices certainly plays an important role here (see, e.g., Anania 2021; Hadas 2020; Johnson 2013; Salter and Stanfill 2020; Wolf 2012; and the contributions in Gray and Johnson 2013), yet it should also be noted that the question of canonicity does not entirely coincide with the question of authorship.

As has already been mentioned, the franchises of *The Matrix* and *Halo* at least initially appeared to be primarily defined by an attempt at the non-contradictory expansion of a single transmedia storyworld, despite the fact that their individual works are still created by different author collectives. Of course, this observation already draws a distinction between who is and is not authorized to contribute to the representation of the transmedia storyworld in question. It seems clear, for example, that the authors or author collectives of officially licensed works such as the video game *Enter the Matrix* (2003) or Eric Nylund's novel *Halo: The Fall of Reach* (2001) are more likely to have the authority to expand the transmedia storyworlds that are at the "canonical core" of the *The Matrix* and *Halo* franchises than, say, the authors or author collectives of the substantial corpus of *The Matrix* and *Halo* fan fiction that can, for example, be found on *An Archive of Our Own*. However, we can also find licensed works such as the video game *The Matrix: The Path of Neo* (2005) or the last of the seven short anime films collected in *Halo Legends* (2010) that are explicitly marked as apocryphal despite being created by officially licensed author collectives (see also, once more, the more detailed explorations of the two franchises in Atkinson 2018; Jenkins 2006, 93–131; Ryan 2015; as well as Harvey 2015, 93–115; Jaagola 2019; Rosendo 2015).

As Mark J. P. Wolf remarks, "for a work to be canonical requires that it be declared as such by someone with the authority to do so" (2012, 271), but the importance of the canonical/apocryphal distinction for the analysis of transmedia franchises' narrative functions should also not be over-emphasized. Indeed, it would seem that the relevance of the question of a given licensed work's canonicity remains largely limited to those cases where that work's storyworld could, at least in principle, be comprehended as a noncontradictory expansion of a previously represented storyworld (whether it is a work-specific, a transtextual, or a transmedia storyworld). Yet, in the case of the *A Song of Ice and Fire/ Game of Thrones* and *The Walking Dead* franchises, it is obvious that both the *Game of Thrones* and *The Walking Dead* television series constitute modifying rather than redundant adaptations of George R. R. Martin's novel series and Robert Kirkman's comics series, respectively. In those cases, asking which of the works is "more canonical" seems to miss the point—which is that neither the *Game of Thrones* television series and the *A Song of Ice and Fire* novel series nor the *The Walking Dead* television series and the *The Walking Dead* comics series contribute to the representation of a "single world," to begin with.

However, while there seems to be neither an immediate need nor theoretically solid ground to exclude any work—whether canonical or apocryphal, licensed work or fan creation—from consideration as contributing to the representation of a franchise's transmedia universe, the fact remains that the canonical/apocryphal distinction often plays an important role in the intersubjective construction of these universes. This has been forcefully illustrated by the discussions surrounding Disney's acquisition and subsequent re-ordering of Marvel Studios in 2009 and Lucasfilms in 2012 (see, e.g., Fandino et al. 2018; Flanagan et al. 2016; Yockey 2017; as well as, once more, Guynes and Hassler-Forest 2017; Nardi and Sweet 2020; Proctor 2019). Indeed, while Marvel thus far continues to promote their "multiverse" canon system, of which the *Marvel Cinematic Universe* forms only a small part (see Marvel Database 2022), the *Star Wars* franchise's 2014 move from the six "canonical levels" of the "Holocron continuity database" to the simpler binary distinction between canonical *Star Wars* content and apocryphal *Star Wars Legends* content (see Wookieepedia 2022) not only likewise reaffirms the necessity to go beyond the model of the "single world" in analyzing transmedia franchises' narrative functions but also exemplifies rather well that the relations between a transmedia universe's storyworlds are in constant flux.

Conclusion

This chapter has presented a broadly narratological perspective on work-specific storyworlds, transmedia storyworlds, and transmedia universes as a theoretically as well as methodologically productive way of transcending the model of the "single world" in the analysis of transmedia franchises' narrative functions. As has further become clear, the "toolbox" of transmedial narratology can be fruitfully applied to a variety of different cases, ranging from the gradual expansion of a single transmedia storyworld in comparatively small-scale franchises such as *The Matrix* or *Halo* via the more complex combination of redundancy, expansion, and modification that defines the transmedia universes of franchises such as *A Song of Ice and Fire/Game of*

Thrones or *The Walking Dead* to the synchronically complex and diachronically variable transmedia universes that long-running transmedia franchises such as those of Marvel or *Star Wars* generate. One way or another, though, the narratological perspective presented here is meant to complement rather than contradict the wide range of existing approaches to the study of transmedia franchises, thus leading to a richer understanding of these franchises specific brand of narrative complexity without in any way dismissing other aspects of their production, aesthetics, and reception.

Note

This is a shortened and revised version of: Thon, Jan-Noël. 2015. "Converging Worlds: From Transmedial Storyworlds to Transmedial Universes." *Storyworlds: A Journal of Narrative Studies* 7 (2): 21–53 (published by the University of Nebraska Press). An earlier version of this chapter has also been published as: Thon, Jan-Noël. 2018. "A Narratological Approach to Transmedial Storyworlds and Transmedial Universes." In *The Routledge Companion to Transmedia Studies*, edited by Matthew Freeman and Renira Rampazzo Gambarato, 375–382. New York: Routledge.

References

Anania, Valentina. 2021. "The Author Is Cancelled, Long Live the Author(s): Alternative Authorial Authorities and Fluid Authorship in the *Wizarding World*." *Makings: A Journal Researching the Creative Industries* 2 (1). Accessed August 22, 2022. https://makingsjournal.com/the-author-is-cancelled-long-live-the-authors-alternative-authorial-authorities-and-fluid-authorship-in-the-wizarding-world/

Atkinson, Sarah. 2018. "Transmedia Film: From Embedded Engagement to Embodied Experience." In *The Routledge Companion to Transmedia Studies*, edited by Matthew Freeman and Renira Rampazzo Gambarato, 15–24. New York: Routledge.

Beil, Benjamin, and Hanns Christian Schmidt. 2015. "The World of *The Walking Dead*—Transmediality and Transmedial Intermediality." *Acta Universitatis Sapientiae* 10: 73–88.

Blodgett, Bridget, and Anastasia Salter. 2018. "*Ghostbusters* Is for Boys: Understanding Geek Masculinity's Role in the Alt-Right." *Communication, Culture and Critique* 11 (1): 133–146.

Brenner, Lisa S. (ed.). 2015. *Playing Harry Potter: Essays and Interviews on Fandom and Performance*. Jefferson: McFarland.

Brummitt, Cassie. 2023. *From* Harry Potter *to the* Wizarding World: *The Transfiguration of a Franchise*. London: Bloomsbury.

Carroll, Shiloh. 2018. *Medievalism in* A Song of Ice and Fire *and* Game of Thrones. Cambridge: D. S. Brewer.

Chatman, Seymour. 1978. *Story and Discourse: Narrative Structure in Fiction and Film*. Ithaca: Cornell University Press.

Currie, Gregory. 2010. *Narratives and Narrators: A Philosophy of Stories*. Oxford: Oxford University Press.

Doležel, Lubomír. 1998. *Heterocosmica: Fiction and Possible Worlds*. Baltimore: Johns Hopkins University Press.

Ecenbarger, Charlie. 2016. "Comic Books, Video Games, and Transmedia Storytelling: A Case Study of *The Walking Dead*." *International Journal of Gaming and Computer-Mediated Simulations* 8 (2): 34–42.

Eder, Jens. 2008. *Die Figur im Film: Grundlagen der Figurenanalyse* [*The Character in Film: Foundations of Character Analysis*]. Marburg: Schüren.

Ensslin, Astrid, and Alice Bell. 2021. *Digital Fiction and the Unnatural: Transmedial Narrative Theory, Method, and Analysis*. Columbus: Ohio State University Press.

Evans, Elizabeth. 2011. *Transmedia Television: Audiences, New Media and Daily Life*. London: Routledge.

Fandino, Daniel, Julian C. Chambliss, and William L. Svitavsky (eds.). 2018. *Assembling the Marvel Cinematic Universe: Essays on the Social, Cultural and Geopolitical Domains*. Jefferson: McFarland.

Firestone, Amanda, and Leisa A. Clark (eds.). 2018. *Harry Potter and Convergence Culture: Essays on Fandom and the Expanding Potterverse*. Jefferson: McFarland.

Flanagan, Martin, Andrew Livingstone, and Mike McKenny (eds.). 2016. *The Marvel Studios Phenomenon: Inside a Transmedia Universe*. London: Bloomsbury.

Frankel, Valerie Estelle. 2014. *Women in* Game of Thrones: *Power, Conformity and Resistance*. Jefferson: McFarland.

Genette, Gérard. 1988. *Narrative Discourse Revisited*. Translated by Jane E. Lewin. Ithaca: Cornell University Press.

Gerrig, Richard J. 1993. *Experiencing Narrative Worlds: On the Psychological Activities of Reading*. New Haven: Yale University Press.

Gjelsvik, Anne, and Rikke Schubart (eds.). 2016. *Women of Ice and Fire: Gender,* Game of Thrones *and Multiple Media Engagements*. London: Bloomsbury.

Gray, Jonathan, and Derek Johnson (eds.). 2013. *A Companion to Media Authorship*. Chichester: Wiley-Blackwell.

Guynes, Sean, and Dan Hassler-Forest (eds.). 2017. Star Wars *and the History of Transmedia Storytelling*. Amsterdam: Amsterdam University Press.

Hadas, Leora. 2020. *Authorship as Promotional Discourse in the Screen Industries: Selling Genius*. New York: Routledge.

Harvey, Colin B. 2015. *Fantastic Transmedia: Narrative, Play and Memory across Science Fiction and Fantasy Storyworlds*. Basingstoke: Palgrave Macmillan.

Hassler-Forest, Dan. 2014. "*The Walking Dead*: Quality Television, Transmedia Serialization and Zombies." In *Serialization in Popular Culture*, edited by Rob Allen and Thijs van den Berg, 91–105. New York: Routledge.

Herman, David. 2002. *Story Logic: Problems and Possibilities of Narrative*. Lincoln: University of Nebraska Press.

Herman, David. 2009. *Basic Elements of Narrative*. Chichester: Wiley-Blackwell.

Hills, Matt. 2015. Doctor Who: *The Unfolding Event—Marketing, Merchandising and Mediatizing a Brand Anniversary*. Basingstoke: Palgrave Macmillan.

Hills, Matt. 2017. "Casting a Female Doctor Who Wasn't So Bold—Choosing Another White Male Would Have Been Really Risky." *The Conversation*, July 26. Accessed August 22, 2022. http://theconversation.com/casting-a-female-doctor-who-wasnt-so-bold-choosing-another-white-male-would-have-been-really-risky-81410

Jaagola, Karl. 2019. "Seriality in Transmedia Storytelling: A Case Study of *Halo*." *Ekphrasis: Images, Cinema, Theory, Media* 22 (2): 152–168.

Jenkins, Henry. 2004. "Game Design as Narrative Architecture." In *First Person: New Media as Story, Performance, and Game*, edited by Noah Wardrip-Fruin and Pat Harrigan, 118–130. Cambridge, MA: MIT Press.

Jenkins, Henry. 2006. *Convergence Culture: Where Old and New Media Collide.* New York: New York University Press.

Jenkins, Henry. 2007. "Transmedia Storytelling 101." *Confessions of an Aca/Fan*, March 21. Accessed August 22, 2022. http://henryjenkins.org/2007/03/transmedia_storytelling_101.html

Jenkins, Henry. 2011. "Transmedia 202: Further Reflections." *Confessions of an Aca/Fan*, July 31. Accessed August 22, 2022. http://henryjenkins.org/blog/2011/08/defining_transmedia_further_re.html

Johnson, Derek. 2013. *Media Franchising: Creative License and Collaboration in the Culture Industries.* New York: New York University Press.

Klastrup, Lisbeth, and Susana P. Tosca. 2004."Transmedial Worlds—Rethinking Cyberworld Design." *Proceedings of the International Conference on Cyberworlds 2004.* Accessed August 22, 2022. www.itu.dk/people/klastrup/klastruptosca_transworlds.pdf

Larrington, Carolyne. 2016. *Winter Is Coming: The Medieval World of* Game of Thrones. London: I. B. Tauris.

Marvel Database. 2022. "Multiverse/Universe Listing." *Marvel Database.* Accessed August 22, 2022. https://marvel.fandom.com/wiki/Multiverse/Universe_Listing

Nardi, Dominic J., and Derek R. Sweet (eds.). 2020. *The Transmedia Franchise of* Star Wars *TV.* Cham: Palgrave Macmillan.

Packard, Stephan. 2015. "Closing the Open Signification: Forms of Transmedial Storyworlds and Chronotopoi in Comics." *Storyworlds: A Journal of Narrative Studies* 7 (2): 55–74.

Parody, Clare. 2011. "Franchising/Adaptation." *Adaptation* 4 (2): 210–218.

Pavel, Thomas. 1989. *Fictional Worlds.* Cambridge, MA: Harvard University Press.

Perkins, Claire. 2020. "Ghost Girls: *Ghostbusters*, Popular Feminism and the Gender-Swap Reboot." In *Film Reboots*, edited by Daniel Herbert and Constantine Verevis, 157–170. Edinburg: Edinburgh University Press.

Proctor, William. 2017. "'Bitches Ain't Gonna Hunt No Ghosts': Totemic Nostalgia, Toxic Fandom and the *Ghostbusters* Platonic." *Palabra Clave* 20 (4): 1105–1141.

Proctor, William, and Richard McCulloch (eds.). 2019. *Disney's* Star Wars: *Forces of Production, Promotion, and Reception.* Iowa City: University of Iowa Press.

Rajewsky, Irina O. 2010. "Border Talks: The Problematic Status of Media Borders in the Current Debate about Intermediality." In *Media Borders, Multimodality and Intermediality*, edited by Lars Elleström, 51–68. Basingstoke: Palgrave Macmillan.

Ronen, Ruth. 1994. *Possible Worlds in Literary Theory.* Cambridge: Cambridge University Press.

Rosendo, Nieves. 2015. "The Map Is Not the Territory: Bible and Canon in the Transmedial World of *Halo*." *IMAGE: Zeitschrift für interdisziplinäre Bildwissenschaft* Thematic Issue 22 (2): 54–64.

Ryan, Marie-Laure. 1991. *Possible Worlds, Artificial Intelligence, and Narrative Theory.* Bloomington: Indiana University Press.

Ryan, Marie-Laure. 2006. *Avatars of Story.* Minneapolis: University of Minnesota Press.

Ryan, Marie-Laure. 2008. "Transfictionality across Media." In *Theorizing Narrativity*, edited by John Pier and José Á. García Landa, 385–417. Berlin: De Gruyter.

Ryan, Marie-Laure. 2015. "Transmedia Storytelling: Industry Buzzword or New Narrative Experience?" *Storyworlds: A Journal of Narrative Studies* 7 (2): 1–19.

Ryan, Marie-Laure. 2022. *A New Anatomy of Storyworlds: What Is, What If, As If.* Columbus: Ohio State University Press.

Salter, Anastasia, and Mel Stanfill. 2020. *A Portrait of the Auteur as Fanboy: The Construction of Authorship in Transmedia Franchises.* Jackson: University Press of Mississippi.

Schröter, Felix. 2015. "The Game of *Game of Thrones*: George R. R. Martin's *A Song of Ice and Fire* and Its Video Game Adaptations." *IMAGE: Zeitschrift für inter-disziplinäre Bildwissenschaft* Thematic Issue 22 (2): 65–82.

Thon, Jan-Noël. 2014. "Mediality." In *The Johns Hopkins Guide to Digital Media*, edited by Marie-Laure Ryan, Lori Emerson and Benjamin J. Robertson, 334–337. Baltimore: Johns Hopkins University Press.

Thon, Jan-Noël. 2015. "Converging Worlds: From Transmedial Storyworlds to Transmedial Universes." *Storyworlds: A Journal of Narrative Studies* 7 (2): 21–53.

Thon, Jan-Noël. 2016. *Transmedial Narratology and Contemporary Media Culture.* Lincoln: University of Nebraska Press.

Thon, Jan-Noël. 2017. "Transmedial Narratology Revisited: On the Intersubjective Construction of Storyworlds and the Problem of Representational Correspondence in Films, Comics, and Video Games." *Narrative* 25 (3): 286–320.

Thon, Jan-Noël. 2018. "A Narratological Approach to Transmedial Storyworlds and Transmedial Universes." In *The Routledge Companion to Transmedia Studies*, edited by Matthew Freeman and Renira Rampazzo Gambarato, 375–382. New York: Routledge.

Thon, Jan-Noël. 2019. "Transmedia Characters: Theory and Analysis." *Frontiers of Narrative Studies* 5 (2): 176–199.

Thon, Jan-Noël. 2022. "Transmedia Characters/Transmedia Figures: Drawing Distinctions and Staging Re-Entries." *Narrative* 30 (2): 140–147.

Tosca, Susana P., and Lisbeth Klastrup. 2019. *Transmedial Worlds in Everyday Life: Networked Reception, Social Media, and Fictional Worlds.* New York: Routledge.

Walton, Kendall L. 1990. *Mimesis as Make-Believe: On the Foundations of the Representational Arts.* Cambridge, MA: Harvard University Press.

Wolf, Mark J. P. 2012. *Building Imaginary Worlds: The Theory and History of Subcreation.* London: Routledge.

Wookieepedia. 2022. "Canon." *Wookieepedia.* Accessed August 22, 2022. http://starwars.wikia.com/wiki/Canon

Yockey, Matt (ed.). 2017. *Make Ours Marvel: Media Convergence and a Comics Universe.* Austin: University of Texas Press.

PART IV

New Perspectives

16

TWO PHILOSOPHIES OF THE SCREENPLAY

Enrico Terrone

The philosophical investigation of artifacts is among the most lively areas of 21st-century philosophy. This area of research exhibits interesting affinities with aesthetics and the philosophy of art since both works of art and technical artifacts are entities brought into existence by human agency. Although it is debatable whether works of art are instances of the ontological kind of technical artifacts or rather constitute a self-standing kind, their dependence on human creation surely makes them ontologically closer to technical artifacts than to other kinds of entities, such as organisms or inanimate natural entities. From this perspective, the screenplay is an especially interesting object since its ontological location seems to lie somewhere at the boundary between the work of art and the technical artifact.

There are two main ways in which the screenplay can be studied. The first consists in focusing on the relationship between the notion of screenplay and that of narrative, conceiving the screenplay as the artifact that is meant to turn a narrative into a film. Let me call this the "narrative-oriented" approach to the screenplay. This is the approach one can find in screenwriting handbooks written by story analysts, for instance, Syd Field's *Screenplay* (1979), Christopher Vogler's *The Writer's Journey* (1992) and Robert McKee's *Story* (1997). As David Bordwell points out, "The flood of manuals that broke forth in the late 1970s responded to a new process of story development [...] Syd Field, Robert McKee, Christopher Vogler, and other script gurus all started their careers as story analysts" (2006, 27–28). On the other hand, one can study the screenplay as an object that is not, in principle, linked to storytelling in spite of the fact that most screenplays surely deal with narratives. Let me call this the "narrative-independent" approach to the screenplay. This is the approach favored by Ted Nannicelli in his 2013 book

DOI: 10.4324/9781003197911-21

A Philosophy of the Screenplay. Nannicelli draws on the work of classical theorists, such as Béla Balázs, Hugo Münsterberg, and Sergei Eisenstein but he notices that the sorts of theoretical and philosophical questions those authors raised about the very nature of the screenplay "disappeared from view almost entirely once the heyday of classical film theory ended" (2013, 1).[1] Recent books such as Steven Maras's (2009) *Screenwriting: History, Theory and Practice* and Steven Price's (2010) *The Screenplay: Authorship, Theory and Criticism,* however, Nannicelli acknowledges, "have explicitly set out to reinvigorate theoretical debates about the screenplay" (2013, 2). Specifically, Maras stresses the primacy of screenwriting as a practice compared to the screenplay as an object while Price insists on the constitutive openness and incompleteness of the screenplay as a text. Nannicelli critically engages with those contributions to propose his own narrative-independent conception of the screenplay.

In this chapter, I will offer a narrative-oriented alternative to Nannicelli's proposal. First, I will analyze the notion on narrative on which my account of the screenplay will be based. Second, I will present Nannicelli's account. Third, I will rely on recent developments in the philosophy of artifacts to challenge that narrative-independent account, and to outline a narrative-oriented alternative to it.

Screenplay and Narrative

In the fourth chapter of his book, "From Playwriting to Screenwriting", Nannicelli explains how the norms of screenwriting emerged out of the norms of playwriting during the first three decades of the 20th century. The emergence of the screenwriting norms was enabled by the standardization and the centralization of production methods, and the publication of screenwriting manuals, which led to "standards of screenwriting practice based on the narrative principles of the legitimate theater" (2013, 95). I contend that such standards contribute to the normative essence of the screenplay, just like the rules of soccer contribute to the normative essence of soccer. Hence, to understand what the screenplay is, we need to understand what "the narrative principles of the legitimate theater" are. Nannicelli does not elaborate upon those principles. He rather assumes that their individuation is not a concern of an account of the screenplay since they are not specific to the screenplay but rather inherited from playwriting. Still, the connection between screenplay and narrative is so central to the screenwriting practice—as Nannicelli himself acknowledges—that it would be hard to offer a compelling account of the former notion without saying something substantive about the latter.

I conceive of screenwriting as a normative practice aimed to produce objects, namely screenplays, that are meant to govern the passage from the design of a film to its production by articulating a narrative in a way that favors its transformation into a film. Although there might be screenplays that are meant to lead to the production of non-narrative films, narrativity is so central a feature of our screenwriting practice that allegedly non-narrative screenplays end up in challenging the constitutive norm of that practice, as the label "experimental cinema" that is usually deployed to encompass them somehow suggests.

In the very framework of experimental cinema, a non-narrative screenplay might be seen as nothing but a production-guiding verbal object.[2] Yet, in the broader framework of film as a historically established cultural practice having the narrativity of the screenplay as its core feature, non-narrative screenplays can be cast as challenges to the normativity of the practice.

If all this is right, we should understand what a narrative is to understand what screenplays are expected to do. The first step is to state that a narrative is a representation of events, which has an order of its own that may be distinct from the objective order of the events represented. Such distinction between the narrative order and the objective order underlies some popular distinctions in the theory of narratives, namely, syuzhet/fabula (Propp 1968), discourse/story (Chatman 1978; Genette 1980), narration/narrated (Prince 1982), emplotment/plot (Ricoeur 1983–1985), game-world/story-world (Walton 1990), periphery/story-world (Predelli 2020).

However, this first step is not sufficient. We now need to differentiate narratives from other representations of events, such as registers, timelines, annals, or chronicles. Drawing on Timothy Williamson's (1996) conception of assertions as speech acts constituted by a Norm of Knowledge, I conceive of narratives as speech acts constituted by a Norm of Connection. Just as the Norm of Knowledge mandates one to assert only what one knows, the Norm of Connection mandates one to represent events as connected.[3] Both assertions and narratives can fail to follow their constitutive norm: an utterance may belong to a speech-act kind just by virtue of being expected to follow the norm constituting that kind. All this explains why certain modernist or surrealist works count as narratives despite not following the Norm of Connection. The fact that those works are *expected to follow* this norm is what makes them *narratives*, though their *breaking* the norm prevents them from being *canonical* narratives.

The notion of connection that is at work in the Norm of Connection requires qualification. For this purpose, let us compare two "mini-narratives" (Williams 2002, 233). The first (STATUE) draws on the story of Mitys told by Aristotle: "We may instance the statue of Mitys at Argos, which fell upon his murderer while he was a spectator at a festival, and killed him" (1907, § IX). The second (COMPANIONS) is a counterfactual variant of that story.

(STATUE) Mitys was killed (E1) and then his statue fell on his murderer (E2s).

(COMPANIONS) Mitys was killed (E1) and so his companions killed his murderer (E2c).

On the one hand, E1 and E2c are causally connected: Mitys' companions killed his murderer (E2c) *because* Mitys was killed (E1). On the other hand, E1 and E2s are not causally connected: the statue did not fall *because* Mitys was killed. Yet, both STATUE and COMPANIONS appear to be narratives. This suggests that the Norm of Connection makes room for two sorts of connections. One surely is causality, as shown by philosophers, such as Noël Carroll (2001, 2007) and Susan Feagin (2007). But what is the other?

Philosophers, such as David Velleman (2003), Ismay Barwell (2009), Gregory Currie (2010), and Peter Goldie (2012) have looked for the answer in the cognitive or affective attitudes of the audience toward the events represented. Currie casts the relevant connection as a "relation of reasons", Barwell characterizes it in terms of "evaluative significance", Velleman speaks of the closure of an "emotional cadence", and Goldie insists on "meaningfulness and emotional and evaluative import". Yet, I argue, such attitudes of the audience are enabled by a feature of narratives themselves: teleology, that is, the property of having valuable ends. Just as the causal dimension of narratives represents events as effects of causes, the teleological dimension represents events as means in view of an end. The value of this end can be assessed in term of reasons and significance, as Currie and Barwell point out, but also in terms of affects and emotions, as stressed by Velleman and Goldie.

Narratives like STATUE represent events as governed by teleological connections: the fall of the statue was not *caused by* the killing of Mitys but rather *aimed to* punish the murderer. From this perspective, Currie's "relation of reasons" and Barwell's "evaluative significance", as well as Velleman's "emotional cadence" and Goldie's "meaningfulness and emotional and evaluative import", all rest upon a teleological relationship between events.

A narrative like COMPANIONS involves both causal and teleological connections. Mitys' companions did kill his murderer not only *because* Mitys was murdered but also *with the aim of* avenging him. Teleology and causality, here, are strictly intertwined: the companions' *intention* of avenging Mitys is caused by Mitys' murder and, in turn, motivates their actions. What is special in a narrative like STATUE is that the teleological connection does not need to rest upon a causal link: the falling of the statue achieves the goal of avenging Mitys without being caused by Mitys' death in the way the goal-oriented actions of his friend are caused by his death in COMPANIONS. There is no character in STATUE to whom one can ascribe the intention of avenging Mitys by pushing his statue on his murderer.

In Oscar Wilde's *The Picture of Dorian Gray* the eponymous picture plays a role analogous to that of the statue in the story of Mitys: just as the statue falls in order to punish the murder of Mitys, so the picture decays in order to sanction Dorian's hedonism.[4] Likewise, in James M. Cain's crime novel *The Postman Always Rings Twice*, there is no character to whom one can ascribe the intention of avenging the husband murdered by his wife and her lover, and yet, when the woman is killed in a car crash and her lover is wrongly convicted of having murdered her, the audience can feel that those apparently fortuitous events have somehow restored the moral balance in the fictional world.[5] The fact that both *The Picture of Dorian Gray* and *The Postman Always Rings Twice* have been adapted a number of times in the history of film suggests that the teleological connection may play an analogous role in screenwriting.

Focusing on teleology and causality enables us to figure out in which sense a narrative involves "a beginning, a middle, and an end", as Aristotle (1907, § VII) puts it. Both STATUE and COMPANIONS represent events as teleologically oriented since in both cases the death of Mitys' murderer is a means to the end of restoring the moral balance that the murder of Mitys has disturbed at the beginning. Yet, in STATUE teleology directly bears upon the events, without the mediation of causality, so that the fall of the statue (the middle) lacks a causal connection to the murder of Mitys (the beginning). In COMPANIONS, instead, the end of restoring justice is obtained through the causal connection between the murder of Mitys (the beginning) and the killing of the murderer (the middle). Thus, in paradigmatic narratives, such as COMPANIONS, teleology is realized through causality and disguised as causality. The causal order is curved, as it were, by the teleological orientation. Narratives, such as STATUE, on the other hand, are exceptional since they use the middle to achieve the end that was implicit in the beginning, despite the fact that there is no relevant causal connection between the beginning and the middle. At most, if one takes the narratological expression "deus ex machina" literally, one might ascribe the crucial event constituting the middle to the agency of a supernatural entity like a demon or a god.

We are now in the position to express the Norm of Connection, the constitutive norm of narrative as a speech act. Events should be organized through a causal-teleological narrative. If a speech act fully abides by the Norm of Connection, the result is a canonical narrative, such as COMPANIONS. Yet, a narrative can be produced also if the norm is only partially followed. We have already seen a way of producing a narrative in the latter way, namely, the merely teleological narrative exemplified by STATUE. Still the Norm of Connection might be partially followed also in another way, that is, by subtracting the teleological component from the causal-teleological model. Consider this other variant of the story of Mitys:

(WIDOW) Mitys was killed (E1) and then his widow faced economic difficulties in raising their children (E2w).

Even though one cannot find any teleological orientation in this case, one can still see this as a narrative by virtue of the causal connection between E1 and E2w. WIDOW is a narrative that limits itself to representing events as causally connected without imposing a teleological orientation on them.

In sum, both causality and teleology play a role in the Norm of Connection that constitutes the narrative as a kind of speech act. If they both are instantiated, a paradigmatic narrative takes place. If one of them is instantiated and the other is not, a non-paradigmatic narrative takes place.

It is only when neither causality nor teleology are instantiated that there is no narrative at all. Consider this last variant of Mitys's story:

(NAPOLEON) Mitys was killed (E1) and then Napoleon was defeated at Waterloo (E2n).

Since the events E1 and E2n, albeit temporally ordered, are represented as completely disconnected, NAPOLEON is not a narrative. There is no glue unifying its events, neither a causal one nor a teleological one. While COMPANION is a paradigmatic narrative, and STATUE and WIDOW remain narratives despite instantiating only one of the two constitutive features, NAPOLEON is rather an object that violates the constitutive norm in such a radical way that prevents it from belonging to the kind constituted by that norm: NAPOLEON is not a narrative but just a mere chronology.

By properly drawing the distinction between narratives and chronologies, the causal-teleological account enables us to unpack the notion of "narrative principles" which remained implicit in Nannicelli's intentional-historical conception of the screenplay. It is now time to analyze that conception more closely, with the aim of developing a narrative-oriented alternative to it.

The Intentional-Historical Approach

What is the screenplay? What kind of thing is it? Is the screenplay a work of art on its own? These are the three main questions that Nannicelli addresses in *A Philosophy of the Screenplay*. His answer to the first question is an attempt to clarify, amend, and systematize the commonsense intuition that the screenplay is "a sort of outline or blueprint from which a film can be made" (2014). He then answers the second question by tracing screenplays back to a kind of document to which architectural plans also belong. Finally, his answer to the third question is that screenplays can be works of art; in fact, sometimes they are so and sometimes they are not, and when they are so they should be cast as literary works.

Being in agreement with the proposal that screenplays are works of art, I will not elaborate further on the issue here. I limit myself to making some remarks concerning an interesting consequence of Nannicelli's statement that the screenplay, when it is art, it is an instance of literature. The consequence is that, although particular screenplays can be works of art, the screenplay is not, as such, an autonomous form of art. This commits Nannicelli to a quite weak version of the thesis that the screenplay is art. A screenplay can be a work of art in the same sense in which a newspaper article can be art if it exhibits sufficient literary qualities. As Nannicelli (2013, 136) puts it: "a screenplay is a kind of literary work just in case it meets whatever criteria one normally applies for a verbal object to count as a literary work. Its relationship to the film is irrelevant in this regard". This does not seem to be a so fruitful sense in which the screenplay can be art. More interesting would be a defense of the strong version of the thesis that the screenplay is art, namely, the claim that the screenplay is a self-standing form of art which is rooted in our appreciative practices, constituting what Dominic Lopes (2014) calls an "appreciative kind". Yet, our culture does not seem to have room for a practice of appreciation of screenplays over and above our practices of appreciation of films and works of literature, as suggested by the fact that most screenplays remain unpublished.[6]

In sum, the thesis of the screenplay as art can be read in two ways which are both unsatisfying: the weak reading is true but trivial, the strong reading is interesting but surely false. Is it possible to draw a middle way which might be both interesting and true? It might be argued that the screenplay is a form of literature just like the poem or the novel. Yet, such a "moderate" reading seems to still suffer from some disconnection from appreciative practices since we do not have—outside the circle of specialists—a practice of appreciation of screenplays on a par with our appreciative practices of novels or poems or even plays. I thus prefer to focus on Nannicelli's question about the definition and the categorization of the screenplay rather than on his thesis that the screenplay is art.

Nannicelli treats the definition of the screenplay and its categorization separately, beginning with the former and then considering the latter. The definition he proposes is the following: "x is a screenplay if and only if x is a verbal object intended to repeat, modify, or repudiate the ways in which plot, characters, dialogue, shots, edits, sound effects, and/or other features have historically been suggested as constitutive elements of a film by a prior screenplay(s) or screenwriting practice (in accordance with recognizable and live purposes of that practice)" (2013, 31).

The key elements of this definition are a formal constraint, a functional basis, and an intentional-historical recursive mechanism inspired by Jerrold Levinson's (1990) attempt to define art. The formal constraint is that the screenplay must be a "verbal object", that is, a text, an object made of words; this aptly excludes storyboards from the definition. The functional basis is that a screenplay is meant to suggest "plot, characters, dialogue, shots, edits, sound effects, and/or other features [...] as constitutive elements of a film". Although Nannicelli acknowledges that this is the main function that screenplays have fulfilled along the history of film, he does not commit himself to the claim that fulfilling this function is an essential feature of the screenplay. There are two main reasons for this. First, he observes that verbal objects such as treatments and shot lists also fulfill this function and yet are not screenplays. Second, he proposes that there are verbal objects which do not fulfill that function and yet deserve to be cast as screenplays. As examples, he considers "fan-fiction screenplays" (2013, 16), and a couple of Cormac McCarthy's 1984 screenplays "which had the intended function of suggesting the constitutive elements of novels rather than films" (2013, 17). Nannicelli also proposes a thought experiment in which a little girl called Lou "grows up in a house that has no books, no television, and no form of entertainment except screenplays" and one day "creates a perfectly formatted screenplay". Nannicelli's conclusion is that "Lou has created a screenplay without intending it to have the historically typical function of screenplays, or, indeed, a function that is plausibly specific to screenplays" (2013, 17–18).

To accommodate cases such as Lou's or the fan-fiction screenplays or McCarthy's screenplays, Nannicelli's definition nests the screenplay's alleged function (that is, suggesting the constitutive elements of a film) within the scope of the screenwriter's intention "to repeat, modify, or repudiate" the ways in which this function has been fulfilled "by a prior screenplay(s) or screenwriting practice (in accordance with recognizable and live purposes of that practice)". The author of a fan-fiction screenplay or Lou in the thought experiment or McCarthy's work create screenplays despite not intending to suggest the constitutive elements of a film because they intend to create verbal objects that are linked to the screenwriting tradition (the main function of which has been to suggest the constitutive elements of a film). On the other hand, an author of a treatment or a shot list does not create screenplays, because they *do not* intend to create verbal objects that are linked to the screenwriting tradition. In this way, Nannicelli's definition seems to properly draw the boundaries of the screenplay.

A basic categorization is, to some extent, already at work in this definition since Nannicelli casts the screenplay as a "verbal object". Still, the categorization to which he ascribes ontological relevance is a more nuanced one. Screenplays, he argues, are to be traced back to the kind of documents to which architectural plans belong rather than to that to which musical scores and theatrical scripts belong. The latter are, as Stephen Davies (2001) calls them, "work determinative documents", that is, documents whose existence entails the existence of the corresponding work of art. If a musician creates a score, she has made a work of music. If a playwright creates a script, she has made a work of theater. On the other hand, architectural plans and screenplays are not work-determinative: creating an architectural plan does not amount to making a building, just as creating a screenplay does not amount to making a film. However, as Nannicelli points out, the fact that a screenplay is not work-determinative does not entail that it cannot be a work of art. Although the screenplay, as such, does not entail the existence of a work of cinematic art, it might nevertheless constitute a work of literary art.

The Hylomorphic Approach

In his 2016 book *Making Objects and Events: A Hylomorphic Theory of Artifacts, Actions, and Organisms*, Simon Evnine offers a contemporary avatar of Aristotle's classical conception of entities (or "substances") as constituted by both their form and their matter. For Evnine, form and matter are relational notions. First, he conceives of the matter as whatever set of elements, either concrete or abstract, that are properly organized by the form to constitute an entity. Second, he conceives of the form as the principle of organization of the matter of an entity that is essentially connected to both the origin and the functioning of the entity in question. Although Evnine's theory is meant to apply also to organisms and actions, artifacts are the paradigm case on which he focuses.

I propose to apply Evnine's hylomorphic theory of artifacts to screenplays, casting the words of a certain language as the screenplays' matter, and the principle whereby these words are organized by a screenwriter for a given purpose as the screenplay's form. The claim that words are the matter of a screenplay is roughly equivalent to Nannicelli's claim that screenplays are verbal objects. Yet, the hylomorphic approach diverges from Nannicelli's intentional-historical approach when it assesses borderline cases, such as fan-fiction screenplays or McCarthy's 1984 screenplays or Lou's screenplay in the thought experiment.

Nannicelli casts all such objects as screenplays since they are intended to belong to the screenwriting tradition even though they are not intended to suggest the constitutive elements of films. The hylomorphic alternative is subtler since it enables us to explain why those are borderline cases rather than just putting them on a par with paradigmatic screenplays. According to Evnine's hylomorphism, an object belongs to the artifactual kind K if it is made with the intention that it be a K. The latter intention usually goes hand in hand with the intention that the object be used as a K, fulfilling the K-function. Yet, there may be cases in which only the intention that the object be a K is present, while the maker does not intend that the object fulfill the K-function. This might happen because the maker ignores what the K-function is, and just defers the function assignment to the relevant practice. This is arguably what happens in Nannicelli's thought experiment in which Lou participates in a screenwriting practice and produces a screenplay despite ignoring what screenplays are for: she does so by deferring the function assignment to that practice. Still, fan-fiction screenplays and McCarthy's 1984 screenplays cannot be traced back to this model since their makers, unlike Lou, are aware of the function of the screenplay. Whether those objects are screenplays or not depends, according to the hylomorphic approach, on whether their makers intend to defer the function assignment to the relevant practice or, instead, intend to bestow a different, "idiosyncratic" function on the object (Evnine

2016, 120). McCarthy's 1984 putative screenplays instantiate the latter option since, as Nannicelli (2013, 17) stresses, they have "the intended function of suggesting the constitutive elements of novels rather than films".

The right conclusion to draw from these premises, I contend, is that McCarthy's 1984 putative screenplays are not screenplays since they are not intended to be so. Nannicelli notices that one of those two putative screenplays "was, in the end, *used to* make a film—*No Country for Old Men* (2006)" (2013, 17, my emphasis). Yet, the fact that an object is used as a K does not mean that this object is a K.[7] Nannicelli himself insists on this distinction when, later in the book, he writes: "we typically think of the identity of an artifact as being determined by the intentions of its creator [...] I might use a bowl to drink orange juice. But this does not make the bowl a cup" (2013, 82). Just like the bowl can *be used as* a cup and yet *is not* a cup, McCarthy's text can *be used* as a screenplay for the film *No Country for Old Men* and yet *is not* a screenplay since it was not intended to be so. The same of line of reasoning can be applied to fan-fiction screenplays, which resemble screenplays and might be *used as* screenplays, but *are not* screenplays since their makers do neither intend them to fulfill the function of screenplays nor intend to defer the function assignment to the screenwriting practice. Rather, the fan-fiction writers bestow a different, "idiosyncratic" function on their texts which is arguably connected to the ludic purposes of the fan-fiction practice.

In sum, the hylomorphic approach enables us to account for the relationships of resemblance and interchangeability between mock screenplays (such as the fan-fiction ones or McCarthy's ones) on the one hand and, on the other, the verbal objects that our cultural practices cast as genuine screenplays (included limit cases such as Lou's screenplay in the thought experiment). We can account for these relationships without being forced to put the former, which can at most be *used as* screenplays, on an ontological par with the latter, which are designed *to be* screenplays. In this sense, the hylomorphic approach seems to have an explanatory advantage in comparison with the intentional-historical approach: the former allows us to distinguish two kinds of things which the latter conflates.

Still, Nanicelli offers another compelling reason in favor of his intentional-historical proposal, namely, its capacity to draw a sharp distinction between screenplays and other verbal objects such as treatments and shot lists which also contribute to the making of a film but are not screenplays. One might wonder whether the hylomorphic alternative is yet another variant of the kind of essentialist functionalism which, according to Nannicelli, is doomed to failure when it comes to draw the distinction between screenplays and other verbal objects, such as treatments or shot lists.

Although I acknowledge that the hylomorphic approach has much in common with functionalism and essentialism, I contend that it has the theoretical resources to properly draw the distinction between screenplays and other film-related verbal objects, such as treatments or shot lists. For this purpose, it is helpful to connect the definition of the screenplay to its categorization in a tighter way than Nannicelli does.

I agree with Nannicelli that, from an ontological perspective, screenplays are like architectural plans rather than as "work-determinative" documents, such as musical scores or theatrical scripts. Yet, I contend, this ontological characterization should contribute to the definition of the screenplay since it enables us to distinguish it from other film-related verbal objects. In the light of Nannicelli's insightful analogy between screenplays and architectural plans, the problem of distinguishing screenplays from treatments or shot lists can be compared to the problem of distinguishing architectural plans from the architect's initial sketches or from the bricklayers' notes. The architectural plan is *the ultimate output* of the design process and *the original input* of the concrete process of building, whereas the architect's initial sketches are only a phase of the former process, and the bricklayers' notes are only a phase of the latter. Likewise, the screenplay is the *ultimate output* of the film-design process and the *original input* of the concrete making of a film, whereas treatments are only a phase of the former process, and shot lists only a phase of the latter. The screenplay individuates the point where writing can stop and shooting can start, just as the architectural plan individuates the point where designing can stop and building can start. Such individuation of the point where writing can stop and shooting can start is a functional dimension of the screenplay as a verbal object. A treatment differs from a screenplay since the film shooting is not supposed to start at that point: a verbal development of the treatment is still required. And a shot list differs from a screenplay since it occurs when the film has already entered its production stage, otherwise it would be premature to make such a list.

Normative Essentialism

Although the hylomorphic alternative succeeds in differentiating screenplays from other film-related verbal objects, one might object that it falls short of accounting for the varieties of screenwriting. Nannicelli (2013, 46–48), for example, points out that standard screenplays in the Thirties and the Forties were "continuity scripts" involving a description of each shot whereas standard screenplays nowadays just involve indications about scenes and dialogues. Moreover, he insists that creative filmmakers are free to break the putative rules that are meant to govern the screenwriting practice. For instance, "Su Friedrich's screenplay 'But No One' for her 1982 movie of the same title [...] does not look like a prototypical screenplay. Indeed, it seems quite clear that it is a kind of poem" (Nannicelli 2013, 49–50). The intentional-historical approach can effectively accommodate all such cases because, despite their macroscopic differences, they are all intended to be part of the historical tradition of screenwriting. It may be objected, on the other hand, that the hylomorphic alternative is problematic here because a, say, 1940 standard screenplay individuated the point where designing can stop and shooting can start in a way rather different than a 2021 standard screenplay would; furthermore, experimental filmmakers like Su Friedrich individuate that point in yet other vastly different manners.

I contend that the hylomorphic alternative can accommodate the varieties of screenwriting at least as effectively as Nannicelli's intentional-historical proposal does. For this purpose, let me introduce the notion of normative essentialism. The traditional versions of essentialism, those that Nannicelli examines in his book, are formulated in terms of necessary and sufficient conditions. Something is water if and only if its molecules consist of two atoms of hydrogen and one atom of oxygen. This sort of essentialism, however, is at odds with artifactual kinds which depend on human attitudes and thus, in principle, might accommodate an object O within a kind K even if O lacks the features that are meant to be essential to K—and even if O cannot perform the function which the instances of K are normally designed to perform. For example, an object can nowadays count as a phone despite not having some features (e.g., cable, wheel, handset...) that were meant to be essential to phones one-century ago, and it would arguably still be a phone even if it could not perform the function of transmitting sounds which was essential to old phones: it might still work for exchanging text messages or navigating the internet.

Recent developments in the philosophy of artifacts have shown another way of conceiving of the essence of an artifact which can deal with such issues (Thomasson 2014; Newman and Knobe 2019; García-Carpintero 2022). From this perspective, the *essence* of an artifact is not a matter of necessary and sufficient conditions but rather of *norms* which, just like social norms, should be followed but might be broken. That is why I dub this view "normative essentialism".

A paradigmatic case of norm-constituted entities, that is, entities whose essences are norms, is provided by games (see Suits 1978). Soccer, for example, is constituted by a cluster of rules which tends to be quite stable even though some rules may change—and indeed have changed—over time. Something counts as an instance of soccer if it is meant to follow those rules. However, the fact that the rules of the game are meant to be followed does not entail that they will be followed in any case. Some instances of a game, indeed, might involve rule-breaking. For example, Maradona's "hand of God"—the goal he scored with his hand against England in 1986—is an instance of soccer despite breaking a fundamental rule of soccer. Philosophers of languages like John Austin (1962) and Timothy Williamson (1996) have argued that speech acts are like games in this respect. For example, according to Williamson, the essence of assertion involves a norm which prescribes one to assert only what one knows. This normative account makes room for cases in which the norm is violated and yet the speech act remains an assertion. Austin calls the latter cases "abuses" and distinguishes them from "misfires" in which, instead, the relevant speech act is not performed in any relevant sense. If I say "Rome is the capital of France" to my students, my speech act is an assertion since this is what I meant to do in that context and is also an *abuse* since it violates the norm of knowledge which constitutes assertion as a speech act—what I said is false, and only what is true can be known. On the other hand, if I am making some noises to test a microphone and end up saying the German sentence "Rom ist die Hauptstadt Italiens" (Rome is the Capital of Italy) while ignoring its meaning, I am not making any assertion despite the apparent truth of that content: this is just a *misfire*. Likewise, Maradona's "hand of God" is an *abuse* but remains an instance of soccer, while a naïve stadium spectator who jumps in the field during an official soccer match and starts kicking the ball is not producing any instance of soccer but only a *misfire*. Abuses have the proper sort of context and intentions despite breaking the rules, whereas misfires are such because they lack the proper sort of context and intentions even when they may appear to follow the rules.

I argue that this sort of normative essentialism can be effectively applied not only to games and speech acts but also to screenplays. From this perspective, screenwriting is a norm-constituted practice, that is, a sort of cultural game whose rules specify how one should write the document, namely the screenplay, that is meant to connect the design of a film to its concrete making. The rules of the screenwriting game, just like those of games, such as chess or soccer, may change in time. For example, as Nannicelli emphasizes, in 1940 the rules of the screenwriting game prescribed to specify each shot whereas the rules of the same game in 2021 just prescribe to specify scenes and dialogue. Yet, the screenplay can preserve its identity through changes in their constitutive rules just as games such as chess or soccer preserve their identity through changes in their constitutive rules. An intentional-historical definition à la Levinson is not required to account for such changes. Defining soccer as a game that is intended to be in continuity with the soccer tradition would be just a cumbersome and convoluted way of saying that soccer is a game constituted by a cluster of rules that can change in time. Likewise, the intentional-historical definition of the screenplay that Nannicelli proposes can be replaced by a normative account according to which the screenplay is constituted by a cluster of rules governing the passage from the design of a film to its production which can change in time.

We can thus apply Evnine's hylomorphic account of artifacts to the screenplay, supplementing Evnine's conception of the form as essentially connected to intentions and purposes with a norm which intentions are expected to follow in order to achieve the purposes. In short, the form needs the norm (see Passinsky 2021). This basic idea leads us to a hylomorphic account according to which the screenplay's matter consists of words while the screenplays' form is the organization of words by an intentional activity that engages with norms to achieve the purpose of connecting the design of a film to its production.

Just like the rules of games, the constitutive norms of screenwriting can not only be changed but also broken. When experimental filmmaker Su Friedrich wrote her screenplay "But No One" as if it were a poem, she intended to produce the document that governs the passage from the design of film to its production in a way that challenges the norms of screenwriting, just as Maradona did his "hand of God" goal against England by breaking the rules of soccer.

Rule breaking in screenwriting, however, unlike typical rule-breaking in sports or other games, does not amount to cheating or to some other morally reprehensible action. It is just that screenwriters are expected to follow the rules in force, but might also attempt to challenge them. The rules of grammar are a better analogy in this respect, considering that the poet who tries to challenge them is not doing anything morally objectionable.

The normativity of the screenplay as a norm-constituted social object is also to be distinguished from the sort of theoretical normativity which Nannicelli proposes when he introduces his attempt to define the screenplay by signaling: "My goal here will be to develop a descriptive definition rather than a normative one" (2013, 13). A "descriptive" approach to the screenplay, in Nannicelli's sense, aims to account for actual screenwriting practices while a "normative" approach is rather meant to revise actual practices by means of new norms of screenwriting established by the theory itself. According to this reading of the normative-descriptive divide, my proposal is as descriptive as Nannicelli's. The difference is just that I contend that the best way to account for screenwriting practices is to investigate their implicit normativity, making it explicit. Hence, the norms of screenwriting that are crucial to my proposal are not those that philosophers would like to impose on the practice, but rather those established by that very practice.

Finally, the proposed approach enables us to properly distinguish screenplays from teleplays, which Nannicelli tends to conflate when he writes: "I take the term 'screenplay' to refer not just to film scripts, but to a rather broad category of objects, including—but not limited to—teleplays and other manuscripts for screen works (i.e., films, videos, television shows, and the like)" (2013, 3). Although the teleplay historically derives from the screenplay which in turn—as Nannicelli aptly shows—derives from the theatrical script, the screenplay and the teleplay are distinct objects since the former is meant to connect the design *of a film* to its production whereas the latter is meant to connect the design *of a TV show* to its production. If a film and a TV show belong to distinct appreciative kinds (cf. Nannicelli

2016; Bandirali & Terrone 2021), the screenplay and the teleplay should belong to distinct kinds of verbal objects. Hence, the account that I am proposing is supposed to apply only to the screenplay: an account of the teleplay might be developed along similar lines, but that would go beyond the scope of this chapter.

Conclusion

Both the narrative and the screenplay can be ultimately characterized in normative terms. A narrative is a representation of events that *should* order them through causality and teleology. A screenplay is the verbal object that *should* enable one to turn a narrative into a film thereby governing the passage from the design of a film to its production. Here is the double normativity of the screenplay, which, on the one hand, relies on the constitutive norm of the narrative to prescribe how to build a story, and, on the other, adds constitutive norms of its own that prescribe how to write the story in order to turn it into a film. Screenwriters can violate the first normative dimension by refusing to build a narrative as it happens in experimental cinema, or by building a narrative that seems to lack the proper causal-teleological order as it happens in modernist films, such as Alain Resnais' *Last Year in Marienbad*. The second normative dimension also can be violated by screenwriters who create verbal objects that govern the passage from the design of a film to its production in a way that significantly departs from the standard, as Su Friedrich did when she wrote the screenplay for her film *But No One*. The history of screenwriting involves not only the establishment of these two normative dimensions but also their gradual changes, and even the various violations of them by either incompetence or creativity.

Notes

1 An interesting exception is Pier Paolo Pasolini 1965 essay "La sceneggiatura come 'struttura che vuol essere altra struttura'" ("The screenplay as 'structure wanting to be another structure'", in Pasolini 1972). Thanks to Luca Bandirali for drawing my attention to that.
2 Thanks to Ted Nannicelli for pushing me to consider this issue.
3 While the Norm of Knowledge refers to the content of one single speech act, the Norm of Connection refers to the interconnectivity of speech acts, that is, to the combination of a number of speech acts into a higher-level speech act that one can call a narrative. The two norms operate at different levels of analysis. In historical narratives, the Norm of Connection rests upon the Norm of Knowledge. In fiction, the Norm of Connection rests upon a variant of the Norm of Knowledge that one might state as follows: "One must assert that P (within the narrative world) only if one knows that P (within the narrative world)". Thanks to Catalina Iricinschi and Paul Taberham for drawing my attention to this.
4 Thanks to Adam Sennet for suggesting this example.
5 Thanks to Greg Currie for suggesting this example.
6 Thanks to Luca Bandirali for this suggestion.

7 At most, it might be argued that McCarthy's text *became* a screenplay when the Coen Brothers used it to make *No Country for Old Men*. Thanks to Manuel García-Carpintero for this suggestion. On deviant uses of artifacts and practices of reappropriation of them, see Juvshik (2021) and Evnine (2022).

References

Aristotle. (1907). *Poetics* (S. H. Butcher, Trans.). London, UK: Macmillan.
Austin, John. (1962). *How to Do Things with Words*. Oxford, UK: Clarendon Press.
Bandirali, Luca; Terrone, Enrico. (2021). *Concept TV: An Aesthetics of Television Series*. Lanham, MD: Lexington Books.
Barwell, Ismay. (2009). "Understanding Narratives and Narrative Understanding". *The Journal of Aesthetics and Art Criticism*, 67(1), 49–59.
Bordwell, David. (2006). *The Way Hollywood Tells It: Story and Style in Modern Movies*. Berkeley, CA: University of California Press.
Carroll, Noël. (2001). "On the Narrative Connection". In *Beyond Aesthetics*. New York, NY: Cambridge University Press, 118–133.
Carroll, Noël. (2007). "Narrative closure". *Philosophical Studies*. 135, 1–15.
Chatman, Seymour. (1978). *Story and Discourse: Narrative Structure in Fiction and Film*. Ithaca, NY: Cornell University Press.
Currie, Gregory. (2010). *Narratives and Narrators: A Philosophy of Stories*. Oxford, UK: Oxford University Press.
Davies, Stephen. (2001). *Musical Works and Performances: A Philosophical Study*. Oxford, UK: Oxford University Press.
Evnine, Simon. (2016). *Making Objects and Events: A Hylomorphic Theory of Artifacts, Actions, and Organisms*. Oxford, UK: Oxford University Press.
Evnine, Simon. (2022). "The historicity of artifacts: use and counter-use". *Metaphysics*. 5 (1), 1–13.
Feagin, Susan L. (2007). "On Noël Carroll on narrative closure". *Philosophical Studies*. 135, 17–25.
Field, Syd. (1979). *Screenplay: The Foundations of Screenwriting*. New York, NY: Dell.
García-Carpintero, Manuel. (2022). "How to understand rule-constituted kinds". *Review of Philosophy and Psychology*. 13(1), 7–27.
Genette, Gérard. (1980). *Narrative Discourse: An Essay in Method* (J. E. Lewin, Trans.; original edition 1972). Ithaca, NY: Cornell University Press.
Goldie, Peter. (2012). *The Mess Inside: Narrative, Emotion, and the Mind*. Oxford, UK: Oxford University Press.
Juvshik, Tim. (2021). "Artifacts and mind-dependence". *Synthese*. 199, 9313–9336.
Levinson, Jerrold. (1990). "Defining Art Historically". In *Music, Art, and Metaphysics*. Ithaca, NY: Cornell University Press, 3–25.
Lopes, Dominic. (2014). *Beyond Art*. Oxford, UK: Oxford University Press.
Maras, Steven. (2009). *Screenwriting: History, Theory and Practice*. London, UK: Wallflower Press.
McKee, Robert. (1997). *Story: Substance, Structure, Style, and the Principles of Screenwriting*. New York, NY: Harper-Collins.
Nannicelli, Ted. (2013). *A Philosophy of the Screenplay*. New York, NY: Routledge.
Nannicelli, Ted. (2016). *Appreciating the Art of Television: A Philosophical Perspective*. New York, NY: Routledge.

Newman, George E.; Knobe, Joshua. (2019). "The essence of essentialism". *Mind and Language*. https://doi.org/10.1111/mila.12226

Pasolini, Pier Paolo. (1972). *Empirismo eretico*. Milano: Garzanti.

Passinsky, Asya. (2021). "Norm and object: A normative hylomorphic theory of social objects". *Philosophers' Imprint*. 25, 1–21.

Predelli, Stefano (2020). *Fictional Discourse: A Radical Fictionalist Semantics*. Oxford, UK: Oxford University Press.

Price, Steven. (2010). *The Screenplay: Authorship, Theory and Criticism*. London, NY: Palgrave MacMillan.

Prince, Gerard. (1982). *Narratology: The Form and Functioning of Narrative*. Berlin: Mouton.

Propp, Vladimir. (1968). *Morphology of the Folktale* (L. Wagner, Trans.; original edition 1928). Austin, TX: University of Texas Press.

Ricoeur, Paul. (1984–1988). *Time and Narrative* (K. McLaughlin and D. Pellauer, Trans; original edition 1983–1985). Chicago, IL: University of Chicago Press.

Suits, Bernard. (1978). *The Grasshopper: Games, Life and Utopia*. Toronto: University of Toronto Press.

Thomasson, Amie L. (2014). Public Artifacts, Intentions, and Norms. In *Artefact Kinds*, edited by M. Franssen, P. Kroes, T. Reydon, P. E. Vermaas. Berlin: Springer, 45–62.

Velleman, David. (2003). "Narrative explanation". *The Philosophical Review*. 772 (1), 1–25.

Vogler, Christopher. (1992). *The Writer's Journey: Mythic Structures for Storytellers and Screenwriters*. Studio City, CA: M. Wiese Productions.

Williams, Bernard. (2002). *Truth and Truthfulness: An Essay in Genealogy*. Princeton, NJ: Princeton University Press.

Williamson, Timothy. (1996). "Knowing and asserting". *Philosophical Review*. 105, 489–523.

17

THE ABSORBED VIEWER'S ACTIVITY

Ed S. Tan and Katalin E. Bálint

Introduction

Most people love to get lost in a story and be absorbed in the lives of fictional beings. It is safe to say that the feeling of being absorbed in a story is one of the best predictors of people's enjoyment and appreciation of a narrative. But what does it exactly mean to be absorbed in a narrative? In media psychology, as well as in empirical film and literary studies this experience of beholders has gained increased attention and systematic investigation. This is due to its essential role in the enjoyment, appreciation (Oliver & Bartsch, 2010), and persuasive power (Moyer-Gusé, 2008) of a narrative. Additional gratifications and effects of narrative absorption pointed at by researchers include perceived realism (Busselle & Bilandzic, 2008), making sense or meaning of a story, belief change (Fitzgerald & Green, 2017), disengagement from immorally acting characters, and changes in the self (Cohen & Tal-Or, 2017; Tal-Or & Tsfati, 2015). Film viewers and readers can experience the story world as if immersed in it and observing all narrative events from within. A common form of engagement with the story, however, occurs by experiencing the events "through the perspective of a protagonist" (Cohen & Tal-Or, 2017, p. 133). Fiction films present their viewers with a story world inhabited in the first place by characters acting with some psychological motivation. Absorption in a story world is a multi-dimensional concept and is largely driven by absorbed engagement with story characters. Thus, absorbed character engagement deserves dedicated study aiming at conceptual clarification and empirical validation of concepts. Moreover, an understanding of absorbed character engagement can help screenwriters and filmmakers in creating enjoyable and convincing stories.

DOI: 10.4324/9781003197911-22

An important step in understanding viewers' narrative absorption was the realization that viewers are not passive observers of projected stories but actually active co-creators of narratives. The idea of an active viewer is not new. In 1916, Hugo Münsterberg, the first film psychologist, held that the exceptionally vivid and intense experience that film audiences typically have is not caused by automated psychophysical responses to what is perceived as a replica of the real world. He proposed that it is viewers' engagement in constructive acts of imagination that enables the sense of absorption in a fictional world. This constructive view of the phenomenon of absorption in the film has not been followed-up for many decades. Research into media effects has until the 1990s neglected the film experience and the spectator's contribution to the very experienced.

Constructivism has received renewed interest in the psychology of film and cognitive film scholarship. For example, Bordwell (1985) discussed the viewer's cognitive share in the construction of fiction film story worlds. Adding to, or rather contradicting, mimetic (e.g., Eisenstein) or diegetic theories that assign minimal cognitive involvement to the mainly passive viewer, Bordwell (1985) calls in the Constructivist theory that deems the mere sensorial input insufficient for any world knowledge due to its ambiguous nature outside a contextual interpretation. As Bordwell puts it, "plainly, many cognitive activities are performed in making sense out of narrative." The viewer makes assumptions and inferences, uses memory, and hypothesizes, all against the backdrop of the real and narrative worlds (Bordwell, 1985, p. 37).

More recent findings in the psychology and empirical study of narrative fiction have furthered a detailed understanding of the audience's participation in the construction and experience of an imagined story world (Green et al., 2004; Kuijpers et al., 2017; Oatley, 1999, 2012). These authors point out how viewer activity is associated with an experience of absorbed engagement with the story world. Tan and Visch (2018) presented a process model of the viewer's playful construction of story worlds, and argued that viewers' constructive activities in absorbed film viewing seem to match with what professional filmmakers intend them to do and to feel.

This chapter gives an overview of the conceptualization of absorbed experience of film viewers, addressing the following questions: what is narrative absorption, and what is the nature of viewer activities underlying this state; what is absorbed engagement with characters; and what is the role of narrative film form and style in inducing absorbed character engagement?

What Is Narrative Absorption?

Narrative absorption is an experiential state emerging during exposure to and interaction with a story, and can be defined as a spontaneous temporary change in the state of consciousness due to an exceptionally intense awareness of the content of a fictional narrative. The experience of narrative absorption can be described by its intensity ranging from lower to higher level (full or complete) absorption. Narrative absorption is part of the broader category of aesthetic absorptions, a term used by empirical scholars in media psychology, empirical literary studies and cognitive film studies. Absorption can also be experienced in non-aesthetic activities, such as sports, cooking, conversations, and so on. However, narrative absorption as we define it here, is an experience emerging from the interaction with aesthetic narrative objects. It is closely related to terms, such as narrative engagement (Busselle & Bilandzic, 2009), transportation (Green et al., 2004), and identification (Cohen, 2001).[1] All of these terms refer to an intense emotional and cognitive engagement with a story and its characters. Story world absorption, our concept and focus in this chapter, refers to the absorption with the story content, which has to be distinguished from artefact absorption, that is the absorption with the form of the narrative (e.g., the way it was constructed (Kuijpers et al., 2017).

When viewers try to describe what narrative absorption feels like, they describe it as a journey from the outside world into the centre of the story world portrayed in the narrative, during which the boundaries of the outside world and the fictional world are blurred, and the self is being in the portrayed world (Bálint & Tan, 2015). The accounts of absorbed narrative experiences often contain words like *being pulled in, wrapped up, grabbed by, caught up in, captured by, sucked in by, tied in by, hooked into the story* (Bálint & Tan, 2015), suggesting that this experience is very dynamic, characterized by the interplay of internal and external forces. Viewers often feel a sense of being forcefully pulled into the story world by the power of the story or by the creator itself.

People differ in the extent to which they tend to get lost in a narrative. This trait is often referred to as trait absorption (Tellegen & Atkinson, 1974), transportability (Dal Cin et al., 2004) or narrative engageability (Bilandzic et al., 2019), and has to be differentiated from state narrative absorption, our focus in this chapter. Trait absorption has a strong impact on the level of state narrative absorption that people experience while following a narrative. However, there are narrative devices effectively engaging media consumers even with lower levels of trait absorption. These will be discussed in the section on film form and style.

Narrative absorption is a multidimensional concept that consists of several components that make up the experience. In the following, we briefly summarize Kuijpers' conceptualization (Kuijpers et al., 2014) focusing on four essential components: attentional focus, transportation, emotional engagement, and mental imagery. *Attentional focus* refers to a beholder's sense of prolonged concentration on the story, due to devoting their cognitive capacity to the narrative, as opposed to doing something else or multitasking. *Transportation* denotes the sensation of stepping into the fictional world from the real world (see also Green et al. 2004). In this process the reader or viewer does not lose contact with the actual world but experiences a partial relocation of the self into the story world. It is the sense of being in the story or being surrounded by the fictional story world. The component of *emotional engagement* is closely associated to empathy (Shen, 2010), but it has a narrower scope, i.e., it refers in particular to the bond readers have with characters. Emotional engagement is the state of having "feelings for or with characters, such as sympathy, and empathy, and identification" (Kuijpers et al., 2014, p. 93). Increased emotional engagement is associated with higher overall narrative absorption. When absorbed in a story, viewers often engage in *mental imagery*. This essential component of narrative absorption refers to the process of visualizing setting, characters, situations, and actions while reading or watching a story (Kuijpers et al., 2014). It is closely associated to the process of imagination that is relevant both for visual and textual narratives. Finally, *narrative comprehension*, the ease or fluency with which the viewer is able to understand the thread of the story, is also considered to be an important part of narrative absorption (Busselle & Bilandzic, 2008). However, recent theorization suggests that challenges to comprehension of actions, characters and settings in plots that are non-linear, puzzling, or ambiguous may also contribute to viewers' absorption (Kiss & Willemsen, 2017).

Substantiating the strictly theoretical concept, several self-report scales have been developed to measure narrative absorption along the dimensions of observer's focused attention, emotional engagement, vivid imagery (more applicable in the case of textual narrative) and transportation or presence, thus introducing multidimensionality in narrative absorption. A detailed overview of narrative absorption scales (i.e., Story World Absorption Scale (Kuijpers et al., 2014), Narrative Engagement Scale (Busselle & Bilandzic, 2008), Transportation Scale (Green et al., 2004), Absorption-like States Questionnaire (Kuiken & Douglas, 2017)) is offered in the chapter by Kuijpers et al. (2021).

What Is Absorbed Engagement with Characters?

Engagement with fictional characters on screen is found to be one of the most reliable predictors of the overall enjoyment of the story (Tal-Or & Cohen, 2010). Engaging with fictional characters, viewers build a mental model of each one in an effort to understand and evaluate their motivations, intentions and feelings, and attempt to grasp the (often complex) relationships among them. Understanding characters takes a certain amount of cognitive and emotional investment (Tan, 1996).[2] A special type of character engagement is called absorbed character engagement, which goes beyond the understanding of characters' minds. Absorbed character engagement is an experience characterized by the sense of having a deeply personal and meaningful bonding with the character (Bálint & Tan, 2019). It is a rather complex and dynamic experience, meaning that it emerges from the ongoing interaction among the textual features of the character, activated psychological processes, the steady personality traits and life experiences of the viewer, as well as the context in which the narrative experience is taking place.

In a previous interview study, we identified the most frequently mentioned phenomenological experiences making up absorbed character engagement (details of the study are reported in Bálint & Tan, 2019). In the following we briefly introduce the findings on four aspects of absorbed character engagement, namely mind modelling, self-character comparison, self-character merging, embodied simulation and parasocial relations.

Mind modelling is the psychological process through which people infer mental states in (real and fictional) others and in the self, often also referred to as mindreading, mentalization, or cognitive empathy.[3] Two main paths of how people understand each other are distinguished in psychological models of social cognition. One is a top-down process, called person perception, in which we apply readily available stereotypes and schemas, and draw inferences based on this prior knowledge. In the cinema, this is when viewers understand who the bad guy is just by their appearance, and assign features as evil, cruel, selfish to (most often) him. Immediate person perception comes about without actually having a lot of information on the character involved. Mind modelling is a bottom-up process, when viewers understanding of characters emerge from their focused attention, deep reflection and intense connection to that character. It is not driven by a preexisting schema but built on the complex narrative information shared with the viewer. The process of understanding the character's feelings, thoughts, wishes and wants is not just a byproduct of grasping the story as a whole. In contrast, it determines the pleasure the viewer derives from the entire story. Some scholars claim that mind modelling is the most important pleasure one can take from a narrative (Keen, 2010; Zunshine, 2006). It should be born in mind that individual viewer can differ considerably in their trait motivation for discussing and elaborating on the complexities of fictional characters' inner lives, as several studies have shown (Carpenter et al., 2016; Davis, 1983).

In our study, people reported an experience we called "enforced access to a character's subjectivity." It is when the beholder feels that the story overwhelms them with details of an antipathic character's psychological perspective to such an extent that they have no choice but empathize with said character. Viewers have to make an active attempt to create an optimal distance from the characters. Enforced character engagement may be experienced while watching the TV shows *Breaking Bad* and *You*, or reading the book *Lolita*. In these stories, the morally ambiguous characters are presented in a way that poses a challenge for the viewer or reader to disengage, and can't help but cheer for them every now and then. This push-pull dynamic is an important aspect of absorbed character engagement and narrative absorption in general (Bálint & Tan, 2015).

While building mental models of characters, beholders often compare characters (or the constructed image of them) with their own self-image. This self-character comparison can be about explicit or implicit characteristics of characters or about their life situation. Self-character comparison is closely associated with personal relevance and self-referencing (Kuzmičová & Bálint, 2019). In order to compare self and character, viewers need to activate self-relevant information in their minds, increasing their personal investment in the fictional story. Viewers not only compare themselves on observable features, but they also contemplate how they would act in the situation the character is in. In general, perceived similarity enhances absorbed character engagement, whereas perceived dissimilarity can either lead to a sense of detachment from the character, or just the opposite, a desire to be similar to the character, called wishful similarity or wishful identification (Hoffner & Buchanan, 2005). These responses are not only elicited by superhero or James Bond type of characters, but also by any kind of character who displays a feature a viewer finds admirable. In absorbed character engagement, observers sometimes have the sense that they enact the desired characteristic of the character (e.g., they feel more relaxed and confident when reading about a relaxed character). Our study demonstrated (Bálint & Tan, 2019) that self-character comparison processes can bring about extraordinary and profound emotional connections to characters.

In absorbed character engagement, viewers sometimes reach such a high level of absorption that they experience a sense of self-character merging. The sense of self-character merging can be characterized by the viewers' experience of lacking boundaries between self and character, as well as experiencing emotions identical to the character's emotions. The notion of self-character merging is closely related to the concept of identification (Slater et al., 2014), entailing the internalization of the character's feelings, thoughts, and motivations. Oatley (1999) notes that in identification story recipients may "become" the character. In extraordinary cases, these shared emotions can extrapolate to the actual self of the viewer (e.g., being scared of the character turns into a scare of oneself) creating a feeling of close proximity (Bálint & Tan, 2019). However, absorbed character engagement is not a constant and static feeling of proximity, rather a dynamic process in which viewers can experience a fluctuation from extreme closeness to distancing and vice versa. Importantly, in absorbed character engagement distancing does not correlate with a lack of care or indifference, but rather with need for self-protection and differentiation evading too much closeness.

The experience of self-character merging is often accompanied by embodied responses. Beholders can experience a strong bodily reaction in response to stories and these embodied responses are essential parts of their absorption experience. According to Hess and Fischer (2013), there are two kinds of embodied responses. The first is mimicry, which consists of automated resonance processes due to automatic motor responses, matching perception with action, resulting in imitation of the non-verbal display of another person (Matched Motor Hypothesis). Movements, especially ones in the face, are immediately copied. The resulting expression is independent of appraisals and intentions on the part of the observer or those of the expresser. This kind of mimicry is, we believe, part and parcel of responding to popular action films. Additionally, Hess and Fischer have proposed a more complex form of mimicry involving an understanding of intentions and emotions in perspective of a social context by the expresser (in our case: the viewer). Emotional mimicry, as they call it, presupposes the engagement of the observer with the expresser. We propose that emotional mimicry both makes for and results from a unique and deep intimacy with the character. Understanding of the situational context in the case of fiction film implies that the fictionality of the scene is part of the viewer's appraisal. For example, in our research, a film viewer reported "I felt the excitement the boy was feeling, and I was wishing I could be there and wishing it was real. You are breathing with them and you're just getting real excited, I think I felt what the characters were feeling so to speak" (Bálint & Tan, 2019, p. 219).

Parasocial relation to characters is a key component of absorbed character engagement. Viewers very often perceive fictional characters as real people with whom they can interact as they would do with a friend, while being aware of their fictional nature. A typical indicator of a parasocial relationship is when viewers address the characters directly, talking to them, shouting at them, trying to warn them, and so on. Reports of a sense of friendship with the character or the author, or a desire to have a friend like the character or the author were very common in our interview study (Bálint & Tan, 2019). Importantly, parasocial interaction is not always valued positively, but can result in irritation and feelings of antipathy towards the character. In absorbed character engagement, these negative feelings arise as a result of deep caring for the character. For example, viewers can feel strong irritation when a character makes the wrong choices in life, because he or she would deserve better. Experiencing a parasocial relationship with characters, viewers are often confronted with their inability to control the course of narrative events. This can be a very emotional realization, as a parasocial relationship comes with feelings of responsibility towards the character, and the desire to change the events of the fictional story to the benefit of the character.

As a natural consequence of a parasocial relationship, separation from a character can elicit a strong feeling of loss and bereavement. This phenomenon is often discussed in the context of parasocial breakup (Cohen, 2004). Beholders can experience strong negative feelings when their beloved character dies or when the story comes to an end. Relatedly, in absorbed character engagement, beholders maintain a mental relationship with characters even when the story ended. Through this prolonged connection, fictional characters can become part of the everyday life of beholders. One of our participants referred to his prolonged connection to the main character of the film *Moulin Rouge*, and how he was thinking of him while he was struggling in his own romantic relationships.[4]

Absorbed character engagement and parasocial relationships in particular can bring about the most profound experiences of self-affirmation in viewers. In our study, viewers talked about a sense of acknowledgment, of being seen, understood and empathized with. An experience that comes with great satisfaction and the feeling of belonging. A character who is like us, whose struggles are like ours, who goes through similar life situations does more than only serve as an example to vicariously learn from. The character also shares with the viewer the feeling of being recognized: "I am seen – someone knows me, someone wrote a story about me."

Aspects of absorbed engagement with characters as just discussed constitute the complex and deeply personal experience of absorbed character engagement. The list is not exhaustive, and not all aspects are present all the time during a narrative experience. Rather, absorbed character engagement is a dynamic experience, characterized by clashes of internal and external forces, resulting in the oscillation of feeling proximity vs. distancing in viewers.

What Is the Role of Narrative Film Form and Style in Absorbed Character Engagement?

Narrative film form structures the presentation of a central character in conflict. Film style lends rhythm and depth to that presentation, determining the concrete visual and auditory qualities of the ongoing presentation. Narrative formal elements that cue viewers' perception of engagement with, and absorption in film characters are characterization and character development. We first illustrate narrative conventions of characterization and development in operation in the three prototypical cinematic genres: comedy, action, and drama, and then highlight the contribution of film style to absorbed character engagement.

Film comedy has numerous subgenres, from slapstick to romantic comedy. The narrative structure of comedy hinges on surprise and comic suspense, or expectation, and the presentation of comic events. A popular category is gross-out movies. They present gross actions, evoke disgust showing bodily fluids, and deal with taboos, such as sex. The teen sex comedy Blockers tells the adventures of three parents whose daughters have a sex pact; they will lose their virginity at prom night. Gross scenes ensue as they try to track the girls and "rescue" them. For example, the parents wind up in a peepshow of sorts when they inadvertently come to watch one of the girls' boyfriend's parents involved in lustful lovemaking, and enjoy it. Later on, the parents are admitted at an afterparty where the girls are, only if they pass a butt chugging contest. By accident, the bodily fluids of one of the dads splashes full in the face of the other dad. The fun of comedy is not only in gross scenes, but also in more profound subversion of cultural norms. Blockers is a girl-centric satire of parental obsession with their daughters' sexuality. The perspective of crampedly overprotective parents is taken, and their attempts to police the daughters are ridiculed. The viewer's awareness of the parent's norm – no "premature" intercourse – has a central place in mind modelling, rendering it top-down. The parents may be perceived as driven by the norm, the girls as escaping it. The fun is in understanding each character's particular way of dealing with it. Self-character comparisons, too, hinge around the norm. Because the girls are setting a new norm – sexual autonomy, wishful identification with them seems easier than with the poor parents, especially for a young female audience. Merging of the viewer's self with the girls may occur especially at the emotional denouement of the film, when the girls step into sexual adulthood, each in their own and self-determined way. The emotional mimicry involved contrasts with the primary mimicry viewers will exhibit in response to the gross-out scenes. The film's typical audience may develop parasocial feelings of friendship towards the girls, and perhaps towards the filmmaker because of shared views of female sexuality. Finally, this audience may find fun in the subversion of a more profound cultural norm. Blockers reverses the norm of teen sex comedy as set, e.g., in American Pie: Sex-hungry male adolescents succeed in getting rid of their loser-status virginity. The typical audience of blockers may enjoy downward comparison with American Pie characters and their fans.

Action films present spectacular events, and the plot develops to absorb the viewer in the protagonist's actions, aiming at concrete goals. Sympathy is high from the start due to the hero's moral stance, immediately recognized by viewers (Zillmann, 2000). Admiration or awe dominates engagement with action heroes or heroines, due to their extraordinary capabilities and often surprising perception of a situation's affordances , according to Lankjaer and Sun Jensen (2019). These authors present an example sequence from "First Blood" featuring Rambo. Rambo has found shelter behind a tree while being shot at by a police officer from a helicopter, as shown in one widely framed moving shot. Then he is shown in medium close-up looking down and reaching out with an arm, followed by a close-up of picking up a stone. "Obviously, Rambo perceives what the stone can afford before the audience does but the audience may perceive what it affords – throwing it as a missile against the helicopter – before the villain knows and before the action is executed" (p. 279). In the example we see an unfolding of affordances, first perceived by the hero, then by viewers, and then by the villain. When viewers come to share the perception with the hero, they recognize the hero's superiority and admire him. They can also enjoy the shared superiority vis-à-vis the villain. The result may be wishful identification, especially in a young male audience.

In action films, automated embodied simulation and perception of action and plan schemata suffice for following the action and the protagonist's reactions. However, some mind modelling may be required. For example, Rambo's skilful action can be explained by his extraordinary combat and survival instinct developed in the Vietnam war. Being a troubled veteran proves to be a blessing in disguise. The sympathy for Rambo as a misunderstood veteran develops early in the film. Over the complications, sympathy may increase along with the obstacles and complications met by the protagonist in reaching goals. The effect can be that viewers engage in parasocial interactions, as sympathetic witnesses commenting on actions. These efforts can, but do not necessarily give way to profound mental imagery of the hero's or heroine's mental and emotional life. In the example provided it could be the imagination of being capable to restore justice. A more complete wishful identification with the protagonist may result in the end.

Drama develops characters in more depth and detail. Drama characters respond to events that have psychological meaning in the first place, like conflict involving significant others, or the self. Think of relationships in jeopardy with lovers, parents, children and friends, and dilemmas they pose to characters. Characters are less immediately enjoyable than in comedy and action. They develop across the story. Difficulties and internal conflicts they face are more existential than in action films. They can be appreciated for their vulnerabilities or moral courage. Oskar Schindler, the protagonist in Schindler's List (1993) develops from an opportunist factory owner in Poland who hires Jews from the Nazis as cheap labour, to a saviour of lives risking his own. Moreover, drama films can elaborate the perspective of main and secondary characters to highlight how they perceive situations. Oskar Schindler is gradually won for his accountant Stern's project to save lives by enlisting a multitude of Jewish workers as "essential." Witnessing the violent evacuation of the Krakow ghetto (featuring the girl in the red jacket) appears decisive for Schindler's conviction to save lives. In the end he buys lives. Elaborate perspectivization has been shown to increase identification with characters (De Graaf et al., 2012). We would argue that it can in particular scaffold self-character comparison and merging with the character. Viewers of Schindler's List may wonder what it is like to have the fate of your personnel in your hands, and how much they themselves would put at stake in the confrontations with his opponent SS-officer Goetz who is in charge of the "final solution" in Krakow. The development of Schindler may be paralleled by the viewer's comparison shifting from downward critical to upward admiring. Outcomes of drama characters' actions and experiences can be poignant, bittersweet or even tragic, and make viewers reflect on their meaning (Oliver & Bartsch, 2010). See Schindler's farewell address to the community of his workers when he leaves after the liberation. [Taking a Nazi brooch of honour from his lapel]: "This pin. Two people. This is gold. Two more people. He would have given me two for it, at least one. One more person. A person, Stern. For this. I could have gotten one more person ... and I didn't! And I ... I didn't!"

Drama characters exposed to conflict with significant others explore their relations, and their own place in it. In the process, they may find the meaning of their relationship. Schindler's collaboration with Stern matures into trust and affection that expands to all his workers. Finally, drama frames conflict between and within characters in a specific historical or social context. Schindler's List is known as a lesson on the Holocaust, taught through dramatic means. Absorbedly engaged with Schindler, viewers may appreciate both the possibility and exceptionality of a single individual's resistance to an utterly destructive system. In all, the conventions of drama as a narrative form allow for absorbed engagement.

Characterization in comedy, action and drama genres is subject to genre conventions. Characterization in art films is non-generic (Bordwell, 1985). Bordwell signals the ambiguity of characterization in this mode of narration. In line with this ambiguity, Bálint and Tan observed dynamic and conflicting approach-avoidance tendencies as part of absorption with art film characters. Complex and possibly abstract themes with trans- cendent meaning are prom- inent in art films (Grodal, 2009), and they support reflection-based character construction. Moreover, art films focus on characters' experiences in an inner rather than an external world. In Grodal's account, engagement with art film characters even involves a blocking of emotional responses to a character's experiences in an exter- nal world.

In sum, the viewer's engagement with characters is associated with formal narrative parameters like depth of characterization and character development. Increasing depth in subsequently discussed genres comedy, action and drama is associated with rising levels of engagement. The higher levels of engagement can imply absorbed engagement. Art films allow for engagement consisting of reflection and complex emotional interaction with characters.

Film style can moderate the potential impact of film form on character engagement, making for more or less absorbed forms. However, it would be overly simplistic to list any direct "effects" of specific stylistic options in cre- ating engaged absorption. Recent empirical research, in which a larger num- ber of film-technological parameters were analysed, suggests that there may not be any singular cinematic style conducive to empathy with characters

(Lankhuizen et al., 2020). These researchers found instead that complex patterned use of many parameters may influence a variety of factors of empathy. One may think of the reduction of perceived distance to characters through combinations of shot scale and face depiction, or the balancing of arousing image features with levels of visual complexity.

Perhaps the basic principle is that engaging film style enhances the impact of engaging film forms, by managing the viewer's attention to either details of the story world, or of the film artefact.

Continuity film style is known to facilitate smooth comprehension of character action and reaction, and goals, plans and reactions. This style generally undergirds smooth story world construction operating in the background of film narration, rather rarely becoming salient to viewers (Bordwell, 1985). Continuity style tends to control the viewer's attention to the effect that at any moment of a sequence or scene: exactly those details are selectively perceived that matter most for the course of story-action, to the exclusion of numerous other on-screen details. For example, movement direction or sound in one shot can cue the viewers' gaze to the portion of the screen in the next shot where story-action relevant details are shown (Smith, 2012). In this example, the gaze is irresistibly attracted to details that the narration deems "must see." Importantly, the cut between the shots, as well as the guidance of one's gaze are not noticed by viewers. The cues are perceptually low-level film-stylistic devices only noticeable through purposeful analytic inspection that is not part of regular film audiences' viewing attitudes.

The power of low-level feature control of attentional shifts has inspired Loschky et al. (2015) to speak of the "tyranny of film." They start from research findings suggesting individual viewers of a scene gaze at exactly the same portions of the screen at exactly the same time. Remarkable degrees of inter-viewer synchronization of visual attention to story-relevant details have also been established in studies of localizations of brain activity in film (Hasson et al., 2003). Applying the insights on stylistic control of viewer attention to the perception of characters, we could say that stylistic devices of acting, mise-en-scène, photography, and editing, as well as of sound and music amplify or finetune selective attention to story details already selected by the narration. The selected details matter for engagement with a character, and a fortiori for absorbed engagement. For example, engagement with the dramatic lead character known to struggle with an internal conflict, can become absorbing when mise-en-scène and photography slow down the pace of action. Actors sitting still or moving slowly, low cutting rate and minimal camera movement may give viewers time to imaginatively empathize, identify and share in the conflict.

The result of more or less invisible stylistic boosting of attention to story details that matter for perception and feeling of the inner life of characters, is optimal absorption of the viewer in the story world. It would seem that a

FIGURE 17.1 The Immigrant (2013; Dir. James Gray; writers James Gray & Ric Menello; DOP Marius Khondji), final shot. Note: filmmaker Cameron Beyl comments: "The last shot in particular is a knockout, and without giving too much away, uses both a window and a mirror to depict both of the protagonists facing the world before them, armed with new discoveries about themselves and each other."

conspicuous use of style detracts attention from the story world and disrupt engagement with it. We argue however that film style can be foregrounded, and yet serve absorption by characters (see also Bálint et al., 2016). As an example, consider a common figure of style, the use of mirrors for dramatic scenes that are telling of character fates and feelings.

Hanich's (2017) analysis of complex mirror shots in art and mainstream films is most instructive of foregrounding effects. Figure 17.1 shows the last shot where, according to Hanich "Ewa Cybulska (Marion Cotillard) sails away with her sister into freedom, Bruno Weiss (Joaquin Phoenix) walks into a confined, narrow world, symbolised by the constricting composition with various lattices and frames-within-frames-within-frames" (p. 148). The shot is foregrounding in that it presents us an image that poses an immediate challenge to perception. A proper perception entails differentiation of three surfaces, from left to right a wall, a window, and a mirror. Subsequently, it can be noticed that the characters seemingly leave the scene in the same direction, i.e., from screen, but in fact move away from one another. This perception may come with a flash of meaningful insight: the characters part definitively. It may be that some viewers will be torn apart in their embodied simulation of the two characters leaving in opposite directions, exactly because it follows on contemplation of the artefact. We argue that the foregrounding effect pays off: Perhaps the cognitive effort of comprehending and contemplating the shot is more than compensated for by the meaning it adds to characterization (opposites and yet connected) and character development (freedom vs. confinement). Engagement with the two main characters in this final scene is already high because of the film's form, an ending scene answering the questions we the spectators have about their destination. We hypothesize that the foregrounding photography and mise-en-scène can contribute to the viewer's higher absorption in the artefact ("the shot is a knock-out") as well as in the story world. Absorbed engagement is with characters in the first place. ("I am happy for Ewa, and Bruno gets what he deserves. But there is a tragedy to this.") To conclude, absorbed engagement is not only elicited by narrative and visual fluency, but also by challenging scenes and images. The latter requires an extra effort and cognitive-emotional investment from the viewer, that leads to a deeper level of absorption.

Hanich in his analysis of the final shot of *The Immigrant* signals the viewer's tendency to oscillate between views of what is before and behind the camera, and the screen frame. The latter view is a view of the film as an artefact, the former two are views of the story world. Oscillation between the former and the latter views imply transitions in viewer attention to story world and artefact, perhaps a frequent effect of foregrounding film style. Elsewhere (Kuijpers et al., 2017), we proposed an essentially dynamic conception of absorption. When watching a film, viewers exhibit a trade-off between attention to story world details and attention to the make-up of the artefact (Tan et al., 2017). At one moment, for example during a sequence or shot, they may attend to the event ignoring how it has been staged, photographed etc., or reversely, attend completely to its film-technological make-up. In the former case the effect is absorption in the story world, in the latter absorption in the artefact. Alternatively, their attention can be divided between story world and artefact, resulting in absorption in both, with possibly lesser intensities. Story world and artefact-absorption may oscillate not only within a film scene, but also between scenes or parts of an entire film. We propose, in line with the argument on absorption in general, that character engagement is also a dynamic state. It fluctuates over a film, from distanced following of a lead's plight to absorbed interactions of the viewer's self with the character in the story as a quasi-live world, and from passive neglect of characterization procedures and techniques to active co-construction. The proposal is consistent with earlier conceptualizations of emotional flow and identification, respectively, by Nabi and Green (2015) who highlighted the narrative experience as a series of emotional shifts, and Cohen (2001) who noted the temporariness and fleeting nature of identification. As attention required for absorption is cued by narration and style, absorption in characters is in large part film-driven. Film style adds to, or moderates depth of absorption in characters provided by plot and character development in the story. And the dynamics of film style over an entire film or within its segments lend rhythm to character absorption. However, recent studies showed that individual differences among spectators related to character absorption abound (Bilandzic & Busselle, 2011; Bilandzic et al., 2019).

Conclusion

Absorbed character engagement is a major component of absorption in the story world of a film, and thus a form of narrative aesthetic absorption. The present research on character engagement leads us to conclude that absorbed character engagement is involvement with a character that feels more intimate and intense relative to more basic varieties of character engagement. These basic varieties are associated with sympathy based on liking and similarity, especially of the schematic moral kind. In contrast, self-character merging, the most intense sense of absorption in a character, is associated with the viewers' profound emotional understanding of the character, to the point of recognizing their selves in the character. Characterization, character development and perspectivization are the formal narrative techniques that engender engagement with characters, and possibly absorbed engagement. Film style can further boost the engaging potential of character narration. Classical film style can amplify engagement to the point of absorbed self-character merging. Foregrounding film style may inhibit absorption because of its prominence. However, it can also function to induce absorption in the character. Absorbed character engagement is a dynamic state, fluctuating over the duration of a film. Its occurrence is sometimes paired with absorption in the artefact.

Although progress has been made in our understanding of the seeming magic of absorption in characters, and especially in the division of labour between film-viewer and film narrator, there is a lot about it that is as yet ill-understood. Firstly, more research is needed into stable viewer characteristics that contribute to absorbed character engagement. Transportability has been identified as an antecedent of absorption (Bilandzic & Busselle, 2011), but generally there is a paucity of research into viewer correlates of absorption (Cohen & Tal-Or, 2017, p. 146). One can think of trait absorption (Tellegen & Atkinson, 1974), and trait empathy (Davis, 1983), but also of gender, age, educational profiles and levels. Life histories, as well as the personal relevance of the story (Kuzmičová & Bálint, 2019) appear to play a role in absorption. Secondly, more research is needed to assess the absorbed character engagement potential of various categories of film. Do art films stand out in affording self-character merging due to foregrounding strength? Or do mainstream drama films surpass art films in this respect because of their more engaging character development, and more efficient use of foregrounding? And last but not least, filmmakers and film scholars are in need of a better understanding of how absorbed character experiences can contribute to prolonged sense making of a film. Oliver et al. (2017) recently argued that meaningfulness of narratives holds a two-way relationship with absorption. On the one hand, absorbed character engagement, and in particular self-character comparison and self-character merging help viewers to reflect on questions of life addressed by films more effectively. On the other, meaningful contents such as transcendent themes of a film narrative guide the viewer in recognizing and being moved by existential dilemmas that characters face, and so become absorbed in the character's inner life. More research is needed to explain how the viewer's comprehension of a film's thematic meaning interacts with character engagement and its absorbed manifestations.

Notes

1 For an overview see Bilandzic and Busselle (2017).
2 Tan (1996) offers a few clear illustrations: "As a viewer I do not only entertain the illusion that I am present in the scene – the diegetic effect –; I may even feel that, to a greater or lesser degree, the adventures of the protagonist are actually happening to me. [...]. In La Peau Douce (1964) we fill in Nicole's thoughts after Lachenay has turned his back on her in the street in order to keep their love secret. We have a different experience when Reuven is struck full in the face by a baseball in The Chosen (1981); we almost feel as if we ourselves are the victim. And watching King Kong (1933), one sympathizes with both the girl and the huge gorilla as the animal majestically undergoes his fate, amid a rain of bullets fired by stupid, insensitive human beings. In describing such experiences, people often speak of identification or empathy" (p. 153).
3 North American readers/scholars will most likely associate the concepts of mind modelling and mind reading with computational approaches to cognitive science/ cognitive studies (e.g., Rescorla, 2021).
4 See further examples in Balint and Tan (2019).

References

Bálint, K., Hakemulder, F., Kuijpers, M. M., Doicaru, M. M. & Tan, E. S. (2016). Reconceptualizing foregrounding. *Scientific Study of Literature*, 6 (2), 176–207. https://doi.org/10.1075/ssol.6.2.02bal

Bálint K. & Tan, E. (2019). Engagement with Characters from Social Cognition Responses to the Experience with Fictional Constructions. In J. Riis & A. Taylor (Eds.), *Screening characters: Theories of character in film, television, and interactive media* (1st ed., pp. 209–230). Routledge.

Bálint, K. & Tan, E. S. (2015). "It feels like there are hooks inside my chest": The construction of narrative absorption experiences using image schemata. *Projections*, 9 (2). https://doi.org/10.3167/proj.2015.090205

Bilandzic, H. & Busselle, R. W. (2011). Enjoyment of films as a function of narrative experience, perceived realism and transportability. *Communications*, 36 (1), 29–50. https://doi.org/10.1515/comm.2011.002

Bilandzic, H. & Busselle, R. W. (2017). Exploring the Conceptual Boundaries of Narrative Engagement. In F. Hakemulder, M. M. Kuijpers, E. S. Tan, K. Bálint, & M. M. Doicaru (Eds.), *Narrative absorption* (pp. 11–27). John Benjamins Publishing Company. https://doi.org/10.1075/lal.27

Bilandzic, H., Sukalla, F., Schnell, C., Hastall, M. R. & Busselle, R. W. (2019). The narrative engageability scale: A multidimensional trait measure for the propensity to become engaged in a story. *International Journal of Communication. 13*, 32.

Bordwell, D. (1985). *Narration in the fiction film*. Methuen.

Busselle, R. & Bilandzic, H. (2008). Fictionality and perceived realism in experiencing stories: A model of narrative comprehension and engagement. *Communication Theory, 18* (2), 255–280. https://doi.org/10.1111/j.1468-2885.2008.00322.x

Busselle, R. & Bilandzic, H. (2009). Measuring narrative engagement. *Media Psychology, 12* (4), 321–347. https://doi.org/10.1080/15213260903287259

Carpenter, J. M., Green, M. C. & Vacharkulksemsuk, T. (2016). Beyond perspective-taking: Mind-reading motivation. *Motivation and Emotion. 40* (3), 358–374.

Cohen, J. (2001). Defining identification: A theoretical look at the identification of audiences with media characters. *Mass Communication & Society. 4,* 245–264.

Cohen, J. (2004). Parasocial break-up from favorite television characters: The role of attachment styles and relationship intensity. *Journal of Social and Personal Relationships. 21* (2), 187–202.

Cohen, J. & Tal-Or, N. (2017). Antecedents of Identification: Character, Text, and Audiences. In F. Hakemulder, M. M. Kuijpers, E. S. Tan, K. Bálint & M. M. Doicaru (Eds.), *Narrative absorption* (Vol. 27, pp. 133–153). John Benjamins.

Dal Cin, S., Zanna, M. P. & Fong, G. T. (2004). Narrative Persuasion and Overcoming Resistance. Narrative Persuasion and Overcoming Resistance. In E. S. Knowles & J. A. Linn (Eds.), *Resistance and persuasion* (pp. 175–191). Lawrence Erlbaum Associates Publishers.

Davis, M. H. (1983). Measuring individual differences in empathy: Evidence for a multidimensional approach. *Journal of Personality and Social Psychology; Journal of Personality and Social Psychology. 44* (1), 113.

De Graaf, A., Hoeken, H., Sanders, J. & Beentjes, J. W. (2012). Identification as a mechanism of narrative persuasion. *Communication Research. 39* (6), 802–823.

Fitzgerald, K. S. & Green, M. C. (2017). Narrative Persuasion: Effects of Transporting Stories on Attitudes, Beliefs, and Behaviors. In F. Hakemulder, M. M. Kuijpers, E. S. Tan, K. Bálint & M. M. Doicaru (Eds.), *Narrative absorption*, pp. 49–67. Amsterdam: John Benjamins.

Green, M. C., Brock, T. C. & Kaufman, G. F. (2004). Understanding media enjoyment: The role of transportation into narrative worlds. *Communication Theory. 14* (4), 311–327. https://doi.org/10.1111/j.1468-2885.2004.tb00317.x

Grodal, T. (2009). *Embodied visions: Evolution, emotion, culture, and film*. Oxford University Press.

Hanich, J. (2017). Reflecting on Reflections: Cinema's Complex Mirror Shots. In: M. Beugnet, A. Cameron & A. Fetveit (Eds.), *Indefinite visions: Cinema and the attractions of uncertainty: Indefinite visions: Üinema and the attractions of uncertainty* (pp. 131–156). Edinburgh University Press.

Hasson, U., Nir, Y., Levy, I., Fuhrmann, G. & Malach, R. (2003). Intersubject synchronization of cortical vision during natural vision. *Science. 303,* 1634–1640.

Hess, U. & Fischer, A. (2013). Emotional mimicry as social regulation. *Personality and Social Psychological Review. 17* (2), 142–157.

Hoffner, C. & Buchanan, M. (2005). Young adults' wishful identification with television characters: The role of perceived similarity and character attributes. *Media Psychology, 7* (4), 325–351. https://doi.org/10.1207/S1532785XMEP0704_2

Keen, S. (2010). *Empathy and the novel*. Oxford University Press. http://www.amazon.com/Empathy-Novel-Suzanne-Keen/dp/0199740496/ref=sr_1_1?ie=UTF8&qid=1444043952&sr=8-1&keywords=empathy+and+the+novel

Kiss, M. & Willemsen, S. (2017). *Impossible puzzle films*. Edinburgh University Press. https://doi.org/10.3366/edinburgh/9781474406727.003.0003

Krutnik, F. & Neale, S. (2006). *Popular film and television comedy*. Taylor & Francis. https://books.google.nl/books?id=wMyHAgAAQBAJ

Kuijpers, M., Hakemulder, F., Bálint K., Doicaru, M. & Tan, E. S. (2017). Towards a New Understanding of Absorbing Reading Experiences. In M. Kuijpers, F. Hakemulder, K. Bálint M. Doicaru, & E. Tan (Eds.), *Narrative absorption*. John Benjamins Pub. Co.

Kuijpers, M. M., Douglas, S. & Bálint, K. (2021). Narrative Absorption: An Overview. In D. Kuiken & A. M. Jacobs (Eds.), *Handbook of empirical literary studies* (pp. 279–304). De Gruyter. https://doi.org/10.1515/9783110645958-012

Kuijpers, M. M., Hakemulder, F., Tan, E. S. & Doicaru, M. M. (2014). Story World Absorption Scale. In *PsycTESTS dataset*. American Psychological Association (APA). https://doi.org/10.1037/t52695-000

Kuiken, D. & Douglas, S. (2017). Forms of absorption that facilitate the aesthetic and explanatory effects of literary reading. *Narrative Absorption*. 27, 219–252.

Kuzmičová, A. & Bálint, K. (2019). Personal relevance in story reading: A research review. *Poetics Today*. 40 (3), 429–451.

Lankhuizen, T., Bálint, K. E., Savardi, M., Konijn, E. A., Bartsch, A. & Benini, S. (2020). Shaping film: A quantitative formal analysis of contemporary empathy-eliciting Hollywood cinema. *Psychology of Aesthetics, Creativity, and the Arts*. https://doi.org/10.1037/ACA0000356

Lankjaer, B. & Sun Jensen, C. (2019). Action and Affordances. The Action hero's Skilled and Surprising Use of the Environment. In J. Riis & A. Taylor (Eds.). *Screening characters* (pp. 266–283). Routledge.

Loschky, L. C., Larson, A. M., Magliano, J. P. & Smith, T. J. (2015). What would jaws do? The tyranny of film and the relationship between gaze and higher-level narrative comprehension. *PLoS ONE*. https://doi.org/10.1371/journalpone0142474

Moyer-Gusé, E. (2008). Toward a theory of entertainment persuasion: Explaining the persuasive effects of entertainment-education messages. *Communication Theory*, 18 (3), 407–425. https://doi.org/10.1111/j.1468-2885.2008.00328.x

Münsterberg, H. (1916). *The photoplay*. Dover.

Nabi, R. L., & Green, M. C. (2015). The role of a narrative's emotional flow in promoting persuasive outcomes. *Media Psychology*, 18(2), 137–162.

Oatley, K. (1999). Why fiction may be twice as true as fact: Fiction as cognitive and emotional simulation. *Review of General Psychology*. 3 (2), 101.

Oatley, K. (2012) *The passionate muse. Exploring emotion in stories*. Oxford University Press.

Oliver, M. B. & Bartsch, A. (2010). Appreciation as audience response: Exploring entertainment gratifications beyond hedonism. *Human Communication Research*, 36 (1), 53–81. https://doi.org/10.1111/j.1468-2958.2009.01368.x

Oliver, M. B., Ferchaud, A., Yang, C., Huangc, Y. & Baileyd, E. (2017). Absorption and Meaningfulness: Examining the Relationship between Eudaimonic media Use and Engagement. In M. Kuijpers, F. Hakemulder, K. Bálint M. Doicaru, & E. Tan (Eds.), *Narrrative absorption*, pp. 253–269. John Benjamins Pub. Co.

Shen, L. (2010). Mitigating psychological reactance: The role of message-induced empathy in persuasion. *Human Communication Research*, 36 (3), 397–422. https://doi.org/10.1111/j.1468-2958.2010.01381.x

Slater, M. D., Johnson, B. K., Cohen, J., Comello, M. L. G. & Ewoldsen, D. R. (2014). Temporarily expanding the boundaries of the self: Motivations for entering the story world and implications for narrative effects. *Journal of Communication. 64* (3), 439–455.

Smith, T. J. (2012) The attentional theory of cinematic continuity. *Projections* 6(1), 1–27.

Tal-Or, N. & Tsfati, Y. (2015). Does the co-viewing of sexual material affect rape myth acceptance? The role of the co-Viewer's reactions and gender. *Communication Research.* https://doi.org/10.1177/0093650215595073

Tal-Or, N. & Cohen, J. (2010). Understanding audience involvement: Conceptualizing and manipulating identification and transportation. *Poetics, 38* (4), 402–418. http://www.sciencedirect.com/science/article/pii/S0304422X10000355

Tan, E. S. (1996). *Emotion and the structure of narrative film.* Erlbaum.

Tan, E. S, Doicaru, M. M., Bálint, K., & Kuijpers, M. M. (2017). Into film. Does absorption in a movie's story world pose a paradox? In F. Hakemulder, M. M. Kuijpers, E. S. Tan, K. Bálint, & M. M. Doicaru (Eds.), *Narrative absorption* (pp. 98–118). John Benjamins.

Tan, E. S. H., & Visch, V. (2018). Co-imagination of fictional worlds in film viewing. *Review of General Psychology, 22*(2), 230–244.

Tellegen, A. & Atkinson, G. (1974). Openness to absorbing and self-altering experiences ("absorption"), a trait related to hypnotic susceptibility. *Journal of Abnormal Psychology, 83* (3), 268–277. https://doi.org/10.1037/h0036681

Zillmann, D. (2000). Basal Morality in Drama Appreciation. In I. Bondebjerg (Ed.), *Moving images, culture, and the mind* (pp. 53–63). University of Luton Press.

Zunshine, L. (2006). *Why we read fiction: Theory of mind and the novel.* Ohio State University Press.

18

NARRATIVE EVENTS

Segmenting, Parsing, and Story Comprehension

Catalina Iricinschi

A Brief Preamble

We see the world in motion. As we actively look at the world, we interact with our surrounding environment – never immutable[1] – through movement. Despite the saccadic movement of our eyes looking at a world, itself in motion, the impression that our visual experience affords is one of smooth continuity, a rather coherent flow, not a cadenced sequence of perceptual bits.

> I look at the landscape, my gaze ranges over it, I see all sorts of distinct and indistinct movement; this impresses itself sharply on me, that is quite hazy. After all, how completely ragged what we see can appear! And now look at all that can be meant by "description of what is seen".
>
> *(Wittgenstein, 1997, p. II, xi)*

How *do* we actually look at the world?

The neurologist Oliver Sacks (1995) recounts the case of a patient who regained sight after being blind from early childhood until late adulthood. Sacks describes the moment following the patient's surgery: "The dramatic moment stayed vacant, grew longer, sagged. No cry ('I can see!') burst from [his] lips. He seemed to be staring blankly, bewildered, without focusing, at the surgeon, who stood before him, still holding the bandages. Only when the surgeon spoke – saying 'Well?' – did a look of recognition cross [his] face. [He] told me later that in this first moment he had no idea of what he was seeing. There was light, there was movement, there was color, all mixed up, all meaningless, a blur" (pp. 113–114). Sacks comments: "We are not *given* the world: we *make* our world through incessant experience,

DOI: 10.4324/9781003197911-23

categorization, memory, reconnection" (Sacks, 1995, p. 114; my emphasis). The world around us does not present itself in predetermined organized patterns. As we interact with the environment, we translate the raw input into consistent "motifs" that enable comprehension; we impose boundaries on the indistinct continuity of visual input thus defining stand-alone meaningful units, static objects, moving entities. And referring back to Sacks' patient, imposing boundaries on a continuous stream of information requires time and, in this particular example, perceived and sustained effort: First, "[...] he said that trees didn't look like anything at all". Later, "[he] finally put a tree together – he now knows that the trunk and leaves go together to form a complete unit" (Sacks, 1995, pp. 123–124).

Three goals motivate and structure this chapter: A perusal of definitions for the concept of *event* prefaces an overview of existing research on event segmentation in narrative discourse. Segmentation in cinematic narrative, the main focus of this chapter, calls for a discussion of medium-specific methodological designs employed in research studies, as well as their corresponding experimental findings. The existing empirical evidence promotes event segmentation as a prerequisite for (film) narrative comprehension and memory encoding. Event segmentation is indeed a necessary cognitive process for narrative understanding, but it is by no means sufficient. The implied correlation between event segmentation and narrative comprehension is debatable due to a potential logical gap between existing experimental methods and their inferred theoretical conclusions. Understanding the architecture of narratives with their intricate, multi-level event connectivity may require cognitive processes more complex than linear segmentation. The terminological distinction between *segmentation* and *parsing* contextualizes the argument that research methods consistent with event *parsing* (extending beyond event segmentation) may afford a more accurate account for the cognitive processes underlying narrative comprehension.

Framing the Event: An Overview of Event Definitions across Disciplines

"What is an event?"[2] Referring to Quine's (1985) definition of an event, Zacks and Tversky (2001) offer "the simplest proposal as to what events are [...]: Simply treat events as objects. That is, regard events as bounded regions of space-time" (p. 4).[3] From informal approximations such as "the stuff that fills our lives" (Tversky et al., 2010, p. 216), or "what happens to us, what we do, what we anticipate with pleasure or dread, and what we remember with fondness or regret" (Radvansky & Zacks, 2014, p. 1), to more formal statements such as "a segment of time at a given location that is conceived by an observer to have a beginning and an end" (Zacks & Tversky, 2001, p. 3), events have received an impressive array of construals within many domains of study. Given the multitude of definitions that the concept of event accrued, it seems pertinent to begin this exploration with a very brief index of the disciplines that contributed to our current understanding of events.

Philosophical accounts identify events as logic, linguistic, and ontological constructs. Approaching events as referents for linguistic entities (i.e., sentences *about* events) whose structural connectivity obeys laws of cause-effect logic, Davidson (1969) held that identical events have identical causes and effects. Subsequently, however, Davidson agreed with Quine's proposal that, for events to be identical, they must occupy, or referentially stand in, the same space-time location. It is, therefore, this theory of event as a space-time co-incidence that motivated the event-as-object definition referred to by Zacks and Tversky (2001; see above), since objects are indeed spatio-temporal confines.[4]

Studies in perception within the Gestalt framework conceptualize the *event* as "an organized whole, a whole built up of parts between which there are mutual influences", therefore ascribing a dynamic internal structure to events that suggests hierarchical architectures and adaptable boundaries (Jansson et al., 1994, p. 38).[5] Gestalt theories also contend that consistent patterns in spatio-temporal clusterings determine the extent of internally consistent arrays of events: "an orderly march of events" – seen as a sequence of coherently arranged actions, or of occurrences rendered orderly by spatial-temporal contiguities – affords meaning and form sustained patterns (Koffka, 1935, p. 9). Johansson (1950) offers a visual illustration: A birch tree in the wind will present the viewer with rather erratic small motions of the foliage and branches. "This is an example of unceasing motion, unceasing change" (p. 11). Despite the continuous and inconsistent change in the branches and leaves of the viewed birch, the visual system recognizes the tree as a coherent whole thus extracting a "relatively undifferentiated unit". An event whole specifies unity even in the face of constant movement, if this movement does not violate the natural spatial-temporal agreement among parts (Johansson, 1950, p. 12).

The field of discourse analysis, mainly concerned with textual, semiotic, semantic, and pragmatic analyses, highlights the temporal dimension of events as linguistic constructions encoding past, present, and future occurrences, as well as event configurations that form synchronic and diachronic temporal structures.[6] Hans Kamp (1979, 1981, 2017) proposes the Discourse Representation Theory in which sentences composing larger texts connect with each other through "discourse representation structures" where *"representations are pictures of the world described by the sentences which determine them"* (Kamp, 2017, p. 3; Kamp's emphasis).[7] I am presenting this particular theoretical proposal because of its relevance (although not overtly stated) to cognitive aspects of events. The Discourse Representation Theory appears akin to a cognitive mental model that affords incremental updates with each incoming sentence in a sequence. For instance, the following sequence of sentences use past tense verbs to denote and elicit representations of fully completed past events: "First Marie did the dishes. Then she cleaned the bathroom. Then she took a rest" (Kamp, 2017, p. 16, citing Kamp, 1979, 1981). This example, provided to illustrate a Discourse Representation Structure (Kamp, 2017, p. 3), contains a sequence of events neatly arranged in chronological order, with the past tense of the verb denoting the completeness of the events. As Kamp (2017) asserts, "the function of these tenses is, in part at least, to provide guidance to the recipient of the discourse in which they occur as to how he is to represent the information this discourse contains" (p. 17). The three-sentence sequence above "recounts a number of successive events: doing the dishes, cleaning the bathroom, having a rest. It appears to me […] that the way we process a discourse of this kind involves the successive introduction, into the representation which we build up as the discourse proceeds, of 'events'. These events are represented as (i) succeeding each other in time, and (ii) as the kinds of events they are said to be by the sentences which provoke their introduction" (Kamp, 2017, p. 16).

Syntactic and formal semantic analyses of discourse events (seen as similar to structural units in linguistics, e.g., Carroll & Bever, 1976)[8] consistently brought into focus their temporal connotation in an atomic bottom-up approach with marginal allusions to non-linguistic top-down interpretations. Theoretical approaches to *narrative* discourse specifically add a new dimension, albeit also temporal: Narrative becomes a "doubly temporal sequence" that exceeds the classic distinction between story time and time in the telling of the story. The double temporal structure "invites us to consider that one of the functions of narrative is to invent one-time scheme in terms of another time scheme" (Metz, 1974, p. 18). Referring to Metz's dual-time narrative configuration, Gerard Genette (1980) construes "order" in narrative discourse as "the temporal order of succession of the events in the story and the pseudo-temporal order of their arrangement in the narrative" (p. 35). Narrative events, seen here as "temporal sections", establish connections and cross-references between two-time orders: one chronological, the other violating the time logic with a non-chronological re-arrangement that creates discourse effects. These two-time orders map on to the story/discourse distinction (or, to use terminology proposed by Russian Formalists, syuzhet and fabula distinction) proposed in narratology studies. Bordwell (1985) presents the syuzhet and fabula with clear referents to spatio-temporal event cognition:

"The imaginary construct we create, progressively and retroactively, was termed by Formalists the *fabula* (sometimes translated as 'story'). More specifically, the fabula embodies the action as a chronological, cause-and-effect chain of events occurring within a given duration and a spatial field" (p. 49). "The syuzhet", Bordwell continues, "(usually translated as 'plot') is the actual arrangement and presentation of the fabula in the film" (p. 50). Chatman (1980) opens the story/discourse discussion with an obvious question: "But what is an event, in the narrative sense? Events are either *actions (acts)* or *happenings*. Both are changes of state" (p. 44).[9] Narrative events, therefore, are the actions and happenings that construct the "plot": "The events in a story are turned into a plot by its discourse, the modus of presentation" (Chatman, 1980, p. 43).[10] Gerard Genette (1980) defines narrative by outlining three meanings of the term, each with reference to events: "the oral or written discourse that undertakes to tell of an event or a series of events"; "the succession of events, real or fictitious, that are subject of [...] discourse"; "narrative refer[s] to an event: the event that consists of someone recounting something: the act of narrating taken in itself" (pp. 25–26). The proposal of story grammars as systems regulating the connections among narrative events, whether causal, spatial, or temporal, affords the translation from the discourse we are presented with into the chronological and causal story we reconstruct. Comprehending a narrative is precisely this reconstruction of the logical sequence of story events from the discourse format. Any act of narrative comprehension is inherently dependent upon this reconstruction, and therefore requires event identification and cognitive abilities to form logical configurations of events.

Working with Events: Segmentation as a Prerequisite for Narrative Comprehension

Research on segmenting continuous streams of information into discrete events gained relevance in cognitive psychology due to attention mechanisms, memory, and comprehension of sequential stimuli. "Proper segmentation" of events, as a precursor of more complex functions (e.g., object recognition, memory, planning), organizes our initial perceptual input famously described by William James (1890, p. 488) as "one great blooming, buzzing confusion".[11] "Without proper segmentation, [...] recognition of objects and actions is difficult [...], and planning breaks down [...]" (Zacks et al., 2010, p. 1).

Proposals for event representation of discourse were initially developed for text comprehension, with subsequent theoretical and empirical approaches to film narrative. I will, therefore, highlight here research on events in text to preface studies on events in cinematic discourse. Models – mental, situational, representational – prevail as explanatory frameworks for narrative comprehension or, more generally, discourse comprehension (e.g., Bailey & Zacks, 2011; Bower & Morrow, 1990; Kurby & Zacks, 2008; Morrow et al., 1989; Schwan & Garsoffky, 2008; Zacks et al., 2009). Understanding discursive information presupposes an internal representation, a "working model" for the information one processes "in much the same way as, say, a clock functions as a model of the earth's rotation" (Johnson-Laird, 1983, p. 2). Referred to as mental or situational models, these constructs were established (in the 1970s) as theoretical accounts primarily of textual discourse comprehension, and were (arguably) based on top-down semantic or inference-making processes *in conjunction with* the bottom-up sentence-level syntactic analyses (see Kintsch and Van Dijk's (1978) for mental model in text representations over time; Glenberg et al.'s (1987) for text content models; Graesser et al.'s (1994) for their "constructionist theory for knowledge-based inferences", etc.).[12] Text readers build an internal model for the situation depicted at a given moment, and revise the constructed model when new 'bits' of incoming information signal a situational change. These bits of discursive information are precisely the events that, as Chatman (1980) proposed, "change[s] the state" and thus elicit a model update. "As narrative events unfold, readers update their mental model, moving characters from place to place, introducing new objects into the model or deleting old ones, and perhaps shifting attention to a new location or situation entirely" (Bower & Rinck, 2001).[13]

Individual events' internal structure and content usually provide text comprehension measures, while between-events spatio-temporal contiguities are used as memory metrics: If spatial and temporal distance is inserted between events, content memory tends to decrease (e.g., Bower & Rinck, 2001; Glenberg et al., 1987; Hanson & Hirst, 1989; Morrow et al., 1989; Rinck & Bower, 2000).[14] In sum, it looks as though measures for text memory and comprehension tend to come in two flavors: either within-event structure, or between-event spatio-temporal contiguity. Despite their claims of narrative comprehension at the semantic macro-structural level of narrative (e.g., Magliano & Zacks, 2011), most of these studies (with few exceptions in the early empirical endeavors, such as Kintsch and Van Dijk (1978), to a degree) construct, even if implicitly, a discourse comprehension model with a rather linear design: event one followed by event two, followed by event three, etc.

A helpful visualization here depicts events arranged like beads on a string: conspicuously marked, and ready to slide over and to alter the previous event sequence. Much like an abacus, if you wish. This linear architecture applies to most experimental methods in existing research: participants are presented with sequences of events, one after another, and are subsequently tested for discourse understanding and memory. Radvansky (2012) states this compellingly: "Life is just one thing after another. We entertain ourselves with various approximations of life – video games, books, films, theater, and so on – more things, one after another. These things consist of events. How we break up all of these streams of action into events influences how we think about things and what we remember later" (Radvansky, 2012, p. 269). Does such "beads-on-a-string" serial presentation in research methods truly reflect the way we understand and remember, say, *Alice in Wonderland*? If so, then we should remember, with fair accuracy, whether the Tweedledum and Tweedledee event occurred before or after the Humpty Dumpty event. Unless strict causal relationships apply, most readers would fail this task. Most readers of the book, however, remember the event depicting Alice seeing that "the Rabbit actually *took a watch out of its waist-coat pocket*" (Carroll, 1971, p. 7). The "Rabbit event" is causally related to all the other events and is, therefore, the most densely connected discourse event.

The complex network of relations that events (all events in a given discourse) establish among themselves and the density of event connectivity are largely overlooked in discourse processing experimental designs. High-level cognitive processes of discourse (i.e., comprehension of the discourse as a unified whole, beyond the event's internal structure) require, I argue, a representational architecture that features all connections among events, including (or especially) non-contiguous, long-distance dependency ones. Whether created in text or film medium, most discourse formats place relevant events in non-adjacent positions (flashbacks, flashforwards), in long-distance dependency positions (plot twists at the very end as in *The Sixth Sense*), or in "puzzle plot" intricate structures (see M. Kiss's chapter for a detailed discussion on puzzling narrative structures). To extract these stories from their discursive arrangement one has to keep track of the connections among these events in a non-linear fashion.

The Argentine writer Julio Cortázar urges the readers to approach his novel *Rayuela* (*Hopscotch* in English translation, 1966) with disregard to the order of chapters, even begin with the last chapter and go backwards, or let chance decide where to start by simply opening the book randomly. The book does features two large structures defined by spatial location: one collection of events occurring in Paris, the other in Buenos Aires. The novel has been described as a mosaic of an era, with its inherent accidents of history and culture that could occur at different points in time. The episodes in the book, however, are not disconnected, not random disjointed 'happenings'. Imagine that readers of this novel are asked to segment the book into events as they read it. Imagine also that these readers are experienced literature consumers and claim a high degree of narrative comprehension. To what extent the results of the segmentation task would reveal readers' comprehension of the whole novel? Can the linearity of the segmentation *task* (i.e., methodological procedure) measure the intricacy of event connections necessary for comprehension? The most obvious flashback must be, in re-constructing the story from its narration discourse, re-placed in a precise location for the story to be encoded as a logical flow of events. The reader, therefore, must maintain active a representation of all relevant events within their connection network. The segmentation task, as described in most event cognition studies, is necessary, but not sufficient to reveal the cognition underlying discourse processing.

Event Segmentation in Film Narrative: Main Theories and Findings

Film viewers are equally perceptive of meaningful "chunks" in the continuous influx of the moving image as readers are in text.[15] More so than text, aren't movies already visibly segmented, cropped, cut, structured, organized, and nicely trimmed? Composers of narrative, whether filmmakers or writers, edit and punctuate (i.e., insert breaks and boundaries in) their work with the intent of directing the audience's attention and eliciting certain impressions. For most film form, editing consists in a somewhat counterintuitive endeavor: cutting the film in order to hide those very cuts. Film edits that are inconspicuous to the human eye articulate a set of rules referred to as continuity editing (see Magliano & Zacks, 2011 for a discussion on event segmentation as a function of continuity editing; Smith (2012) for the cinematic continuity and attentional theory proposal; Berliner and Cohen (2011) for a model of spatial continuity as "reality of illusion" induced by cinema; Smith and Henderson (2008) for eye tracking data on "edit blindness"[16] due to continuity in film editing). Viewers are not blind to edits; they just don't lose track of the continuity in narration because of film edits. Do spectators segment narratives along the pre-established event boundaries (i.e., filmmakers' edits)? Or do they cut-and-paste the story in ways peculiar to the individual viewer? Moreover, do film viewers agree in their segmentation, or is event segmentation an individual, experience-driven exercise?

Event segmentation studies in film narrative share the underlying assumption that the stimulus is not (in most cases) over-specified; that is, it does not pre-determine viewers' segmentation by imposing overly conspicuous edits and rigid event markers. Therefore, "[...] important elements and structure of an event are often, in some way, imposed by a person. [...] Thus, the components and structure of an event are not deterministically derived from the components of the world itself" (Radvansky & Zacks, 2014, p. 9). With strict relevance to segmenting the moving image, Newtson (1973) provided the initial paradigm for studying event segmentation empirically: presented with videos of simple actions, participants were asked to press a button whenever a "situation" changed and initiated another state of affairs (i.e., an event ended and another began). The resulting segmentation indicated that people agree significantly in their event boundary identification, Cutting et al. (2012) shows 90% agreement in Hollywood film; Sasmita and Swallow (2022) show agreement in fine- and coarse-grain segmentation. Using Newton's general paradigm, Zacks et al.'s (2001) fMRI study forwards a hierarchical event organization with fine-grain subevents within coarse-grain events. The fine-grain segmentation task elicited the smallest event units, whereas the coarse-grain task marked the larger events. The observed pattern of brain activity displayed a gradual increase before event boundaries with activity peaking immediately after boundaries. Therefore, information present in the stimulus affords the anticipation of event boundary and elicits a situation update.[17]

Discretizing the environment is a necessary and automatic effort because "the continuous input is so rich and complex that much of it must be, and is, ignored; the input must be categorized to be effectively processed and understood" (Tversky et al., 2008). As memory and attention increase in the vicinity of event boundaries (e.g., Kurby & Zacks, 2008), the Event Segmentation Theory (EST) (Zacks et al., 2007, 2010; see also Kurby & Zacks, 2008; Zacks et al., 2007) construes segmentation as "a side effect of prediction during ongoing perception" (Zacks et al., 2010, p. 11). The EST thus contends that information consolidation processes occur at each event boundary and engage attention and memory mechanisms (Zacks et al., 2010, Zwaan, 2016, etc.).[18] fMRI event segmentation studies report significant transient activity in passive film viewers when situational changes occur in the stimulus (i.e., interactions between characters, spatial shifts, etc.), and higher activity in memory-relevant brain regions immediately after a situation changes (i.e., an event boundary) thus revealing the automatic nature of event segmentation (Swallow & Jiang, 2010; Zacks et al., 2010). In sum, EST puts forth three main findings: segmenting events is automatic, attention and memory increase at event boundaries (Swallow et al., 2022, etc.), and the increased memory performance suggest that "events form the units of memory encoding" (Zacks & Swallow, 2007, p. 83).[19] When presented with uninterrupted perceptual input, perceiving it as such – uninterrupted – is an almost impossible task for the visually developed human brain, so tuned to perk up when a change occurs in the environment.[20]

The theoretical proposal advanced in the Event-Indexing Model supports similar principles for event segmentation regardless of the discourse mode (Magliano et al., 2001). In both text and film narrative, events are identified when the situation changes along five main indices: time, space, protagonist, causality and intentionality (Cutting & Iricinschi, 2015; Rinck & Weber, 2003; Zwaan et al., 1995). Hollywood film viewers identify events with a predilection for spatial and character shifts as boundaries, followed by the more unobtrusive time shifts (e.g., Cutting, 2014).[21] Subsequent occurrences of relevant locations in Hollywood film gradually decrease the contextual information provided thus revealing, although obliquely, the assumption that viewers need less time and information to update the narrative model for reoccurring events (Cutting & Iricinschi, 2015).[22]

Although various empirical studies consistent with the theoretical and empirical proposals discussed above (i.e., the generic Mental Model, Event-Indexing Model, and Event Segmentation Theory) interpret their results as informing directly the process of film narrative comprehension (e.g., Magliano & Zacks, 2011; Zacks et al., 2009, 2010) these model-based designs do not test directly the comprehension of narrative globally, at discourse level, across individual events (but see Kurby and Zacks's (2012) proposal for *incremental updating* versus *global updating* of situation models). The event inter-connectivity architecture necessary for understanding discourse as coherent and cohesive forms of meaning is not addressed methodologically in systematic ways: the generic research task's surface linearity does not map onto the deep-level semantic processes required for film narrative comprehension and long-term memory.

The Cut-and-Paste Narrative Processing

Early "theories of filmic narration [...] have little to say about the spectator, except that he or she is relatively passive" (Bordwell, 1985, p. 29). In discussing early mimetic and diegetic accounts of narrative, Bordwell highlights their focus on inherent compositional story make-up and narration techniques at the expense of the cognitively engaged spectator. These approaches result in descriptive accounts of narrative with limited prescriptive features or predictive affordances. Perspectives and points of view, among other narration tools, do indeed take the spectator into account but only to assign them a place from which they can *witness* the story. "A film, I shall suggest, does not 'position' anybody. A film cues the spectator to execute a definable variety of *operations*" (Bordwell, 1985, p. 29).

Presented with a film narrative – an apparently continuous flow of moving image – the engaged viewers identify the internally coherent narrative events and – as many event segmentation methodological approaches seem to imply – perform a cut-and-paste story re-construction very much akin to the old-fashion roll film: cut the film strip in relevant places, rearrange the bits in a linear format, and paste the rearranged bits. Or, if I may use a rather domestic metaphor, this segmentation task is as if items on a clothes line are shifted to match colors, simply re-arranged along the same line. The "clothes-line segmentation" is a bit too simplistic of a process to add up to understanding which of those cut bits, placed just so in the pasted version, explains with utmost clarity why James Bond faked his own death and sided with the bad guys.

"The viewer must take as a central cognitive goal the construction of a more or less intelligible story. But what makes something a story? And what makes a story intelligible?" (Bordwell, 1985, p. 33).

Well, film discourse is intelligible as long as the engaged viewer is provided with sufficient information to rearrange the narration events in a logical and memorable format. However, for such rearrangement to afford a comprehensive representation of the discursive material, connectivity among *all* events – not only adjacent ones as in the cut-and-paste story reconstruction – must be featured. Most studies reviewed above (and others not mentioned) use the cut-and-paste linear method to test narrative comprehension. An example mentioned earlier, *The Sixth Sense* (Shyamalan, 1999), ends with a plot twist: the main character was actually dead throughout the film. And the punch line goes even further: the protagonist himself is just as surprised to find out he was dead all along. This final plot twist elicits not just an update of a mental model, but a complete override of viewers' narrative representation and a discourse-to-story reconstruction from scratch. A naïve viewer asked to perform a 'traditional' event segmentation of the film would certainly and effortlessly identify the final plot twist as an independent narrative event. This segmentation task, however, fails to capture the viewer's final rewrite of the narrative after the narration twist. Event segmentation does not seem to answer Bordwell's question: "What makes a story intelligible" to the cognitively active spectator?

Several studies approach this gap between the surface-level linear event segmentation task and the non-linear theoretical inferences by importing "depth" from hierarchical narrative representations. Statistical analyses of film reveal a scene-subscene hierarchy defined with reference to theater: "Subscenes [...] mark somewhat finer boundaries by allowing for the entrances and exits of characters and changes in tone within a scene – neither of which are instances of change in time or place. But more importantly, subscenes also allow for the crosscutting of events within parallel action, which demonstrate clear changes in time or place. Crosscutting occurs when a film follows, in parallel, two or more storylines with those narratives temporally interleaved" (Cutting et al., 2012, p. 3; see also Cutting, 2014; Cutting & Iricinschi, 2015).

In empirical studies, when asked to segment events in a narrative, participants spontaneously identify event within events as "fine-grain events clustering into larger units" (Kurby & Zacks, 2008), or events "being organized into partonomic hierarchies reflecting relations between parts and subparts" (Zacks & Tversky, 2001; see also Garsoffky & Schwan, 2020; Zacks et al., 2001). The EST proposal (described above) contends that participants segmenting continuous stimuli "*perceive* event boundaries on multiple timescales simultaneously, but selectively *attend* to one timescale in response to instructions or other experimental manipulations. According to this view, when activity is coherent participants segment it at multiple timescales, and can choose to attend to finer or coarser grains" (Zacks et al., 2007, p. 278; see also Swallow et al., 2018). Garsoffky and Schwan (2020) address the "part-whole relationship" among events (partonomic event organization) by manipulating time scale or psychological distance between naturalistic activities presented as experimental stimuli. Two film versions depicting an activity labeled as "cleaning a room" were presented: "a long gaps version" featuring "longer leaps in time between successive actions", and an equivalent "short gaps version" featuring "shorter leaps in time between successive actions" (p.

1869).[23] Without being explicitly prompted, viewers' segmentation was consistent with the scale implicitly provided in the two versions of filmed activities. In addition to segmenting activities (which suggests a focus on boundary identification), viewers narrated the filmed stimuli mentioning the events at a large scale in the long gaps version, and a smaller scale for the short gaps version and thus indicating an implicit hierarchical segmentation. The resulting architecture approximates an *event pyramidal construction* that affords relational event configurations on a vertical dimension, within each pyramid. These hierarchies would feature disconnected 'event pyramids' with clear internal structure, but no stipulated connections among them.[24] To illustrate this with a film example, *Ordinary People*'s (Robert Redford, 1980)[25] main character (Conrad, played by Timothy Hutton), a high school student, struggles with the traumatic event of seeing his brother drown in stormy waters during a boat accident. The boat accident event, only subtly hinted at in a few brief nightmare images, is connected with a high number of other segmented events: the protagonist's suicidal attempt, his hospitalization (also never actually shown), the brief encounter with his friend from the hospital, the mother's cold and distant demeanor, the father's visualization of his son's suicidal attempt, the protagonist's therapy sessions, to give only a brief list.

An event that is barely shown and features on the lowest number of film frames is, however, the highest in event connectivity and causal chain presence. Mere segmentation tasks do not capture the *importance* or *relevance* of events within the fabric of the entire narrative. Event connection density within a network design is a more adequate measure of the complexity involved in story-from-discourse reconstruction and memory encoding. As Graesser (1981) concludes, based on text research: "It is believed that causal conceptualizations are normally organized in a network fashion in contrast to the hierarchically structured, goal oriented conceptualizations" (Graesser, 1981, p. 128; see also Graesser et al., 1980).

"Going beyond the Information Given": Segmenting versus Parsing and the Issue of Narrative Comprehension

> The activity of constructing formal models and theoretical constructs is a prototype of what we mean by the creation of generic coding systems that permits one to "go beyond" the data to new and possibly fruitful predictions.
>
> *(Bruner et al., 1957)*

Parsing algorithms in computational implementations of grammars (e.g., Earley, 1970) or parsing strategies in human sentence processing (Chomsky, 1965; Fodor, 1998, etc.) afford deep-level connections among units.

Borrowing terminology from generative linguistics, the surface structure of a sentence consists of the order in which the words (or clauses) are sequenced (very much like the narrational discourse in film), while the deep structure allows for meaning construction by connecting the individual units in coherent ways[26] (Chomsky, 1965, etc.). Only accompanied by deep-surface semantic relationships between units, the outcome of parsing, does segmentation afford sentence comprehension. Segmenting and parsing continuous visual input denote significantly different processes with equally different outcomes. Segmentation provides data on viewers' identification of event boundaries and event internal structure, therefore focusing on surface sequences of individual events. Reconstructing stories from discursive structures, I argue, presupposes the representation of *event networks* that entertain many-to-many connections in a complex, multi-level architecture.

Drawing from earlier studies on text showing that "the importance of a statement depends directly on its *relational* role to other statements in the text", Trabasso and Sperry (1985) tested participants' judgments of statements/ events as correlated to the event's direct causal connections and its presence on a causal chain throughout the text narrative (Trabasso & Sperry, 1985, pp. 595–596). The findings show that "judgments of importance are predetermined, in part, by local linking of one event to another by causal and/or logical inferences. The result of these individual links is a *network* of events and event relations" (p. 610, my emphasis; see also Graesser, 1981; Graesser et al., 1980, cited above).

In film narrative research, a theoretical account that approximates representations of event importance and the event "weights" in carrying the narrative forward comes from the Scene Perception and Event Comprehension Theory (SPECT) (Loschky et al., 2020). Using eye tracking, Loschky and colleagues measured attentional load as a function of frequency of fixations dedicated to film narrative. The theory thus outlines a dual-level processing in visual narratives: the dynamic between front-end and back-end processes provides an explanation for event model construction. Front-end processes "are involved in extracting content from the image" and map onto specific bits of information from single eye fixations. Back-end processes operate "across multiple eye fixations" by sampling information that, cumulatively, sustain and continuously update the "current event model" throughout the narrative. Cross-referencing these two levels of processes results in intersections between low-level perception and high-level cognitive comprehension. "The basic architecture of SPECT distinguishes between stimulus features and front-end and back-end cognitive processes involved in visual event and narrative cognition" (Loschky et al., 2020, pp. 5–7). The configuration outlined in SPECT does *not* map onto top-down and bottom-up processes. Rather, in its schematic diagram (p. 6), SPECT seems to allow for feedback loops which place the front-end and back-end processes in a dynamic informational exchange, and not in a feed-forward linear structure.[27] To my knowledge, this theory of narrative processing is unique in stipulating nodes that allude to network architectures: "Laying the foundation is the process of constructing the first nodes in an event model, where a node reflects a basic unit of representation (e.g., proposition, simple grounded simulation)" (p. 11). The empirical evidence underlying this theory accounts for narrative comprehension at both single event and discourse level.

To sum up, what makes story consumers go "beyond the word" (to use Graesser's book title)?[28] Or beyond the moving image to obtain a representation of the narrative discourse that is both comprehensible and memorable? As Jerome Bruner puts it, what enables us to "go beyond the information given?" The information given is at the mere sensorial level, it meets our sensorial modalities still empty of meaning; we make the meaning, we impose significance onto the bare stimuli by connecting the input bits in ways that support unifying laws, in ways that are (mostly) impenetrable to internal logical contradictions. To afford prescriptive mechanisms (following Bruner's proposal of coding systems) and generalization, these connections must be flexible and vulnerable to additions, edits, redactions. Only a complex network structure of connections, I would claim, affords efficient comprehension processes applicable to all forms of discourse, from the mere chronological event series to the puzzle plot.

Notes

1 A question was raised by my undergraduate student Raluca Rilla: Does the property of immutability apply equally to environments that are "stationary" (e.g., indoor environments) and, as such, do not display movement/change to our immediate visual perception?

 The question is worth addressing: My immutability statement is proposed in the framework of Gestalt psychology that did not attribute explanatory power to simple, independent local sensations; rather, explanations of perception come from processes that interact among themselves, and with the environment. Wolfgang Köhler (1969) affirms: "The Gestalt psychologists' next question was whether interactions [...] occur only in the case of movement. Are there also observations which demonstrate the dependence of local facts upon conditions in their environment when the observed perceptual objects remain at rest?" (p. 41). The answer highlights the contextual dependence of color perception (changing with light in the environment). Color, shadow, etc. are perceived as change and follow the same explanation as the perception of motion in Max Wertheimer's stroboscopic movement (two adjacent lights alternating on/off states).

 I take this opportunity to express my gratitude for all Raluca's comments, questions, and patience during our lengthy discussions.

2 "What is an event?" is the opening question in *Understanding Events* (Shipley & Zacks, 2008). The authors continue: "An event may be miraculous, mysterious, seminal, even divine – and, of course, to paraphrase Ecclesiastes, there is one event that happeneth to us all. Of what do we speak when we say event?" (p. 3).

3 W.V.O. Quine (1985) states: "A physical object, in the broad sense in which I have long used the term, is the material content of any portion of space-time, however small, large, irregular, or discontinuous. I have been wont to view events simply

as physical objects in this sense" (p. 167). Insofar as it is evaluated within the more complex Davidsonian account of events as logic, linguistic, and ontological categories, Quine's definition may indeed be considered "the simplest proposal as to what events are", as Zacks and Tversky (2001) note.

4 The Davidson-Quine debate goes beyond the space-time issue; it hints at the uniqueness of event instances: it is rather difficult for two particular events to share comprehensively all their causes and effects. Similarly, two distinct objects (i.e., *tokens*, not exact copies within categorical *types*) cannot share the same space-time simultaneously.

5 Jansson et al.'s (1994) definition of the concept of the event falls within the broader proposal of *event configuration*: "Firstly, we can say that [event configuration] approximately coincides with the definition given for the term *whole*. But when using the term *configuration*, we wish to point out, [...], that we are dealing with an *organized* whole, [...]" (p. 38).

6 I am referring here simply to synchronic/simultaneous events and diachronic/representation of events over time without direct reference to the terms synchronic and diachronic introduced by Ferdinand de Saussure (English edition 1959/2011). in linguistic analyses. For Saussure, synchronic linguistics, a prerequisite of the inferential diachrony, refers to syntactic structures in a static language instance, while diachrony refers to language change over time. "The synchronic and diachronic phenomenon, for example, have nothing in common. One is a relation between simultaneous events, the other the substitution of one element for another in time, an event" (p. 91, 2011 English edition).

7 Kamp (2017) is the first English translation of Kamp (1981a) which, in turn, revisits and revises his 1979 proposal.

8 "A motion picture sequence attempts to portray an event by imposing a structure of cuts, zooms, tracks, pans, framings, and the like on that event. Analogously, a sentence represents an idea by imposing a syntactic and phonological structure on a set of lexical item" (Carroll & Bever, 1976, p. 1053).

9 Chatman (1980) borrows the terms *action* and *happening* from Boyd and Boyd (1977). To Lose the Name of Action: The Semantics of Action and Motion in Tennyson's Poetry. *PTL 2*, 21–32. Happenings allude to non-agentic accidents, while actions appear to imply an agent. As such, actions and happenings afford different degrees of causality. For a more detailed discussion, see Sternberg, M. (2003). Universals of narrative and their cognitivist fortunes (II). *Poetics Today*, 24(3), 517–638.

10 Jonathan Culler (1981) offers the same distinction with a reference to story grammar (necessary in narrative studies, as theorists seem to agree) that are rule-based systems linking the story and the discourse. Culler states: "[..] the theory of narrative requires a distinction between what I shall call 'story' – a sequence of actions or events, conceived as independent of their manifestation in discourse – and what I shall call 'discourse', the discursive presentation or narration of events" (p. 117).

11 "The baby, assailed by eyes, ears, nose, skin, and entrails at once, feels it all as one great blooming, buzzing confusion" (James, 1890, p. 488).

12 Kintsch and Van Dijk (1978) tested their model – one of the early research proposals for model-based text representation – on text comprehension and recall at three different time delays (immediately following the study, one month later, and three months later). Text reproductions decreased over the three test times, text reconstructions increased slightly, and metastatements increased significantly. The results suggest a macro-representation of the text based on a general semantic processing model. Glenberg et al. (1987) measured recognition and reading times to indicate that mental models "represent what the text is about (the events, objects, and processes [...], rather than features of the text itself". Mental models thus suggest semantic (not just structural) representations of text.

13 As Bower and Rinck (2001) emphasize, the "integrated model", proposed by Zwaan and Radvansky (1998), goes beyond the available discourse by incorporating the reader's background knowledge (especially if consistent with discourse content), as well as visual stimuli complementing the textual information, resulting in faster text comprehension.

14 Hanson and Hirst (1989) confirmed "the ability of observers to segment an action sequence into meaningful units" (p. 146). The segmented meaningful units, however, depend also on the intrinsic features of the stimulus. Observers of an action showing a person categorizing questionnaires identified an event boundary when a black page was inserted in the sequence. Although the behavior displayed was identical in both conditions, a change in low-level perceptual features resulted in an additional event boundary (Newtson et al., 1978).

15 Baggett (1979) constructed a text structurally equivalent to *The Red Balloon* (Lamorisse, 1956) with each narrative containing 14 content-identical episodes. In a subsequent cued-recall test, readers and viewers agreed on the location of structural boundaries, identical in both narrative formats, even when the test was administered with a seven-day delay.

16 The edit blindness in the film is an application of studies on inattentional and change blindness in the real world (Simons & Chabris 1999 and Simons & Levin 1997, respectively).

17 Such anticipation is in part possible because of the simplicity and familiarity of the activities shown in the stimuli. The feature film is a more complex stimulus, one that does not grant boundary anticipation easily. Moreover, contemporary films tend to be structurally complex and thus even more opaque to boundary anticipation.

18 Radvansky and Copeland (2006) provide similar results for a virtual reality environment in which participants explore different rooms. Walking through a door appears to elicit a representational model update and consolidation of the space event left behind.

19 Loschky et al. (2015) test the mental model hypothesis against the "tyranny in film" hypothesis. Viewers exhibit higher eye-movement attentional synchrony and lower cognitive load when provided with context than in the absence of context. The findings support the assumptions that some films are over-specified thus exercising a stimulus-driven exogenous control of viewers' eye movements.

20 Schwan and Garsoffky (2004) show that redacting out chunks of film that contain event boundaries impairs memory, whereas redacting chunks of film between boundaries does not change significantly memory performance.

21 Initially developed for text comprehension (Zwaan et al., 1995, etc.), the event-indexing model purports to inform situational models irrespective of the discourse medium. The model focuses on the indices marking situational changes, i.e., the nature of event boundaries (time, space, protagonist, causality, and intentionality). Testing the same model, Rinck and Weber (2003) show longer reading times for protagonist and temporal shifts, with no significant difference in space shifts. Given the prevalence of space shifts in film, this may suggest a potentially different event indexing in the two media.

22 We can venture here, rather safely, a "good-enough representation" account (proposed by Ferreira et al. (2002) in linguistics) for the faster processing of re-occurring events once the "gist" is extracted from the first, content-rich depiction of location. Alternatively, the filmmaker's intention in reducing contextual spatial information might be to minimize the psychological distance between viewers and characters by gradually 'pulling' the viewer into the story space. This, however, does not explain the shorter shot duration.

23 The long gaps version, more precisely, shows sequences of activities normally performed with significant amounts of time separating them (i.e., dusting the cabinet,
cleaning the floor, washing the window), whereas the short gaps version depicts
activities at a fine-grain scale (i.e., pick up paper towel roll, tear one sheet, prepare
the window detergent).

24 Hierarchical architectures stipulated in textual discourse provided similar results:
text units placed higher in the hierarchy were recalled, recognized and summa-
rized more accurately (Kintsch & Keenan, 1973; Rumelhart, 1977; both cited in
Trabasso in Sperry, 1985). Two notes here: 1. Kintsch's research dealt, in part,
with story grammars (following J. Mandler's proposal). A grammar in text linguistics, according to Kintsch and van Dijk (1978), includes "a parser, which is
necessary both for the interpretation of input sentences and for the production
of output sentences" (p. 363). 2. David E. Rumelhart is a proponent of connec-
tionism (see Rumelhart, 1998, among others). It is apparent that both Kintsch
and Rumelhart's later work favor parsing and network architectures in discourse
processing.

25 I cannot help but notice, genuinely baffled, the rather grim nature of the film illustrations I chose.

26 A clear illustration: The following sentences, frequently used to illustrate the deep-
versus surface structure difference, have identical surface structures (noun follows
verb follows argument): *Jack is easy to please*, versus *Jack is eager to please*.
The segmentation of these two sentences at the surface level fails to provide the
semantic deep-level structure that distinguishes the meaning of two syntactic
constructions.

27 The authors convey their intention to motivate further research that "explores the
interplay between multiple levels of front- and back-end cognitive processing". A
model mapping single eye fixations at front-end level onto series of fixations at
back-end level would, potentially, devise a complex network of focal points of
information between the two levels. Linear segmentation would not "fit" such a
model; parsing would be more adequate.

28 Graesser (1981). *Prose Comprehension Beyond the Word.*

References

Baggett, P. (1979). Structurally equivalent stories in movie and text and the effect of
the medium on recall. *Journal of Verbal Learning and Verbal Behavior. 18* (3),
333–356.

Bailey, H. & Zacks, J. M. (2011). Literature and event understanding. *Scientific Study
of Literature. 1* (1), 72–78.

Berliner, T. & Cohen, D. J. (2011). The illusion of continuity: Active perception and
the classical editing system. *Journal of Film and Video. 63* (1), 44–63.

Bordwell, D. (1985). *Narration in the fiction film.* University of Wisconsin Press.

Bower, G. H. & Morrow, D. G. (1990). Mental models in narrative comprehension.
Science, 247, 44–48.

Bower, G. H. & Rinck, M. (2001). Selecting one among many referents in spatial situation models. *Learning, Memory. 27* (1), 81–98.

Boyd, Z. & Boyd, J. (1977). To lose the name of action: The semantics of action and
motion in Tennyson's poetry. *PTL: A Journal for Descriptive Poetics and Theory
of Literature. 2*, 21–32.

Bruner, J. S., Brunswik, E., Festinger, L., Heider, F., Muenzinger, K. F., Osgood, C. E. & Rapaport, D. (1957). Contemporary approaches to cognition. A report of a symposium at the University of Colorado, May 12–14, 1955.

Carroll, J. M. & Bever, T. G. (1976). Segmentation in cinema perception. *Science. 191* (4231), 1053–1055.

Carroll, L. (1971). *Alice in Wonderland.* W. W. Norton &Company, Inc.

Chatman, S. B. (1980). *Story and discourse: Narrative structure in fiction and film.* Cornell University Press.

Chomsky, N. (1965). Aspects of the Theory of Syntax Cambridge. In: *Multilingual matters.* MIT Press.

Culler, J. (1981). Story and discourse in the analysis of narrative. The Pursuit of Signs: Semiotics. *Literature, Deconstruction. 169*, 169–187.

Cutting, J. E., Brunick, K. L. & Candan, A. (2012). Perceiving event dynamics and parsing Hollywood films. *Journal of Experimental Psychology: Human Perception and Performance, 38* (6), 1476–1490.

Cutting, J. E. (2014). Event segmentation and seven types of narrative discontinuity in popular movies. *Acta Psychologica. 149*, 69–77.

Cutting, J. & Iricinschi, C. (2015). Re-presentations of space in Hollywood movies: An event-indexing analysis. *Cognitive Science. 39* (2), 434–456.

Davidson, D. (1969). The Individuation of Events. In *Essays in honor of Carl G. Hempel* (pp. 216–234). Springer.

Earley, J. (1970). An efficient context-free parsing algorithm. *Communications of the ACM. 13* (2), 94–102.

Ferreira, F., Bailey, K. G. & Ferraro, V (2002). Good-enough representations in language comprehension. *Current Directions in Psychological Science. 11* (1), 11–15.

Fodor, J. D. (1998). Parsing to learn. *Journal of Psycholinguistic Research. 27* (3), 339–374.

Garsoffky, B. & Schwan, S. (2020). Same action, different level: Descriptions of perceived or predicted actions depend on preceding temporal gaps in event streams. *Journal of Experimental Psychology: Learning, Memory, and Cognition. 46* (10), 1868–1880.

Genette, G. (1980). *Narrative discourse: An essay in method* (Vol. 3). Cornell University Press.

Glenberg, A. M., Meyer, M. & Lindem, K. (1987). Mental models contribute to foregrounding during text comprehension. *Journal of Memory and Language. 26* (1), 69–83.

Graesser, A. C., Robertson, S. P., Lovelace, E. R. & Swinehart, D. M. (1980). Answers to why-questions expose the organization of story plot and predict recall of actions. *Journal of Verbal Learning and Verbal Behavior. 19* (1), 110–119.

Graesser, A. C. (1981). *Prose comprehension beyond the word.* Springer-Verlag New York Inc.

Graesser, A. C., Singer, M. & Trabasso, T. (1994). Constructing inferences during narrative text comprehension. *Psychological Review. 101* (3), 371–395.

Hanson, C. & Hirst, W. (1989). On the representation of events: A study of orientation, recall, and recognition. *Journal of Experimental Psychology: General, 118* (2), 136–147.

James, W. (1890). *The principles of psychology.* Henry Holt. & Co.

Jansson, G., Bergström, S. S., & Epstein, W. (1994). *Perceiving events and objects.* Lawrence Erlbaum Associates, Inc.

Johansson, G. (1950). Configurations in the perception of velocity. *Acta Psychologica.* 7, 25–79.

Johnson-Laird, P. N. (1983). *Mental models: Towards a cognitive science of language, inference, and consciousness* (No. 6). Harvard University Press.

Kamp, H. (1979). Events, Instants and Temporal Reference. In Bäuerle, R., Egli, U., & von Stechow, A. (eds.), *Semantics from different points of view.* Springer Series in Language and Communication 6, 376–417. Springer.

Kamp, H. (1981). A Theory of Truth and Semantic Representation. In Groenendijk, J. A. G., Janssen, T. M. V. & Stokhof, M. J. B. (eds.), *Formal methods in the study of language: Part 1.* Mathematical Centre Tract 135, 277–322. Mathematisch Centrum.

Kamp, H. (2017). Events, discourse representations and temporal reference. *Semantics and Pragmatics. 10* (2), 1–68.

Kintsch, W. & Van Dijk, T. A. (1978). Toward a model of text comprehension and production. *Psychological Review.* 85, 363–394.

Koffka, K. (1935). *Principles of gestalt psychology.* Harcourt, Brace.

Köhler, W. (1969). *The task of Gestalt psychology.* Princeton University Press.

Kurby, C. A. & Zacks, J. M. (2008). Segmentation in the perception and memory of events. *Trends in Cognitive Sciences. 12* (2), 72–79.

Kurby, C. A. & Zacks, J. M. (2012). Starting from scratch and building brick by brick in comprehension. *Memory & Cognition. 40* (5), 812–826.

Loschky, L. C., Larson, A. M., Magliano, J. P., & Smith, T. J. (2015). What would Jaws do? The tyranny of film and the relationship between gaze and higher-level narrative film comprehension. *PloS One. 10*(11), 1–23.

Loschky, L. C., Larson, A. M., Smith, T. J. & Magliano, J. P. (2020). The scene perception & event comprehension theory (SPECT) applied to visual narratives. *Topics in Cognitive Science. 12* (1), 311–351.

Magliano, J. P., Miller, J. & Zwaan, R. A. (2001). Indexing space and time in film understanding. *Applied Cognitive Psychology: The Official Journal of the Society for Applied Research in Memory and Cognition. 15* (5), 533–545.

Magliano, J. P. & Zacks, J. M. (2011). The impact of continuity editing in narrative film on event segmentation. *Cognitive Science. 35*(8), 1489–1517.

Metz, C. (1974). *Language and cinema.* De Gruyter.

Morrow, D. G., Bower, G. H. & Greenspan, S. L. (1989). Updating situation models during narrative comprehension. *Journal of Memory and Language. 28* (3), 292–312.

Newtson, D. (1973). Attribution and the unit of perception of ongoing behavior. *Journal of Personality and Social Psychology.* 28, 28–38.

Newtson, D., Rindner, R., Miller, R. & LaCross, K. (1978). Effects of availability of feature changes on behavior segmentation. *Journal of Experimental Social Psychology. 14* (4), 379–388.

Quine, W. V. O. (1985). Events and Reification. In *Actions and events: Perspectives on the philosophy of Donald Davidson* (pp. 162–171). Blackwell.

Radvansky, G. A. (2012). Across the event horizon. *Current Directions in Psychological Science. 21*(4), 269–272.

Radvansky, G. A. & Copeland, D. E. (2006). Walking through doorways causes forgetting: Situation models and experienced space. *Memory & Cognition. 34* (5), 1150–1156.

Radvansky, G. A., & Zacks, J. M. (2014). *Event cognition.* Oxford University Press.

Rinck, M., & Bower, G. H. (2000). Temporal and spatial distance in situation models. *Memory & Cognition.* 28(8), 1310–1320.

Rinck, M. & Weber, U. (2003). Who when where: An experimental test of the event-indexing model. *Memory & Cognition.* 31 (8), 1284–1292.

Rumelhart, D. E. (1977). Understanding and summarizing brief stories. In D. Laberge & S. J. Samuels (Eds.), Basic processes in reading: Perception and comprehension (pp. 265–303). Hillsdale, NJ: Erlbaum.

Rumelhart, D. E. (1998). The architecture of mind: A connectionist approach. *Mind Readings.* 207–238.

Sacks, O. (1995) *An anthropologist on Mars.* Random House, Inc.

Sasmita, K. & Swallow, K. M. (2022). Measuring event segmentation: An investigation into the stability of event boundary agreement across groups. *Behavior Research Methods*, 1–20.

Saussure, Ferdinand de. (1959/2011). *Course in General Linguistics.* Translated by Wade Baskin. Edited by Perry Meisel and Haun Saussy. Columbia University Press.

Schwan, S. & Garsoffky, B. (2004). The cognitive representation of filmic event summaries. *Applied Cognitive Psychology: The Official Journal of the Society for Applied Research in Memory and Cognition.* 18 (1), 37–55.

Schwan, S. & Garsoffky, B. (2008). The role of segmentation for perception and understanding of events. *Understanding Events: From Perception to Action.* 4, 391–414.

Shipley, T. F. & Zacks, J. M. (Eds.). (2008). *Understanding events: From perception to action* (Vol. 4). Oxford University Press.

Simons, D. J. & Chabris, C. F. (1999). Gorillas in our midst: Sustained inattentional blindness for dynamic events. *Perception.* 28 (9), 1059–1074.

Simons, D. J. & Levin, D. T. (1997). Change blindness. *Trends in Cognitive Sciences.* 1 (7), 261–267.

Smith, T. J. (2012). The attentional theory of cinematic continuity. *Projections.* 6(1), 1–27.

Smith, T. J. & Henderson, J. M. (2008). Edit blindness: The relationship between attention and global change blindness in dynamic scenes. *Journal of Eye Movement Research.* 2(2), 1–17.

Swallow, K. M. & Jiang, Y. V. (2010). The attentional boost effect: Transient increases in attention to one task enhance performance in a second task. *Cognition. 115,* 118–132.

Swallow, K. M., Kemp, J. T. & Simsek, A. C. (2018). The role of perspective in event segmentation. *Cognition. 177,* 249–262.

Swallow, K. M., Broitman, A. W., Riley, E. & Turker, H. B. (2022). Grounding the attentional boost effect in events and the efficient brain. *Frontiers in Psychology. 13,* 892416.

Trabasso, T., & Sperry, L. L. (1985). Causal relatedness and importance of story events. *Journal of Memory and Language.* 24(5), 595–611.

Tversky, B., Zacks, J. M. & Hard, B. M. (2008). The Structure of Experience. In T. Shipley & J. Zacks (Eds.), *Understanding events: How humans see, represent, and act on events* (pp. 436–464). New York, NY: Oxford University Press.

Tversky, B., Zacks, J., Morrison, J. B. & Hard, B. M. (2010). Talking About Events. In J. Bohnemeyer & E. Pederson (Eds.), *Event representation in language and cognition.* Cambridge University Press.

Wittgenstein, L. (1997). *Philosophical investigations.* Blackwell Publishers.

Zacks, J. M., Speer, N. K., Swallow, K. M., Braver, T. S. & Reynolds, J. R. (2007). Event perception: A mind-brain perspective. *Psychological Bulletin. 133* (2), 273.

Zacks, J. M. & Swallow, K. M. (2007). Event segmentation. *Current Directions in Psychological Science*, 80–84.

Zacks, J. M., Speer, N. K. & Reynolds, J. R. (2009). Segmentation in reading and film comprehension. *Journal of Experimental Psychology: General. 138* (2), 307.

Zacks, J. M., Speer, N. K., Swallow, K. M. & Maley, C. J. (2010). The brain's cutting-room floor: Segmentation of narrative cinema. *Frontiers in Human Neuroscience. 4*, 168.

Zacks, J. M. & Tversky, B. (2001). Event structure in perception and conception. *Psychological Bulletin. 127* (1), 3–21.

Zacks, J. M., Tversky, B. & Iyer, G. (2001). Perceiving, remembering, and communicating structure in events. *Journal of Experimental Psychology: General. 130* (1), 29.

Zwaan, R. A., Langston, M. C. & Graesser, A. C. (1995). The construction of situation models in narrative comprehension: An event-indexing model. *Psychological Science. 6* (5), 292–297.

Zwaan, R. A. & Radvansky, G. A. (1998). Situation models in language comprehension and memory. *Psychological Bulletin. 123* (2), 162.

Zwaan, R. A. (2016). Situation models, mental simulations, and abstract concepts in discourse comprehension. *Psychological Bulletin Review. 23*, 1028–1034.

INDEX

Note: Page numbers in bold denote tables, page numbers in *italics* denote figures. Page numbers of the form XnY denote footnote Y on page X.

400 Blows, The 18, 108
8 ½ 13, 105, 114

Abre los Ojos (Open Your Eyes) 71
Adaptation 64, 73, 81
Adventures of Prince Achmed, The 181
Alfred Hitchcock Presents 164–165
Amélie 20
American Psycho 13
Amour 18, 109
animation 175–197; humorous phases
    in 176; personality animation
    179; *see also* narrative
Annie Hall 12, 45
Antonioni, M. 19, 99, 101, 104, 109
Arabian Nights 15, 115
art cinema 20, 65, 76, 95, 98, 138;
    avant-garde, and 142; film
    enigma 96, 106–116; minimalism
    104; non-unified theory of 95;
    parametric narration 99; realism
    98, 106; realist art cinema
    108–109, 111; slow cinema 102,
    106–116; subjective/objective
    realism in 112
A Song of Ice and Fire/Game of Thrones
    franchise 230
attention 12, 14, 16, 22, 64, 111,
    116n6, 199, 125, 267, 279, 282;

and memory 79, 283; attentional
    focus 258, 259; attentional
    shift 267; attentional synchrony
    290n19 (*see also* Loschky, L.)
Atlanta 171–172
auteur/auteurism x, 88, 103, 108, 138
avant-garde film: as quasi-narrative 116;
    in animation 176

Babel 73
Baby's Meal 16
Back to the Future 11, 13, 19
Bad Boys for Life 20
Badlands 13, 109
Bal, M. 8n2
Bambi 11
Barry Lyndon 11
Batman 222
Battleship Potemkin 17, 115
Beautiful Leukanida, The 180
Before Sunset 13
Being John Malkovich 64
Bellville Rendez-Vous 13
Bergman, I. xvii, 19, 99, 104, 109, 112,
    116, 123
Berliner, T. 18, 282
Bicycle Thieves 18, 106, 109; social
    realism of 106 (*see also* art
    cinema)

Big Lebowski, The 58
Big Sleep, The 33, 42, 44
Black Mirror 165–166
Black Mirror: Bandersnatch 21
Blackton, J. S. 177
Blade Runner 15, 33, 41
Blood of a Poet, The 112
*Bobby Bumps and His
    Goatmobile* 177
Bonnie and Clyde 18
Bordwell, D. xiii, 2, 12, 17, 29, 65,
    73, 76, 86, 88, 95, 97, 123,
    140, 180, 188, 239, 257, 266,
    278, 284
Branigan, E. 2, 15, 188
Bresson, R. 19, 67, 99, 101, 104, 109
Bringing Up Baby 13, 39
Buckland, W. 2, 21, 73, 95, 97,
    110, 188
Buñuel, L. 19, 112
But No One 249, 252

Cabinet of Dr. Caligari, The 14
Carroll, N. 15, 31, 108, 187, 230, 242,
    278, 281
Casablanca 12
Chatman, S. 2, 31, 39, 223,
    241, 279
Cheers 22, 157, 167, 169
Chinatown 19, 45
Citizen Kane 34, 40
City of God 20
classical Hollywood 5, 18, 20, 29, 35,
    49, 55, 63, 178; narration 33;
    narrative model 53, 65
Close Encounters of the Third Kind 56
Cocteau, J. 19, 102, 112
cognition 3, 29, 36; and aesthetic
    pleasure 30; cognitive effort
    37, 45; cognitive engagement/
    involvement 35, 256–274;
    cognitive play 4, 6, 38, 40;
    distributed xi; situated xi
cognitive narratology 212; *see also*
    narratology
cognitive play 4, 40–41
Columbo 161–162
counterpoint 127; *see also* narrative
    structure
cut-and-paste narrative processing 284;
    see also narrative comprehension
Cutting, J. 2, 126, 282
Cries and Whispers 18, 107, 109

Dancer in the Dark 96
Dark 21, 72
Deadwood 158, 159–161
dialogue abstraction 127; *see also*
    narrative structure
diegesis/diegetic 13, 60, 71, 84, 144,
    284; extra-diegetic inferences 76;
    intra-diegetic 213
diegetic fictionalization 71–92
diegetic theories 257
Dirty Dancing 19
Dirty Harry 12
discourse 2, 5, 7, 13, 89n1, 95, 138,
    178, 185, 212, 276, 288;
    Discourse Representation Theory
    277; vs. story 2, 200, 201, 241,
    279, 285, 289n10 (*see also*
    syuzhet-fabula distinction); *see
    also* fabula
Disney, W. 176, 190
Disney studio 180, 190n1, 214, 232
Dog Day Afternoon 18
Donnie Darko xvi, 21, 71, 78
Down by Law 54
Dragnet 152
*Dreams of Chaos, Visions of
    Order* 143
Dune 144; complex vs. complicated 145

Easy Rider 18
Edward Scissorhands 39
Eisenstein, S. 17, 240, 257
Elephant 20, 101, 111
Elephant Man, The 139
Ellen 153
Elsaesser, T. 18, 74, 188
Enchanted Drawing, The 178
Enter the Matrix 21, 231
Eraserhead 19, 115, 138, 143
European Rest Cure, The 16
event 288; defined 276; discourse 278;
    Gestalt 277, 289; linguistics 278;
    memory of 283
event boundary 282, 286, 290n14,
    290n17; *see also* event
    segmentation
Event-Indexing Model 283, 290n21;
    see also event segmentation
event segmentation 8, 75, 77, 82, 84,
    126, 184, 276, 282, 291n26,
    291n27
*Everything Everywhere All at
    Once* 20

Evnine, S. 247, 251, 254n7;
hylomorphic theory 247 (*see also* screenplay)
experimental cinema 49, 115, 120, 122, 124, 139, 241, 250, 252; as complex plot 71, 74, 76; experimental animation 175, 186; experimental television narrative 153; experimental video game 200

fabula 2, 241, 278; defined 29
Fargo 20, 166
Field, S. 10, 19, 97, 239
Fight Club 14, 20, 42, 143
film enigma 96, 106–116; defined 111; *see also* art cinema
film-based franchise 222; *see also* transmedia(l) narrative
Five Easy Pieces 19
Fleabag 13
Fellini, F. 13, 99, 105, 114, 123
franchise: comic-based 222; film-based 222; novel-based 222
Fresh Prince of Bel Air, The 22
Friends 156
From Dusk Till Dawn 15
Full Metal Jacket 11

Game of Thrones 12, 222, 229
Garsoffky, B. 285
Genette, G. 85, 88n1, 215n6, 223, 241, 278,
Gertie the Dinosaur 179
Girls 168–169
Godard, Jean-Luc 123–135; counterpoint 127; dialogue abstraction 127; parallel soundtrack 127
Godfather, The 13, 19, 33, 41
Goodfellas 13
Grand Theft Auto 203
Grodal, T. 4, 113, 115, 266
Groundhog Day 19, 31
Guardians of the Galaxy 12
Gummo 15, 20, 50
Gunning, T. 16, 177
Gunsmoke 155, 158–159

Hannah and Her Sisters 11
Harold and Maude 18, 39
Harry Potter 7, 12, 222, 226
Harry Potter/The Wizarding World franchises 227

Heartstopper 157
Heaven's Gate 19
Heavy Rain 22, 201
Hélas pour moi! 127
Hitchcock, Alfred 15, 42, 77, 163, 218
Hollywood cinema xvi, 24n5, 30, 33, 42, 71; cartoons 183; *see also* classical Hollywood; new Hollywood
Hollywood narration 30, 33, 36, 41; *see also* narration
House of Cards 154
House that Jack Built, The 13
How a Mosquito Operates 179
How to Train Your Dragon 12
Humorous Phases of Funny Faces 178
Hunt for Red October, The 19

Illusionist, The 189
I Love Lucy 22, 167
Immigrant, The 268, 269
Inception 15, 21, 33, 71, 73, 81, 88n1, 179
Incongruity-Resolution Theory 37–40
independent cinema 20, 49, 55; multi-part narrative 64; multi-strand narrative 6, 58, 62 (*see also* narrative structure); narrative thread 51, 58, 113
Indiana Jones 19, 222
Infernal Affairs 21
Inland Empire 111, 138, 141
interactive narrative 7, 21, 72, 197, 199, 203, 212, 219; *see also* (video) game
In the Mood for Love 21

Jarmusch, J. 19, 55, 64, 104, 111
Johnson-Laird, P. 78, 280
Julien Donkey-Boy 51
Jurassic Park 12
Jurassic World: Fallen Kingdom 20

Kiki's Delivery Service 11
Killing, The 33, 42, 43
Kurosawa, A. 18

LA Confidential 13
L.A. Noire 209
La Strada 18
Last Year at Marienbad 18, 33, 76, 105, 108, 112
Law & Order 156
Legend of Zelda, The 203

L'Enfant 18
Le Voyage dans la Lune 178
Les Vacances de M. Hulot 13
Lightning Sketches 178
linear narrative 31, 55, 177
Little Nemo in Slumberland 182
live-action cinema 15, 21, 177, 180, 189
Locket 18
Lord of the Rings, The 222
Loschky, L. 267, 287, 290n19
Lost Highway 65, 71, 113, 139,
    141, 222
ludonarrative 198, 215n5; dissonance/
    consonance 199
Lumière Brothers 16, 178
Lydia 18
Lynch, D. 102, 112, 137–146; Lynchian
    narrative 137

Magliano, J. 280, 282
Magnificent Ambersons, The 13
Magnolia 12, 20, 45, 59, 61
Maltese Falcon, The 29, 32
Mare of Easttown 162–164
Marvelous Mrs. Maisel, The 13
Mary and Max 13
Matrix, The 12, 21, 33, 222, 227;
    franchise 230
McCarthy, C. 119, 165, 246, 254n7
McCay, W. 179
Méliès, G. 177
Memento 21, 45, 65, 71, 73, 75, 81,
    87, 143
mental model 277, 280, 283, 289n12,
    290n19; *see also* situation(al)
    model
Merrie Melodies 182
metalepsis 73, 85, 89; *see also* puzzle
    film
Mittell, J. 72, 79, 152, 173n1
Modern Family 153
Moonlighting 157
Moulin Rouge! 20
Mulholland Drive 65, 113, 139, 145
Münsterberg, H. 240, 257
Mystic River 13

Nannicelli, T. xiin.2, 3, 239, 244, 247,
    253n2
narration 33; defined 2, 29; erotetic 14,
    31–33, 187; Hollywood classical,
    33; in Godard 122; manipulation
    of 74–78; narrative, vs., 1, 241,
    284; parametric 99 (*see also*

art cinema); post-classical 20;
    pseudo-narration 133; *see also*
    classical Hollywood; Hollywood
    narration; narrative
narrative viii, 1, 16, 19, 49, 71, 103,
    116n6, 122, 154, 177, 200, 219,
    221, 223, 239, 256, 275; as
    speech act 243; canonical 241;
    causality 30, 33, 242; defined
    10, 29, 175; in animation 176;
    Lynchian (*see* Lynch, D.); non-
    narrative 10, 15; unity/disunity
    of 5, 30, 34, 40, 44; vs. narration
    1, 5, 10, 29, 32, 58, 65, 197 (*see
    also* discourse; plot; story)
narrative absorption 5, 7, 32, 110, 177,
    256, 261, 263, 266; defined
    257–259; transportation 258
narrative comprehension 279, 287
narrative event viii, x, xiin.1, 2, 8,
    10, 13, 29, 30, 34, 53, 73, 76,
    78, 99, 103, 107, 111, 116n6,
    126, 129, 139, 141, 175, 182,
    197, 204, 208, 256, 262, 275;
    defined, 38, 278
narrative immersion 1, 89, 151, 153,
    163, 198
narrative infusion 7, 210–215; *see also*
    (video)game
narrative situation viii, 55, 75, 78,
    104, 124, 127, 156, 168, 177,
    184, 202, 208, 259, 264; in
    television narrative 166; pseudo-
    narrative situation 133; *see also*
    situation(al) model
narrative structure 18, 31; causality
    30; four-act structure 11; in
    animation 181, 197; in Godard's
    late film 127; multi-strand
    narrative 58–65; multiverse 188;
    narrative thread 51, 58, 113 (*see
    also* independent cinema); of
    interactive narrative 203–210;
    pseudo-narrative 128–135;
    three-act structure 20, 23n1
narrative unity 30–33; disunity 34–36
narratology 138, 144, 172, 184, 198,
    200, 212, 223, 278; classical
    200, 212; defined 1
Nashville 12, 45, 59
Natural Born Killers 20
network narrative 12
new Hollywood 18, 23n4, 24n5, 42;
    see also classical Hollywood

No Country for Old Men 13, 248
North by Northwest 15, 45
Nouvelle vague 122

Ocean's Eleven 12
October: Ten Days That Shook the World 17
Odd Couple, The 12
Oldboy 21, 96
Old Mill, The 180
One Flew Over the Cuckoo's Nest 18
One from the Heart 19
Orange Is the New Black 154
Orpheus 112
Our New Errand Boy 16
Our Town 18
Out of the Inkwell 182
Outrun 22
Ozu, Y. 99, 101, 109

Pac-Man 197
parsing 276, 286, 291n24
PEN15 157
Pickpocket 18
Plantinga, C. 4
plot: dangling cause 15; defined 29; dual plot structure 31; plot points 10, 54; plot vs. story 29, 78
Poirot 22, 39
PONG 21, 197
Popeye the Sailor 182
Postman Always Rings Twice, The 242
Prestige, The 42, 45, 71, 82, 88
Prince, S. 241
Processing fluency theory 33
Propp, V. 241
pseudo-narrative 129; *see also* narrative situation
Pulp Fiction 11, 57, 64, 71, 119
puzzle film 21, 71, 73, 81, 143, 188; defined 42; cognitive approaches to 71–92; complex/complicated 73, 143, 145, 181, 188 (see also *Dune*); metalepsis 73, 85, 89; puzzle games 202

Rashomon 18
realist art cinema 106, 108–109; *see also* art cinema
Red Desert 18
Reservoir Dogs 20, 57
Rick and Morty 21
Room 222 169–170
Rope 13

Run Lola Run 21, 71
Ryan, M.L. 34, 40, 80, 200, 203, 205, 209, 212, 223

Scarface 11
Scene Perception and Event Comprehension Theory 287
screen narrative i, 12, 23; *see also* narrative
screenplay viii–xi, xiin.3, 3, 7, 8n1, 239; and narrative 240–244; defined 244, 249; hylomorphic theory 247–249; narrative-independent approach to 239; narrative-oriented approach to 239
Seinfeld 22
Sex, Lies and Videotape 19
Shaun of the Dead 15
Shutter Island 14
Silence of the Lambs, The 19
Silly Symphonies 182
Simpsons, The 22, 194
Sinking of the Lusitania, The 179
situation(al) model 279, 282, 284, 290n21; global updating 284; incremental updating 284
Sixth Sense, The 14, 41, 77, 281, 285
Slacker 20, 58
slow cinema 102, *106*–116; *see also* art cinema
Smith, M. 142
Smith, T. 267, 282
Snow White and the Seven Dwarfs 181
Soderbergh, S. 19
Song Car-Tunes 182
Sonic the Hedgehog 21
Sopranos, The 12, 152, 159
Sorry, Wrong Number 18
soundtrack 127, 146, 169; in animation 182; parallel 127
Source Code 21
Space Invaders 197
Space Odyssey 33, 45, 111, 114
Spiderman: Into the Spider-Verse 13
Staiger, J. 16, 73
Star Trek 222
Star Wars 12, 19, 226
story 16, 29, 78; aesthetic pleasure of 45; high-concept/low-concept story 12, 19; in animation 176; interactive story 7, 197, 203, 212; story logic 34, 39, 75; story nodes 22; story universes 7; storyworld 73, 78, 81, 152, 207

Straight Story, The 140
Stranger Than Paradise 19, 54
Strike 17
Synecdoche, New York 21, 114
Syriana 79
syuzhet-fabula distinction 2, 29, 241, 278

Tarantino, Q. 57
Tarkovsky, A. 102, 109, 111
Tarr, B. xvi, 96, 104, 109, 116
Taxi Driver 18
television narrative 5, 22, 72, 151; anthology series, the 164–166; genre (defined) 151; police procedural, the 161–164; ration and scale in 152; sitcom, the 166–169; social comedy 157, 169–172; storyworld in 158; western, the 158–161
That Girl 166–168
That Obscure Object of Desire 18
Thompson, K. ix, 11, 15, 19, 73, 86
Titanic 11, 13, 33
Top Gun 19
transmedia(l) narrative 5, 15, 21, 213, 222; transmedia franchise 7, 222, 228; transmedia storyworlds 222, 228; transmedia universes 222
transmedial narratology 223, 232; *see also* narratology
Twilight Zone, The 153, 164
Twin Peaks 72, 142
Twin Peaks: Fire Walk With Me 139
Two-Lane Blacktop 19

Un Chien Andalou 112, 115

Vertigo 15, 41, 45
VFX technology 178
(video)game i, 2, 5, 7, 15, 21, 72, 197, 199, 205, 218, 222, 229, 241, 250, 280; a-narrative 202; and narrative program 197, 200–203; fractal story structure in 210; hyper-narrative 202; hypo-narrative 202; interactive design 197; meso-narrative in 202; modular story structure 210; narrative infusion in 210–215; nonlinear 22; open-world environment in 200, 203–204, 207; spatial story in 214; storyspace of 204
Visitor, The 119

Walking Dead, The 222, 230, 233; franchise 232
Warner Brothers 176, 182
What We Do in the Shadows 157; viewpoint 18
Will and Grace 153
Wings of Desire 113
Winter Light 104, 112
Witch, The 13
Wittgenstein, L. 275, 294
Woman Under the Influence, A 18

Zacks, J. 276, 279, 282, 288n2, 288n3
Zwaan, R. A. 78, 283, 290n13, 290n21